Let Freedom Come

Books about Africa by Basil Davidson

HISTORY

THE AFRICAN GENIUS

THE LOST CITIES OF AFRICA

BLACK MOTHER: THE AFRICAN SLAVE TRADE

THE AFRICAN PAST: CHRONICLES FROM ANTIQUITY
TO MODERN TIMES

THE GROWTH OF AFRICAN CIVILIZATION: A HISTORY OF
WEST AFRICA 1000–1800, with F. K. Buah

A HISTORY OF EAST AND CENTRAL AFRICA TO THE
LATE NINETEENTH CENTURY, with J. E. F. Mhina

GUIDE TO AFRICAN HISTORY

AFRICAN KINGDOMS (with the editors of Time-Life Books)

AFRICA IN HISTORY: THEMES AND OUTLINES

LET FREEDOM COME: AFRICA IN MODERN HISTORY

CURRENT AFFAIRS

CAN AFRICA SURVIVE? ARGUMENTS AGAINST GROWTH
WITHOUT DEVELOPMENT

REPORT ON SOUTHERN AFRICA

THE AFRICAN AWAKENING

WHICH WAY AFRICA? THE SEARCH FOR A NEW SOCIETY

THE LIBERATION OF GUINÉ: ASPECTS OF AN AFRICAN
REVOLUTION

IN THE EYE OF THE STORM: ANGOLA'S PEOPLE

BLACK STAR: A VIEW OF THE LIFE AND TIMES OF
KWAME NKRUMAH

FICTION

THE RAPIDS

Let Freedom Come

Africa in Modern History

by Basil Davidson

An Atlantic Monthly Press Book

Little, Brown and Company · Boston · Toronto

A

LIBRARY OF CONGRESS CATALOGING IN PUBLICATION DATA
Davidson, Basil, 1914–
    Let freedom come.

    "An Atlantic Monthly Press book."
    1. Africa, Sub-Saharan—History. I. Title.
DT352.7.D38   967   78–5924
ISBN 0–316–17435–1

ATLANTIC—LITTLE, BROWN BOOKS
ARE PUBLISHED BY
LITTLE, BROWN AND COMPANY
IN ASSOCIATION WITH
THE ATLANTIC MONTHLY PRESS

BP

PRINTED IN THE UNITED STATES OF AMERICA

amicis carissimis
gentilissimis magistris

CONTENTS

AUTHOR'S NOTE

This is a history of modern Africa, of twentieth-century Africa, by way of the development of African political ideas and practices. It was long in preparation: from the time, really, when in 1950 I first began to study the continent, and since continued through all the years between. So in the first place I have to thank many persons in many African countries for helping me, through more than a quarter of a century, to become less ignorant or mistaken; and this I do most sincerely.

When it came at last to writing I found that the getting from the 1880s to the present day, despite all the preparations I had made, was still like the climbing of a mountain whose summit lay out of sight, whose weather could not be relied on, and whose possible routes up the rock-face were hard to find and harder to follow. I am again grateful to more guides than I can mention here for messages of encouragement or cries of warning along the way; but I owe an especial debt to Christopher Fyfe and Terence Ranger, as well as to Adenekan Ademola, Pierre Alexandre, Bogumil Andrzejewski, Cathérine Coquéry-Vidrovitch, Polly Hill, Thomas Hodgkin, Marion Johnson, Ayodele Langley, Ann Seidman and Jean Suret-Canale. They did their best to keep me safely on my climb to the top, but cannot possibly be blamed for my slips and wanderings on the way.

I am indebted to the Simon Research Council and the Senate of the University of Manchester for a valued research fellowship in aid of this work, and to Peter Worsley for so patiently receiving me into his department at Manchester. I wish to thank a number of African leaders and governments for giving me advice and access to records; the University of Ibadan for allowing me to work on the papers of Herbert Macaulay; the Service des Archives Nationales de France for enabling me to consult files; Mr R. H. Forey of the Army Historical Branch of the British Ministry of Defence for information about African casualties during the Second World War; and Professors Adeboye Babalọla and Lalage Bown, of the University of Lagos, for helping me with the Yoruba proverb on page 14. Professor Babalọla will forgive me for slightly misquoting the adjective. The dictum of Brecht's is from his *Kann die heutige Welt durch Theater wiedergegeben werden?*, in *Sinn und Form*, 2 of 1955.

B.D.

The Centre of West African Studies,
University of Birmingham

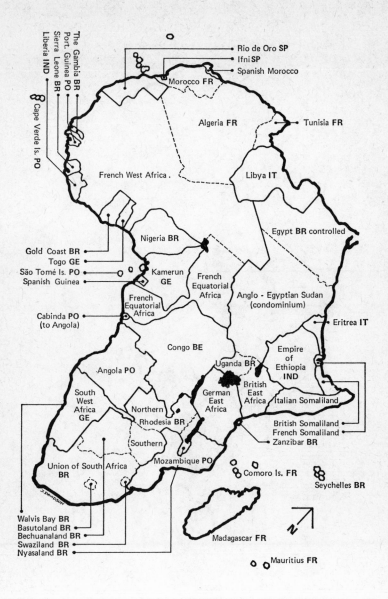

Rio de Oro **SP**
Ifni **SP**
Spanish Morocco
Morocco **FR**

Algeria **FR**
Tunisia **FR**

The Gambia **BR**
Port. Guinea **PO**
Sierra Leone **BR**
Liberia **IND**

Cape Verde Is. **PO**

Libya **IT**

French West Africa

Egypt **BR** controlled

Nigeria **BR**

Gold Coast **BR**
Togo **GE**
São Tomé Is. **PO**
Spanish Guinea

Kamerun **GE**

French Equatorial Africa

Anglo - Egyptian Sudan (condominium)

Cabinda **PO** (to Angola)

French Equatorial Africa

Eritrea **IT**

Congo **BE**

Uganda **BR**

Empire of Ethiopia **IND**

Angola **PO**

German East Africa

British East Africa

Italian Somaliland

South West Africa **GE**

Northern

Rhodesia **BR**

Southern

Zanzibar **BR**

British Somaliland
French Somaliland

Union of South Africa **BR**

Mozambique **PO**

Comoro Is. **FR**

Seychelles **BR**

Walvis Bay **BR**
Basutoland **BR**
Bechuanaland **BR**
Swaziland **BR**
Nyasaland **BR**

Madagascar **FR**

Mauritius **FR**

BELGIAN: **BE** BRITISH: **BR** FRENCH: **FR** GERMAN: **GE** INDEPENDENT: **IND**
ITALIAN: **IT** PORTUGUESE: **PO** SPANISH: **SP**

AFRICA: PARTITION BEFORE WORLD WAR ONE

These maps have been drawn at an unusual angle in order to show the relative positions of the island republics, especially Cape Verde and the Seychelles

Western Sahara

Morocco

Mauritania

Tunisia

Mali

Niger

Libya

Volta

Ivory
Coast

Nigeria

Chad

UAR Egypt

Liberia
Ghana
Togo
Benin

Cameroun

São Tomé
and Principé
Equatorial
Guinea
Cabinda
(Angola)

Gabon

Central
African
Empire

Congo

Sudan

Zaïre

Eritrea

Ethiopia

Djibuti
Ogaden

Uganda

Angola

Kenya

Namibia

Somalia

Zambia

Tanzania

Botswana

Rwanda
Burundi
Zanzibar

Republic of South Africa

Mozambique

Comoros

Seychelles

N

Lesotho
Swaziland
Zimbabwe
Malawi

Malagasy

Réunion

Mauritius

Cape Verde Republic

Senegal
The Gambia
Guinea-Bissau
Guinea
Sierra Leone

countries still under white rule in 1977

contested territories

AFRICA IN 1976

PART 1

INTRODUCTORY: SETTING THE SCENE

History stops in 1830; after that, it's politics.
>   Advice given to Marc Bloch

One can describe the world of today to the people
of today only if one describes it as capable of alteration.
>   Bertolt Brecht

Olóun pàápàá kò gb̞ón tó . . .
Not even God is wise enough.
>   Yoruba proverb

1

THE CENTURY OF NATIONALISM

The history of modern Africa is above all a history of the ideas and development of nationalism through the twentieth century. It will be written in many volumes and summarized in all tranquillity a hundred years from now; and for those historians, strolling on the pleasant shores of hindsight, this particular book will only be another message from the scene of action. But for present use the intention is more ambitious.

This intention is to offer a sufficiently comprehensive survey and explanation of shaping trends, movements, ideas and persons in a period of continental change when the Africans, as a chief branch of humankind, have moved into the modern world and become fully part of it. The central theme is thus a difficult and capaciously dramatic one, perhaps as great as any that the twentieth century has known. Through previous development over many centuries, the Africans of the nineteenth century had organized themselves into a very large number of communities. But now, to the tunes of an extraordinary and perhaps unique experience, profoundly innovating even when severely painful, they became organized into some fifty nations: forty-six on a count of the middle 1970s, but with several more upon the way. One long phase of history came to an end; another, evidently, began. Why did this happen, and how? What ideas have steered this transformation? Where did they come from: where, perhaps, are they going?

Such questions, as we know, are dangerous to answer; but they may still be asked. Others suggest themselves. When setting forth in 1848 upon a famous history of England, Thomas Babington Macaulay remarked that the previous hundred and fifty years were 'eminently the history of physical, of moral, and of intellectual improvement'. These were in fact the years of England's development of nationalism in its modern guise; and in 1848, the 'year of revolutions', there were many who thought poorly of the outcome. 'But no man who is correctly informed as to the past,' replied Macaulay, 'will be disposed to take a morose or desponding view of the present.' Today, as it happens, we are more correctly informed about the African past than any previous generation. This being so, does the outcome of the twentieth century appear a correspondingly great improvement?

And what in any case will it all look like in fifty years' time? The question is less fanciful than it may appear. The best estimates now available indicate that nearly half the population of the continent is under the age of fifteen. Around 2020 these young folk will have become Africa's elder citizens. What will they think about the nationalism through which they have lived as children? As a liberating force: but also, as in Europe its begetter, as another scaffolding for a house of freedom whose walls, when duly built, were found incapable of standing free? Or will they have opened a way out of the trap of nation-state rivalries and reductions, and be living in a time when the unities of African humanity will appear as natural as those of any other great family of mankind?

This book's central concern, meanwhile, is the development of political ideas as a route to understanding what happened, and why it happened. Whether for general reading or for study I have included a fairly adequate framework of dates, while the organization of the chapters is strictly linear: they try, that is, to begin at the beginning, in this case the final decades of the nineteenth century, and to continue until now. The narrative is necessarily selective as to events and trends; but there are plenty of useful books of historical chronology already to hand, and there seems no point in adding to their number. The aim here is to explain as well as to describe.

The geographical limits are those of the continent. Most of the material and discussion concerns all those countries which lie within the tropics and form the main body of Africa. But this un-avoidable concentration should not be seen as suggesting that South

Africa and its immediate neighbours at one end of the continent, or Egypt, Libya and the states of the Maghrib at the other, do not have their great and integral importance. None of them is omitted here, but they are treated under pressures of space as being somewhat peripheral. For this, perhaps, an apology is due, and certainly for the fact that Egyptian political history is given the merest sketch.

Other large difficulties besides those of selection have beset the writer. The quantity of information is one of them. For the twentieth century this quantity is already vast, and will become much larger as archives for the second half of the century are more generally available. Even now, usable source materials are beyond any single brain's capacity for absorption while the books about these materials, among those that are indispensable, already number many hundreds in half-a-dozen languages, not counting a practical infinity of learned papers from a host of scholars in these languages, or in others, including Japanese, which a European seldom knows how to read. The historians of the future may regret our industry: it offers, however, another aspect of the subjects treated in this book.

Then it may be objected that much of the twentieth century is not quite history yet, or, at least, history that can be objective for those who dislike the view that historical synthesis is always subjective because it is always selective. The difficulty is well known. 'Depuis 1830, ce n'est plus de l'histoire,' Bloch recalls being warned at school, in a time when 1830 stood to him as 1900 stands to the students of today: 'C'est de la politique.' Should one heed the warning? Bloch replies with another piece of advice. 'In these parts,' a colleague in a southern French lycée once explained to him, 'the nineteenth century isn't really dangerous. But mind your step when you get back to the Wars of Religion.'[1] Yet perhaps the warning is reversed for Africa, and the twentieth century a touchier thing to write about than medieval Mali? It is far from certain. 'Why did you quote evidence to suggest that the Somalis ate cattle's blood mixed with milk?' an indignant Somali student asked me in 1975: 'They did no such thing.' The offending evidence was from the ninth century.

Safety is not everything, however, and those in love with history can least afford to think it so. A history that is close to a writer's heart will always be a history, in a vital because conceptual sense, which is to some extent autobiographical. In this case, no doubt, the author's involvement with African experience over more than a quarter of this century will add to subjectivity. But it may also reduce subjectivity, through this long and often intimate contact with 'mental climate', more effectively than a studied alienation could achieve. 'I have passionately loved the Mediterranean,' writes Braudel at the beginning of his great book upon that subject.[2] It is a good beginning.

Standpoint makes another problem. I am writing here from the belief that the new history of Africa flows organically out of the old history of Africa, and is otherwise inexplicable. This standpoint sees the 'colonial period' not indeed as an episode but as an interlude of complex and often contradictory consequences, precisely because the new imperialism did not operate in a vacuum but within the packed arena of ongoing African society. While giving primacy to the African 'side of the story', however, one needs to find due place for the European 'side': and this, too, within its own historical context.

Africa today is the product not only of its pre-colonial history, or more recently of the history of the colonial period, but also of a direct trading relationship with the mercantile and early capitalist systems of Europe and America which began before 1500, had become of great influence by about 1650, and continued for two hundred years before the new imperialism sent in its armies. What was started by the old coastal partnership, in terms of mercantile and political influence, the Atlantic slave trade continuously enlarged; and what the slave trade achieved, driving through those sombre years, the non-slave trade of the nineteenth century again enlarged in terms of that same mercantile and political influence. No doubt the influence of this inter-continental relationship went both ways; its influence was in any case profound.

The background to modern history has therefore to be seen as a triptych of pressures and reactions over a period beginning before

1700. On one wing of this triptych there is the evolving nature of capitalism before, during, but especially after the industrial revolution which began in England late in the eighteenth century, together with the evolving interests of that capitalism in Africa. Things did indeed change much in Africa itself during the nineteenth century, above all in coastal and near-coastal regions which embarked on raw-material exports. Yet such changes were not the prime reason for the invasions of the new imperialism. These occurred because the capitalist systems had new demands.

In 1895 the king of a still independent Asante, a state of considerable power then covering most of what is modern Ghana, offered the British government the enormous concession of a chartered company 'for the purposes of opening up and developing the country'. More, this proposed British company was to be patterned on the British South Africa Company which was then, under the hand of Cecil Rhodes, 'opening up and developing' Central Africa.[3] The Asante thereby offered the British everything that an imperialist businessman could conceivably want, except territorial possession. But the British government, by way of Joseph Chamberlain, turned down their offer. Territorial possession was precisely what British imperialism was now determined to achieve. 'Expedition,' Chamberlain cabled to the British commander on the coast, 'must go Kumasi at all costs'; and go it did.

That was one wing of the triptych. On the central panel there is then the economic action in Africa. Effectively studied since the middle 1960s, this can be seen to have moved from response to the demands of an early oversea capitalism, in the shape of the slave trade, to an adaptation to European demands for palm-oil and other raw materials in and after about 1830. The economic action then moves on again to modes which respond to the colonial systems in the period of the new imperialism, the period of rival capitalist monopolies; and then, after the 1950s, to a whole new series of relationships which emerge with the oversea development of transnational capitalism in the West, and of non-capitalist or socialist economies in the East.

On the other wing of this central panel there is a third one to be held in mind when measuring the shift and imbrication of influence and pressure that have built the framework of our history. This other wing is the similarly changing nature of the political and cultural response in Africa as one phase in the underlying relationship gives way to another.

The early relationship had been dominated by alliances and agreements between African and European 'kings, big men, and rich traders', as John Barbot called the dominant partners in the 1680s. These were agreements between negotiating equals. Gradually, because of the advance of western European technology, such agreements came to be controlled more and more by the European side. New polities arose along the coast. Old polities readjusted themselves. All these polities remained independent but felt themselves, increasingly, at risk; and they were right. The period of 'developing under-development' had in fact begun.

This process grows fast after 1880: here and there, earlier still. Invasions follow, then subjection. With this there opens the complex story of resistance and accommodation to colonial systems. That is the African political history of the colonial period: on the African side a long period of search for new solutions to new problems or, for a while, the attempt to solve these new problems by old solutions. The political and moral cultures of the Africans strive with their destiny, and the shrines of the ancestors are assailed with questions never asked before. Seers and prophets return with a host of varied answers as the decades pass; and it is above all in these answers, whether shrewd or ineffective, gathering many followers or few, that the unbroken continuity of African thought may be seen. Meanwhile some Africans, here and there, have acquired a Western-style education and apply to very different shrines. They discover the values of European nationalism. There follow the rise of African forms of that nationalism, and then their triumph, and then, nearing the final decades of our century, the effort to break free from constrictions inherent to those forms and also, in doing that, to restate Africa's relationship with the outside world.

On this view of historical processes, beginning to be quite widely held by the 1970s, the twentieth century acquires a still more dramatic and decisive interest. For this emerges as the century in which the Africans not only come out of their isolation and begin to measure where they stand, but learn to analyse their limits and capacities within the wider scene of the world itself, and embark on new destinations. Much can be explained on this view of interaction between continents, between systems, that otherwise remains inexplicable; much can be understood that must be otherwise obscure. Yet large views of this kind contain a danger; and this one is no exception.

The danger is that giving full importance to this intersystemic view may promote the idea that modern African history – indirectly after about 1700, directly since about 1900 – has been the mere object or reflex of Western history, and that Africans have acted as the more or less passive recipients of whatever others might decide to bring. This simplistic idea also acquired a fairly wide currency, no doubt encouraged by the spectacle of 'neo-colonial' forms of political independence. There were usually percipient writers as late as the 1970s who appeared to think that the 'periphery' or 'Third World' appendages of the world-capitalist system must remain the essentially helpless dependents of the 'centre' where development holds sway. 'Third World' countries might beat their fists against the prison of their plight: they would never escape unless the 'developed' countries were good enough to unlock the door. Just how false this idea could be, historically, was perhaps best shown in 1974 when the utterly 'undeveloped' peoples of the Portuguese colonies unlocked their door for themselves and, incidentally, felled a dictatorship in Europe which the European people in question had failed to overcome in nearly half a century of protest.

In sum, the primacy of Africa's own history blends and interweaves with exterior histories; and there are times, notably between 1920 and 1945, when exterior histories appear altogether to command the scene, and when the history of the Africans seems to become much more a history of the Europeans in Africa than a history of themselves. We shall see how all this happens as we move along and where, in this sinuous and elusive narrative, the points of crucial change stand out and trace the future which we ourselves have lived. First of all, though, a few words about the organization of the evidence.

2

STRUCTURE AND CONTINGENCE

Anyone attempting to sail this course has somehow to keep afloat and moving forward, or at any rate moving, upon a torrent of first-hand information, second-hand interpretation, gusts of opinion, tempests of disagreement, and baffling calms of doubt or sheer bewilderment. But the essential steering task is to spot the difference between what parts of the evidence are to be seen as ephemeral and contingent, and what parts must be accepted as decisive and structural. Braudel, again, has put this well. Which parts belong merely to the confused and often chaotic river of events, and which to the shaping bed of the river? Where does the bed of the river decide the flow of history, and where does the flow itself, wearing and eroding by its sheer unceasing power, shift the bed into a new direction? For there are two histories, the contingent and the structural. And 'the essential problem is to take these two histories in the same grasp: the history that moves from one moment to the next, riveting to the eye of the beholder by the mere fact of its shifts and dramas: and an underlying history, saying little, almost unsuspected by its actors or observers, but a history which nonetheless persists, no matter what may happen, against all the wear and tear of time.'

It would be possible to make a list of structural features; but no such dry abstraction could have much value. Braudel shows, for example, that one of the chief structural features of Western European history in the sixteenth century was the fact, seemingly small in itself, that Spanish troops garrisoned in the Netherlands demanded to be paid in gold, and were able to enforce their demand. Spain could bring gold from the New World, but not enough for the needs of these decisively important troops; and so a torrent of New World silver flowed to the coffers of those European bankers, mostly in northern Italy, who were able to change this silver into gold (obtained, chiefly, from West Africa by the trans-Saharan trade); and with this there came that whole development of monetary technique which opened the way for a maturing capitalism. Yet to follow this subtle and compelling argument in all its rational beauty, one needs to read it in its detailed context.

This kind of structural feature recurs again and again in our history. Coins come in to replace cowries. Railways push through physical and psychological barriers. Far more explosively, so does literacy in several European languages, chiefly English and French. Taxation in cash turns farmers into proletarians, and a trail of devastation marks the course. The motor car appears, most often as a truck and then, later, as the Land Rover which will prove an indispensable aid not only to colonial officials but also to African nationalists carrying their message far from any beaten track. There is a 'revolution' in communications. Every year, by the 1960s, thousands of Africans will be travelling their continent in journeys by aeroplane never thinkable before.

Underlying these again, deeper structural features build their river bed. In some countries they include the massive expropriation of land, cattle and labour to the benefit of European settlers; in others, a similarly massive if very complex shift by Africans to the production of cash crops for export instead of food crops for local consumption. To all this, outside influences add their shaping pressure by the development of new forms of monopoly, by the consequences of ferocious international wars which are the fruit of these monopolizing trends, by the eventual development of trans-national monopoly, by new rivalries between 'West and East'.

It would be possible to make a list of ephemeral or contingent features. The personalities of history would stand near the head of these. They are many and memorable. There are the great and often tragic figures of the 'last-ditch stand': the stern unbending Samori, silent in disaster; Lobengula striving to make sense of Queen Victoria and of those he took to be her servants; the Asante king Agyeman Prempeh with his fraught dilemma of whether to negotiate or fight; the unforgotten Somali, Mohamed Abdille Hasan, and his barbed messages of defiance; a host of others. Then there are the 'morning stars' of nationalism on the European or rather, as they usually saw it, the Christian model: a vivid cluster of men and one or two women who took the brunt of colonial racism: preachers, lawyers, traders, journalists, often writers of an ebullient force and talent. There are all those others who stood against the current of the 'colonial mission', shot the rapids of anti-colonial resistance and were drowned or somehow burst ashore: dissidents, leaders of sects, organizers of illegal strikes, rebels with a cause, conscious revolutionaries. And then there are the men who led the nationalist resurgence, martyrs when they died in the attempt, presidents of new states when they survived; and these, too, run the gamut of human nature.

Or were these vivid personalities decisive and structural, rather than ephemeral and contingent? One had better see them, too, in their context. Perhaps it is easy to think that early spokesmen such as Herbert Macaulay of Lagos with his Bechstein boudoir grand piano and his love of the Pax Britannica, his cosy dinner parties and stand-up collars of an irreproachable whiteness, were not decisive. Yet Macaulay's influence on the evolution of Nigeria was not a small one, and Nigeria is the greatest of all the new nation-states. Shall we in any case think the same of others? What can be understood about the history of Cameroun without Reuben Um Nyobé, of Ghana without Kwame Nkrumah, of Guinea without Sékou Touré, of Egypt without Gamal Abdel Nasser, of Tanzania without Nyerere, of the Portuguese colonies without Cabral, Neto, Mondlane, Machel? The reader may lengthen the list to his taste: clearly, the difference between the river's flow and the bed of the river is sometimes hard to tell.

The plan of this book divides it into parts. These are decided by 'periods'. There is nothing definitive about periodization, but the one adopted here is probably uncontroversial. Placed helpfully along the narrative, as I hope, structural chapters discuss aspects of the river's bed at this or that point in time. Other chapters, and indeed most chapters, track the river's flow. Here and there the 'structural' and the 'contingent' have to jostle with each other as they demonstrate their interplay.

Footnotes are kept to a minimum; references likewise. Most of the numbered references in the text need not distract readers unless they wish to trace sources; only the few numbers in bold type refer to notes which add fact or comment. Readers will find that I have adopted a number of shorthand labels for decisive ideas, modes of action, types of actor: African model, European model, élites, intermediate strata, social struggle as distinct from national struggle, development as distinct from growth, and so on. I feel inclined to ask indulgence for these, but their advantage of brevity is probably worth the annoyance they may cause. Where the meaning of such labels is not obvious there are explanations along the way, sometimes in footnotes; and for ease of interpretation I have added a brief index of terms and definitions.

Being devoted to the twentieth century, this book might be expected to begin with the year 1901. And 1901, for some of the century's early themes, did indeed mark several crucial events, notably in the way of annexations and inter-imperialist agreements about boundaries. Yet these were aspects of a process of enclosure long at work, whether in the economic, political or cultural field. When 1901 dawned, seventy-four years had passed since the (British) Church Missionary Society had launched the earliest college designed to provide a few West Africans with a post-primary and even higher education, and twenty-five since this college, Fourah Bay in Sierra Leone, had become affiliated to the English University of Durham, while its most famous graduate, Bishop Samuel Crowther of the Niger, had died at the age of eighty-four as many as ten years before our century began.

Decades had elapsed since the ideas of contemporary Western Europe, particularly about nationhood and sovereignty, had become familiar along the West coast. Even the process of military enclosure was far advanced by 1901. The British had annexed Lagos Island in 1861, for example; the French had seized Algeria in 1830; more than a century had gone by since Egyptian history took a new turn with the disembarkation of Napoleon's army there, and much more than that since the little European colony at the Cape of Good Hope had spread far to the north and east.

No kind of watershed divided the end of the nineteenth century from the outset of the twentieth. All the same, the years 1900–1901 were ones that do help to set the scene.

3

ON THE EVE

Challenge and conflict were much in the air. There was even a sense of standing on the eve of great decisions. 'The last year of the present century,' wrote the *Lagos Standard* of 17 October 1900, 'will long be memorable to all people of African descent for an event in the history of race movements which for its importance and probable results . . . is perhaps without parallel.' This event was the 'unprecedented spectacle of a Conference of members of the Negro race' met together in London to discuss their wrongs and plead their cause: it was, in short, the first of the Pan-African Congresses, although really it was more of a Pan-Negroist congress. Only four of the thirty-two delegates had come from Africa; eleven were from the U.S.A., and ten from the West Indies, the rest from here and there, chiefly residents in Europe. Yet it seemed much at the time; and its 'appeal to the nations of the world', framed by the American scholar William Burghardt Du Bois (1868–1963), would be remembered.

Others liked the omens less well. 'The feverish rush for plunder and division of Africa,' *The Gold Coast Aborigines* had forecast a few months earlier, 'is about to be consummated on this eventful eve of the Twentieth Century.'⁴ Others, again, used stronger language. 'A sun of disaster has risen in the West,' wrote in 1900–1901 a Muslim poet of interior territory then being annexed by the British to their Gold Coast colony: 'Poetically speaking, I mean the catastrophe of the Christians.

> The Christian calamity has come upon us
> Like a dust cloud . . .'⁵

As one people after another took the impact of invasion, the note of calamity deepened.

But if 1900 was scarcely a good year for Africans, neither was it one of unmixed blessing for the Christians. The British Christians, for their part, were in the midst of a South African rehearsal for the holocausts of the First World War, and were finding it a sorry business. They had generally expected an easy success: or those, at least, who had organized the war. 'My good fellow,' one of Britain's then most prestigious generals had felt able to inform some Doubting Thomas during 1899, 'I intend to put the fear of God into these fellows.'[6] But it turned out that the fellows possessed a God of their own who was evidently better at the game of war, for one British general failed to relieve Kimberley from Boer beleaguerment in the last month of 1899, while two others met with sore defeats in a week deplored by an English politician of the day as 'one of the blackest within the memory of every man amongst us'.

And bleakly dawned the New Year of 1900, with British reinforcements far away in the Cape, slogging northwards to the Transvaal whose Boer (Afrikaner) farmers were everywhere on the offensive. Ladysmith was still under their siege; so were Kimberley and Mafeking. 'None of the ceremonies which mark the season throughout the Christian world were possible,' The Times history of that war would lament; but the officers of the Ladysmith garrison gave a party for the children of the troops, 'an incident of pathetic interest amid the privations and anxieties of the siege'.

Happily for them, Africans were mostly on the sidelines of the Anglo-Boer war, neither side being prepared to recruit them. Yet there were plenty of Africans who found the spectacle depressing. In besieged Mafeking an African who soon afterwards made his mark on the political scene wrote in his diary that the British were making fools of themselves.[7] They had kgotla semane, stirred up a hornet's nest, but without testing 'their abilities to face it'. Sol Plaatje's own people, the Rolong, had ignored the British intention, which was in line with the Afrikaner intention, to keep the war 'all white' in case the blacks, having had a say in the war, might then claim a voice in the peace. The Rolong did not enjoy the prospect of British control. But they greatly preferred it to that of continued Boer control.

They had accordingly declared themselves as fighting allies

of the British, showing in this a sound political judgement on what they should try to make happen afterwards, and had gone into the war without asking anyone's permission. But the British had so far failed to beat the Boers and now, commented Sol Plaatje to his diary, 'they have left us to square the account while they lounge on couches in London City, reading their newspapers and smoking their half-crown cigars.' The account was soon to be squared in ways that Plaatje and his fellow-countrymen, Rolong or not, were to think not blundering but deliberate betrayal. Meanwhile, in Mafeking, the blackmarket price in unexploded shells landed from the Creuzot guns of the Afrikaner besiegers went up to six guineas, unofficially, and the price of whisky, officially, to one shilling and sixpence a glass. The war was the costliest that Africa had yet known.

Elsewhere, with variations, the story was much the same. For all those in contact with the oncoming Europeans, the 1890s had sufficiently explained the future, and the threshold of the new century came only as confirmation. In 1898 Samori had been finally defeated by the French in his territory behind the Guinea coast; in 1900 he died in exile. The same year brought disaster to Rabeh in his dominion near Lake Chad, again at the hands of the French. Further south, five years had passed since the British had bombarded Oyo town with a single field gun which, being the only one on the scene, proved as good as a battery; and a little more since the Royal Navy had much more copiously shelled its way into Ebrohimi on the river of Benin, while other British commanders had shoved their way into Benin itself. Now, in 1900, Lugard was finally subduing the emirates north of the Benue, soon to be Northern Nigeria, and even peoples distant from the main track of imperial progression, such as the Tiv (in central Nigeria), could reasonably take a 'morose and desponding view of the present', no matter how mistaken Thomas Babington Macaulay might have thought them.

The Tiv, as it happened, were one of quite a few peoples for whom the nature of the 'Christian calamity' was not at first apparent. They could be glad enough to have the Christians pounding away at the Muslims north of the Benue, because those Muslims had proved no friends of theirs. They learned better. Finding the same treatment applied to themselves, they objected, and paid a nasty price for doing so. 'I cannot but express my sense of regret,' the Colonial Office was informed by Lugard, still in 1900, 'at the very great loss of life among these ignorant savages and the burning of scores of villages with their food.' But the Tiv, Lugard went on to explain, were a most intractable people, and nothing save severe chastisement could prevent their wickedness, or, more practically, 'induce them to allow the telegraph to be constructed through their country.'[8] The widening technological gap between Europe and Africa was to provide another major theme after 1900. In that year, while the Tiv thought evil of the field telegraph, London was receiving its first underground electric railway.

The great encounter proved much the same in other regions, practically in all regions. The Italians were still smarting under a severe defeat suffered at Ethiopian hands in 1896, and from lesser defeats of ill-equipped or ill-commanded expeditionary forces. But 1900 saw them, eager for national glory, once more probing along the southern flank of the Red Sea and the coast of the Somalis. Farther south, in what was now labelled East Africa, the Germans had joined the British, and here too 1900 was a year of annexation and inter-imperialist agreement on the spoils of territorial enclosure.

Far away in the interior, along the rivers of the Congo basin, the 'Free State' of Belgium's King Leopold was at last beginning to yield profits according to its own peculiar methods. There, perhaps, the spectacle was the most depressing of all, insofar as anyone outside the Congo Free State really knew what was happening inside it. Next door, in France's newly-acquired possessions along the Oubangui and the Chari, concession companies modelled on those of the Congo State were setting out on a career of plunder which soon threatened to outdo even Leopold's depredations. And the list could be continued.

Such were the keynotes. If missionary kindness and scientific interest were still on the scene, violence and aggression had taken control. A profound mutual ignorance accompanied all this:

another fact, even a structural fact, which needs to be remembered. A profound ignorance: but also a pervasive contempt on one side and bewilderment on the other. The Europeans knew a little geography by the time they launched their colonial invasions, but almost nothing of the peoples who inhabited that geography. The whole international enterprise was tackled as though the object, to apply the quip of 1886 of a former British governor of the Gold Coast, seemed to be to seize on territory and then 'as much as possible to rule the country as if there were no inhabitants'.[9] Were they not dealing, as the first British high commissioner of East Africa affirmed, 'with a *tabula rasa*', a blank and untouched page of humankind where they could write whatever they might wish?

Even in small matters this ignorance, and still more the assumption equally widespread that nothing need be done about the ignorance, became what seemed almost a principle of action. In 1900 the British sent large armies to the rescue of their garrisons in the Transvaal. But they sent them without any maps, and the want was supplied only by the lucky accident of finding maps in Cape Town. Eleven years later Italian armies sailed across the Mediterranean to the invasion of Libya not only without maps but even without interpreters.

What Europeans inside Africa knew and had long known was often unabsorbed in their home countries. European traders on the Niger coast had understood the excellence and relative abundance of Yoruba cotton cloth ever since the Portuguese of the early sixteenth century had begun buying it for sale in Europe; and its 'fast-dye' quality long remained without any parallel that Europe could produce. All this was on the record; but the record was forgotten. In 1851 the Bishop of the Niger, Samuel Crowther, was presented to Queen Victoria and her Prince Consort. After discussing this and that, including the abolition of slavery, 'the Prince asked whether the people of Abeokuta', then one of the most prosperous of the Yoruba towns, 'were content at merely getting something to eat, and merely having a cloth to cover themselves?'[10]

Ignorance about Abeokuta's passion for wearing lavish folds of wide varieties of cloth may be excused at Windsor

Castle. Such ignorance is harder to forgive when displayed by the explorers of that high Victorian age. Of these the most travelled was Richard Burton. He was, alas, also the most obtuse: the man, as Henry Nevinson said of him, who saw everything and understood nothing. Burton had every reason to know the success of African peoples in a dozen important skills which Europe could respect, not least in those of the export trade in palm-oil, then a major item in European commerce. Yet Burton could blithely tell his readers – and it was only one of his opinions that echoed down the colonial years – that Africans were in a perfectly hopeless state when left to themselves, 'the removal of the Negro from Africa' being 'his only chance of learning that there is something more than drumming and dancing'.[11]

It is true, of course, that not even the most enlightened European traveller of those days could have found Africa easy to understand or accept. Yet the travellers of half a century earlier, and more, had generally shown a far less blinkered attitude. This new racism of the late nineteenth century went hand in hand with a new and narrower nationalism, and underpinned a new imperialism. One sees this particularly well in the records of territories settled by European immigrants. Their curiosity about the human beings whom they found was practically nil. To the extent that these settlers were neither ruffians nor thieves, the peoples whom they found had to be set down as naturally inferior, as barely human, since otherwise they could not be dispossessed or reduced to helotry on any terms acceptable to Victorian morals. But such nice matters bothered very few settlers. They entered their territories and lived in them 'as if there were no inhabitants' but themselves. Answering their 'call to the wild', with few exceptions such as F. C. Selous they saw with any keen attention only the animals they tried to shoot.

'"Up country" – there's magic in those words,' recalled a sympathetically romantic English memoir of the old Transvaal on the eve of the 1900s. '"Up country" will bring back to the Pioneers of the nineties a recollection of the creaking wagon; the patient, straining bullocks; the unearthly scream of a hyaena breaking in on the soft silence of the veld at night; the camp fire at the outspan, and the cool, early trek when the morning star is paling...'[12] A whole generation of English middle-class schoolboys was reared on that kind of nostalgia, and the prose of Rider Haggard and the verse of Rudyard Kipling, however more subtle and ambiguous their real messages may have been, confirmed the scene. Except for strange and usually menacing savages, no Africans appeared upon it. What stayed in mind, apart from all the 'rod and gun' affair, was an idyll of bucolic life and rural pleasures, enlivened now and then by small amusements such as the 'arrivals and departures of Gibson's coaches, which plied between Kimberley and the new-born city of gold – Johannesburg ... lumbering vehicles usually drawn by ten mules with a pair of horses...' It is for us another age. But it was very much the age which presided over Europeans in the Africa of this century.

There is the instructive case of Theodore Bent, an Anglican clergyman of irreproachable Victorian probity whose income allowed him to pursue an antiquarian interest in the ruins of ancient Greece. The period of Gibson's coaches also brought Parson Bent to southern Africa. He came a few years before 1901 with the blessing and financial aid of the British Association for the Advancement of Science. His object was to explain the mystery of great stone ruins at Great Zimbabwe, north of the Limpopo, which were then beginning to be heard about in England.

The parson enjoyed his tour and proved a muscular traveller. He got to Zimbabwe, then a rather testing journey, and settled there for several weeks. This was enough for him to become completely sure that Great Zimbabwe's walls and towers could never have been built by any representatives of the 'present Negro race'. About the members of that race he found that he 'could not help saying a few words in their favour', since they were so generally reviled, but he concluded, after sapient calculations as to the alignment of stones and stars, that the builders of Zimbabwe had come from far away, both in space and time. A settlers' idea already around, that these builders had been the people of the Queen of Sheba or King Solomon, he found naive and unacceptable. For Parson Bent the builders had obviously been the Phoenicians; and 'by diligent search among the gigantic ruins' he was confidently able to 'repeople this country with a race highly civilized in far distant ages'.[13]

One may remark in passing that the scientific archaeology of the twentieth century, and from as early a point as 1905, would show all this to be the merest fantasy. The ruins of Zimbabwe are medieval in date and local African in origin. Yet no quantity of archaeological evidence was to shake the descendants of the period of Gibson's coaches from a fixed belief that Zimbabwe was the work of 'some highly civilized race' from beyond the seas who, as it happened, had preceded themselves in occupation of the country by some 2,000 years or so. This was natural: for they had to admire Great Zimbabwe, but they could not possibly allow themselves to admire 'their Africans'.

Much in fact could have been understood about the Africans and some of their cultures even from the limited knowledge then generally available. In several regions, for example, European or African missionaries had set themselves to learn African languages and commit these to an alphabetic script. Such had been the case along the West coast before 1801, let alone 1901, while regular study of important West African languages had begun as early as the 1830s. Even in South Africa, where most whites had contracted acutely racist attitudes long before 1901, Christian texts were available in several languages before 1850, meaning that there was already quite a body of African informants who were literate both in English and their own language, while a newspaper in Xhosa appeared briefly in 1841, another in 1862, and a third in 1876. Yet such channels of cultural contact, even if known to men like Parson Bent, or still more to white settlers who were themselves often barely literate, might as well have not existed.

One should see things as they were. If most of the British on the scene had a perfectly complacent indifference to the human realities of the continent which they were supposed to civilize, there was a large sense in which they could have no other attitude. For Parson Bent with his strictly 'classical' scale of values, civilization outside the periphery and heritage of ancient Greece was barely thinkable, though at a pinch he would go as far as the Phoenicians. Most of the rank and file came from a Britain where elementary education was still a very new thing, and far from universal, while the bulk of Afrikaner farmers read nothing but the Bible, and were often unable to read at all.

Their rivals were in scarcely better case, whether as to illiteracy or provincialism. For those who wish to meditate upon the underlying cultural assumptions of French imperialism there is something to be said for a best-seller more amusing than any of Burton's: and even the rebarbative Burton, when compared with others such as Stanley and Cameron who were widely read, wrote classics of elegance and wit. This is Alphonse Daudet's *Tartarin of Tarascon* (1872), a caricature which explains far more than it tells. In his little city of Provence the bold and famous Tartarin dreams of African marvels to be found. Eventually he goes to Algeria to find them, because to him and his friends even near-by Algeria, though by that time familiar to the French for nearly half a century, composed the wild and curious wilderness of Darkest Africa.

Yet Tarascon lay at the foot of the hills of the Ardèche, and even Tarascon, when compared with these, was a place of light and learning. For there lived in the hills of the Ardèche a population then hardly known to any save themselves, except when some festival might coax them down their trails in *cortèges* to the civilization of the plains. Then other Frenchmen would briefly see them as they walked together in the paved streets, leading their harnessed donkeys, and followed by thin wives and womenfolk whose breasts might glitter with the trinkets of an age before Napoleon. Yet the people of the Ardèche, and others like them in western Europe, also became part of the problem. It might be easy for Africans to think of all these Europeans of 1900, with their field guns and their field telegraphs, as persons of a great and even magical enlightenment; the truth was rather different.

It could be said that the century was born into an atmosphere of complete and completely mutual misunderstanding. If few Europeans knew or could know anything true about Africans, all but a handful of Africans suffered from a contrary ignorance still more profound. The king of the Ndebele had lately taken it for granted that Queen Victoria's power and policy should prefer a treaty directly with himself to the giving of a free hand to some underling like Cecil Rhodes: he himself, after all, would never have conceded such a thing to the most powerful *induna*. The king of Asante could suppose that the same queen's interest in Africa, and specifically in his own country, must stand on all fours with such interests as the king of Asante might develop in Victoria's realm: an understanding between the two of them must sufficiently regulate the behaviour of their respective subjects. The king of Oyo could imagine that his British resident officer, established in his capital in the wake of bombardment, had nonetheless become as much his own vassal as the sovereign of England's. As Atanda tells us he liked to say, 'Whenever he wanted anything done, he would send his friend,' the British resident, 'to do it for him.'[14] For what was a vassal's dignity as between two rulers who had signed, as King Ladugbolo considered that he had signed with Queen Victoria, a treaty of friendship and mutual respect?

Such kings had simply missed the operative truth, while down the rungs of society, among peoples still completely rural and 'pre-industrial', even 'pre-mechanical', the misunderstandings were as large as they were universal. Most Africans could interpret these utterly strange and usually demanding foreigners only in the terms which their own cultures could provide: as agents of Good or as agents of Evil, but in any case as coming from cultures of which they had no reliable knowledge at all.

For the few Africans who managed to acquire a Western education the fact of this misunderstanding on either side was both apparent and decisive. They stood in both camps, at least to some extent, but they stood alone. They had emerged from the assumptions of what we shall call the African model of society, meaning by this the culture or cultures of earlier African history; but they had been schooled in the assumptions of what we shall call the European model, meaning by this the culture of the western European nation-state such as it had developed in the nineteenth century. They alone were aware of the inner workings of the two models, and saw how impossibly these models could be made to fit together.*

These 'hybrids', as Kobina Sekyi called them in 1916, were quite often persons of unusual intelligence and perception, but they found their dual knowledge very hard to deal with, and its component parts impossible to reconcile. This often tore them apart, posing acute dilemmas of loyalty and conduct. 'Born into one race, and brought to live like members of another race,' again in Sekyi's words, they had to settle these inner conflicts as best they could.[15]

This educated few, as will be seen, played in the development of nationalism a part much larger than their real influence at any given moment. For decades they were saying things that most Africans could not hear, or, if they heard, could only think absurd or meaningless. These things flowed from full acceptance of the European doctrine that peoples became worthy of respect only as they became nations, and that they could become nations only on the model of Europe.

Such advice, to begin with, was heavily black and not white. The American emancipationist Martin Delany, a black medical doctor who served in the armies of the North and led an expedition to the Niger, gave it in unequivocal terms. 'Africa, to become regenerated, must have a national character,' he wrote: in the name of progress out of barbarism, Africa must also have her century of improvement.[16] Composing his appeal from the first Pan-African Congress of 1900, Du Bois could find it altogether natural to address 'the nations of the world' on behalf of those who

*'African model' means the cultures or related groups of cultures, with their economic underpinnings and socio-political forms of organization, which had developed by 1900 through the workings of African history over a great many centuries. All this is the subject of an earlier work: Basil Davidson, *The Africans*, Longman and Atlantic-Little, Brown, 1969, Penguin, 1973, to which this present book forms a pendant.

'European model' means the generally Christian and capitalist nation-state which has derived, in the essence of its structures and ideas, from the economic revolution in Britain and the political revolution in France of the late eighteenth and early nineteenth centuries.

were not yet, but manifestly must become, members of the same
club.

This idea became the central ideological theme of the
twentieth century. It carried all before it as a programme which
would come to seem so self-evidently right as to stand beyond
question. In what other way could Africa modernize herself? 'Let us
help one another to find a way out of Darkest Africa,' urged the
Reverend Attoh Ahuma in his book of 1911, *The Gold Coast Nation
and National Consciousness*: 'We must emerge from the savage
backwoods and come into the open where nations are made.'[17] He
spoke for the conviction of all his kind, whether enclosed in one
empire or another.

The nations would be made: but not in any kind of
vacuum. As a model of community borrowed from Europe, they
were made against, but also out of, the existing African model of
community. The first question, then, is the nature of that African
model. Were there no nations in 'pre-colonial' Africa? If not, what
was there instead?

BEFORE NATIONALISM

It was not a despotism, nor a constitutional monarchy, nor an oligarchy, nor a republic, but partook something of the quality of each of these different forms . . .

    Brodie Cruickshank on the Asante state, 1853

Almost all the concepts associated with nationalism are very fuzzy.

    E. J. Hobsbawm, 1976

4

FOUNDING CHARTERS

In 1901 a number of Angolans living in Lisbon published a protest against Portuguese misrule of their country. Portugal had conquered Angola centuries earlier, they charged, but done nothing for the people's welfare. 'The people remain brutalized, as in their former state,' and such neglect was an 'outrage against civilization'.[1] The history of the next decades would have harsher things to say about African brutality, as well as European. But it would also call in question the smoothly borrowed assumptions of the social hybrids about the opposition of 'European civilization' to 'African barbarism'.

It was to be shown, against all previous belief, that the historical cultures of the Africans were neither the fruits of stagnation nor the features of a brutish innocence. On the contrary, these cultures were the most recent stages in a complex evolution of socio-economic forms and corresponding technologies, beliefs, arts and explanations of the world. Grottanelli remarked in 1961, in speaking of African sculptures discovered by Europeans late in the nineteenth century and labelled then as primitive, that in fact these carvings were 'points of arrival' and not 'points of departure', the outcome of a long aesthetic development and by no means the raw materials of a wild imagination.[2] That is also true of their enfolding cultures. Insofar as the term has developmental meaning, these cultures had become mature.

They were embodied in many hundreds of communities of differing size and power, and at differing points of economic or social organization. Some appeared to voyaging Europeans to have become nations, and were reported to be such. Most were placed in a lower category of European esteem; these were called tribes. The decision as to whether a community was nation or tribe appears to have turned mainly on whether it possessed a powerful kingship. Europeans usually thought that peoples with powerful kings were superior to peoples without them.

Later attempts at defining the nature of these communities were scarcely more successful. National consciousness, affirmed a confident Belgian definition of 1960, consists in 'the consciousness of belonging to a nation and of being, thereby, like all other persons ranged in the same category, and different from others not so ranged . . .'[3] Six years later another although sceptical Belgian definition applied almost the same words to a tribe: 'a community which believes that it is culturally different from all other communities around it, a belief shared by the surrounding communities'.[4] The Yoruba of southern Nigeria, to offer only one example among a multitude, have almost always been described as a tribe or group of tribes. Yet they fit perfectly well into any usual definition of a nation or of national consciousness.

In getting beyond such verbal simplicities, European history offers some help. The nationalism of the twentieth century is clearly that of the nation-state deriving from the English and French revolutions: it is, in short, the specific nationalism of the economy of capitalism and the cultural hegemony of the bourgeoisie. The difficulty comes in defining the much less specific sense of nationality or nationhood which preceded those revolutions. How was that conceived? Without going deeply into these matters, one may reply that it was conceived, as in Africa, in terms of a consciousness of community: of membership of 'a community which believes that it is culturally different from all other communities around it'.

This consciousness took shape in distinctive language, religion, habits, memories, literature, though not necessarily in a *political* unity. If definitions were needed, they were supplied in terms such as the German *Volk* or the Slav *narod*, but it is characteristic of the subtle elision between those old terms and the new terms of modern nationalism that this same *narod* has come to mean both 'people' and 'nation'. And when the *narodnosti* or nationalities of the multi-ethnic but German- and Magyar-dominated Austro-Hungarian empire pressed for independence in the same period that saw the onset of the colonial period in Africa, they were called the 'submerged' or 'forbidden' nationalities. Nationality therefore came before nationhood. And what developed the first into the second, or into a demand for the second, the demand that we call nationalism, was the need felt by these 'submerged' communities to achieve an equality of status with the bourgeois-capitalist model of their masters.

Basically, the same progression of consciousness occurred in Africa. The pre-nationalist African model of community also had its strong sense of *narodnost*, of nationality, scaling up from very small communities of people who were believers in the same shrine, speakers of the same language, members of the same culture, to large and multi-shrine communities which nonetheless conserved a sense of cultural unity underlying their political disunities. And the great drama of the twentieth century has lain in what happened to these communities as they wrestled with the sudden and irresistible impact of an entirely different concept of community, that of modern nationalism, and tried to give life and sense to this in circumstances altogether different from those in which it evolved in Europe.

To see this confrontation's depth and range one needs to inspect the nature of the two protagonists. Little need be said about the European model: its nature and its place in history are what the history books all tell us. But the nature and place of the African model, as an historical process that has given a whole continent its own specific if highly various sense of community, has been less obvious. Yet African history, including the history of the twentieth century until now, makes no sense without some understanding of it.

What then, culturally, was this African model in its historic dimensions? A first point to emphasize is that it had become, by the nineteenth century, the product of an immensely long development. The historiographical achievements of the later twentieth century reveal a socio-economic and therefore cultural process that is clearly perceptible for at least six centuries into the past, less clearly though still perceptibly for as many centuries before that again, and even, in some exceptional cases, back into a remote time long before the beginning, around 400 B.C., of the African Iron Age, the 'age' which ushered in the development of most of Africa's historic cultures. The resultant synthesis is weak in many places, even in most, and an educated intuition has often had to serve for certainty in overleaping gulfs of doubt and chasms of ignorance. Even so, the synthesis is no longer a guess.

We have no idea how many communities there were in ancient times. Yet it seems probable that their number grew with population; and the total number of Africans may have grown from a few millions around 2,000 years ago at least to 100 million by A.D. 1800, or quite possibly more.* In any case the communities of 1900 were the long-growing harvest of a specific experience. This experience rested in the solving of the problems of economic production which had enabled these communities to survive and grow in their ecology. The solutions thus evolved, whether in raising cattle, growing crops, developing handicrafts, and in the economic and social relationships that went together with these solutions, comprised Africa's specific form or forms of production. These, in turn, were the groundwork upon which the ideologies of African community were raised.

In practice, according to the minds of men, these ideologies gave themselves first place. The hard facts of life had governed the content of these ideologies; but the ideologies were seen as governing

---

*By what we know now, African demography shows six large probabilities: (a) from Early Iron Age times till 1900, with local exceptions for famines, epidemics, or unnatural causes such as the slave trades, most populations everywhere achieved slow but steady growth from very small initial groups; (b) the continental population in 1900 was somewhere between 115 and 155 millions; (c) the crudities of colonial invasion and early exploitation checked this growth, and in some large regions (notably equatorial) induced a real regression; (d) this check and/or regression ended after 1945 with the introduction of less crude exploitation, and, in smaller degree, with the spread of preventive medicine; (e) the 1950s saw the onset of an 'explosion' when most populations began growing at a rate of between two and three per cent a year; (f) in 1975 the continental population was around 400 millions.[5]

the facts of life. 'In the beginning' there had been the first ancestors, the founding ancestors sent from God. These had led their people to a homeland, explained by application to God just how their people should live and work there: as soon, that is, as the frailty of human nature had forced the gates of Eden, let in work and death, and obliged God to retire into the skies. After that, a people could order its community, distinguish good from evil, cherish the first and battle with the second, only by application to the shrines through which the founding ancestors and their descendants continued to speak on behalf of God. I have greatly simplified the picture, but the essence of the matter is there.

Each living person was thus clasped within a community which identified itself by its own unique 'charter' of belief and behaviour. Handed down from the divinely-accepted ancestors, this 'founding charter' gave its people their sense of personality, legitimized their presence in their homeland by reference to the spirits who spoke for the powers of life, provided rules for everyday conduct, made possible the invention of new rules whenever these seemed desirable, and generally explained the world that each people knew.

The 'sets of rules' varied with the communities, and developed diversely in time and place and circumstance. It remains that in the essence of the matter, in general adherence to a mandatory-explanatory charter of validity and possibility, received by advice from ancestral shrines (or their cultural equivalents) and continually capable of modification by reference to the same source of legitimacy, all these communities belonged to the same model or group of models. When considered together in their often astonishing comparability, they may be said to have embodied Africa's distinctive and original form of civilization: of the civilization, in Matthew Arnold's useful definition, which promotes 'the humanization of man in society'.[6]

Much has still to be explained by further research. Writing about the modes of self-organization of a coastal people of Ghana and Togo, the Ewe, Fiawoo observed in 1974 that scholars were 'only just beginning to realize that they have barely scratched the surface of Ewe social organization'.[7] Yet detailed studies were already available of several dozen communities, the work of patient and often highly skilled observers, and the comparability of all these modes of community organization, and of community consciousness, has become repeatedly apparent. This is true of all the sub-tropical and tropical regions, even where Islam has long wielded another formative influence; but it is also true of the Mediterranean regions, even if the influence of Islam there, or that of other factors of change, has appeared to disinherit older ideas about community membership and cohesion.

The centrally unifying concept, resting on the mode of production which has shaped it but also been shaped by it, is that of kinship. Necessarily so: for the source of wisdom in each of these communities has been attainable only by application to its own ancestors. Community therefore means lineage: a certain group of living people linked to dead people (or, rather, to their spirits) by founding charters initially produced by the 'first ancestors', rather in the manner of Moses descending from the mountain with his tablets of the law, and presuming all those future descendants who are not yet born. For any given community, a lineage is in practice surrounded by other lineages of the dead, the living, and the yet unborn; but all these lineages share a common identity, because they also share an ultimately common ancestry, and, through the community of the yet unborn, a common future.[8]

The community is the sum of all such lineages. Its members' sense of community will be felt in varying degrees according to the individual's closeness to a constellation of lineages or feeling of remoteness to another constellation. Yet kinship within related lineages remains the common denominator of all social relationships, as Ayisi says about Akwapem. The people of that Ghanaian community have a word which gathers up all social ties into one conceptual analysis. They use the term *abusua* – we could translate this as lineage – 'to describe all types of social ties which are produced by affinity and descent'. The sum of all *abusua* is the community of Akwapem.[9] The case has been a general one.

Spiritual wisdom may be conceived in different forms. It

may embody a counterpoint between different categories of persons speaking for different categories of spirits: between those, for example, who legitimize entry into and settlement in a homeland and those who speak for the 'original rights' of that homeland. Correspondingly opposed mythologies may emerge: such as those, among the Yoruba, which hold that the Yoruba came from far away, even from Arabia, and those which explain that Yorubaland is where mankind was first created. Many founding charters allow for 'cross-cutting' links of organization which by-pass separate lineage loyalties so as to reinforce unity. Others, sometimes with great conceptual elegance, provide for a hierarchy of 'founding spirits' which correspond to socio-political and moral realities. Alagoa has shown this very neatly for the Nembe of the Niger delta during the nineteenth century. At the base of Nembe understanding of Nembe society there is Amatuemsuo, the settlement-creating destiny of the Nembe by whose advice the Nembe, around 1830, created four city-states: at a time, that is, when major expansion of the Nembe export trade posed new political requirements. Then there is the spiritual force which guides the life of each of these four states: if you like, its national god. And then, allowing for the twists and turns of daily experience and its constant process of innovation, there is a number of lesser spirits ready to meet such needs.

These systems of advice and explanation have been described as religions. But for us today, living no longer in an age of religious faith, the term can be misleadingly reductive. These systems of inquiry and belief explained spiritual force as comprehending all the science of explanation and prediction then available, all-embracing in its use of ascertainable knowledge, and operative as a practical and political instrument of social control. In Europe's age of faith it was said that no individual could have life outside the Church: *extra Ecclesia nulla salus est*. In these systems it was similarly self-evident that no individual could have life outside his or her community. Within that community, on the other hand, the individual had access to self-identification, self-justification, and self-fulfilment, as well as practical answers to the problems of everyday life.

Perhaps the whole of human history is no more than the

search for harmony between individual and collective. However that may be, the ideological pattern sketched above was practically universal, even if it occurred less obviously in North Africa in forms overlaid by Islam. Generally, because of what Lewis has called Islam's 'truly catholic recognition of the multiplicity of spiritual power', the African model could adapt itself very well to Islam. So long as the beliefs of the African model were adjusted to accept the absoluteness of Allah, Islam did not ask its adherents to 'abandon their accustomed confidence in all their mystical forces'.[10] Nor did it ask them to abandon their concept of lineage as the core of community consciousness within the *umma*, the world-wide family of Islam. The Christian missionaries of the nineteenth century, on the other hand, generally demanded the abandonment of belief in all other mystical forces, while the colonial power they soon supported and often spoke for reduced the concept of lineage to merely decorative status.

'What is a Berber?' Gellner asked in 1969, and proceeded to answer his own question. A Berber 'is a member of the nested series of kin units which constitute his tribe (or what has remained of it in modern conditions), and of the territorial units which may sometimes cut across the kin-defined ones'; beyond that, and in a more general and less immediately operative sense, a Berber is a Muslim.[11] Islam in Morocco, Waterbury found, might provide 'the glue of a new community';[12] but the substructure of community remained the rules of behaviour laid down by the pre-Islamic model. 'So there we are with evil and good,' said Hadj Brahim to Waterbury: 'those who follow the straight path and those who deviate. There is never one without the other.' It is very much the language of the divinely-guided ancestors.

The Sanusi of Cyrenaica (eastern Libya) are another North African people who are said to have made the journey 'from tribe to nation'. They are Bedouin who accepted the leadership of a ruling lineage called the Sanusiyya, initially a Sufi order of Islam. Their 'attachment to the Sanusiyya springs from their personal devotion to the Grand Sanusi and his family,' Evans-Pritchard concluded in 1949, 'and the Grand Sanusi derives his sanctity, and thereby his power, from the fact that he is a Marabout,' a Sufi saint.[12a] For the lineages of the Bedouin, in other words, the Grand Sanusi became the living representative of spiritual forces which have given birth to the Bedouin community. Once more we have an ancestral charter transposed into Muslim guise.

The Somali display another. Politically, they have been a single community acutely and often violently divided into opposed clans (or groups of closely related lineages). Yet all these have a firm sense of common ancestry, just as they have a common language and religion as well as a common oral literature. These march together in a series of concepts, such as *Somaalinnimo*, 'the ideal of the virtues and positive attributes believed to be present in Somali culture and tradition': the moral cement, as it were, of the Somali 'charter' of community over and beyond political divisions. And these ideas are undoubtedly very old.*

One could adduce many examples leading to the same conclusion. Generally, the pre-colonial and pre-nationalist African community offered the individual a moral and psychological identity within his world, and a guide to reality that was rounded and complete, encompassing past, present and future. In a decisive cultural sense, this was the basis on which Africans met the colonial experience. The community of the founding charter within which they stood was firm and trusted ground. Now it shifted beneath their feet, and slid towards what seemed increasingly like chaos. The world they knew 'turned upside down', throwing a tried security into a void of sickening doubt.

This is not to idealize the African past, but to see it in its structural essence. In order to face internal problems or the impact of external civilizations, African society greatly needed modernizing and reorganizing at least by the middle of the nineteenth century, acutely needed rescuing from the incapacity of its founding charters to handle new and often very violent situations. Modernization duly came. But it came in no fortunate way. Its overall impact of the first half-century or so was to undermine this African community in its myriad forms, attack and often destroy its modes of social control,

*I am especially indebted to Dr B. Andrzejewsk ifor enlightenment about Somali ideas of nationality and nationalism. See also Chs 28 and 29.

dislocate its moral systems, and set going everywhere a search for restoration or renewal: but to do all this while offering, as replacement, a perfectly exotic model, fruit of a completely other history, and even this at second hand.

5

DEVELOPMENT WITHIN THE AFRICAN MODEL

It is possible that Africans of several thousand years ago lived in the bliss of primitive communism, warring with nobody but 'walking with God' in a timeless time before the Fall into work and death. The myth is at least a pleasant one. What seems probable is that the Fall into work and death had a good deal to do, in the imagination of hindsight, with the discovery of how to produce and use metals, and above all iron, surely in the ancient world the greatest single agent of work and death. Looking round that world in about 450 B.C., when the Iron Age was still quite new in Europe and just beginning in Africa, Herodotus took it for a fact so obvious as to require no further comment that 'the discovery of iron was a bad thing for mankind'.

In any case many African peoples celebrate a time of innocence on which 'the ancients bestowed the name of golden', as Don Quixote explained to the goatherds, 'not because gold which in this iron age of ours is rated so highly, was attainable without labour in those fortunate times, but rather because the people of those days did not know those two words *thine* and *mine*': for in that blessed age all things were held in common. We may take it as a reasonable hypothesis, in short, that economic development began with systems of collective 'subsistence'. Families or groups of families found or produced their own food, made their own tools, depended only on the small egalitarian circle of themselves.

If so, all this had long vanished from the African scene by the nineteenth century. There might be one or two exceptions in this continent of inexhaustible variety. Perhaps there were Khoi (Bushman) groups in the Kalahari wilderness who still lived only by 'subsistence'; possibly there were Twa (Pygmy) groups who did the same. Otherwise the economy of subsistence was nowhere to be found. From about 400 B.C., or from much earlier in favoured regions such as the lower valley and delta of the Nile, less simple modes of production had evolved. Like all early agricultural economies, these continued to rely on a large amount of 'subsistence' or local self-sufficiency. But their regulator, along a slow continuum of change, was formed by the accumulation of exploitable labour power in the hands of lineage leaders: in those, that is, of the acknowledged heads of communities. A 'community economy' took shape in food production, handicrafts, local trade. Division of labour then developed a political stratification. With this lineage mode of production, as we may call it,* the ancient inequalities of African society began.

They were severe. Women provided the chief source of exploitable labour power: as daughters but even more as wives; and in a large sense these lineage modes of production became systems of tributary labour. In some communities this subjection of women was less complete than in others, but Mohamed Harbi was surely right when he remarked in 1975 that women in that Africa were the true *damnées de la terre*, the real 'wretched of the earth'.

As simple technologies improved in markets of gradually expanding size, new systems of servitude added to exploitable labour power. Lineages adopted patterns of self-enlargement by which 'external' or 'foreign' males as well as females were absorbed into hereditary positions of servility. Such patterns were self-regulating in that the 'slaves' of one generation could sometimes become the 'slave'-owners of a later generation. The inverted commas round 'slave' are necessary in order to emphasize that most of this servile labour was the early forerunner of wage-paid labour, and was seldom in the condition of rightless chattels.

---

*The term 'lineage mode of production' was used early in the 1970s, and remained controversial. Others have preferred to use 'domestic mode of production'. The first seems preferable on the grounds that lineage heads accumulated wealth and status to the point that these lineage heads could become chiefs, and chiefs could become kings, in a process of manipulation of the 'founding charters' which gradually enlarged but also reconstructed the founding charters.

The inequalities were severe, but the social stratification was not. The times when nobody had known those two words *thine* and *mine* might already be remote. The formation of communities, their enlargement, their development of divisions of labour and embryonic classes, their government by lineage heads who gradually became divinely-appointed kings: all this had indeed banished the 'golden age' that myths of creation continued to remember. Yet there evolved, in the easy-going ethos of rural life, a concept and framework of community within which everyone could have their place and personality, even women and 'slaves', and could find their personal identity and value.

Somewhere along the line in this process, one finds the origins of the state in Africa: of the qualitative development from a quantity of lineages to a community equipped with structures of central government or control. States had emerged in the Eastern Sudan much earlier, and in the delta of the Nile, living on the verge of the Mediterranean with its multitude of state-forming influences, at least by 3000 B.C. But in tropical Africa the records suggest that states began to take shape during the first half of the first millennium A.D.

Stratification became less easy-going. Simple states composed of a single community developed into complex states of several or even of many communities. Among factors making for that, the development of long-distance trade was among the most important. Even the simplest state required a measure of security and regulation within its boundaries. But once long-distance trade became important the boundaries of a desirable security, regulation, or monopoly of commercial control were pushed outward by lineage leaders who now ceased to be the first among their peers, and became, by appropriate manipulation of founding charters (and sometimes with the aid of Islam), powerful and ambitious rulers. Using part of their exploitable labour force as soldiers for conquest, these rulers built large systems which the writers of our own time, in some ways misleadingly, have called empires.

Each of the large systems of which we know – the Fatimid empire of the tenth century, those of the Western and Central Sudan between the eighth and seventeenth centuries or later still, the Shona systems associated with Zimbabwe between the fourteenth and the eighteenth, a number of others – appears to have been primarily aimed at enlarging a single area of trade and tribute. These large systems rose and fell with accompanying pains and troubles for those they pestered, but otherwise with little more than dynastic upsets. The community consciousness of the lineage mode of production could survive and hold firm within their various compartments.

There were several Berber empires, for example, yet the Berbers continued to live within a multitude of communities. Mali of the fourteenth century became geographically one of the largest systems in the world of its time; but its constituent communities conserved their separate identities. They did not merge or melt, or lose their languages, beliefs and moral consciousness as distinctive peoples. The Africa of today certainly retains a memory of those great adventures in statecraft. But for all their long-term political effect, they might scarcely have taken place. They were powerful in their time. But the community consciousness of the African model proved stronger still.

Built to exploit the long-distance trade, these empires made economic advances. They presided over the rise of complex systems of credit and commercial investment, especially where the juridical inventions of Islam were able to assist them. Their cities were the home of merchants with a far horizon of activity. Their merchant-kings linked the shores of Morocco to the coasts of Arabia, India, even China. Such was the value and the use of gold in the Fatimid empire based on Cairo (c. 950–1150) that the Almoravid *dinar*, minted in Morocco, formed the indispensable monetary standard of that *économie-monde*. Yet it was the producers and merchants of ancient Ghana or Mali who supplied the metal for that prestigious *dinar*, just as, a little later on, it was the producers and merchants of Asante who enabled the bankers of Florence and Milan to change the king of Spain's silver into gold. Should we not therefore think that these cities and their merchants developed early forms of capitalism? The question has its weight.

Economic history in Africa long remained the Cinderella

of the discipline, and began to be studied seriously only in the 1960s. A résumé of its findings in the 1970s would suggest that no capitalist systems developed either north or south of the Sahara, but that elements of a capitalist mode appeared at any rate by the tenth century in North Africa, and in the cities of the Western and Central Sudan about two centuries later. No full discussion would be appropriate here, but the interesting question of the use of coins may be mentioned.

In 1067 the chronicler of Cordoba, al-Bakri, wrote on good contemporary evidence that the king of ancient Ghana (Western Sudan) operated a regular system of taxes on trade. Al-Bakri gave the quantities in *mitcals*. The *mitcal* then was both a unit of value and a name for the Almoravid *dinar*, but in this case it almost certainly meant the first. Thereafter West Africa continued to use the already existing scale of value which consisted in graded weights of gold dust, but more and more the Indian Ocean cowrie and other standard measures which were not coins. Visiting the Mali capital in 1352, Ibn Battuta exchanged his *dinars* into local currency, the cowrie, at the rate of 1,150 cowries.

The kings of the high period of Sudanese empire-building – broadly, A.D. 800 to 1600 – appear to have minted no coins, a fact which suggests the small degree in which their economies had advanced beyond an adding of capitalist elements of exchange to dominant lineage modes of production. Over on the other side of Africa, the maritime empire of Kilwa did indeed begin to mint coins in the thirteenth century. Yet although Kilwa was a major exporter of gold from the mines of the Shona states of Zimbabwe and its periphery, its commercial system apparently had no place for a coinage based on gold. Save for a handful in silver, all Kilwa coins so far recovered are of copper; only a single report of 1883 makes mention of Kilwa coins in gold, and none has yet been found. Likewise, only one Kilwa coin has yet been found in the great stone-built sites of the Shona states whence Kilwa drew its supplies of gold.[13] For all their local success, Swahili Kilwa and the Shona states manifestly remained at the periphery of the exterior systems they traded with.

The overall picture of these economies is the reverse of stagnant, but within them there were evidently absent those factors by which a purely mercantile assemblage of capitalist and pre-capitalist elements could have developed into a new synthesis. The economies often grew, became more effective, larger, very enterprising; but they did not develop.* What was missing?

Was it that the level of demand could be met by a mere enlargement of existing systems of production and exchange? Or that innovation into a capitalist mode of manufacture required a technological background such as only Europe, for reasons of its special history, could then possess? Or rather that a lineage mode of production, content with wageless labour, crucially inhibited the development of wage-paid labour and thus of new methods of production, and therefore of new relations of production? These arguments seem to have weight. They belong really to a single argument: that capitalism failed to develop from these economies because the market could be sufficiently supplied without it.

Having said this, however, one has to bear in mind the real complexity of economic life. The habits of Hausa tobacco traders investigated by Hill in the 1970s make an instructive illustration. During the nineteenth century, but from a long history of commercial enterprise, these traders were farmers who produced tobacco as an export crop. Their trading system was a wide one. Having cropped their tobacco, they stored it for six months or more until they judged its selling price had reached an optimum. Then they loaded their tobacco on donkeys and drove these north to Zinder (now in southern Niger, just north of the Nigerian frontier), or as far as the great oasis of Agadès in the southern Sahara. There they sold their crop for cowries and *kanwa* (natron, a natural salt of several useful qualities), and returned home again. Back at home they completed their seasonal farming, and fattened cattle for export. Some weeks later they set out again, this time southward on *fatauci*, or

*The reader is asked to bear with another definition. 'Growth' in this book means the extension or enlargement of existing structures. 'Development' means the qualitative change of existing structures into different and more advanced structures.

long-distance trading caravan enterprise, now with their donkeys carrying the *kanwa* of the north and with their cattle on the hoof. The cattle and *kanwa* they sold throughout the markets of Yorubaland as far as Lagos Island. With the proceeds of these sales, the Hausa traders bought Yoruba *kola* nut for sale at home. The whole 'circuit' made up their year, and covered a marketing area of not much less than a thousand miles from north to south.

Other examples tell the same tale. These economies contained many elaborations of the lineage mode in its 'ideal' and ancient condition. Yet these elaborations remained marginal to the mode which had evolved them. Even when they became complex and ingenious, as with these Hausa traders, they did not accumulate into a change of essential mode. Perhaps we may conclude, with Rodinson, that they should be seen as contributing toward a series of partial modes of capital-using formation, often widely important and very long-lived (as with the medieval gold trade), yet never acquiring the motive force to build fully capitalist formations.[14] For these economies, however responsive to the needs of the markets they served, continued to lack those two prerequisites which elsewhere would enable 'the historic conditions of capital' to dominate the scene: 'free labour and the exchange of free labour against money', and, secondly, 'the separation of free labour from the objective conditions of its realization': that is, from its means of production.[15]

If this was true of the older systems linked to the world of North African, Southern European, and Indian Ocean trade, it was evidently true of newer systems linked to Western Europe after about A.D. 1600. Here, too, we find the imbrication of partial capitalist modes within the fabric of existing modes. There appeared a coastal partnership with European commerce, at first chiefly in gold and ivory and then, predominantly after 1650, in the sale of captives and other servile persons for enslavement oversea. This partnership induced the rise of advanced forms of mercantile initiative. Some of these forms made a decided mark upon the scene, most notably on the Gold Coast and somewhat later in the delta of the Niger and neighbouring areas. The rise of the forerunners of a capitalist bourgeoisie is manifest as early as the 1640s.

Importing guns and exporting gold and captives, John Claessen of Fetu on the Gold Coast dominated local affairs, and disposed of a fleet of war canoes and up to 2,000 musketeers. Others followed him. 'Ruler, trader, farmer, owner of lucrative salt pans, and a successful broker,' in Daaku's words, Claessen's contemporary John Kabes of Komenda (also on the Gold Coast) grew powerful in partnership with the Dutch and afterwards the English. John Konny of neighbouring Ahanta had even more success, defending his shoreward monopoly against an Anglo-Dutch coalition mounted to reduce a man who possessed, says Daaku, 'by far and away the largest force of any single power on the coast'.[15a] All locally-based long-distance trade passed through the hands of such men, and this trade was large and important. In the three years 1658–61, for example, the Dutch sold 5,531 muskets to Gold Coast business partners, while the cities of the Netherlands (like those of northern Italy before them) were ultimately dependent for the maintenance of their monetary systems on gold that now came largely from the Gold Coast by way of the sea. Other coastal regions, such as Senegambia on the far western bulge of the continent, displayed the same general picture. There had appeared a 'new class' of coastal merchants, thrusting intermediaries of African or Afro-European origin, and they seemed to hold the future in their hands. Emerging in the seventeenth century, their ranks were replenished down the years. Yet these generations of flourishing merchants, for all their political and economic power, in fact remained as peripheral elements within their enclosing systems.

It is not difficult to see why. They were agents of export and import between partners who were ultimately too strong for them. On one side of them, the great chiefs and kings of the inland country found state-controlled trading, which was theirs to command, always more desirable than the private enterprise that could escape their control. This, too, was why private merchants in Asante, although working at the source of gold and captives for export, were never able to assert themselves to the point of carving out a 'private sector' of any size and significance. On the other side of the coastal businessmen, there were the Europeans who controlled not only shipping and oversea markets, but also oversea sources of import items now practically indispensable, such as guns and gunpowder. These Europeans, like the kings of Asante, had no interest in seeing coastal middlemen grow any stronger than they were. The business partnership accordingly remained within narrow limits of sale and purchase.

Lastly, confining their possible development, these coastal businessmen had no economic incentive to invest in production rather than in trade. This was universally true among them until the serious decline of the Atlantic slave trade after about 1820. But that decline brought another point of change within the development of the African model. With the nineteenth century new pressures appeared, new opportunities; and new potentials were revealed. As much as the early twentieth century, the nineteenth was the cradle of the Africa we know today.

6

NINETEENTH-CENTURY GROWTH AND CRISIS

Back in 1775 a British minister rejected pleas for British banning of the Atlantic slave trade on the grounds, he explained to the House of Commons, that no responsible British government could allow any check or discouragement to 'a traffic so beneficial to the nation'. Yet in 1807 it was found, after all, that the thing could be done and even should be done; and the infamous trade was declared illegal in British vessels. Other slaving nations slowly followed suit in the rank of their relative economic backwardness: logically, the Portuguese and North Americans came last. Sanctions over many decades were required to bring the trade completely to an end; these were applied principally by the British Navy.

In major eastern African areas, the trade became in fact much larger in the middle of the nineteenth century than it had ever been before. This was partly by Portuguese slaving in the Zambezi Valley, and partly by that of Zanzibari entrepreneurs in cooperation with Swahili and other mainland traders; and the consequences of their depredations took effect in a profound and widespread crisis of security and control within communities far into central Africa. But in major western African areas the British ban induced a large and growing decline by the 1820s. Local export economies geared to the oversea trade were consequently in trouble. With their export market for captives stopped or seriously hampered, they had to find alternatives.

Europeans believed then, and indeed for long afterwards, that their intervention must be indispensable to the reorganization of these economies. In 1926 a book about the British West African colonial economy even explained that an 'economic revolution' had taken place. In point of time, however, this 'revolution' had begun a hundred years earlier; these economies had proved able to reorganize themselves. For the fact is that the early and middle decades of the nineteenth century were years of crucial mutation in many fields of African life. In one sense, within existing structures of society, this mutation occurred as a crisis of growth induced by a variety of internal pressures of growth, possibly including growth of population. In another sense the mutation responded to the changing demands of oversea markets. In a third sense it brought a search for more effective political controls over situations which now began to be markedly destructive.

Much of this may be seen most easily in what happened with the decline of the oversea slave trade on the western seaboard. After a short while, other export products were found and pushed. Palm-oil was chief among them. A physically filthy Britain, busy with her dark Satanic mills and mines, needed vegetable oil as never before, not least for soap. Palm-oil was the best that could be got. There was little to be had, but more, it transpired, could be found in that same delta of the Niger where so many slaving ships had bought their cargoes. Exporting palm-oil, the trading states of the delta became known as the Oil Rivers; petrol would not repeat the name for another century and a half.

Palm-oil exports boomed. In 1830 Britain bought some 10,000 tons of oil, chiefly from Oil Rivers' producers and traders; in 1842, 20,000 tons; in 1855, 40,000 tons, and so on through the century at about the same level. On the neighbouring Dahomey seaboard, long known as the Slave Coast, local entrepreneurs went in for the same expansion, selling 6,600 tons in 1891. The Gold Coast came in with a growing contribution, and lesser areas along the coast. Other export crops joined the boom. Peanuts proved another source of oil wherever ecology prevented the production of palm-oil. In the 1840s, for example, Senegalese producers were selling a few tons every year to French traders. By the 1890s they were selling an annual average of 68,000 tons, after which the colonial system was able to induce a steep rise to an annual average of 374,000 tons in the 1920s, and so on upwards.

British technology invented margarine made from palm-kernels. Oil Rivers' export of kernels climbed to more than 50,000 tons a year in the late 1880s: through Lagos alone, in the last years of the century, the British were importing about 37,000 tons a year. The Gold Coast's trade with Britain, all of it now 'legitimate' (i.e. non-slave), more than quadrupled in the decade of 1862–72 alone, chiefly from palm-oil exports and cotton-cloth imports. Then came cocoa.

In the 1860s, local Basel missionaries had shown that cocoa beans could do well in the Gold Coast. Local producers, Tete Quarshie being the best remembered, made experiments. With cocoa trees requiring seven years to come into bearing, they were able to export 80 lbs in 1891. This marked the onset of another boom that would make the Gold Coast into the world's greatest supplier. By 1905 cocoa exports had risen to 5,093 tons; by 1908 to 13,000 tons; by 1919 to 176,000 tons.[16]

Imports kept pace. Between the early 1850s and 1900, the value of total British trade with West Africa (i.e. Nigeria, Gold Coast, Sierra Leone, the Gambia) grew from less than a million pounds a year in contemporary values to more than nine millions a year.[17] Such figures are indicative of the absorptive capacity of economies that were still largely 'pre-colonial' save for coastal Sierra Leone. In 1831 these West African economies imported 2,384,000 yards of British cotton valued at £75,000; by 1850 the quantities had risen to 16,929,026 yards and £270,069. Another set of figures shows cotton imports into Lagos, nearly all from Britain, as being worth £22,483 in 1862, but £194,332 in 1890.[18] French trade with their 'spheres of interest' also rapidly expanded.

These 'pre-colonial' economies thus proved capable of large and continuous expansion within structures purely indigenous to themselves. There were, of course, external factors of stimulus. New forms of demand were the most important among these. The advent of the steamship was another. A monthly mail steamer began to ply between Britain and the Oil Rivers in 1854, harbinger of a steady enlargement of transport by steam. In that year of 1854 the total tonnage of British shipping to West Africa was 54,000, nearly all under sail. Steam began overtaking sail in the 1860s, and by 1904 total British tonnage had risen to 4,674,000. In 1863, ninety-seven vessels of a total of 29,591 tons entered the port of Lagos; in 1900, 526 ships and 531,871 tons.[19]

Other regions displayed the same trend in lesser degree. The Zanzibari Arabs developed a major industry in the export of cloves. Peoples of the central Angolan plateau organized themselves to collect 'wild rubber' and were highly successful till expropriated by the local colonial system. Even in areas where slaving remained dominant, as in parts of Mozambique, there were hints that the same trend could develop if oversea shippers would accept it.

Summarizing, one may conclude that the new export booms were made possible not by any 'revolution' in the indigenous economies, but by the fact that oversea economies had managed to get themselves beyond the slave trade. Once that immaturity was sufficiently overcome, and the oversea demand for captives largely cleared away, African economies could develop growth-potentials which they already possessed. What the colonial enclosures then did was to exploit these potentials, while making sure that export-led economies became export-monopolized economies, and that fixing of the terms of trade passed entirely into European hands.

It may be well to emphasize that these export-production booms were the work of African innovation within *existing* structures. Even in the matter of transport by steam the initiative was not invariably on the European side, although the shipbuilding was. Latham has shown that early mail steamers carried Sierra Leonean traders to Old Calabar in the Oil Rivers.[19b] There these traders, most of them the descendants of captives taken in some region of what was to become Nigeria and 'recaptured' at sea by the Royal Navy so as to be set ashore as free men in Sierra Leone, set up local businesses. Some of them began to ship palm-oil to the United Kingdom on their own account.

Long before the huge migrations of labour induced by the colonial systems, small migrations were already occurring in response to the opportunities of the export boom. A Gambian colonial report of 1848 describes how 'the Sera-Wollies and Telli-Bundas frequently (come) from distances of not less than 500 or 600 miles in the interior, and on paying a small custom (tax) to the chief of the country in which they settle, are permitted to cultivate the ground under his protection for one or more years . . . and to sell the produce to the European merchant. The greater proportion of the ground nuts exported is raised in this manner.'[20]

Writing long afterwards, Meier and Baldwin have argued that economies must be judged as backward whenever they are 'relatively unsuccessful in solving the economic problems of man's conquest of his superior environment'.[21] If that is good doctrine, then these economies were backward in relation to the industrialized economies which were shortly to enclose them, but not backward in relation to the needs of the societies they supplied and fed. Save in very barren regions, existing populations probably fed better than they ever would later, if only because the pre-colonial export booms had not yet cut seriously into land and labour resources available for growing food. The relative backwardness of these economies would not diminish with the colonial systems, but would become steadily greater. Meanwhile they revealed their ability to meet new demands.

Their success in solving problems occurred not only along the coast in direct contact with the export trade. As Hopkins remarked in 1973, 'pre-colonial Africa had a range of manufacturing industries which closely resembled those of pre-industrial societies in other parts of the world.'[22] These manufactures expanded wherever large markets could be tapped across state boundaries. This was most strikingly the case in the interior of West Africa. Returning from Hausaland (northern Nigeria) in 1857, Heinrich Barth reported that the city of Kano and its environs – but chiefly, as Hill's researches of a century later have shown, its environs – were producing cloth of the annual value of £40,000 in the prices of that time. This was sold to markets as far as Senegal.

The 'pre-colonial' salt trade with Saharan deposits was organized in such a way that some 50,000 camel-loads could be carried every year from Bilma during the second half of the nine-teenth century, while the twice-yearly salt caravan to and from Taoudéni usually had 25,000 to 35,000 camels carrying four to five thousand tons on their return journey. In those years when philanthropic foreigners fondly believed they were introducing 'legitimate trade' to the otherwise helpless inhabitants of the interior, traders in Timbuktu were handling between eight and ten thousand tons of salt a year as well as great quantities of African cloth and other goods.

All this portrayed flexibility as well as growth. Did it also indicate more than that: the beginnings of systemic change, of development from one mode or modes to more advanced ones, such as earlier centuries had not produced?

No conclusive answer seems possible because the processes in play were expropriated by colonial systems before they had time to work themselves out; and this was shown conclusively in the destruction of those groups of nascent bourgeois who commanded the shoreward side of the new export trade, as their non-bourgeois predecessors had commanded that of the old. What seems likely, on a general review of the evidence, is that existing modes more or less easily contained these processes of expansion, but that their confrontation with oversea capitalism was tending to induce at least the beginnings of structural change. This can be seen, for example, in the matter of currency.

The trades of West Africa had long been conducted with the use of Indian Ocean cowries bought from overseas shippers. Huge quantities had been thus imported, and the effective 'cowrie zone' covered a vast area. When the British banned the shipping of slaves, in 1807, they alone were exporting some 100 tons of cowries to West Africa every year. The sharp economic crisis which followed that ban was reflected in a fall in these cowrie exports to an average of about six tons a year in 1810–15. But the palm-oil trade brought recovery, and cowrie exports rose rapidly again: by 1850 the Gold Coast alone was importing cowries at the rate of some 150 tons a year. Steady inflation followed until silver coins came gradually into circulation in the 1870s: between 1872 and 1911 the four British West African colonies imported these to the value of some £6.5 million, 38 per cent of which went to Nigeria. Paper money was not introduced until 1916; but it was already clear by then that the principal contribution of the early colonial system to the further expansion of these economies, aside from some minimal improvement in communications, lay in modernizing the currency.

One can only speculate on the use that these economies might have made of that modernization if they had remained independent. Except at certain points along the seaboard, production remained at its handicraft and 'family' stage; if servile labour was also used, this labour was absorbed into the lineage systems of those who used it. There was as yet no process of proletarianization, no paying of wages, and, for the most part, no use of savings as capital divorced from its immediate process of production. The traditional mode, the lineage mode in all its variants, still held the upper hand: because of its potentials for expansion and flexibility, but also because of its cultural prestige.

This cultural dimension stood in the centre of the picture, and would long remain there, retaining its force through all the strains and changes of the nineteenth century. Wealth should be gathered, because, as the Akan proverb taught, there was nothing more important than wealth: *sika sene, biribiara nsen bio*. But the accumulation should be collective, should reinforce the lineage, should benefit the individual only as part of his collective. Great and chronic inequalities might exist in practice. They were frowned on in theory, and the theory was more than a gesture to the ancestors. Individual greed should be discouraged, even punished, and the instrument of punishment was there to hand. 'To find one wild bees' nest,' held the Bemba of Zambia, 'is good luck. To find two is very good luck. But to find three is witchcraft': is the consequence, that is, of inviting the force of Good to act in punishment of greed.

Another Hausa example, again from Hill's researches, may help to illuminate this fabric of thought. Although examined in the 1960s and 70s, it casts a reliable light into earlier times. The typical Hausa unit of production is a *gandu*, essentially a family farm controlled by a family head. It is a unit of accumulation. Yet *gandu*, or *gandaye* in the plural, almost always were and often still are dissolved when the family head dies. The sons each take a share. In other words, the accumulation is periodically dispersed in favour of a kinship group in its individual parts. And it is difficult to dissociate this repeated dispersal of accumulation from a ruling Hausa concept, that of *arziki*, which held and still holds that a man's individual fate must be subject to the luck of his birth, his behaviour, his place in society.[23] 'Lay not up treasures on earth, where the moth and rust corrupt . . .' How many generations of individualism in Europe were required before that old lesson could entirely lose its power?

Here and there along the coast, around the 1850s and after, modes of operation were certainly beginning to appear upon a threshold of systemic change. With a corresponding development of political institutions such as kingship, leading merchant-rulers in the Niger delta embarked on a whole new range of productive and trading techniques and relationships. They showed a sharp under-standing of the potentialities of their own economies, but also of the nature of the European market. They defended their shoreward monopoly against the intrusion of European merchants, and they sought to circumvent the European seaward monopoly by opening up relations with their own shippers in Europe.

Again one may speculate on what might then have devel-oped without the colonial enclosure. As it was, each of these inno-vators was broken on the wheel of colonial policy, even though each of them behaved precisely as the kind of modernizing agent which colonial policy was supposed to promote. King Ja Ja of Opobo was tricked by the British into allowing himself to be arrested in 1887, and was forthwith deported from the scene. Nana of Itsekiri was literally blown out of his trading base by the British Navy. Others suffered the same fate, then or later; and when they were not deported they were dispossessed.

Short of speculation, it is in any case clear that the nine-teenth century induced situations and responses that were quali-tatively new. Previous centuries had known plenty of upheaval. But now there was an atmosphere of strain and search that betokened something more than readjustment within the systems of the past. Partly this was the fruit of the external partnership: the changes brought about the decline and termination of the oversea slave trade in western Africa, the contrary changes wrought by the onset of a new slave trade in eastern Africa. Partly it was the fruit of the import of very large quantities of firearms. Partly, in southern Africa, it derived from the stubborn northward shove of settler farmers from the Cape and Natal, pushing for African land and cattle, and taking both whenever they were able.

Yet the purely internal factors of change were probably dominant in creating this new atmosphere. Though reliable statistics are altogether lacking, one has the repeated impression that population growth began to rub awkwardly against extensive modes of farming. There is a comparable impression that the success of internal trading systems had reached a maturity where new rivalries could no longer be contained within them, and new initiatives were on the way. If nineteenth-century Africa was not moving toward capitalism, the weight of the evidence still suggests that it was moving toward a large if slow and diffused reorganization.

Reviewingt his evidence in his important book of 1973, Hopkins wrote of 'a crisis of the aristocracy in 19th century West Africa' – but the words could apply much more widely – 'a social and political crisis stemming from a contradiction between present and past relations of production'.[24] The word 'aristocracy' can be misleading here, but the essential judgement is surely right. Not only in West Africa, kings fell into conflict with king-makers through conflicts which increasingly shook the assumptions of the lineage mode and its political systems. They reached for more power, even for despotic power, in defence against rivals or in ambition for larger trading monopolies. More complex systems of civil government emerged. Professional armies bestrode the scene. Old states collapsed into long and painful wars of succession. New states came on the stage. Such things had happened before: now they happened with an increasing note of stress between the assumptions of the past and the challenges of the present.

However one may explain it, this nineteenth-century crisis of society formed an essential factor in the background of the twentieth century. One may see it as the outcome of long centuries of Iron Age growth within lineage modes no longer adequate to needs and possibilities. One may see it as the fruit of an interplay between the lineage concept of community, developed during those centuries, and the growing impact of the outside world. One may see it as the early onset of a process of development toward new concepts of community. But now, in any case, it had to meet and if possible absorb the colonial enclosure with its huge and many consequences. In doing this, the crisis of the nineteenth century led onward to the groundwork of nationalism.

PART 3

THE COLONIAL MODEL:
1890–1939

The old slavery is dead, but a more subtle slavery may take its place.
The demand of the capitalist everywhere is for cheap and
docile labour . . .

> *Gold Coast Aborigine*, 31 August 1900

History shows that nations reach their zenith in their periods
of greatest colonial development.

> Belgian Congo Yearbook, 1934

7

THE REASONS WHY

There were those who welcomed the coming of European rule: usually, this was after the invasions were over. Few who were present at the time seem to have enjoyed it. 'I hear your countryman done spoil West Indies,' said a Niger Delta ruler to some British visitors in 1841, long before the invasions had begun: 'I think he want come spoil we country too.'[1] With few exceptions the existing states of Africa found it well to defend themselves. They did this by diplomacy wherever they could, by warfare whenever they must: there were many wars of resistance to invasion.

The Ethiopian emperor Tewodros II spoke for a whole generation of African rulers as early as the 1860s, not long before his suicide after defeat in 1868 by an invading British force. 'I know their game,' he affirmed. 'First, the traders and the missionaries: then the ambassadors: then the cannon. It's better to go straight to the cannon.'[2] Even so, there was much puzzlement about why Europeans should behave as they did. There was most puzzlement, perhaps, over the question as to why Europeans should be so determined to possess countries where, without possession, they could enjoy all the commercial advantages of their forerunners: all these, and sometimes more.

But if Africans found it hard to explain European behaviour and still harder to understand European ideas, the Europeans were often in the same difficulty about themselves. For some, of course, the motives for 'going into Africa' could never be in doubt. At one end of the spectrum of certainty stood the best of the missionaries. To Mary Slessor, a Scottish mill-girl who answered her missionary call in 1876, the thing was obvious. A sternly Caledonian God told her to help save the heathen from damnation, wean them from their perversity, and open the gates to a Christian civilization. To others, at the opposite end of the same spectrum of certainty, it was rather a matter of seeking a fortune, or at least an escape from embarrassments at home. In 1790 Daniel Houghton volunteered to explore West Africa as a means of evading the duns and picking up a suitable reward in cash. Many followed in his trail; and not all of them, like Houghton, were never seen again.

Not a little of the confusion in men's minds, then and later, as to why Africa should be partitioned, seems to have arisen from this nature of the agents on the spot. For a long time Africa was 'opened up' by persons of small standing in their home countries, and, the missionaries apart, often of dubious reputation. Much of the initial drive for conquest and enclosure came from those segments of middle-class European society that stood outside the ring of real economic power. Received with contempt in bankers' parlours, they had to be careful to knock twice and wipe their feet. Those who went in as of right were the men and interests concerned with India and the 'white colonies' in Britain's case, or with Indo-China if they were French.

For long they toiled in vain. By the 1880s, however, nationalist rivalries in western Europe had begun to give them a new lever of influence. They waved the banner of 'Christianity and Commerce' but banged far more effectively upon the drums of 'national interest'. There began what the French imperialist Jules Ferry described in 1885, when an international conference in Berlin enshrined the principle of European 'spheres of interest' in Africa and laid down rules for the share-out that was to follow, as 'this immense steeple chase into the unknown'. Hard-riding men on the make were now to the fore. A somewhat later participant, and rare in having a sense of humour, wrote a novel about the 'steeple chase' that was published in 1919; it deserves to be remembered for its insights as well as for its wit. Discussing these 'new men' who then came forward, Harry Johnston explains in his *Gay-Dombeys* that 'the middle 'eighties contained some very forceful if unpleasant personalities'. Ambitious soldiers short of a career in the stagnant hierarchies of European military promotion; small entrepreneurs with dreams of grandeur; disinherited younger sons of the rising middle class and landed gentry; misfits, adventurers, mere rogues

> qui un beau soir, de leur maîtresse
> ont plein le dos:
> ils fichent le camp, pleins de tristesse,
> pour le Congo ...[3]

All these added powerfully to the chorus of missionary zeal and patriotic rectitude.

They had to be taken notice of even when this was distasteful. The press of the middle class and of the newly literate 'masses' was their great weapon. The new men worked this press for all it was worth. Lord Wiltshire in the *Gay-Dombeys* – he is Johnston's amusing portrait of the great Lord Salisbury – 'lived in a serene and rarefied atmosphere, and soared high above all the groundlings (as he thought) in shaping the Nation's policy, yet the tail' – of these 'forceful if unpleasant personalities' who were now on the scene – 'was already beginning to wag the dog, just beginning.'

It wagged to effect. 'When I left the Foreign Office in 1880,' Lord Salisbury himself recalled in 1891,[4] 'nobody thought about Africa. When I returned to it in 1885, the nations of Europe were almost quarrelling with each other as to the various portions of Africa they could obtain.' And the press had much to do with that. 'The Treasury is rather stubborn about spending money in African adventures,' Lord Wiltshire is made to explain to another empire-builder in Johnston's novel. 'But if the Treasury sees those ventures warmly supported in *The Times* and *The Spectator*, they will think Providence must have decided we should go in for them.'

Others thought no such thing, but were carried with the tide. 'Mr Gladstone could not honourably suppress the fact,' Queen Victoria was advised during the 'share-out' Berlin conference of 1884–5, 'that he himself, for one, is firmly opposed on principle to such a system, and he believes that herein he is only a humble representative of convictions, which were not general only but universal among the Statesmen of the first thirty years of his political life.'[5]

Others who found the partition worse than distasteful were

ignored. These were the spokesmen of working-class movements which the development of capitalism also brought to birth in the closing decades of the nineteenth century. They form a minority tradition, but their critique of imperialism was to become far more influential than Mr Gladstone's. Here is the founding issue of *The Commonweal* edited by William Morris, writing about that same conference of 1885: 'Populations to rob and ensnare; markets to shoot bad wares into; lands to invest capital upon: to obtain these is the be-all and end-all of modern statemanship. For this has the stock-jobbers' republic of France waged war successively on Tunis, Madagascar, Tonquin and China; for this does the congress sit in Berlin, partitioning the plunder . . .'

Most of the anti-colonial themes of later times found their way into the excoriating columns of *The Commonweal*, briefly and obscurely though it lived. Pitching into Henry Stanley and the Leopoldian adventure in the Congo Basin (out of which came the so-called Congo Free State), E. Belfort Bax writes in an issue of 1885 that 'the plundering goes merrily on. The explorer reconnoitres the ground, the missionary prepares the soil, the "trader" works it. The time is then ripe for protectorates and annexations . . .' Stanley is 'the market-hunter's pioneer', 'the harbinger of the gospel and shoddy goods' against whom and whose fellow-brigands 'every true Socialist may "drink damnation" . . .' In an issue of 1888 Bax even goes so far ahead of the general thinking of his time as to pose the 'dread possibility' that 'the capitalistic world' may take 'a new lease of life out of the exploitation of Africa'. It was the line of thought that Hobson and Lenin would develop: essentially, all the central themes in their arguments of 1906 and after are shadowed forth in *The Commonweal* of the 1880s.

A comparable progression occurred elsewhere in western Europe. One finds the same shifting debate in France and Germany. In 1884 the Italian Foreign Minister Mancini informs the Italian Senate that the acquisition of 'commercial or economic colonies' may be permissible, but 'any effort to acquire political colonies by annexation or conquest' must be 'repugnant to the true interests of the Italian nation'. Less than a year later he is singing a different tune.

Defending his government against criticism of a minor colonial disaster, he argues that 'it would not in any case have been possible for Italy to watch, idle and indifferent, the peaceful crusade undertaken by all the great powers in order to civilize the populations of Africa, without seeing Italy's good name disgraced in Europe.'[6] The prestigious *Nuova Antologia* comments in the same year that 'there is above all this irresistible need, felt by every Power, to advance its own action against that of other Powers . . . We can be certain that if we do not now begin to prepare the ground [for Italy's oversea expansion], we shall within a year or so find that ground entirely occupied by others . . .' A newly united Italy must therefore turn its back on the very principles of national freedom in whose name the Risorgimento had triumphed, and fasten upon others the chains she had struck from herself.

Once again, there were radicals to oppose this. Still in 1885, the socialist deputy Andrea Costa condemns Italy's ventures in the Red Sea, and calls on the Italian government 'to recall our troops from Africa, where we have sent them with such irresponsibility; and before thinking about taking civilization to other countries, let us get rid of the remnants of a sorrowful past in our own.'[6a] Like other socialists of that time, he stuck to his guns through later years. But they were pop-guns when compared with the cannon that the imperialists could now deploy.

These cannon had been hard to come by. The financiers proved difficult to convince. Not for lack of funds: the British banking system had become larger, more concentrated, governing huge assets. New banks had appeared in France: the Crédit Lyonnais in 1863, the Société Générale in 1864, the Banque de Paris et des Pays-Bas in 1872. Imperialist Germany displayed the same trend; on a lesser scale, so did the banking cities of northern Italy. Secondly, the general recession of the 1870s had reduced interest rates and now argued for capital export. Yet this export went very reluctantly to Africa, save in one or two special cases such as South Africa, where diamonds and gold were found in the 1880s. In Britain's case, capital went to the future dominions of Canada, Australia, New Zealand, as well as to the United States. In the French case, it preferred the 'semi-colonies' of Tsarist Russia and Ottoman Turkey, where it built their railways, took possession of their banks, and lived off their national debt.

Little was left for the huge areas now being carved into African colonies, and even that little became available only where mineral wealth could be proven. Otherwise the gap was filled by limping chartered companies, or by hand-to-mouth remedies elsewhere. Leopold's Congo State was the sole exception. It was certainly the scene of fearful scandals of robbery and violence. Yet compared with much that happened elsewhere, and most of all in the neighbouring French Congo, the Leopoldian State eventually became a serious financial enterprise. Leopold actually invested European money in order to promote an eventual profit. Next door, in the French equatorial colonies, they copied the methods of Leopold but lacked his resources in money, and the result for a long time was little different from simple piracy. At least in their settler colonies, the British and the Germans (not to speak of the Portuguese) might claim to be doing differently. But the claim was largely an empty one.

The bankers gave way in the end, their arms suitably twisted by the frenzy of end-century European nationalism, as well as by appeals to their sense of security at home. Colonies could be 'a safety valve for states menaced by internal agitations', Italy's *Nuova Antologia* was noting as early as 1884.[7] Cecil Rhodes offered the same argument in Britain, pointing to the perils of London's riotous East End and the need to export trouble. Bismarck got hold of much the same idea, while a prominent French historian remarked at about the same time that 'oversea expansion can be a remarkable means of assuring internal peace,' because the French nation, if deprived of any 'grand design', might allow 'its warrior instincts to turn into intestinal quarrels, bloody intrigues, class hatreds, even civil wars'.[8] The Paris Commune, after all, was still warm in memory. Let mischief-makers depart for some lost corner of the Dark Continent, and there lose themselves in pursuit of national glory, however described or justified.

Looking back, it is possible to trace a number of decisive

underlying motives. One was the ambition of European traders to extend and secure their monopolies or break those of the African monopolies that opposed them. Another was the mounting rivalry between European powers, and most of all between a Britain now on the defensive and a France determined to find psychological and material compensation for the disasters she had suffered at the hands of the Prussians in 1870. A third was the push and pull of a whole variety of special interests. A fourth was the evidence that big capitalists could invest profitably wherever minerals could be discovered. All these were part of the process.

Another factor paved the way, the agreed political partition of almost the entire continent, and the acceptance of an obligation to subdue and 'occupy' these many prospective colonies. Conductor of the orchestra of this new imperialism was the ideology of nationalist aggrandizement which appeared with the 'new men' and their 'mass appeal', and which, soliciting now one order of interests and now another, proved able to carry all before it.

Seen from now, nothing could appear less rational or useful. Huge territories of which nothing was known were taken and occupied, or at least claimed, for no real reason other than to deny them to rivals. Huge claims for their 'natural wealth' were made for such territories by otherwise dubious adventurers who could adduce no solid evidence, and such claims were accepted without question. The perversity of all this was noted at the time. 'We have been engaged,' Lord Salisbury sardonically told a London audience, 'in drawing lines upon maps where no white man's foot has ever trod; we have been giving away mountains and rivers and lakes to each other, only hindered by the small impediment that we never knew exactly where they were.' But it made no difference by the 1890s: national interest had become identified with colonial possession, and the dictates of national interest were supreme.

Out of this flowed many ambiguities. The new colonies were said to be vital to the national interest of the imperial powers which got hold of them. Yet it soon became clear that many colonies were nothing of the kind. Enormous territories were 'held' simply because they had been formally enclosed; having got them, the imperialist countries clung on to them until, long afterwards, they discovered that they did not need them after all.

These territories had to be administered, but not at the expense of the metropolitan tax-payer. Even those that could yield large profits, sometimes annually of fifty per cent or more of invested capital in mineral exploitation, had to pay for their own administration and also, in large part, for their own infrastructure. Railways had to be built by forced labour or dirt-cheap labour even while mineral companies were pocketing huge dividends. Meanwhile nothing was to be allowed to stand in the way of permanent European control even when, as in parts of West Africa, all the principles of occupation had declared otherwise.

Culturally this new imperialism, this enlargement of the nation-state developed from the English economic revolution and the French political revolution of a hundred years earlier, was said to represent all that Africans must achieve if they were to 'come out into the light of day'. Africans were being dispossessed, affirmed the more high-minded of imperialists, only in order that they might eventually build such models of their own. In point of fact, however, the new imperialism did not usher in a time of liberty and enlightenment, but one of a cruder racism than any known before. During the nineteenth century Africans could be governors of British colonies: after the 1890s they could not even become department heads.

Making sense of this experience in all its verbal ambiguity was to need time. The South African Sol Plaatje in besieged Mafeking was better placed than most of his contemporaries to know a silk purse from a sow's ear, if only because he was faced with the luridly racist night-thoughts of the *Mafeking Mail*, 'which regards the native as a mere creature'. Yet even he could long nourish a belief that British success against the Boers would also be an African success. Not until a decade later, when he saw the terms of the Act of Union between the Cape Colony, Natal, and the former Boer Republics, did Plaatje see the enormity of his error.

Most Africans in Western-educated groups were in the same predicament. They held to the liberal Victorian vision of civilization kindling its light from one new nation to the next, drawing each within its blessed fold, long after the local facts depicted a very different prospect. Yet to write off these men and women as merely naive or foolish would be to read back into history the lessons that history had not yet taught.

8

COMPLETING THE ENCLOSURE

Many outside influences had come into the continent during previous centuries, sometimes by peaceful infiltration, at other times by conquest. Those that came with the colonial invasions were different in scale but above all in their underlying assumptions. These supposed, invariably, that Africa should be enclosed within the processes of an altogether different history, that of the Western Europeans. Dispossession was not to be the prelude to an absorption of the newcomers by Africa and its cultures, but the reverse. The intended alienation was to be complete.

The invasions themselves were carried through over several decades, but essentially in the last fifteen years of the nineteenth century. They were widely and bitterly resisted. Often brutal, the invading campaigns were with few exceptions ill-organized, poorly planned, and done on the cheap. All this reflected the reluctance of European treasuries, as of European capital, to spend money on enterprises which governments disliked or privately deplored, as well as the general conviction, which often led to sharp reverses, that 'native resistance' was unworthy of serious attention.

There were some large exceptions. The British invasion of Asante in 1874 was a costly affair and a major effort.[9] The French campaigns against the rulers of the Western Sudan were long and expensive. The Ethiopian defeat of an invading Italian army in 1896 cost the Italians more killed than all those who had fallen in the battles for the unification of Italy itself. There were other large expeditions.

Mostly, however, the invasions were carried through by small numbers of European troops backed with levies from the West Indies or elsewhere in the already colonial world, and, increasingly, by conscripts or mercenaries levied in Africa itself. In this, too, the invasions were to have their formative effect: they brought into existence the first of all those 'sub-élites' who were to prove indispensable to colonial government as local agents, interpreters, and policemen. These troops now became the backbone of every military expedition. It was already an old tradition: the Portuguese in western Angola had recruited their earliest *guerra preta*, or black army, during the early decades of the sixteenth century.

They were easily obtained by a mixture of bribery, corruption or the local use of force. Africa 'before nationalism' had no psychological barriers against recruitment of men from one ethnic group to fight against men of another. Chiefs could be browbeaten or bought into agreement to raise men; and there were plenty of individual adventurers willing to serve for a rifle or the loot that it could win.

Thus the earliest French black troops, origin of the multi-ethnic Tirailleurs Sénégalais created in 1857, were formed early in the nineteenth century by agreement with local chiefs. These chiefs supplied as troops the men they had previously supplied as captives for enslavement, and the French were able to send two companies of such soldiers, Wolof in origin, to fight in Madagascar as early as 1828, and another such company to French Guyana ten years later. For the British it was rather their Indian empire which formed the precedent, in this as in other elements of their colonial policy; and African troops were raised and regularly used in every colonial campaign upon which the British embarked.

In 1896 it was thought necessary to launch another invasion of Asante, and troops were sent from England. But these were much outnumbered by troops raised in the West Indies and by local levies, the latter consisting of 1,000 Hausa soldiers, recruited in what was shortly to become Northern Nigeria, and about 800 others from the coastal peoples of the Gold Coast colony. In the next and last campaign against Asante, that of 1900, it was found possible to dispense with British troops altogether, save for officers. All the invading force was African in origin except for a detachment of Sikhs from India.

Along the coast, in the Niger region now being invaded

by Britain, it was much the same. One of the first acts of the Royal Niger Company after its establishment as an economic and political monopoly in 1886 was to acquire a force of 424 Hausa and Yoruba soldiers under British officers. This was duly incorporated and enlarged into the West African Frontier Force, initially under Frederick Lugard's command, with which the invasions of the north were carried out. Its strength lay in its discipline and experienced military command, but even more in its use of lately-invented quick-firing guns, and of light artillery.

Like the Portuguese, the Italians always relied heavily on local levies. Raised initially by General Baldissera in 1888, their Eritrean *ascari* provided the main body of their army of invasion against Ethiopia. The Tigray invasion was carried out by 3,500 *ascari* under Italian officers. Later, at Adowa, Baratieri had some 7,000 Italians with as many *ascari* as well. Generally, in all this, one parochialism marched against another, but at Adowa the Ethiopian emperor showed that he understood the Italian general better than the Italian understood the Ethiopian. The utter futility of Baratieri's battle at Adowa could scarcely have occurred if this had not been the case.

Baratieri was not alone in making a fool of himself. A history of the Europeans at this time would have a good deal to say about the ignorance and complacency of invading commanders. They marched off into the unknown as though upon parade, knowing next to nothing of the country through which they had to pass, nor of its peoples, nor of its languages; without their African guides, they could scarcely have marched at all. Perhaps the one large exception was that of the French marshal Bugeaud who carried through the occupation of Algeria against resistance led by Abd al-Kader. He had learnt about irregular warfare while fighting Spanish guerrillas during the wars of Napoleon, and was Europe's first colonial exponent of what was to become known, long afterwards, as 'counter-insurgency'.

The pattern was improved upon. In French Africa the Tirailleurs Sénégalais drew rank and file from many territories, becoming Senegalese in little more than name. Their use was extended to equatorial territories, and developed a callousness typical of mercenaries. Thus Oubangui was enclosed with the commitment of four companies of Tirailleurs and local auxiliaries. Most of these Tirailleurs were equatorial in origin.

The British list of similar ventures, whether for enclosure or 'pacification', was also a long one. Here, too, mercenary callousness became the general rule; and with this 'tradition', in due course, an independent Africa would have to settle its accounts, or, failing in that, take over the same heritage. In 1905-6 the British in Kenya moved against the recalcitrant Nandi for the sixth time, using twelve companies almost all African, assisted by Masai and Somali auxiliaries. The Nandi lost an official count of 1,117 killed, many wounded, some 26,000 cattle, 36,000 sheep. Later in 1906 the Embu got the same treatment, losing 407 killed. Back in London they were a little shaken by all this bloodshed, but rallied their spirits. 'Unless we are going to abrogate our civilizing mission in Africa,' commented an official, 'such expeditions with their attendant slaughter are necessary.'[10]

The settlers certainly thought so. Others began to wonder. In 1908 another Kenya people, the Kissi, were beaten up for recalcitrance, losing about 100 killed. An under-secretary at the Colonial Office thought things were going too far, and sent a warning to the Kenya governor. 'Surely,' he commented, 'it cannot be necessary to go on killing these defenceless people on such an enormous scale.' His name was Winston Spencer Churchill. 'One might almost say,' concluded another official comment of 1906, 'that there is no atrocity in the [Leopoldian] Congo – except mutilation – which cannot be matched in our [East African] Protectorate.'[11] All this was to echo down the years.

German practices were of the same order. They too relied upon African levies. They too bought slaves and turned them into soldiers: in Dahomey, for instance, for use in Kamerun. Such 'slave mercenaries' were generally not paid by the German command. Their punishment was accordingly physical whenever thought to be required, usually by lashing with a hippo-hide whip. Brutalized, such troops became the colonial scourge of generally defenceless peoples.[12]

Long afterwards, in the time of the African warlords that began around 1965, the Emperor Bokassa and his kind would continue with the good work.

How far were such men volunteers? Some were, undoubtedly: the prospect of loot, and sometimes of wage payment, proved attractive in a period of generalized violence. Many, and probably by far the greater part, were got by the coercion or corruption of their chiefs or lineage headmen; or else they were men who passed from one form of bondage to another. Recalling the French invasion of Dahomey, a French officer described this familiar form of transfer:

So we hastily got hold of the 300 natives from Senegal who were said to be volunteers. Recruited in response to a payment of 40 francs or because of the power of the illusion, in which they were encouraged to believe, that they were going on 'looting raids' or to 'make captives' [whom they would duly be able to sell as slaves], or else, with many of them, thanks to the more persuasive and forceful arguments of village headmen in overcoming any who hung back, these blacks were hauled out of the bush, given intensive training for a month, and then declared to be soldiers.[13]

Old servitudes had simply acquired a new form.

The great enclosure was mostly complete, at least in outline, by 1904 when the Germans undertook their destruction of the Herero and Nama in South-West (Namibia); but many lesser campaigns had still to be fought against the recalcitrant. 'Pacification' of resisters like the Nandi continued in all regions until the eve of the First World War, and here and there until the 1920s, even in a few cases into the 1930s. Most of these many and even countless campaigns of 'pacification' appear in the records as 'police actions' or 'administrative measures'; but some were big affairs. In 1915, for example, the Portuguese had to send 7,000 metropolitan troops against Cuanhama (Ovambo) resistance in south Angola, while many years of sporadic fighting by the British and Italians were required to end the resistance of the early Somali nationalist leader, Mohamed Abdille Hasan, in 1920. Again in the 1920s, the French and Spanish had to wage a major campaign in Morocco against another nationalist forerunner, the innovating Abd al-Krim.

After that there was a kind of peace; and not until the 1950s would there be a need for large European contingents to fight new forms of resistance. By the 1910s, or soon after, the emergent system could handle its problems of law and order with little call on home resources. African troops and police forces were raised on a permanent basis, and paid for from local taxation; the latter, it was quickly realized, could also cover the cost of European personnel.

Having thus acquired and subdued enormous territories, the imperialist Powers duly recognized their system, however little value or importance they attached to it in the general run of their world affairs. They now set about inventing appropriate doctrines of colonial rule.

9

DOCTRINE AND REALITY

The great administrative and other differences in colonial Africa were between territories chosen for white settlement, and territories where white settlement did not occur. This contrast was barely affected by the original nationality of the settlers, since all of them, whether British or French or German, Belgian or Italian or Portuguese, evolved the same instrumental mythologies of race, aimed at the same maximization of their standards of life at the cost of 'the natives', and wished to reach the same position of supreme internal power achieved by their earliest forerunners and exemplars, the Afrikaner and English-speaking whites of South Africa.

For Africans, accordingly, cultural suffocation and social dismantlement were always more severe in the settler territories. Elsewhere, as especially in parts of British West Africa, the colonial period could afterwards appear as little more than an episode, so abundantly did local cultures manage to survive it. But no suggestion that the period was episodic in regions of white settlement has come to hand, nor seems likely to. In comparison with this major contrast, differences between the policies of the various colonial powers mattered far less.

All the same, these differences existed and continued to grow. Like the presence or absence of white settlement, they form part of the structural history of the twentieth century. They took effect at many levels. In economic policies, as will be seen, all the powers adopted much the same methods and objectives. Here the differences lay in the relative backwardness of the power in question. The most backward of all, Portugal, retained forced labour for long after it had vanished elsewhere; France, less backward than Portugal, abolished forced labour in 1946; Britain, the least backward in its own economic structure, did so much earlier.[14] In other ways, politically and culturally, these intra-colonial differences produced varying attitudes to law, education, local government and the possible assimilation of Africans into this or that European culture. Above all, they took shape in European languages and their use, and in what may be called the style of life.

At one level the inner history of the colonial period was always one of adjustment by ruling Europeans to the framework of possibilities laid down by the Africans they ruled: even if, as was often the case, these Europeans were persuaded that it was they and not the Africans who held the initiative. But at another level, less profound yet seldom merely superficial, the cultures of the colonizing countries were to have a persistently formative influence. Neighbouring 'Anglophones' and 'Francophones' became more different from each other in their manners, dress and much else, than anything that separated the peoples of widely situated regions. By a nice inversion of cultural usage, this or that European attitude comprised in the term 'our Africans' would eventually become embodied, after the colonial period was over, in this or that African attitude to 'our Europeans'.

Like the enclosure itself, the elaboration of policy had to be piecemeal, haphazard, hand-to-mouth. In this business of governing territories whose use or value to the colonial power was often hard to see, opportunism reigned supreme. This opportunism flowed from the situation in any given place; it also flowed from the quirks of individual character of those who were sent to rule that place. Imperialist ideology endowed these rulers with the prestige of unchallengeable patrons; and they had to have, in any case, a wide measure of local power. Distances were enormous, communications often by foot. Eccentrics flourished, sometimes charmingly, at other times not.

There were fascinating cases. In 1895, for one example among a multitude, a small Hausa force under a British officer, and equipped with one piece of field artillery and a Maxim machine-gun, subdued the *alafin* (king) of the ancient but much decayed Yoruba state of Oyo (western Nigeria). A missionary eye-witness described how Commander Bower's first shell was an over-shoot, but his second 'burst in the outer courts of the palace'. It was soon over, but not before a third to a half of Oyo town was sadly battered.[15] This use of force was much condemned by missionaries and the Lagos worthies, but officially was thought appropriate. 'In a country like this,' a senior British official informed the Colonial Secretary (then Joseph Chamberlain), 'radical changes are not made entirely with the aid of a silk glove, the iron gauntlet must appear at times . . .'[16] The *alafin* and his advisers saw the force of that argument. They remained convinced that their treaty with the British gave no right to territorial invasion. But they sensibly capitulated. The interesting thing is what happened next.

In 1903 a young man called Captain William Alston Ross arrived from Britain as a recruit to the colonial service. He seems to have been a characteristic product of a Victorian 'public school', which meant that an upper-class ambition was grafted to a middle-class origin: in the British colonial service, the case was not uncommon. In 1906 Ross was posted to Oyo as its first district commissioner. There, as Atanda has told the story, he found an *alafin* who was perfectly convinced of his own continuing sovereignty, and exercised this through lineage heads and appointed persons of authority (chiefs) as for long into the past. Oyo, in short, was being governed as before and Ross, though formally in charge, had nothing to do nor indeed could do anything, save give orders to the *alafin*.

Remembering the lesson of the field gun, the *alafin* accepted these orders. But since government remained exactly as before, it soon transpired that what Ross was really doing was little more than make the *alafin*'s dispositions appear to be his own. This became all the more convenient to Ross, as the records indicate, because every addition to the *alafin*'s prestige was necessarily an addition to his own. Happy in his eminence, Ross set about helping the *alafin* to create what Atanda has called 'a new Oyo empire' to replace the one that had fallen into ruins early in the nineteenth century. Ross could preen himself on playing God to the *alafin*'s Angel Gabriel; the *alafin*, meanwhile, could see things in reverse. They worked together in much amity and impressive ceremonial.

This practice of accepting the local governing situation upon condition that local rulers in turn accepted British overlordship became known as Indirect Rule, though not because of Ross. The latter continued in Oyo, as God or the Angel Gabriel according to point of view, until 1931, when new needs broke up the partnership in favour of a certain degree of modernization. But Indirect Rule was widely promoted wherever there was no economic interest and therefore no 'close administration'; and huge areas of enclosed Africa were now in that position.

The origins of British Indirect Rule had been in India where part of that empire remained under the local government of kings and princes. As colonial doctrine, it was codified for Africa in 1922 by Frederick Lugard, the conqueror of the north and then governor-general of Nigeria, in a book called *The Dual Mandate in British Tropical Africa*. A full analysis would belong to a history of the British in Africa; here one need note only two relevant points. The first is that the 'system' arose from local accommodation between the British and the Fulani emirate governments they had subdued in what now became Northern Nigeria. The second is that the essential arguments were all set forth in 1918, and in rather better prose, by one of Lugard's principal lieutenants, Charles Temple.[17]

Temple's father had served in the severely élitist Indian Civil Service, and it was natural that Temple, charged with governing Northern Nigeria, should apply the lessons and the standards of that Service in its relations with Indian princely rulers. As Chief Secretary and afterwards Governor of a vast peripheral area enclosed partly to deny it to the French and partly from sheer vanity of enclosure, he envisaged his task as merely to hold the ring and keep the peace. He predicated three possible systems of colonial rule, 'any of which may be adopted by the dominating European race for the control of a native race'. One was Direct Rule, with all government in the hands of European officials, and Africans 'in minor posts only, such as clerkships', while 'the policing of the country is entrusted to European officials, with coloured subordinates in Government employ wearing Government uniforms.' Most colonial rule was like that. But it would clearly not do for Northern Nigeria: there the

British had neither the power to substitute themselves for emirate rule, nor any interest in trying to do that.

A third method was a mixture 'whereby the white man, realizing that he has not the force necessary to enable him to deprive the native governing class of all their power, at least whittles it down to a great extent'. But this could end in nothing better than a messy form of Direct Rule, although it too was widely practised or at least attempted. Temple's preferred system was his second alternative, Indirect Rule, by which 'the native governing class' and all its political, juridical and executive institutions 'remained as real, living forces, and not as curious and interesting pageantry', while 'European influence is brought to bear on the native indirectly, through his chiefs, and not directly through European officers'. As good aristocrats, or even deities, the British lords of this system would stay 'a good deal in the background', the underlying object being 'to assist the native to develop that civilization which he can himself evolve'. Decades later, white South Africans trying to resolve some of the more inconvenient contradictions of *apartheid*, or 'separate development', would call their 'Bantustans' into being with something of the same thought in mind.

Opportunism thus emerged as doctrine. But as with Ross and the king of Oyo, it became unclear as time went by just who was God and who was Gabriel. The emirs were in some sense the prisoners of the Temples, but the same was true in reverse. As Temple himself noted, the typical emir manipulated his situation so as to increase his autocratic power. But the typical British official, for long under instructions never to go outside his emirate capital except on pleasure bent, could only stand back and applaud, or even actively assist in this process. He had no local power unless he cared to send for a punitive column (an admission of failure liable to break his career), and he could seldom have any clear notion of what happened in 'his' emirate. The result became an unembellished autocracy, with the emirate states increasingly cordoned against any infiltration of 'disturbing ideas' from the ebullient and subversive southern regions of Nigeria.

Becoming governor-general of Nigeria in 1931, a former

Tanganyika administrator called Sir Donald Cameron disgustedly described the system as one of 'Sovereign Rule by Native Chiefs ... an unhallowed policy insidiously introduced in the later twenties of this century'. His own policy, developed in Tanganyika after 1925, was 'indirect administration'. This variant of Indirect Rule was desirable, he held, because officials then ruling directly were hopelessly overworked, and could govern only by rule of thumb from one day to the next. But it was also desirable since it opened the way to fulfil, eventually, the promises of the League Mandate under which Britain held Tanganyika (having taken it from the Germans in 1918), and could meanwhile give Africans at least a distant prospect of governing themselves. Cameron was duly lambasted by the leaders of the Kenya settlers who then ruled the roost in British East Africa: they believed, as Cameron complained, that 'the Africans of Kenya must never at any time have any political rights',[18] and were, accordingly, tremendously indignant at any suggestion that the Africans of Tanganyika should eventually acquire some. Cameron's reforms in Tanganyika helped to shield Africans there from settler ambitions.

        Variants of this or that form of Indirect Rule were tried elsewhere. They were even tried, disastrously, in parts of Nigeria where local peoples possessed no chiefs of their own. They were always predicated on the same racist assumption set forth so well by Temple: that 'the number of posts [in administration] which could be filled by educated natives must always remain few and must be posts which do not carry high responsibility'. Usually, they ended as Temple had predicted: with a more or less messy form of Direct Rule in the wake of local objections, sometimes violent, to the appointment of chiefs who were despised or distrusted as puppets of the nearest white official. Such accommodations could succeed, really, only where a region was both peripheral to colonial economic interests and possessed a traditional ruling group. Otherwise colonial rule was direct autocracy mediated through African policemen and interpreters.

        Opportunism reigned on the French scene as well, just as did the instrumental attitudes of racism: but from a different background. With the major exception of South Africa after the discovery of diamonds and gold in the 1880s, territorial occupation for the British was a reflex of weakness. Forcefully challenged by new industrializing powers, the British Empire was driven off the ground of 'international free trade', always to Britain's advantage so long as Britain remained 'top nation', and was reduced to the monopolist imperialism of its rivals. Britain's decline really came with the period of greatest territorial expansion: the first process, however ironically, led straight into the second.

This was scarcely seen at the time. The rush for African colonies might seem perverse and even silly to 'lords of creation' like Salisbury: to their successors like Chamberlain, it appeared the reverse. To add to Britain's 'imperial estates' now appeared as a proof of Britannia's waxing power. Culturally, in any case, the British continued to regard the colonized peoples as mere objects of use or experiment: in no way could they ever become part of the British nation, no matter what passports might declare, nor should they be given the least encouragement to try. Hence, for example, British indifference to the teaching of English, and their tolerance of 'native vernaculars' as media of instruction or even of administration. Hence again, somewhat later, the relative ease with which the British ruling classes were to accept the idea of decolonization: the British nation was losing no part of itself.

Although as blinkered in Africa as any other European colonizing people, Frenchmen in France had a different idea of 'the nation'. Generally, the French nation was thought to exist, imma- nently or in fact, wherever people could speak French and French culture played a dominant role: partially, Belgium and Switzerland provided the only and perverse exceptions. This was partly a heritage from Jacobin ideas of the 1790s. More immediately, it was the product of a belief that getting hold of colonies could compensate France, in size of territory as well as in other ways, for what she had lately lost in Europe. French adventures in the late nineteenth- century Africa were always inseparable, in their ideological moti- vations, from the trauma in 1870 of the disaster at German hands and the German amputation of Alsace-Lorraine.

Those who argued for colonies promised rich rewards to France, but it was long before French bankers and investors would believe them. Meanwhile the 'colonialists' were opposed by others who denounced them as anti-patriotic 'for going to fight at the end of the world, for spending hundreds of millions, for killing thousands of Frenchmen' – never mind the Africans – instead of keeping their eyes fixed steadfastly on the real enemy in Germany and his odious occupation of two sacred fragments of the national soil. 'I have lost two sisters,' superbly cried the arch-nationalist Deroulède, spurning the colony-seekers, 'and you offer me twenty flunkeys.'[19]

There was at least a refreshing absence of the thought, so often expressed in England, that colonial enterprises were a sacrifice accepted by Europeans for the benefit of Africans. Even the great Cardinal Lavigerie saw the affair in terms of what would be good for the French. Addressing himself to the 'Christian population of Alsace and Lorraine' on the morrow of 1870, he told them that 'Algeria, French Africa, opens its doors and its arms to you. Here you will find for yourselves, for your children, for your families, lands wider and more fertile than those you have left in the hands of the invader.'[20]

'You have been horribly mutilated,' a French admiral then governing Cochin-China argued against nationalists of the Deroulède school of sentiment. 'But is that a reason to fold your arms and make no effort to compensate, however feebly, for the painful loss that you have suffered?' Others reshaped the same argument. 'There can be no compensation,' another prominent pro-colonialist of the 1880s, Paul Bert, sought to reassure the anti-colonial nationalists: 'Do not fear that this idea of colonial development' – of the development of France, and not, as the term would afterwards be made to suggest, the development of the colonized peoples – 'can distract me for an instant from what no Frenchman can ever forget,' the loss of Alsace-Lorraine. As time went by the 'compensators' carried the day. Bankers were induced to rally less reluctantly; so were politicians. By the 1890s the French were leading the game, and rivals had to quicken their step.

French colonial doctrine took shape, accordingly, as

'enlargement of the French nation'. Dressed in Jacobin guise, and duly launched in the dithyrambic prose of politicians of the Radical Party who now 'made the empire' as a party fief, this doctrine supposed that all the colonial peoples were in some magical sense members of the nation or community of France. This was called Assimilation, a sort of counter-doctrine to Britain's Indirect Rule.

The cultural implications of Assimilation had some importance. One of its principles was that all education had to be in French, since no other access to civilization was thinkable. So doggedly was this maintained that not even the Algerians of Algeria were able to receive any non-Koranic education in Arabic. At least this meant that the French language was relatively well taught when compared with English in the British colonies. Provided that they could get to France, and then stayed clear of radical gestures, Africans could also move about in French society somewhat less uneasily than in British society.

Otherwise, Assimilation was a mere fantasy. It existed, true enough, in the privileged 'four communes' of coastal Senegal: Dakar, Gorée, Rufisque, St Louis. Yet the number of Africans with French citizenship in Senegal was only 48,973 in 1926, out of a total (estimated) population of 1,358,000, and fewer than double that number even in 1945. The same totals for the whole of French West Africa, in 1926, were 50,722 out of 13,499,000; and, in 1945, 97,707 out of 15,955,000. In Madagascar, where much was also talked of Assimilation, there were fewer than 8,000 Malagasies with French citizenship as late as 1939. The assimilated total for the French equatorial colonies was smaller still.

As with the British, varieties of direct or indirect rule were practised wherever convenient; but preferred policies invariably discouraged change. Generally, as Deschamps has remarked of the middle colonial period in Madagascar, everything was 'frozen' into an accepted pattern. There might be a 'crumbling away of social structures, the birth of individualism, the transformation of the old outlook by missionary and educational action, the influences of European modes of life and thought': but 'movement was rejected': as in British Africa, 'things had to stay within the *status quo*.'[21]

The Belgian practice also had some specific differences from Britain's. Settlers were allowed into the Congo. But they were not encouraged, nor given the politically privileged position they rapidly achieved in Kenya and the two Rhodesias. This flowed not from any Jacobin tradition, for Belgium had no such two-faced animal in its brief ancestry, but from a strictly commercial approach. This in turn derived partly from the ethos of Belgian society, and partly from reaction against the condition of the Leopoldian State taken over as a Belgian colony in 1908.

What the condition of this Congo Free State really had become by 1905 or so was described in public by a famous commission of inquiry, as well as by the more general criticism of the Congo Reform Association launched in Britain by the liberal reformer, Edmund Morel. And whatever that report concealed from a sense of tact, since Leopold was still king, a prominent specialist in colonial law set forth in 1906. 'The truth about the Congo,' Félicien Cattier then concluded, 'is that this state is not a colonizing state, and scarcely a state at all . . . The colony is administered neither in the interests of the natives, nor even in the economic interests of Belgium. To win a maximum revenue for the King: that is the regulator of its administrative action.'[22]

The Belgian state took control with a realistic determination to reduce Leopoldian horrors and put their new colony into working order. There could be no question of avoiding 'undue interference', or of 'staying in the background'. Bureaucratic obsession became the most enduring though not endearing characteristic of Belgian administration. Everything possible must be labelled and filed for reference; everyone possible must be named and noted down for work passes and movement passes. Out of this came an administration whose severely authoritarian attitudes were bolstered by a ministering Catholic church of bottomless paternalism – like all paternalists, it could rarely afford much affection for its wards – and geared to the interests of a series of trustified mining and other corporations, headed by a monster called the Société Générale, whose headquarters were in Brussels. The general aim was well expressed in a report of 1917. 'The former power of the (African) chiefs,' this explained, 'will pass into the realm of memory. They will become civil servants applying the laws and regulations of the State.'[23]

But the Belgian state retained control, in contrast with what happened in Southern Rhodesia, where control passed to settler hands in 1923 (as it had in South Africa in 1910), or even in Kenya or Northern Rhodesia, where British colonial government continued to share power with small settler minorities. And in course of time, settlers in the Congo being few, Belgian policy allowed Africans to graduate to skilled jobs as part of a consistent policy. But not more: because more 'advancement' might lead to trouble, and the Belgians in their vast colony were understandably obsessed by fear of trouble. A trickle of Africans from British and other non-settler territories could graduate in European universities, and form the educated groups that were to play a large part in the rise of nationalism. But the Belgian doctrine began and continued in line with a colonial minister's statement of 1954: 'We have seen that those Natives who have been shown Europe, and given a very advanced education, do not always return to their homelands in a spirit favourable to civilization and to the Mother Country in particular.' In such situations it became inevitable that nationalism, when it appeared, should be in the hands of those who, in less restrictive colonies, became known as the 'sub-élites', the clerks and male nurses and primary schoolmasters; and that mass movements of messianic content should particularly flourish.[24]

The variants continued. Little need be said about the Germans, for their colonizing time was cut short by defeat in the First World War, when all their colonies passed as mandates of the League of Nations to Britain, France, or Belgium. Their attitudes were generally authoritarian although not unusually brutal, except in South-West Africa (Namibia). They too shared the racism of other colonizing powers, and used it as an instrument of domination, while their understanding of African reactions proved no greater. In 1906, for example, they deprived the Herero of life, liberty, land and cattle, while the Nama neighbours of the Herero suffered the same disastrous fate. Yet the *Deutscher Kolonial Lexikon* of 1920, though edited by a man as relatively enlightened as their last governor of German East Africa, Heinrich von Schnee, could still fail to perceive that the Herero war of resistance, like that of the Nama, was one of national self-defence. The cause of that 'rebellion', declared the *Lexikon*, lay 'in the consciously freedom-loving mentality of the Herero'. This 'felt itself ever more acutely threatened'; not, however, by loss of land and cattle to intrusive settlers backed by German power, but 'by the progress of civilization (*Kultur*)'. And it was this 'progress' that provoked 'their all-out resistance to the colonizing intruder'. Later on, during the great Kenya Emergency of the 1950s, otherwise intelligent Europeans would say just the same about the Kikuyu fighters of the so-called 'Mau Mau'. The trouble with these rebellious Kikuyu was not that they had lost land, cattle, and freedom; it was simply, as was portentously explained, that they were unable to adjust to the 'psychological strains' of modern life.

Of the other colonizing powers, there is little to be said about the Spanish. Their Moroccan enclave was small. Their West Saharan holdings had a very sparse population, mostly nomads who could be 'administered' only whenever Spanish officials were able to get sight of them. Their equatorial holdings, consisting of the small enclave of Rio Muni and the offshore island of Fernando Poo, were run by the principles of a down-at-heel and therefore not intolerant authoritarianism.

The Italian contribution to doctrine deserves more attention. Undertaken against the general indifference of the rising bourgeoisie of Milan and other northern cities, and prosecuted in a series of violent lurches caused chiefly by the ambition of southern politicians, notably Crispi, or else by the simple thought that a newly united Italy must somehow or other keep up with the Jones's and find colonies, Italy's colonization was in one sense the real thing. Whether in Eritrea or Ethiopia, Somalia or Libya, it was always intended to establish colonies of emigrants who should thus continue to live under the Italian flag and remain part of the Italian nation unlike all the millions lost to the Americas in these years and later.

The first question was: where to go? Ousted from political

control of Tunisia, where a French Protectorate declared in 1881 found 700 French citizens but 11,000 Italians, Tripoli seemed an obvious answer. Yet British patronage in the Red Sea turned Italian eyes that way. The Red Sea port of Assab was thus declared an Italian possession in 1882 and opened the way to other Red Sea adventures; while Eritrea, duly invaded, became an Italian colony in 1890. In 1905, as part of the share-out on the East Coast, Italian sovereignty was claimed over the Banadir Coast (the lower part of the coast of modern Somalia) and, against local resistance, an Italian colony of Somalia was declared in 1908.

Three years later Italian troops invaded the Turkish possessions of Tripolitania and Cyrenaica. These were declared Italian colonies in 1913, again over many dead bodies, and were eventually joined together in 1935, as Italian Libya, after a long war of resistance by the Sanusi. Such official figures as are available from records still sparsely known indicate that the population of Cyrenaica was reduced from 225,000 in the 1920s to 142,000 in 1931 after the Fascist commanding general, Rodolfo Graziani, had completed his work. Ethiopia was invaded in 1935 and held until 1941.

Italian humanism could boast of an absence of 'social racism'. But Italian Fascism, fully installed by 1926, saw to it that a strictly ruthless racism should be applied wherever settler or other national economic interests were in play. A basic law providing for 'the defence of the race in contact with the natives of Italian Africa' was not in fact passed until 1939; but Fascist practice by that time had long ensured that there should be a minimum of assimilation and, of course, a complete absence of civic rights and political freedoms. Attitudes swung in practice from an empty paternalism to an outright repression.[25]

Portuguese theory and practice began as assimilationist but became increasingly restrictive after the First World War. With Salazar's installation of his Fascist-inspired *Estado Novo* early in the 1930s, both theory and practice came to resemble those of Italy's. Much was claimed for the régime's 'non-racism' on the grounds of its doctrine of assimilation. All this was largely mythical. Census figures as late as 1950 show that the assimilated proportion of the non-white inhabitants of Angola was smaller than one per cent, that of Mozambique still more minute, and that of Guiné barely one third of one per cent. All the rest were treated as *indígenas*, natives, against whom the grossest forms of discrimination were applied by law and common practice.

Inhabitants of the Cape Verde Islands were regarded as *assimilados* and so, theoretically, as Portuguese citizens, but in fact they suffered a systematic discrimination. The same was true of the indigenous inhabitants of the islands of São Tomé and Principe. In so far as it deserved the name, colonial doctrine in the Portuguese empire was defined accurately by Salazar's successor at the head of the dictatorship, Marcello Caetano, when a professor of Lisbon University early in the 1950s. 'The blacks,' he taught, 'are to be organized and enclosed as productive elements in an economy directed by whites.'[26] From an African standpoint, a form of slavery might be another accurate definition.

The men who had to administer these systems were as mixed in capacity and character as the circumstances in which they had to work. In the early years of makeshift they were anyone who happened to come to hand; later, with the systems more or less regularly installed by the 1920s, they were usually selected by examination. Inevitably, they reflected both the class structures of their mother-countries, and the relative degree of importance attributed to this or that territory.

Those of middle-class or assimilated upper-class formation, having less need to assert their own importance and superiority, tended to be less intolerant of African cultures than those of petty-bourgeois origin. This was noted at the time, and the Belgian missionary who complained in 1911 that among the dozen *chefs de poste* he knew there were 'not more than two gentlemen', while the rest were generally not 'the type of man who will assure the success of our native policy', probably spoke for many observers beside himself. Those who were 'gentlemen', and need fear no comparison with 'natives', could occasionally take a cautious interest in their subjects. Each of the colonial services, but above all the British and the French, produced a handful of distinguished students of Africa, as well as a number of outspoken critics of the system they had served.

Many laboured devotedly for the improvement of their districts. One can see this in a multitude of examples when reading such records as the 'district books' kept in British colonies, recording small events, discussing immediate worries, entering into the detail of a shilling spent or saved. Ill-paid themselves, they had a constant problem in finding money for administrative improvement. There was never enough; almost always there was far too little. This remained true even of mineral-rich colonies: company taxation was generally extracted, when at all, in Europe and not in Africa. The 'district books' arouse an immediate sympathy for the sheer poverty in which these men were obliged to work. There are 'some gadgets which only you are able to produce', appeals an agricultural officer in the British Somaliland Protectorate (northern Somalia) to the Public Works Department as late as the 1950s, and goes on to describe his modest wants: a pulley for a grain silo, a set of 'lugged channel irons' for the sliding gate of a small dam.

Like so many of his colleagues, this agricultural officer felt a paternal love for his district. 'On the subject of handing over,' he says in his 'farewell note', also in the distant dusty files of Borama, 'it has been said by Police and Administrative Officers of my acquaintance that once the new incumbent signs, the departing Officer's worries, responsibilities and ideas on the district must cease'. But no: he can't see things that way. His advice must surely continue to be useful, not least because of 'this special feeling that I have for the future of what I shall always regard as my district'. Such attitudes were not rare. They belonged to that strange relationship of admiration and respect for Africans which flowed from human nature into the interstices of a system which insisted, in its essence, that there was no place for either.

Even so, large proportions of such revenues as could be raised by direct taxation of Africans or by customs dues – the two chief sources of all colonial revenue – went to pay for administration. Shortly before the Second World War, by which time the systems were thoroughly 'run in' within a *status quo* envisaged as likely to endure for all foreseeable time, the proportion of Nigeria's state revenues allocated to administration was 30 per cent. Elsewhere in British Africa it tended to be as high or higher: 38.8 per cent in Kenya, 33.4 per cent in Uganda, 30.18 in Nyasaland (Malawi). Most went on law and order, with social services tailing far behind. Nigerian public education in 1938 received 5.9 per cent of state revenue; 9.9 per cent in Kenya (high because of local white settlers, only 5 per cent going to African public education); 6.7 per cent in Uganda; 4.7 per cent in Nyasaland.

Yet colonial administrations were scarcely over-staffed. The whole of Nigeria, in 1938 when total population had possibly achieved the forty-million mark, was being administered by 386 British political officials and another 1,663 in service departments, only 109 of whom were in education. Other territories, *pro rata* of population, showed a similar sparsity. It was the same in the French system. The whole vast extent of French West Africa, today composing eight independent states,* was governed at the end of the 1930s by 118 French *commandants de cercles* whose task was to operate through 48,049 African *chefs de village*, 32 *chefs de province* or *groupes de canton*, and 2,206 *chefs de cantons* or *de tribu*. Other systems told the same tale of an administrative standstill guaranteed by the principle of minimal expenditure. The doctrines spoke of progress and trusteeship for the benefit of Africans. Realities had to be different.

*Not counting Togo, administered between 1919 and 1960 as a mandate or trusteeship territory and formally outside the French West African colonial federation.

10

THE SYSTEM TO 1930:
1. LABOUR

These realities behind the doctrines of colonial rule derived partly from the political circumstances of Africa's partition. Rivalry between the invading powers led them to seize vast territories for much of which they had yet to find any use or purpose. Given that the peoples of these territories must be made to pay for their government by Europeans, the new rulers had to govern them by such taxation as could be got from inhabitants who, for the most part, still lived outside a cash economy. The results varied in detail according to ecologies and sizes of population, just as they also varied with the national and social origins of the administrators, but were in substance much the same.

Another and larger factor shaped these realities. Increasingly after the end of the First World War this consisted in the economic requirements or expectations of the various 'mother countries', as European parlance now generally if rather curiously called them. These underpinned the structures and cultural assumptions of foreign rule through which African political thought had somehow to find its way to new strategies of resistance and self-assertion. At this point, accordingly, there is need for some analysis of the crucial ways in which the colonial economic system worked.

Its formative nature can be divided into three fields of action: those concerning African labour, African land, and African trade. As the whole system evolved in its central period between the end of 'pacification', roughly 1920, and the far-reaching upheavals of the Second World War beginning in 1939, these fields of action occurred within two complementary 'zones'. The first of these were zones of mineral and cash-crop production for export; it was into these that such small European investments as were available all went.

The second were all those other areas, for a long time much larger than the first, which produced little or nothing for export and received no investment, but were indispensable to the whole system (or group of systems) because they could and did supply the zones of extractable profit, the 'export zones', with cheap labour and cheap food.*

Functioning in this way, the system already had a history of its own, being the 'modernized relay' of much older relationships between Europe and Africa. Early capitalism in western Europe had needed slaves for the Americas. These had been obtained from African 'export zones' which relied on their hinterland for a sufficient supply of captives for enslavement. Capitalism in the nineteenth century could dispense with slaves in the Americas, but wanted palm-oil and other tropical products. These in turn were produced in African 'export zones' which relied on their hinterland for cheap labour, if not for cheap food. What the colonial system essentially did was greatly to intensify and extend the range of export enterprise and its consequent exploitation, again relying on a hinterland of cheap labour as well as cheap food. Its need for military enclosure and direct political control came partly from this drive to intensify and re-organize, and partly from its being the projection of capitalist monopolies which had yet to become sufficiently mature to dispense with direct control. That need would begin to disappear when the imperialist monopolies developed into their trans-national phase after about 1950.

Whatever they were to do with the colonies they had acquired, and opinions often differed, the new rulers were clear about one thing: it would have to be done with African labour. No quantity of settlers could alter this, because Europeans, as a British official in Kenya explained as early as 1905, speaking for the whole prospect and perspective, 'will not do manual labour in a country

*Never more clearly explained than by a Belgian missionary expert on the Congo to the Royal Colonial Institute in 1951: 'The Congo economy makes two essential requirements of the rural population: to provide labour, and to provide this labour with cheap food.' J. van Wing, S.J., *Le Congo Déraille*, Bull. Inst. Roy. Col. Belge, I, 1951.

inhabited by black races'.[27] Most of what was initially achieved, administratively, was done by forced labour: dirt roads, administrative buildings, porterage, the first railways, and the rest.

This labour was obtained by directly purloining it from other villages, or, as time went on, by having it purloined through the agency of chiefs. Where chiefs proved recalcitrant or non-existent, they were replaced or installed by colonial nominees. Of Kikuyu chiefs listed in 1909 by the Kenya administration, 'almost all appear to have secured their official status through the practical test of the degree of their loyalty to Government, and not to their position in Kikuyu tribal society.'[28] The case of 'loyal chiefs' was very common. This was another part of the colonial heritage with which nationalism, later on, would have to reckon.

Coercion was universal. Often it applied to little more than extracting a few days' work from a few people. Sometimes it went far beyond that. Thus the French equatorial stretch of railway known as the Congo-Océan, linking Pointe Noire with Brazzaville, was built by the more or less forced recruitment between 1921 and 1932 of 127,250 'fit adult males'. These provided 138,125 'years of absence' from their village. Official figures reported 10,200 deaths among them up to 1928, when conditions were somewhat improved, and another 3,900 deaths after that. Such figures were invariably conservative.[29]

That kind of recruitment was generally masked as 'contract labour'. This in turn was based on labour codes which provided that every 'fit adult male' must 'work' for a specific number of days each year. The thought behind such codes was characteristic if peculiar. In all the many territories where 'contract labour' was widely used, colonial attitudes took it for granted that Africans were 'working' only when doing so for wages: when, that is, they were working for Europeans. Otherwise, no matter how laboriously they might produce within their own non-cash economies, they were held to be 'idle'; and 'idling', it was regularly explained, was tantamount to a punishable 'refusal of civilization'.

To quantify the total amount of labour taken in these ways is impossible, but it was large in most territories, and very large in several. The loss of labour to indigenous systems of rural production was increasingly accompanied, moreover, by loss of health for those 'recruited'. Both losses were the subject of adverse comment by official and other sources during the 1930s and later, although the effect had begun to be felt much earlier. There is a mass of evidence.

Italian forced labour in Somalia is one example. 'Masked in 1929 under a form of labour contract', a worried secretary-general of the Italian Fascist Party in Somalia reports to Mussolini early in the 1930s, this coercion had become 'a good deal worse than slavery'.[30] A slave would be cared for 'as a carter cares for his donkey', because of his purchase cost: if a slave died, his owner would have to buy another one. 'But when a Somali native dies after being assigned to an employer, or becomes unfit for work, it is merely a matter of his employer's asking the government to provide another one for nothing.'

Such 'contract workers', the same official goes on, might be marched hundreds of kilometres to their places of work under armed guard, chained or tied together whenever there was reason to fear they might otherwise be able to escape. They were then presented with their 'contracts', sometimes read aloud but often not, 'to which they must apply their finger print in signature'. If they fell ill or idled they were deprived of their rations 'in the hope that hunger will teach them better'. Seventeen years later a senior administrator in Angola reacted in the same way to similar abuses. 'Under slavery, after all, the native is bought as an animal: his owner prefers him to remain as fit as a horse or ox. Yet here [in Angola] the native is not bought – he is hired from the State, although called a free man. And his employer cares little if he sickens or dies, once he is working, because when he sickens or dies his employer will simply ask for another.'[31]

Worst in these Fascist colonies, forced labour practices were pervasive elsewhere. Up to 1946, in French West Africa, all 'natives' had to give 'statute labour' for ten or twelve days a year unless they could buy their way out of it. 'For forty years,' comments a French administrator in Guinea in 1940, 'statute labour has taken the form of arbitrary forced labour.'[32] In the Belgian Congo of 1923 an official commission finds that the obligatory labour service of sixty days a year for 'fit adult males' should mark 'the extreme limit' of such 'service', but hears that some natives have had to work for ninety or even 104 days, and goes on to ask that natives should at least be provided with 'the tools and materials necessary to carry out the work imposed on them'. In 1928 the same Commission notes 'with vivid satisfaction' that women are now to be exempted from obligatory porterage services, but takes care, having local realities in mind, to suggest 'an absolute ban on the use of women, old men and children in the building and maintenance of roads'.[33]

These methods of extracting labour from rural workers occupied with their own farms and other enterprises were inadequate in territories which had mines and plantations. Such methods could not be made to yield long-term labour. Besides this, they were much resisted. Innumerable small acts of rebellion, and some large ones, were provoked by demands for labour. Less direct and more effective methods of transferring men from rural areas to 'export enclaves' were clearly desirable. In finding these, as an historian of East Africa would afterwards remark, the starting point was that the peoples of Africa, unlike the working classes of Europe, 'were in possession of the means of subsistence'.[34] They would continue to work at home unless fetched. But could they not be fetched without direct use of force?

The answer was found in South Africa, where a Cape Colony Act of 1894 imposed a tax in cash, of ten shillings, on 'fit adult males', so that, as Prime Minister Cecil Rhodes blandly explained, rural producers might be removed from their life of sloth and idleness, and made to give some return 'for our wise and good government'.[35] The idea took on fast. To pay cash taxes, Africans would have to earn cash: almost invariably in that period, this meant leaving their villages for European employment. If they failed to pay, they must naturally be punished, and would work as prison labourers instead.

Cash taxation as a means of extracting long-term labour chimed with administrative needs for revenue. The latter usually came first. In Bechuanaland, for example, a hut tax had been paid since

1899. Initially at ten shillings a year, it was raised with the need for mining labour to 20 shillings in 1909, to 25 shillings in 1920, and to 28 shillings in 1931, after which the great depression brought it somewhat down again. In Kenya a rudimentary hut tax raised about £5,000 in 1901; in the years 1902–4 it raised £73,943. Poll taxes followed, mainly for the extraction of long-term labour rather than administrative revenue. Throughout East Africa, according to former governor Sir Donald Cameron, each 'fit adult male' (over the 'apparent age' of 18) was paying from 2s. 6d. to 5s. a year, 'although his gross cash income for the year may not amount to forty or even twenty shillings'.[36]

Major mining centres thus found their labour without direct coercion and at the lowest price they cared to pay in wages. The gold and diamond mines of the South African Transvaal were pioneers in this respect. They recruited single men on one-year contracts (but the details varied through time) not only from South Africa but from all neighbouring areas: eventually they were drawing labour from all the territories of southern Africa. Between 1921 and 1925 the Union Minière in Katanga (Belgian Congo) took as many as 10,000 men a year from their villages, or about ninety-six per cent of the labour force. In 1926, however, the Union Minière began changing to a stable mining force settled with its families at the mines; at the same time, the contractual period was lengthened from one to three years. With this, annual recruitment could begin to tail off: between 1936 and 1940, only eleven per cent had to be recruited every year. The contrast with the South African situation was very evident.

But the South African situation was typical of what generally evolved in the 1920s and 1930s. Sponsored at first by various forms of pressure, long-term migrant labour slowly acquired a momentum of its own. Men left their homes to earn cash to pay taxes. As things evolved, they also left – and especially the young – in order to find the cash to buy some of the things that wage-employment in towns or mines could now offer: bicycles, sewing machines, clothing, eventually radio sets. There were occasions when 'going to Goli', to the mining Witwatersrand became with all its physical trials and tests a kind of substitute for the initiation procedures whereby the young became recognized as adults in village life. Many new ambitions added to the flood; and a desire for a means of acquiring the power that could derive from possessing a Western education was not always the least of them.

Long-term or semi-permanent migrants (for survivors usually tried to return to their villages at the end of their working life) flowed not only into the zones of European enterprise. They also went into those 'export zones' where African producers were now growing more and more cocoa, peanuts and other cash crops. In West Africa, as in some other regions, inland territories relatively poor in their capacity to produce for export began to be drained of men to the advantage of coastal cash-crop colonies. By 1936, for example, more than 76,000 *navétanes* (from the Wolof word for rainy season, when migrants were needed) from a wide inland area were producing peanuts for Senegalese landlords, whether African or European. This local pattern was initially an easy-going one, contractually, and had attractions for 'subsistence' farmers who needed cash; but gradually it blended into the wider pattern, and led to a systematic impoverishment of inland territories in comparison with their near-coastal neighbours.

Between 1912–38 – and the trend continued after that – the population of the Gold Coast (Ghana) grew from an estimated 1,700,000 to four millions, partly through the continual migration of cultivators from the neighbouring (French) Volta territory. This migration was evidently not the consequence of Volta's 'natural poverty'. A distinguished French official gave four reasons for it. These were military conscription of Africans (not imposed in the Gold Coast), the abuse of obligatory labour regulations, the compulsory growing of cotton, and a monetary policy less favourable to Africans than that of the British in the Gold Coast.[37]

In these ways the French system reflected a certain backwardness of French capitalism compared with British capitalism, not fully overcome perhaps until the 1950s. This was especially shown in forced labour usages. Between 1921 and 1930, for example, more than 42,000 Africans were levied in the Ivory Coast for the Abidjan-

Ferkessedégou line of rail, though under conditions less mortal than for the equatorial Congo-Océan at the same time, and more than 16,000 men for timber-felling, transport and plantation work. 'Even by official figures,' comments Delavignette, it could be said that in these ten years 'nearly 189,000 healthy men in the prime of life, the best twentieth of the population, were dragged from their homes, from marriage, from their villages, from cultivation.' Governors protested, but the settlers in Ivory Coast had the whip hand, and protesting officials were liable to be dismissed by Paris. One of these was the liberal Governor Richard Brunet, of whom indignant settlers asked, it seems, 'whether he thought he was Jesus Christ?'[38]

Over very wide areas, by 1930, a long and complex transition from outright forced labour to tax-induced migrant labour had begun to dominate the scene. The results were destructive. Such health records as are available, notably for South Africa, point to the spread of syphilis, tuberculosis and other diseases incurred by migrants in mines or in peri-urban slums and shanty-towns. Many official reports inveighed against this wholesale migration. Of Nyasaland in 1935 an official committee reported that 'the whole fabric of the old order of society is undermined when thirty to sixty per cent of the able-bodied men are absent at one time.' The old community had been stable, with responsibilities counter-balanced by rights. But 'emigration, which destroys the old, offers nothing to take its place.'[39]

In these years, and in many territories, migrant labour became a *via crucis* for countless millions of uprooted rural people over decades, generation by generation; and this feature of the system probably did more to dismantle pre-colonial cultures and economies than most other aspects of the colonial experience put together.

The imperialist powers were successful in resolving their rivalries in Africa. That was the essential achievement of the Berlin conference of 1884–5. Its chief agreements on 'spheres of interest' and of intended occupation – the British securing monopoly over the lower Niger, the French over the Western Sudan, Leopold being given the Congo Basin, the Portuguese being allotted their limits of expansion in Angola and Mozambique – were followed by detailed border settlements. The bulk of these were made by 1901.[40] With one or two exceptions – Anglo-French rivalry in one place, Franco-German in another – the occupation and partition were made in amity among the powers. But what these powers could achieve in Africa they failed to manage in Europe. There came the First World War of 1914–18.

African involvement in that holocaust reflected colonial attitudes to African labour. There was much recruitment by one means or another. In West Africa the British raised some 25,000 troops, about half of these in Nigeria and some 10,000 in Gold Coast (Ghana). Most were retained in West Africa, but some were sent to the East African war against the Germans in Tanganyika. In British East Africa – Kenya, Uganda – recruitment was on an altogether different scale. A small number of Africans were recruited for British fighting units, but some 350,000 were used as unarmed carriers. In 1924 it was still possible to state that of the 46,618 Africans who thus lost their lives, 'the relations of 40,645 are still untraced, and unclaimed balances of pay and wages amounting to £155,447 are still owed to them.'[41] On their side the Germans in Tanganyika began the war with 216 white officers and 2,450 African rank and file, not counting police, and ended it with 3,000 whites and 11,000 Africans.

France was the largest user of African troops. Were they not, after all, inhabitants of that 'greater France' called in to compensate for the loss of Alsace-Lorraine and, now, to rescue those 'two sisters'? From first to last, some 211,000 black troops were raised, partly by the aid of the Senegalese black deputy for the 'four communes', Blaise Diagne, who justified recruiting with the argument, completely vain as it turned out, that if Africans fought in the war they might be given a say in the peace. About 170,000 were flung into the murderous battles of the Western Front; in these, 24,762 were eventually listed as dead.[42] Others never seen again were listed as missing. The total losses may have been as many as one-fifth of all recruited: even by the official list of dead, losses greatly exceeded one-tenth.

There was much resistance to recruitment, but it went

ahead. Madagascar provided some 40,000 men; about 4,000 of them died. French North Africa – Algeria, Tunisia and Morocco since 1912 – provided the immense total of 270,000 combatants; some 40,000 were listed as killed or missing, which usually amounted to the same thing. Money, too: local taxation in the French African colonies contributed 6,000 million francs in the values of that time. British colonies produced lesser but still substantial amounts. And then, of course, there was the war effort in the Portuguese, Italian, Belgian, and German colonies.

The First World War sharpened the monopolist functions of the various empires, confirmed their need for territorial possession, further inflamed their ideologies of race, and set the winners, after it was over, still more firmly to the work of installing their colonial systems.

11

THE SYSTEM TO 1930: 2. LAND

For most of Africa south of the Maghrib, wherever white settlement occurred in quantity, the pattern in land expropriation and the use of labour was set by the Union of South Africa. Formed in 1910 from the British colonies of the Cape and Natal and the defeated Afrikaner republics of Transvaal and Orange Free State, the Union was fully self-governing and white-controlled from the start. From the start, in all its basic structures and assumptions, it was also racist and segregationist. In this the Union confirmed the attitudes of the earlier Afrikaner republics and Natal, but extended these in line with growing labour needs. A Native Labour Regulation Act codified a rigid colour bar in wage employment only a year after the declaration of union. Subsequent laws merely lowered and reinforced this bar.

This pattern heralded a long period of rising white prosperity still continuing in the 1970s, if with some checks and hiccups in the 1920s and 1930s. By 1912, two years after Union, mining personnel totalled 325,000, only 36,000 of whom were white; black mining wages would thereafter fall steadily for decades. By then, too, the country already had some 2,600 miles of railway. White farming diversified from its prosperity in wool; ancillary industry began to appear in Johannesburg and several other towns. Everywhere the great cry was for more labour. Indians had begun to be brought in as indentured labour already in the 1860s: by 1899 they numbered 19,084 with 41,672 free Indians. They were not enough. We have noticed Rhodes's solution by poll tax. That too was not enough.

In 1913 there duly followed a Land Act which abolished all African land ownership in rather more than 90 per cent of South

Africa. This was to become one of the chief instrumental tools of segregation and *apartheid* ('separate development'). But its immediate motivation was to increase the labour supply. That was achieved by banning the then existing system of 'farming on the half', or 'Kaffir farming', by which Africans could use land in white areas on a system of *métayage* with white landowners, or else as squatters. It was also a way of reducing the wage-rate for land workers. Both aims were achieved. They were maintained, even though Africans outnumbered whites at least by four to one.

The same system of proletarianizing self-sufficient peasants, and of driving them into a labour market where they could have no bargaining power, was used elsewhere with local variants. In Southern Rhodesia, seized by the British South Africa Company in the 1890s, Crown Colony government was established in 1923, but on a pattern which gave all effective control to local settlers, numbering then some 34,000. Offered the option of joining South Africa as a province of the Union, the settlers voted by 8,774 to 5,998 for colonial autonomy. They at once set about installing a South African pattern of segregation, whether as to land or to labour. After much tergiversation a 'final allotment' was made in 1936: this awarded nearly half the total area to white settlement (even if there were nothing like enough whites to settle it), and 'reserved' about a quarter for African ownership. Not surprisingly, the whites got the best areas.

As in other such patterns, this segregation achieved three purposes. It enforced a measure of physical separation, so that Africans in white-reserved areas could be there only on sufferance: they had to come as supplicants, or they could not come at all. Pass regulations made sure of that. Secondly, it opened the way for a more effective pressure on rural Africans, by hut or poll tax, to quit their own economy for the cash-and-wage economy of their new masters: the reserves being relatively small or barren, they soon became grossly overcrowded. Thirdly, more land became available for white settlers. Northern Rhodesia (Zambia) witnessed all this, too, though in relatively small degree, given the sparsity of settlers and the discouragement to more settlement by a widespread incidence of malaria. Yet even here, by 1936, about a million African peasants had title in 71 million acres (of which 37 million were in the Barotseland Protectorate, banned to white settlement), while a few hundred white farmers had nine million.

Colin Leys has described the process in Kenya.[43] In 1901 the British completed a strategic railway from the port of Mombasa to Lake Victoria, headwaters of the Nile. The Kenya–Uganda Protectorate thus acquired had to be made to pay for itself. White farming settlement appeared the only route to solvency, if not to prosperity. Out of this came a settler-built economy in Kenya whose expansion supposed that Uganda (and afterwards Tanganyika) would act as ancillaries. By 1915 about four and a half million acres of excellent land in central Kenya had been taken from its African inhabitants and settled by about 1,000 white farmers. This was another dominant pattern: by the early 1950s the same figures would reach a maximum of 4,000 farmers on 7.3 million acres.

Here, too, land and labour expropriation went hand-in-hand as structural imperatives. By the mid-1920s, Leys tells us, more than half the able-bodied men in the two largest agricultural communities, those of the Kikuyu and the Luo, were estimated to be working for Europeans. This was a process of proletarianization at very cheap rates. As elsewhere the principle applied here was that whenever men came without their families they should be paid as though they had no families, it being supposed that these could sufficiently subsist in their home villages, even when these villages were deprived of a large part of their labour power. Driven into a cash economy, these peasants were also driven into impoverishment. Even so, they had to pay relatively high taxes. Of a gross one million pounds a year earned by Kenya Africans in registered employment, direct and indirect taxes for the sample period of 1920–23 annually subtracted £750,000: only a quarter of their earnings remained to the earners.

These examples show how the colonial model worked in the period of its installation up to 1930; the full results would not be seen till later years. Lesser examples of the same system occurred in Tanganyika, Angola, Mozambique, Nyasaland (Malawi). Other major examples occurred in North Africa, though not in Egypt, where British suzerainty induced the growth of an Egyptian land-owning and trading class which depended largely on peasant-grown cotton for export within the British imperial system. Here, in the north, Algeria was the parallel to South Africa.

'Wherever good water and fertile land are found, settlers must be installed without questioning whose land it may be.' Thus Marshal Bugeaud, Algeria's conqueror, to the Chamber of Deputies in 1840. The advice was taken. For a long time there was little settle-ment, but the way was prepared. 'Natives unable to prove their ownership,' notes an official text of 1856, 'have been treated as mere users of the land, or tenants who may be displaced at will, so as to free land for colonization.' Speculative buying of such land fol-lowed the rise of the Third Republic from the defeat of 1870. An informed guess of 1906 held that some 1,600,000 hectares (3,520,000 acres) had passed into European ownership by 1890. By 1940, with much effective settlement, this total had risen to more than 2,700,000 hectares (5,940,000 acres), or about a third of all land reckoned as profitably cultivable. This third was owned by about two per cent of the whole population, chiefly immigrant Europeans.[44]

In this way Algeria became an 'export enclave' within the French imperial system, chiefly for wine which most Algerians did not drink. In 1870 there were thought to be about 22,500 hectares of vineyard. In 1900 this total had become 154,000 hectares, and in 1953 eventually reached an all-time high of 378,000 hectares. Nine-tenths were in European ownership. As elsewhere – and it is a theme we shall return to – this cut savagely into food resources for local consumption. It could be calculated in the middle 1950s that cereal production stood at the same level as in the 1880s, although the population had tripled. With cereals a staple of Algerian diet, this meant deepening hunger. If each inhabitant in 1871 could have five quintals of cereal a year, according to another informed guess, this total had been halved by 1940. One structural aspect of colonization, a growing application of preventive medicine, was thereby more than cancelled by another. Tunisia revealed the same pattern, though to a lesser extent; Morocco, less again.

Unsuitable for white settlement, the equatorial African regions were at first plundered for wild rubber and other products. This was done partly by piracy and partly by land expropriation. Later on, King Leopold was able to induce the Belgian state to lend him 25 million francs in 1890, and other such loans followed. With these he built railways and other infra-structures, but the characteristic mode of exploitation remained one of extracting labour and food from the African 'non-cash' economy.

Enclosed in the 1890s, the French equatorial possessions of Middle Congo, Gabon, Oubangui-Chari, and Chad, had a somewhat different fate. In 1899 they were parcelled out among forty companies whose thirty-year 'concessions' amounted to seventy per cent of their whole area. The largest concessions covered 14,000 square kilometres; even the smallest was 1,200 square kilometres. Within their concessions the companies' property rights and freedom of action were extensive, and in some respects virtually complete. In exchange for such prerogatives the companies were obligated to pay an annual rent – varying from 500 to half a million francs – and fifteen per cent of annual profits, as well as performing some other duties such as installing telegraph lines.

There followed what modern French historians have called a period of pillage, notably in those northerly districts where companies could go into partnership with 'warlord' sultans of recent pre-colonial installation. Perhaps Oubangui-Chari suffered worst: over the years to 1930, according to Pierre Kalck, its populations were 'so hard hit that they were never to recover'.[45] The reasons were various. Though adopting Leopoldian methods of pillage of natural products, the companies were mostly too small, ill-managed, and irresponsible to be able to adopt his schemes of capital investment. By 1904 only thirty companies remained in place; with the few that prospered, as Coquéry-Vidrovitch has shown in her masterly study of the subject, methods were not only crude or inhuman, but aimed at securing an immediate profit no matter what might happen in the future.

Only one out of seven companies in Gabon could show a profit after seven years, and this was 'thanks to the brutality of its working methods', while not a single one of them had made 'the least serious effort at investment'.[46] Most of the profits that were made came from buying natural produce, chiefly rubber, at dirt-cheap rates and selling it in Europe for ten or twenty times as much; otherwise forced labour and forced crop-growing were the basis of the operation. Great damage had been done by the early 1920s; and in 1930, when the concessions ended, they were not renewed.

German policy in Kamerun, as in Togo and Tanganyika, looked chiefly to the establishment of white-owned and managed plantations. They had some success in the highlands of northern Tanganyika and also in Togo, but their main effort in this direction went into Kamerun. Dispossession of African land began in 1896 after some three years of armed resistance; by 1913, fifty-eight German companies were exploiting land and labour. As elsewhere, early conditions were deplorable. Official figures for Kamerun plantations show a general mortality figure, in 1905–6, of ten per cent of workers obtained by various forms of coercion; later, mortality became higher still.

No coercion on this scale was applied to British West Africa, where white settlement was never seriously attempted and a white plantation system was happily avoided.

British West Africa escaped white settlement for three reasons. Tough opposition to any large-scale alienation of land, shown repeatedly by peoples well organized to make their opposition effective, was the primary reason. Secondly, British interests concerned with overseas production of tropical crops, such as cocoa, came fairly soon to the view that they could be very well satisfied with monopolizing the purchase of an already flourishing local production. Thirdly, malaria and the climate were feared as being deadly to Europeans, a reputation that continued even after quinine and other remedies had practically removed the danger. Settlers might find it hard to survive, but in any case they were not required.

Plantations were tried here and there, but without success. In Hancock's explanation for the years after 1918, 'the British Cotton Growing Association discovered by experience that peasant production was generally a more economic proposition than plantation production . . . [while] it needed only a little experiment to convince would-be cocoa planters that they would be wise to avoid competing with the Native cultivators.'[47]

Lever Brothers thought otherwise, arguing that palm-oil and kernels could be produced more profitably by European plantations. In the circumstances they had in mind, they were right about this. Barred from Nigeria, they went to the Belgian Congo and there installed plantations with the full backing of the administration. These showed a rate of productive expansion much steeper than that of African production in Nigeria, where the crucial factors of labour coercion and punitive repression were comparatively absent.

Why were Levers barred from Nigeria? The story leads into an instructive area of temperamental and political comparison between colonizing powers. In West Africa, at least, the British doctrine of enclosure had not entirely obscured the older conception of colonial trusteeship which had presided over Victorian councils: these peoples, it was held, should not be expropriated, and eventually they should be led to govern themselves. More practically, they should not be provoked into a resistance whose control must be costly; and land alienation would certainly provoke resistance. Thirdly, by the 1920s, there was a fear that land alienation on any scale – European plantations – would create a 'landless proletariat' in Nigeria. With the Bolshevik Revolution only a few years old, fears of opening a door to 'communism' in any of its forms was by this time a vivid and continuing factor in the official mind.

With a finally decisive memorandum of 1926 the then governor-general of Nigeria, Sir Hugh Clifford, mustered the arguments against Lever Brothers and other contenders. Land alienation would lead to trouble. Large-scale palm-oil production having begun in southern Nigeria as early as the 1850s, there was in any case very little idle land in those densely populated forests. Planters would have to get labour by force, taxation, or the import of workers from elsewhere. Each of these methods would create a landless proletariat with all its potentials for instability. Finally, alienation was at odds with the principle of trusteeship.

But the absence of a European plantation system made no difference to the overall result. The British West African colonies, like those of France, became firmly clasped within the export-enclave pattern by means of an African plantation system. This formed another structural feature of the period to 1930, in the economic field, perhaps the most influential of all.

12

THE SYSTEM TO 1930:
3. TRADE

'Trade follows the Flag,' urged the new imperialists, eager to persuade their treasuries and taxpayers that national blessings must flow from public money spent on forwarding private profit. But in Africa, as it happened, the flag invariably followed trade: often reluctantly, sometimes disgustedly, but always with obedience in the end. The consequences of the West African boom in palm-oil and other produce are particularly revealing in this respect.

With some exceptions, the African end of this boom had been entirely in the hands of African merchants, whether in buying local produce or in selling it to European shippers. Up to the 1880s these shippers had tried vainly to break into this African landward monopoly. By the 1880s, however, they could draw on the fervours of a mature and therefore most aggressive nationalism. Backed by thrusting consuls, they called for the army and the navy, and invasion followed. The central feature of the colonial system to the 1920s, in the field of trade, was then the transfer of the landward monopoly from African to European hands. Thus would be deferred, for some three-quarters of a century, any further unfolding in any significant degree of the development of those elements of an African capitalism which had appeared before the 1880s.

Here and there, much force had to be applied. When the British navy was finally sent in to destroy the greatest of the African traders of the Benin river districts (southern Nigeria), the Itsekiri leader Nana Olumu, Admiral Bedford and his men were up against an opponent who was well aware of the dangers which threatened him. He had long fortified his headquarters on the Ebrohimi creek of the Benin river. After taking it, the naval attackers counted 106 cannon, one machine-gun, 445 heavy blunderbusses mounted on swivels, and some 1,700 assorted flint-locks and other small arms, an arsenal which also says a good deal for the scale of Nana Olomu's trading operations.

One monopoly, many-handed, was then replaced by the single-handed monopoly of Sir George Goldie and his chartered Royal Niger Company. A dispatch from an indignant British official encapsulates the process. Commenting in 1895 on the similar destruction of another merchant prince of the delta palm-oil trade, Ja Ja of Opobo, Sir Claude Macdonald notes that the British had deported Ja Ja 'because he was a monopolist'. They had gone on to 'wipe the floor' with trading chiefs in the Brass river because these chiefs had got in the way of the Royal Niger Company's trading interests. What were these interests? 'As I daresay you know,' Macdonald points out caustically to the Foreign Office, which of course knew it very well, 'in the vast territories of the Niger Company there is not one single outside trader, black, white, green or yellow. The markets are all theirs. They can open and shut any given market at will, which means subsistence or starvation to the native inhabitants . . . They can offer any price they like to the Producers, and the latter must either take it or starve . . .'[48]

This new monopoly took shape in 1879 when British firms and individual traders concerned with the Niger delta trade gave up ditching each other and accepted Goldie's firm leadership. The Royal Niger Company was formed seven years later, in 1886, when it achieved control by charter of the newly-proclaimed British Protectorate along the lower Niger river. Other competitors then appeared with the same objective of imposing export and import prices, while excluding rivals, but Goldie quickly persuaded them to become shareholders in the Niger Company.

One monopoly naturally begot another. The year 1895 saw the formation of the West African shipping ring, a combination of shippers judged by a royal commission of 1906 to be so strong as to hold the West African trade 'as in a vice'.[49] These two monopolies gradually becoming interlocked, the ring then applied its 'vice' only to such smaller merchants who managed to survive the excluding pressures of the major interests. These were reorganized after 1920.

A new pattern of concentration evolved, largely through the intervention of Lever Brothers. Having failed to win the right to open plantations in Nigeria, Levers now contented themselves with engrossing control of exports and imports. In 1920 they bought the Royal Niger Company, and in 1929 crowned their bid for control of the trade by combining thirty-seven firms into the United Africa Company, henceforth a giant which colonial governments, as was remarked by a British economist in the 1940s, were quite powerless to deal with. The trend therefore continued: by 1936, the United Africa Company had more than 56 per cent of all Nigerian exports of palm-oil and kernels, cocoa and peanuts.

Between 1891 and 1895 the average annual value of British West Africa's exports and imports rose from about £4 million to about £26 million, and French West African trading expansion showed a comparable rise. This was the boom that British economists liked to herald as a 'revolution'. But any revolution must have meant a development of African capitalism, and none occurred. The basis for that development may have existed, as earlier years had shown; but the basis was not built upon now, it was merely destroyed. Coins might assist exchange, communications improve,* new regiments of small traders might come upon the scene. But no capitalists appeared, nor indeed could appear. Even many years later the size of African banking deposits in Nigeria and the Gold Coast remained insignificantly small.

Other fields of action show the same result. Nigerians had smelted tin for many centuries by handicraft methods. But modernization of the economic system did not advantage them. On the contrary, in large measure it expropriated them. Seventy foreign companies received Nigerian tin-mining concessions in 1902 and 'took off' in 1909 with fresh London capital; by 1910, fifty surviving companies were employing 15,000 African miners. So little available ore-body remained to 'native producers' that in 1911 it was thought well to allocate them a 'reserved' 100 acres, later commuted into an annual money payment . . . of £26 10s.

*The first railway locomotive, for example, puffed its way into Kumase, the Ghana 'cocoa capital', as early as 1903.

Local production certainly continued in other sectors, notably in the weaving of cloth, and even expanded. But it did so for another half century and more within the 'traditional' mode of production and exchange, the latter being modified only by the use of coins. Not until the 1970s would there be any real prospect of revolutionizing the mode of production with the use of modern machinery, and thus give Nigerians their own access to cheap cottons. Other weaving industries were less fortunate; they simply disappeared. In 1400 Ibn Khaldun had reported the Algerian city of Tlemcen as possessing 4,000 handlooms; after a century of colonial occupation in 1954 the total was 105. Yet no Tlemcen textile mill had taken the place of all the handlooms which had vanished.

This transfer of trading initiative and profit destroyed the budding middle-class groups of West Africa, even though they had decades or even centuries of trading enterprise in their history. Famous old families such as the Brews, famous newer ones such as the de Graft Johnsons, long prominent on the Gold Coast for their local influence and initiative, men of stern Victorian ambition and great innovators enthusiastic for Western education, fought a long battle to survive. One or two persisted even into the 1920s. Other trading centres such as Lagos and Onitsha, Ibadan and Abeokuta in Nigeria, were the scene of similar efforts. But the odds were against them.

Individuals could win out here and there, but not as an economic group, not as an embryonic class of capitalists. What developed instead was a multitude of petty traders who were the intermediaries between cash-crop producers and European or Levantine export–import companies. As these economies expanded with the markets of the early twentieth century, these small trader intermediaries held the centre of the African scene. Just how active were they and the system within which they worked may be seen in their relatively huge demand for silver coins. Import of these, for 1906–10 alone, totalled about half the silver coins issued within the United Kingdom itself. These 'petty-bourgeois' intermediaries had a large political future ahead of them. They would provide nationalism with the bulk of its early troops and, later, with most of its officers. And nationalism would duly reflect their origins and ambitions.

The French West African scene was no different in this respect. Here too there was expansion. The Dakar–St Louis railway was completed in 1885, and seven years later Dakar received an autonomous though French chamber of commerce, following earlier chambers at St Louis and on Gorée Island. The concept of monopoly as vital to colonial enterprise took shape, and with it a new metropolitan willingness to invest. Systemic enclosure followed. In 1887 there was formed the Compagnie Française d'Afrique Occidentale (CFAO) with a capital of 30 million francs; in 1906 the initially much smaller Société Commerciale de l'Ouest Africain (SCOA); and in 1913, making a third in the 'big three' of French West Africa, the Compagnie du Niger with largely British capital. Credit facilities kept in step: in 1884 the Banque du Sénégal was upgraded in its status and transferred from St Louis to Dakar, while other banks were founded by metropolitan capital as the Senegal peanut boom swung into its stride.

The scene was thereby set for liquidation of local trading groups; and this was carried through. Their number in Senegal in 1900 appears to have been about 500 Africans engaged in export–import, and some 300 others who were mostly local Frenchmen. Up till then, as Samir Amin has explained, French policy had favoured the development of a local trading bourgeoisie as being a 'natural aspect' of this fragment of the French nation. Now, with the new imperialism, policy was reversed. This nascent middle class was displaced by a projection of the metropolitan middle class in the shape of the 'three giants' and their lesser kind.[50] Its end came finally in the great depression of 1930. Another thirty years were to pass before the prospects of a middle-class or 'petty bourgeois' revival could be improved.

The case is still more striking in the Maghrib, and of course in Egypt. North African traders had led the western world in long-distance trade in ancient times; Fatimid Egypt had done so in the period of the European Middle Ages. Now, with partial exceptions in Egypt, the inheritors of that long tradition of international trade and credit were likewise liquidated or reduced to peripheral sub-sidiaries: in Tunisia by a multi-national community of foreign entrepreneurs, in Algeria by French settlers, in Morocco by intrusive French banking and mining interests.

Morocco offers an illuminating variant on this theme. It had long been divided under various dynasties into two major areas. These were the *bilad al-makhsen*, or area of Muslim kingship rule, and the *bilad as-siba*, or area of 'dissidence' inhabited by more or less autonomous but Muslim Berber clans. Having declared a protec-torate in 1912 over the whole of Morocco (save for a Spanish-held enclave in the far north), the French under Lyautey's firm guidance adopted a system of indirect rule for the *bilad al-makhsen* that some-what resembled Lugard's in Northern Nigeria. Here, in the ports and cities of the *makhsen*, notably Fez, there existed a skilled trading community whose economic traditions were many centuries old. This community's political position was weak within the Moroccan kingship system. But its potential as a future capitalist class, provided that it could now achieve scope within the international markets of the early twentieth century, was clearly large. Given that the king-ship's power was undermined by French over-rule, this potential for development could be expected to grow rapidly stronger. The reverse occurred.

The businessmen of Fez and their kind were able, after 1912, to consolidate a subsidiary position on the fringes of the colonial economy. They were unable to do more, since any further development was prevented by French interests; and even their growth as a group was stunted. Local capitalism developed, but this was little more than an oversea branch of the capitalist system in France. Looking back across the protectorate years (1912–56), an inquiry of 1970 found that Moroccans had at best become marginal participants in an expanding French economy based on commercial agriculture, mining, industry and the export–import trade.

The same process occurred in other regions where export–import trade had preceded colonial occupation. Having survived Portuguese depredations in the sixteenth century, the merchants of the Swahili city-ports were unable to meet this new challenge of expropriation, while the Zanzibari merchants fared little better. Harassed on the coast, all were progressively barred from the interior, notably by Leopold's policy of monopoly in the Congo. Leopold and others invariably represented this as 'ending the slave trade'. Aside from the large question as to whether the consequences of Leopoldian policy were any better for Africans than the slave trade, this was an excuse which ignored the very considerable non-slave trade in which Swahili merchants such as Tippu Tip were involved.

13

THE GREAT SLUMP AND THE 1930s

How one cuts up history into periods may often be a matter of personal preference. One man's 'turning point' will seem, at the time, like nothing of the kind to someone else: even in hindsight, there has been seldom much agreement. For the colonial period, however, hindsight by the 1970s and impressions at the time are in fair consensus. Up to 1939, the important point of change since 1890 was not the First World War. It was the great slump which began in Europe and America in 1929 and hit the colonies of Africa a year or so later.

The great slump, Coquéry-Vidrovitch could affirm to very general agreement in 1975, 'upset economic and social conditions throughout the continent',[51] and led from policies of predatory or primary extraction, such as had generally reigned hitherto, onward to policies of modern extraction resting (though not soon) on the investment of capital for infrastructure. Hence the colonial period really falls into two periods, and the great slump is the hinge between them.

Contemporaries certainly felt they were living through a time of profound change. Writing in brief retrospect in his important book of 1940, Hancock could say that the great slump marked 'the end of an epoch', calling into question all those certainties of economic behaviour and prediction which had presided until now over the whole imperialist enterprise, and opening a new period when 'vast tracts of economic circumstance and struggle' could find no optimistic guide.[52]

Many felt they were threatened by something like an earthquake. In Sierra Leone, Cox-George tells us, 'the economy suffered a complete slump, touching every sector.'[53] Egypt, says Vatikiotis, passed through 'a tremendous economic crisis'.[54] These two comments from widely separated countries are representative of countless similar judgements with their implications for the daily scene. My own study of the Belgian Congo began only in 1954, but memories of the great depression were still very much alive there. 'I assure you,' a veteran Belgian administrator recalled for me, 'that in those grim days I had to kill in order not to be killed myself.' Resentments multiplied as produce prices nose-dived and incomes vanished. The total value of the export–import trade of the four British West African colonies stood at £56 million in 1929; in 1931 it was down to £29 million, while the same totals for six British East African colonies (including the Sudan) stood at £40 million in 1929, but £21 million two years later. For the twelve French West African and Equatorial colonies, and the two French mandates of Togo and Cameroun, the same totals were just under £30 million in 1929 and just under £18 million in 1931. Once down, moreover, prices stayed down. Not until the late 1930s was there any real improvement; and only with the furious raw-material extraction of the Second World War was the groundwork laid for the steeply rising totals which followed 1945.

All territories suffered, though with contradictions wherever new minerals were discovered or white-settler domination could protect this or that sector within a given economy. In Northern Rhodesia (Zambia), for example, copper exports began to be large in 1927, and rapidly became larger, moving from 19 to 51 per cent of that colony's total exports. Yet gross expenditure by colonial government in Northern Rhodesia rose very little, moving only from £550,000 in 1929 to £820,000 in 1931, the doctrine being, as elsewhere, that mining revenue must be taxed as little as possible. More white miners were employed at wages that were very high when compared with those paid to African miners. But the bulk of the population can be safely said to have gained nothing from this exploitation of the country's copper, nor would indeed gain anything till after independence.[55]

For the big settler colonies, the Moroccan case appears fairly characteristic. Hitting Morocco a little later than usual elsewhere, the slump lasted longer. It was extremely severe: even in 1936, Moroccan exports were only about half their value of 1929. For the non-French population the implications were disastrous: between 1930 and 1933 Moroccan rural incomes apparently fell by about sixty per cent, and the structures of the colonial economy could offer no relief. Yet it was different for the settlers. Those reduced to bankruptcy or unemployment could at least try their luck in France. Paying neither income tax nor company tax, although at this period about one-fifth of all French overseas investment was going to Morocco, most settlers seem to have survived remarkably well.

Yet they survived in a new frame of mind. Hitherto there had been a feeling that Frenchmen and Moroccans were somehow 'building together', even if the 'pacification' of Morocco was still incomplete by 1930. Now it became increasingly clear in the facts of everyday life that the well-being of Frenchmen by no means implied the well-being of Moroccans, but rather the reverse. The average white income in Morocco during 1934 stood at about 17,400 francs (compared with the average in France of about 5,500), but an employed Moroccan (and he was now a rare bird) would be lucky to get more than 1,000 francs a year. With this, the mental gap also widened. White society, says Gallisot of this period, 'becomes ever more completely isolated in its well-fed indifference' to whatever might be happening within 'native' society. One has the same impression of hardening moral arteries from the evidence for Algeria, Kenya and the two Rhodesias; while there is little doubt that the slump in South Africa was a formative element in shaping the extreme doctrines of *apartheid* that the Afrikaner minority, hit far worse by the slump than the economically favoured English-speaking minority, was to apply after 1948.

In that still pre-Keynesian epoch, axes were struck savagely against all those forms of government spending which, by relieving poverty, would eventually relieve the slump as well. In Britain they were handled by Sir Eric Geddes and his like, jovial men who were sure that the Devil should take the hindmost since they themselves were properly blessed by God. In Africa it was much the same, except that there the cutting was done by administrators who often feared the consequences for the work they were supposed to do, and tried vainly to oppose the cutting axe.

But if social services had to be made to shrink, that was not true of taxation. The general tropical-zone picture was that of Kenya: direct taxation paid by Africans in the period 1924–9 averaged £553,000; in the period 1930–34 it averaged £545,000. Elsewhere, taxation actually rose. Direct taxation in Nigeria, nearly all from rural producers, yielded 38 per cent of all revenue in 1928–9, but 40 per cent a year later, and 43 per cent eight years after that.

The effects on African society were to be long-enduring and deep. Meanwhile the few years remaining to the 1930s played out the sorry dramas of depression. For colonial officials this was a time of hand-to-mouth administration with means that were never adequate even to the little they were intended to achieve. The bluff optimism of the years of invasion and 'pacification', for so many of these Europeans a bracing challenge to a 'mission' in which they sometimes vividly believed, gave way to disillusionment or worse. The novelists of the time, mostly European, reflect all that. At one extreme of indigence and wretchedness there are the Portuguese officials of Castro Soromenho's *Terra Morta*, written about the Angola of the 1930s. At another extreme of relative ease and order, there are the British officials of Joyce Cary's *Mister Johnson*.

At one point in that memorable novel about Nigeria there is a discussion between a junior British official and his senior. The former is well schooled in the beauties of Indirect Rule and the obligations of the British. The latter is an old hand long wearied of enthusiasm. He explains to his junior that 'native civilization' is going to pieces, 'if it hasn't gone already'.

'But what's going to happen then?' asks Rudbeck, the junior. 'Are we going to give them any new civilization, or simply let them slide downhill?'

'No idea,' Bulteel, the senior, says cheerfully.

'I suppose one mustn't talk about a plan,' Rudbeck says.

'Oh no, no, no. They'll take you for a Bolshy.'[56]

That was another contingent feature of the 1930s. All

effective protest against stagnation or repression came now to be
referred, automatically as not even in the 1920s, to the influence of
the Bolshevik Revolution and the Comintern. The French suffered
from this particular hallucination even worse than the British: in
doing so, they were in fact some three decades before the time when
the influence of communist ideas (except to some extent in South
Africa) began to have any real impact on African thought and
action. Reporting in 1931, a confidential French document could
even reach the absurdity of saying of the 1929 'Womens' Riots' in
Eastern Nigeria, a purely local anti-tax protest, that 'the Third
International may not have been foreign to the movement', while
lesser anti-tax agitations in the Gold Coast, in 1930, were ludicrously
referred to as the work of 'educated Negroes acting as communist
propagandists'.[57]

On a level of serious analysis, however, the great slump
marked the end of an epoch in ways that lay beyond the immediate
consequences for those who had to live through it. For the colonial
system or systems, the slump acted as a kind of incubator: it induced
maturity in much that was previously potential, uncertain, or incomplete. Or perhaps it was simply that dominant interests in Britain
now rallied to the practice of the French and Portuguese, for whom
colonies had always been a monopolized national extension of the
economy and society of the 'mother country'. An imperialist British
politician had put the essential idea to the British war cabinet as early
as the ruinous situation that followed the First World War.

'We are in fact,' Amery told his colleagues in 1919, 'no
longer the sort of country that can compete industrially in the open
market except in certain industries. It really comes to this, that we
can both carry out our social reform' – that is, absorb the possibly
revolutionary pressures of mass unemployment in Britain – 'and
develop an immense trade' – that is, restore the old British supremacy
– 'but mainly if not entirely within the Empire.'[58] The *status quo* had
drawn its unassailable strength (as, wrongly, that strength had appeared at the time) from nineteenth-century Free Trade; now it
should be rescued by a lesser free trade, 'Empire Free Trade'; and
Britain, like its rivals, would now build tariff and quota walls around

her possessions. Not much was done about this till the great slump. But a great deal was done then.

British colonial 'protectionism' was one thing that came out of the slump. One of its effects was to deprive the inhabitants of British colonies of cheap imports such as Japanese textiles. But it could do more than that. If British textile exports should be protected against the dangers of competition from Japan, there should be an equal care to protect such exports, whether textile or not, from what might otherwise become the dangers of African competition. 'Ought there not,' Ernest Bevin, a prominent British trade union leader, asked rhetorically of the Trades Union Congress in 1930, 'to be some control against the development of coal in Tanganyika?' When it came to the pinch, what were colonies for if not to sacrifice themselves for the mother country?

The wider crisis of the capitalist system induced at the same time a certain solidarity among the powers. Orthodox belief, however improbably, was that salvation lay in cutting wages while raising prices. One way of raising prices was to restrict production. In a world then acutely short of food, an international agreement of 1937 accordingly imposed a sugar quota on British East Africa. What befell Uganda also happened elsewhere, save in favoured settler colonies; sometimes it even happened there. The quota meant that Uganda could sell abroad less than half the sugar she actually produced in 1937, and less than a third that she produced in 1938. Cotton and other commodities came within comparable restrictions. The slump meant stagnation for these economies; it could also mean regression even from the productive level of the 1920s.

Another strand in the same fabric of 'imperial protection' had more enduring consequences, and led eventually to the large post-1945 programmes of 'aid and development' which would underpin the raw-material booms of the future. This, essentially, was King Leopold's old idea that profits from colonies were closely linked to capital investment. Nobody had followed Leopold, it being generally held that colonial profits were linked to the rate of extraction capable of being obtained from African economies in their existing condition. Minerals and plantations might make an exception: if so, they only proved the rule. Yet the possible advantages of raising the technological level of existing economies had been mooted from time to time. In 1921 the British Cabinet considered a proposal that loan guarantees to colonies 'would lead to the immediate placing of large orders' in a Britain then gripped by mass unemployment. A little came out of this in terms of money, much more in terms of the idea that 'empire development', as it came to be called, might be very helpful in solving Britain's problems.

In time this idea bore fruit, more ambitiously and as a pointer to the way ahead, in the Colonial Development and Welfare Act of 1929. About £6½ million were spent under this Act up to 1939, when it was relayed by a larger arrangement of the same kind. Much of this money went on mining equipment to the primary benefit of mining investors; much went on helping colonial governments to balance their budgets; and interest was payable on all the loans. There were a few 'special schemes' aimed at increasing African production by reorganizing it. These schemes invariably supposed that African farmers were incapable of understanding what was good for them, but could be induced to grow what was good for others; generally, they failed. An obvious example is that of the French plan to irrigate about a million hectares (2.2 million acres) of the 'internal delta' of the Niger above the great bend of its upper half. About one and a half million African cultivators were to be settled on this newly-irrigated land, and grow cotton for French textile factories. By 1937, comments Hopkins, this Niger scheme 'had cost over £1 million; by 1940 there were about 12,000 settlers on three sites which were more like refugee camps than model villages; and by 1953 only about 62,000 acres had been irrigated.'[59]

Some of these schemes collapsed by a mere misunderstanding about what could be made to grow where. Mainly, though, failure derived from hard-headed peasant estimates of profit and loss. If the peasants of Soudan (Mali) did not flock to the irrigated lands of the Middle Niger, this was also because they saw advantage in staying away. If peasants in the southern (Anglo-Egyptian) Sudan refused to grow cotton in the so-called Zande scheme, this was because they found they could do better by growing other crops. If

Nigerian peasants (in this case, the Tiv) likewise refused to grow cotton under administrative pressure or appeal, and turned to the successful production of benniseed (a vegetable oil) without any pressure or appeal, this was because, Dorward has explained, 'Tiv farmers showed an acute awareness of profit factors.'[60]

Even the successful Gezira cotton scheme in the (Anglo-Egyptian) Sudan made no real exception to that rule. Launched in 1913 when colonial government responded to an appeal from Lancashire cotton interests for more long-staple fibre, it grew into a thoroughly good investment by the early 1920s and continued to expand. The Sudan became an important cotton producer thanks to this initiative. Yet the point to notice here is that the Gezira scheme succeeded because it did not seek to displace an existing productive system, but intelligently grafted cotton cultivation into that system. This could happen wherever cultivators were sufficiently convinced of their advantage. The real limits on growth were colonial, not indigenous. Uganda again offers an instructive example. African cultivators in Uganda also took to cotton with success and even enthusiasm, expanding their production from 47,000 bales in 1919 to 96,000 in 1925, and so on upwards. But cotton-ginning was reserved as a European or Asian monopoly, African cooperatives were discouraged, and African middlemen were squeezed out of business. For all this, too, a triumphant nationalism would afterwards exact a price.

Because of the great slump and its consequences, the system rigidified, became structurally more coherent, and led to a more complete enclosure of colonial economies within European economies. Throughout this period, in other words, development meant the growth of these European economies in their oversea extension. It did not mean, nor was ever seriously suggested to mean, the development of African societies from a 'backward' to an 'advanced' condition. That gloss on investment was put forward later. At this period the beauty of the imperial lily was thought to require no gilding, and to be sufficient in itself. Only the Second World War and its huge upheavals would alter that opinion.

14

FACING THE CONSEQUENCES

This brief account of the system up to the Second World War may appear forbiddingly bleak, but forms a necessary background to the history of African responses and initiatives. Aside from all individual intentions whether good, bad, or indifferent, these forty or fifty years installed the system, formed its characteristic imbrication of pressures and resistances, shaped the potentials of the future. There may be moral conclusions to be drawn, and many were drawn at the time. They were voiced by African critics from Casely Hayford and Sol Plaatje to the pioneers of mass nationalism. They were argued by European critics like J. L. Hobson, Vigné d'Octon, Norman Leys, many others and, with a new cutting edge of Marxist provenance, by a growing band of radicals and revolutionaries before and after those 'ten days that shook the world' in October 1917.

Moral conclusions are not the point here, any more than the justifications by which the colonial systems were defended, nor even the counter-rhetoric with which they were attacked. All that apart, these systems each fell into an essentially similar pattern, formed by the evolving interests of European economies or by what these interests were conceived to be by those who steered them. At crucial points, nothing else mattered. The cultural dimension is obviously far more varied and rich in controversy. As often as not, colonial administrators believed that they were doing their best for Africans as well as for their own empires, and were powerfully buttressed in this belief by the general run of missionary and humanitarian enterprise.

The records suggest that few of those who imposed the

pattern, or struggled with African resistance in order to impose it, were aware of the consequences of what they were about. They acted and reacted to immediate problems, working often with self-denial and devotion but ambushed by their ignorance of African realities, distressed by the economic perversities of Europe, harassed by what Hancock in 1940 called the 'farrago of cant and greed' of imperialists at home, chased by anxieties about budgets and careers, and understandably dreaming of retirement to Sussex or Provence. Yet the pattern came into existence, repeatedly shifting the course of African experience. Its land and labour requirements, whether for European export of minerals and plantation crops or of African production of export crops, combined to destroy a self-generating mode of life without introducing another to replace it. This was the central outcome of these years, just as it would be the central cause of the widening structural crisis which accompanied decolonization in and after the 1950s.

Official figures for Northern Rhodesia might show in 1936 that Africans received some £490,000 in wages, and government rejoiced in the benevolence of the copper-mining industry. Yet the same figures showed that between £100,000 and £150,000 was clawed back in annual taxation of 'native males', even though, as a British critic noted then, it was obvious that over large areas the local resources of the country were entirely inadequate to provide the taxpayer with the means of meeting such taxation. Not surprisingly, malnutrition became widespread. Yet government needed the tax revenue, since copper-mining profits were not to be seriously milked, while settler opinion saw no connection. Besides, as a settler remarked to that particular critic, 'it can't be necessary to give growing children milk.'[61]

Other governments took satisfaction in their expanding export figures. They failed to notice, or took no account of it if they did, that the more land and labour were devoted to export crops the less land and labour could there be for growing food. Consequent food shortages, with concomitant rises in the price of local food-stuffs, were nonetheless appearing as early as the 1930s. They were small compared with the endemic dearths which were afterwards to transform these once self-supporting communities into dependants on imported food, but already they were serious. A nutritional inquiry promoted by the Gold Coast government in 1938 found that price rises caused by cocoa production had produced a situation in which 'the general population cannot afford to buy meat', a surprising impoverishment in a colony rightly regarded as among the best supplied.

Colonial government regretted this, but saw the fault in African backwardness. 'This disastrous situation,' concluded that same visiting British expert, 'can only be met by a general improvement in the agriculture of the country,' and she went on to blame African methods of farming. The comment became a refrain. Perhaps nothing better reveals the profound ignorance in which external critics regularly foundered whenever they tried to grapple with reality. Post-colonial researches have proved that 'the general improvement of agriculture' had in fact already taken place, not least in the matter of meat.

Thus the officially recorded cattle population of the stock-raising northern territories of the Gold Coast grew from 60,000 head in 1921 to 170,000 in 1941. This expansion became sustainable, however, only after mass immunization against rinderpest became available, and this was not provided by colonial government until 1930. Once it was provided, African producers simply went ahead. What we now know about cocoa yields the same reply: given opportunity, producers knew how to respond. Far from failing to march with the times, as would be shown in the 1950s, cocoa producers had 'always regarded cocoa growing as a business', and applied 'a thoroughly commercial attitude to land purchase' as well as to land use and the disposal of profits.[62]

They became chronically indebted, but not because they were feckless or incompetent. The reason was that colonial government, which controlled all such matters, did not know that cocoa growing, given such factors as the number of years that trees require to come into bearing, was a capital-intensive business, and therefore needed facilities for credit. Between 1895 and 1919 Gold Coast farmers pushed up their output from thirteen tons to 16,000, and the expansion continued. Yet all this was achieved while being debarred, until the 1960s, from credit facilities such as Europeans in Europe took for granted.

In such cases, the resultant pattern of exploitation thus became as much the outcome of African as of European initiative. African producers not only accepted the pattern; often they enlarged it. This combination of initiatives worked for an ever deeper installation of the pattern, of the system, in the ethos and acceptance of everyday life. Each 'side' responded to the pressures of the system according to its perception of immediate interests. The whole system acquired its own dynamic.

This was equally true of its parts, such as migrant labour. Initially forced into cash-paid employment, great masses of rural Africans began to move out of deepening impoverishment into proliferating towns. Colonial governments had adopted the measures necessary to set this movement going: the great slump took care of the rest, and then the further unfolding of the same system. Yet when this mounting tide became painful to most, and scandalous to many, colonial governments were invariably astonished and dismayed. Who could suggest that they had wanted this? Report after report, onward from the 1930s, inveighs against the evil of migrant labour from rural areas, deplores the calamities of urban squalor and moral decay, looks vainly for remedies. Often enough, like King Canute in the fable, they go right down to the edge of the tide and order it to stop. Irresistibly, it rolls on as before.

This 'flight to the towns' became another structural feature of the mature colonial period. It had far-reaching effects at every level of life. Not least, it gave the nationalism of the Western-educated groups an audience they could never win before. Berque's comment on the Maghrib between the two world wars can be applied to the continent. 'Onwards from the 1930s, the towns are where things happen':[63] the colonial towns and their unplanned African 'quarters', 'locations', *bidonvilles*, *senzalas* where men and women are soon living in hundreds of thousands, even in millions.

Out of this will come a convergence between a 'national struggle' and a 'social struggle'. And this convergence, however brief, partial, and soon destroyed by nationalist leaders, will be the force that carries these colonies to their independence.

PART

AFRICAN RESPONSES:
1890–1939

It is impossible for a nation to civilize itself; civilization must
come from abroad.

> James Africanus Horton, 1868

The people were not pleased with that sort of rule, so they longed
for their old type of government.

> Mzee Amlani, of the anti-colonial war
> in Ungoni during 1905–7

15

THE MANY AND THE FEW: A GREAT DIVIDE

Seen in retrospect, the colonial experience may look simple in its structure, and so in essence it really was. But in its human dimensions it was nothing of the kind. Its effects may appear to have flowed clearly from its causes; but this is not how it seemed at the time. The problem then was that of any great confrontation: to understand what was happening or intended, and what was possible or desirable.

Opinions varied among Europeans as among Africans. Few among the empire-builders achieved a reputation for sound and independent judgement as great among the empire-builders as Frederick Lord Lugard who, in an imperialist sense, shared with Goldie the role of 'father of Nigeria'. But not all Lugard's contemporaries admired his wisdom. Among the dissidents was Mary Kingsley, whose books remain as descriptive classics of West Africa a century ago. Lugard might be a very fine tool, she thought, 'but he ought to be kept for his work, and not shoved in when judgement is required, for he has not an atom of an idea of the elementary laws of evidence'. He did not even have a mind of his own. 'Order him to go anywhere,' she complained, 'tell him such and such a thing is good or bad, and if he recognises the person who tells him so as a proper pious person, he throws all the weight of his authority in backing up what he thinks is the proper pious thing.'[1]

Such contrasts of opinion about leading men and large issues were sharp and many. As to what was actually happening, Africans like Europeans reached innumerable conclusions. In a vast continent peopled by a thousand communities enclosed within the plans and calculations of remote and altogether different communities of which little or nothing was known, while most of what was believed to be known was wrong, people sought to find their way ahead. But in looking at this half-century of history from the standpoint of the stock of political ideas then in play, a distinction between two chief trends at once appears.

The first concerns the thought and action of all but a very small minority of Africans. Ensconced within their historical communities, the vast majority strove to defend or advance their separate interests and identities. At first they did this by defensive warfare or alliance with Europeans so as to win local gains. When superior firepower and organization had got the better of them, they consulted the wisdom of their founding charters and made compromises and accommodations, looked for new policies of life and sometimes discovered them, or, when all else failed, rose in desperate revolt. Onwards from all that experience they pursued new advice, embarked on their own versions of Christianity, and sought once again to defend or re-shape their communities. For a long while they acted, however variously, only within the framework of what we have called the African model, the concept of society that Africa had forged across the centuries. The ideas of nationalism, save in faint foreshadowings, meant nothing to them.

The second trend, initially very small, was composed of men (and a few women) who achieved a Western education and accepted the lessons of what we have called the European model. They existed at the beginning only in South and West Africa, but gradually appeared elsewhere. They are hard to label. The term 'élites', although they often used it about themselves, is far from satisfactory, partly because it has tended to become a mere term of abuse, and partly because these groups were far from being the 'chosen ones' of early imperialist preference. Yet it is also true that they tended to see themselves as the 'chosen ones' of history, as those who were to be the instruments of applying the European model to Africa, and therefore as the saviours of the continent. Being sure of the values of their Western education, they were convinced of their superiority over the vast majority: who but they, after all, possessed the keys to the powerhouse of knowledge whence European technology and conquest had flowed? Perhaps they can best be called the

'Western-educated few'. In this book, generally, I tend to call them simply 'the few' as opposed to the 'many', to the vast majority of Africans, who were neither Western-educated nor contemptuous of their own heritage.

Through most of this half century there was next to no ideological communication between the few and the many. They pursued different paths.

16

FROM PROPHETS TO STRIKE-LEADERS

Many communities resisted colonial intrusion by force of arms. With few exceptions, these included all those communities which had developed kingships or other forms of centralized government. And of the exceptions most were those, like the Buganda kingship, which accepted colonial intrusion as a means of gaining an ally against a neighbouring rival: in Buganda's case, the Bunyoro kingship.

These wars may be called 'primary' resistance. Some of them were large and long, and occurred in all regions of the continent. Others were small and soon over, but were numerous. Several proved appallingly destructive. German official records for South-West Africa (Namibia) show that the Herero people who began their armed resistance in 1904 lost as much as four-fifths of their whole population, while their neighbours, in resistance, the Nama, lost almost half.[1a] Belgium's Commission for the Protection of the Natives, meeting in 1919, considered that the population of the Belgian Congo was then perhaps only half what it had been at the outset of the colonial enterprise. They thought that this reduction, probably in fact an over-estimate, was largely due to the spread of new diseases; but other official records suggest that great numbers must have died in the many annual campaigns of Belgian 'pacification'. The Shona-Ndebele war of self-defence against British intrusion in Rhodesia (Zimbabwe) during 1896–7 cost unrecorded casualties; they were undoubtedly many. The tale of loss in South Africa, from the 'Kaffir wars' to the Zulu wars, has not been counted.

Outright resistance of this kind was mostly over by the end of the nineteenth century. Accommodation followed. Once kings and 'great chiefs' were sufficiently convinced that further fighting would be fruitless, they went for the best terms they could get, often enough rescuing their own positions at the cost of their peoples' more complete subjection. Sharing authority with colonial rule was obviously preferable to having no authority at all. This guaranteed political stagnation, but kings are seldom against that.

'Primary' resistance among non-kingship states was also common, but tended to occur a little later. There were evidently two reasons for this. One was that the lack of kings or their equivalents made initial resistance more difficult to organize, save on a very local scale. The other was that 'lineage-group states' were often subject to a process of 'fraying at the edges', as one or other of their constituent groups accepted the presence or the promises of European explorers, treaty- or concession-hunters, missionaries or traders, and thereby opened the gate to deeper infiltration. They could reach a consensus of rejection only after the early consequences of colonial intrusion became thoroughly understood by all or most of their component groups. This usually happened through the imposition of forced labour and taxation.

Armed resistance by these non-kingship communities often followed. It was invariably seen and treated by colonial power as rebellion against an established colonial government whose legitimacy was said to be enshrined in 'treaties' or 'concessions' to which this or that lineage head or local chief had put his mark. For this reason it has appeared as 'secondary' rather than 'primary' resistance. But the distinction is really a colonial one: from an African standpoint, all such resistances were part of the same reflex of self-defence. It remains that the resistances of the non-kingship states continued into the 1920s and even later.

Afterwards there came true 'secondary' forms of rejection: forms, that is, which followed an initial acceptance of colonial intrusion. Nearly all were by the non-kingship communities; their history of successive forms of resistance, or rather of the search for reconstituted forms of their community life, is a particularly rich one. The case of the Kenya Luo is strikingly instructive.

Bethwell Ogot, their modern historian, tells us that at the time of the 'impact', during the 1890s, the Kenya Luo (as distinct from the Uganda Luo) were organized in twelve or thirteen lineage groups (*ogendini*) with 10,000 to 70,000 persons in each. They were thus a community of perhaps half a million people, one of the larger in East Africa, as indeed they still are. Unlike the Nandi, who were their rivals and neighbours, they offered no armed resistance to the claims of British rule. On the contrary, they welcomed these 'red strangers' because their priests – the guardians of their founding charter, the intermediaries with their world of spiritual power – advised them that the ancestors had sent these strangers to Luoland for purposes of good. So the British were amicably received as the agents of divine intention. And when the newcomers led by C. W. Hobley called upon them to help the British in waging war upon the Nandi, for whom the 'red strangers' were no such good news, the Luo willingly responded. Hobley might not be a Luo; but Hobley had the blessing of the ancestors of the Luo. Though rare in Kenya, the interpretation was not unique.[2]

Hobley and his kind, as it happened, had the blessing of quite different ancestors, and was soon obliged to make plain to the Luo that they had fallen into error. These had supposed that the colonial model of community would reinforce a further evolution of the Luo model. Far from doing this, colonial law and order in fact required a freezing of Luo society within its boundaries and structures of the moment when colonial rule was imposed. The same applied to the neighbours of the Luo. The Pax Britannica intended to preside over a static situation: there would be an end to community re-organization, now invariably seen as 'tribal warfare', and the savages in due course would become civilized. The Luo saw things otherwise.

They saw that their model of community could be improved. Such periodical improvement or readjustment was inherent to a founding charter evolved by a people with a long history of migration, and so of adaptation to new circumstances. At first they believed that the British would bring them useful advice about facing situations which were obviously new. Then they discovered that what the British wanted was not improvement of the Luo model, but the scrapping of an essential part of it. This part consisted in Luo dependence upon a repeated process of secession by lineage fragment (potential clans) and their movement to another homeland. How otherwise could Luo patterns of farming and self-rule be defended against the slow but constant pressures of a steadily growing population? Now they found themselves blocked within existing boundaries, and left to unavoidable internal quarrels. 'Successive generations of Administrative officers from the earliest days,' ran a typical recollection of the 1950s, 'have complained bitterly of the "clan jealousies" of the [Luo] tribe and their disruptive effects on social life.' The Luo model, in other words, could not be made to fit into the colonial model.

The lesson was harsh, and harshly taught. Not, in the Luo case, by outright resistance as with the Nandi and others: but partly by the troubles they now faced at home, partly by the coming of forced labour and taxation, partly by the porterage conscription of the First World War, and then by the triumph of the settlers after 1918. Out of all this experience, beginning in the 1900s, there came 'secondary' resistances. These continued, in successive forms, right through the colonial experience; and they constitute a central part of the history of that period, especially in territories under strong settler influence.

This connection between 'secondary' resistance and settler influence was not a coincidence. For it was in settler territories that African communities suffered their most jagged dislocation. And the guiding motive of this resistance, almost invariably, was an attempt either to defend or to rebuild the sense and fact of community on the African model. This model had always supposed and provided for adaptation to new situations. Now the effort to adapt, far more difficult than before, took successively new shapes. These were directed by that 'science of social control' which Africans had learned from the oracular teachings of the ancestors: in other words, they were efforts at adaptation that were social, political, even economic, but couched in religious guise. This made them hard for Europeans to understand.

Most Europeans, by this time, made a sharp distinction between the teachings of religion and the teachings of practical life: all the history of European thought since the Reformation opposed 'science' to 'religion', or 'religion' to 'politics'. Europeans in Africa were consequently surprised to discover that when Africans acted in the name of religion they were often acting, just as much, in that of politics. Not until the 1960s would it begin generally to be understood, thanks in no small measure to a brilliant school of interpretative historians headed by T. O. Ranger, that the distinction was a false one.

The Luo case continues to be instructive in this respect. Impressed by the advice of their own priests, they were inclined to listen cordially to the priests of the newcomers. But then it turned out that the priests of the newcomers required a still greater scrapping of the Luo model even than that demanded by colonial officials. For these missionaries preached a Christianity which not only denied the validity of the ancestors, but soon became indistinguishable from subjection to each and every demand of colonial government. Yet was this spiritual power of Christianity, very attractive in its offer of a wider community than any allowed by lineage ancestors, to be simply a European possession? Was this power to be a monopoly of the Europeans who had taken the country?

Such questions were being widely asked in the 1910s, and led to ideological developments. There were many who accepted the Christian vision of community above clan and lineage, but rejected the missionary condition that this community must be framed, governed, and controlled by Europeans. In the case of the Luo, as Ogot has continued the story, in 1907 a man called John Owalo declared that God had called him to launch a new religion. Owalo had received a Christian education successively in Italian Catholic, Scottish Presbyterian, and English Anglican missions, and was therefore well qualified to suppose that Christianity was adaptable to differences of nationality. In 1910 he denied the divinity of Christ, proclaimed himself a prophet, and rapidly won thousands of followers. These evidently thought, as he did, that a Luo Christianity must be better for the Luo, and certainly as valid, as an Italian, Scots or English Christianity. They set about building a Luo Christian community with schools of its own and the right to speak for itself.

With conditions worsening as the colonial model in Kenya

took further hold, such efforts proved inadequate. They were followed by others along a typology of ideological development which
can be widely traced in the 1920s and 30s. Some peoples moved
towards a further development of the Owalo version of an indigenized Christianity. Others moved towards a rejection of
Christianity as a promise that was only a trap.

To remain with the Luo for a moment, an example of this
second type of movement appeared in 1913. Onyango Dundo proclaimed a new cult, that of Mumbo, a great serpent 'whose two
homes are in the Sun and in the Lake [of Nyanza]'. Entirely rejecting
Christianity and all its ways, including the wearing of clothes instead
of skins, and denouncing all Europeans as enemies, Dundo and his
Mumboites preached the coming of a liberation that had nothing to
do with Christ. Once again their chief concern was to reconstitute
the shattered fact of community in a new situation. They called
for rejection of everything linked to the European model, Ogot has
explained, but they also looked forward to a complete transformation
of their own model. Like others of their sort, they ended in deportation, prison, or dispersal by an indignant colonial power.

The complexity and development of these movements of
'secondary' resistance, of ideological resistance, defy any brief
account. What the reader has to bear in mind, if he will, is that they
were by any measure the most important and pervasive theme of
African experience throughout these years 'before nationalism';
further, that they continued to be such in the period of conjunction
with or divergence from mass nationalism after the 1940s. Here one
can offer only a sketch of these myriad attempts to save or restore the
sense and fact of community against all the pressures of the colonial
system.

They are often hard to place within the typology of
ideological change. The Maji Maji war is a case in point. It erupted
in 1905 as a protest against German coercion in southern Tanganyika.
A man called Kanjikitile was able to develop a technique for con-
structing unity among neighbouring peoples who were never known
to have previously acted together in any large affair. In this the chief

symbol was a hallowed water, or *maji*, through whose acceptance a unity of purpose was achieved. This purpose was to oppose the further destruction of community life, which meant ejecting German rule. It cost the Germans two years of concentrated warfare to defeat the attempt.

Seen from one point of view, the Maji Maji rising was an attempt at restoration. One of the peoples who joined it, for example, were the Ngoni of the far southern territory of Tanganyika, a people whose forefathers had come from South Africa in the middle of the nineteenth century. 'What humiliated the Ngoni people most,' recalled one of their elders in 1968, a man who could remember the rising, 'was the European domination over them. They were prepared to die rather than continue being ruled by the whites, whose impact had been experienced by their fathers in South Africa.' They rejected German rule, recalled another eye-witness, and 'they longed for their old type of government.'[3]

But seen from another point of view, the Maji Maji rising was also an adjustment to a new sense and fact of community, though one that was still true to the African model. Those peoples who joined the rising had accepted, in their way, what would later on become the principal teaching of nationalism: the need to find the ideological basis for a wider unity than any known before. In due course, answering that need, the rural masses of Africa would breathe life into the nationalism of the élites. Among the first faint foretellings of that answer, the Maji Maji rising has its place.

Other movements, whether before or after Maji Maji, or more or less at the same time, display the same subtle ambiguity of vision. Some were much older. The oldest among them, as one might expect, occurred in the oldest territory of white settlement, the Cape Colony of South Africa. These offer a multitude of examples. An early one was the action of the Xhosa people set going in the 1850s by their prophet Mhlakaza. Characteristically for such movements, Mhlakaza identified the curse of European domination as a punishment of sin. Only a supreme act of expiation could be adequate. The Xhosa were ordered to slaughter their cattle and destroy their crops.

Obedience would be followed by a restoration of the old community in all its independence and self-respect. But already the ambiguity of restoration and reconstruction was present, for the restored community would inherit the goods of the Europeans, and would to that extent become a 'modernized' community.

The belief that certain remedial actions, sometimes involving armed revolt but more often not, would be followed by a Day of Reckoning, a moment of the 'millennium' when everything would change, and the Europeans would be expelled but their wealth and their technology would be left behind for African use, became a very common one. It took many forms: frequently of anti-witchcraft movements which, logically in African thought, sought to use the power of Good against the power of Evil (itself an aspect of the power of Good); often of a rejection of all European-like behaviour; almost always of a denial of European missionary teachings because they were teachings of submission to colonial rule. Not until the 1960s, and then only rarely, was this reliance on oracular wisdom, on African religion as a remedial guide, to be followed by a new and secular comprehension of reality. When that happened, the period of revolution would begin.

That was far ahead in the 1920s and 1930s. Two other types of response were important then. Both spread widely from southern Africa into east and central and even western Africa. One was a movement to form African Christian churches fully independent of white priests and white teachings. This began in South Africa in the 1880s, and soon became known as the Ethiopianist movement, after the Biblical prophecy of Ethiopia's special blessing and mission in the eyes of God – Ethiopia meaning not the country of that name, but Africa. Many communities devoted to this form of Christianity were founded in South Africa, and then in other territories as well. A Nigerian Ethiopian church appeared as early as 1888, again in reaction to the racism of local European missionaries. Another such initiative, in the Ivory Coast, enabled the Prophet Harris to baptize more than 100,000 people in the 1914–15 period alone.

A second trend or cluster of separatist Christian movements, especially strong in the settler territories of Central Africa, including the Belgian Congo and Angola, was that of Watchtower and its near relations. These shared some of the characteristics of the Ethiopianist movement, but added others of their own. Most were markedly 'millennarian' in their beliefs, counting on a Day that would end the world of colonial rule and begin another of liberty and happiness. All were hostile to secular government, whether colonial or by the chiefs of tradition. And they too displayed the ambiguity of restoration and reconstitution. Watchtower in its many rural manifestations throughout wide regions 'was not only concerned with [an] almost desperate belief that Africans were the chosen people' of God and, as such, would inherit their Earth despite all the facts of their disinheritance. They were also concerned with building new communities out of the ruins of the old. 'By rejecting the authority of the chief and the customs of the tribe and at the same time rejecting the authority of the British [or other colonial] administration and the teaching of the missionaries,' in Ranger's sensitive analysis, 'the Watch Tower believers did create new societies on a small scale.'⁴

Such movements gave hope to those who followed them, because they gave a new sense of fraternity. The fear of colonial power and its consequences could be overcome, as well as the fear of witchcraft and other such sanctions of the founding charters. Small in scale though they were, partly because of the rigorous administrative repression which they suffered, and partly because of the nature of their own separatism, they could still do something to relieve anxiety and revive a sense of fellowship. A few of them, somehow surviving, became and have remained wide multi-ethnic movements; among these, perhaps the most successful is the Church of Jesus Christ upon this Earth, founded by Simon Kimbangu in the Belgian Congo during 1921.

How did these movements connect with ideas of nationalism already current among the educated few of the 1920s? Were these voices in the wilderness a contribution to the many-channelled delta that fed the reservoir of protest that fed the sea of political pressure after 1945? Or were they rather a divergence into comforting evasion, a stream of dissent that lost itself in other-worldly dreams and heavenly promises?

There is no clear answer. In one large sense they were eventually fruitless, even futile, for they failed to face the this-worldly consequences of the colonial model, and could therefore make no progress towards realistic strategies of political action. Yet they were more than an evasion. To individuals they could give courage and comfort; to congregations they could open the way towards the mending of a sorely shattered feeling of community. In this respect, at least, they could offer a certain political leadership. And it was not long before they began to produce disciples who looked beyond other-worldly visions to the possibility of direct political action within the realities of every day.

There then occurred a tentative convergence between the protests of the many and the protests of the few: between, that is, the search for a restored or reconstituted African community and the élitist notion that this must be a national or nation-state community. Tentative: because the élites or Western-educated few wherever they existed were still deep in Europeanized isolation, but also because the men who began this convergence were far from having any kind of élitist status. Understandably, these men appeared chiefly in terri-tories where settler domination prevented the emergence of Western-educated leaders who were at home in the language of European nationalism, and where, in consequence, there was only a political void outside the arena of the African model. Now a new kind of spokesman began to fill this void.

In the Kenya of 1911 a young Kikuyu called Harry Thuku, then aged sixteen, left his mission school and went to the already important town of Nairobi, where he found work. There, like the rest, he had to have a pass (*kipande*) and he had to pay tax on a very small wage. In 1921, he recalled later, 'we heard that the settlers were going to reduce African wages by one third.' Thuku organized a protest. But it took a new form: neither that of a separatist church, nor of a return to some restatement of the African model, nor of an application for help to government-nominated or government-approved chiefs. He and others formed the Young Kikuyu Association, and this, beyond any doubt, stood on the threshold of the mass-supported nationalism which was partly to emerge from it.

Thuku's language illustrates this tentative convergence between all those who rejected the European model, and those who now began to think in terms of accepting it but turning it to African advantage. 'I, Harry Thuku,' he declared in February 1922, 'am greater than you Europeans. I am even greater than the chiefs of the country . . . Hearken, neither the Chiefs nor the Europeans have given you the slightest assistance. I do not want them at all in this country of Kikuyu . . .'[5] This was not yet nationalism, not even Kikuyu nationalism; but it was certainly protest of a type that was different from the cult of Mumbo and its kind.

Reacting against an especially aggressive white racism, the politics of protest in South Africa converged on nationalism from relatively early times. This was much like Algerian protest politics, and the history of the African National Congress, or of its contemporaries among Indians and Coloureds, is comparably rich and interesting. So is that of another formative influence, a non-white trade union movement much hampered but not yet crippled by white racism. Notable on this front was the Industrial and Commercial Workers Union formed in 1919 by a Nyasa immigrant, Clements Kadalie, influential in South Africa and later, thanks to Kadalie's skill and courage, in colonies to the northward.

Radical and even socialist ideas were also at work. These came chiefly through a South African Communist party organized in 1921 by influence from immigrant British workers such as the memorable W. H. Andrews.[6] They were vigorously in favour of placing the social struggle at the centre of policy, but their influence was stultified or extinguished through splits and expulsions caused by the destructively doctrinal disciplines of the Comintern in Moscow; and here, too, the parallel with Algeria is strikingly close.* For this reason, among others including administrative harassment and police repression, no unity of theory and practice could emerge to give non-white nationalism the force of mass support.

They were years of tough repression everywhere. The

*See Chapter 18.

extraordinary case of André Matswa ma Ngoma shows what this could mean. Born of peasant parents near Brazzaville (French Congo) in 1899, Matswa achieved some mission schooling, which meant a little literacy and an understanding of the need for more; and, again like the Kenyan Harry Thuku, he was able to secure a job in the lowest ranks of colonial service. In 1921, while Thuku was forming the Young Kikuyu Association, Matswa went to France, like many others later, to see what the world was like. There he became a *tirailleur sénégalais* (himself a Lari from the French Congo), and took part in the colonial war against Abd al-Krim in the Moroccan Rif. That, too, proved a formative experience, and seems to have given him his first radical ideas. Settling in Paris, he became a militant in 1926 of the Union des Travailleurs Nègres, a self-help organization of black immigrants rather than a regular trade union, and began writing occasionally for its journal, *Le Cri des Nègres*.

But in 1926, too, Matswa formed his Association des Originaires de l'AEF (French Equatorial Africa), the *Amicale* which became famous in its time and place, and was afterwards regarded by Congolese nationalists as a chief source of their nationalism. By 1928, much ahead of his time, Matswa was preaching a campaign of passive resistance to colonial discriminatory regulations. Arrested in 1929, he was deported to the Congo where his trial induced demonstrations of protest amid signs of a mass awakening to the possibilities of political action. Duly sentenced on derisory charges, he escaped to Nigeria in 1935, thence to Dakar and Casablanca, and eventually to France.

There Matswa lived clandestinely, somehow surviving, until the outbreak of the Second World War when, acting on the principle of his anti-fascism, he at once volunteered for military service. Among the first wounded who were sent to the rear, he was again arrested in hospital in April 1940, and died in prison during 1942 in grimly suspect circumstances. Yet the influence of his *Amicale* did not die with him. Later, his political work became transformed into a semi-millennarian cult, and 'Matswai-ism' became a source of mystical hope. It remains that Matswa was one of the true forerunners of mass nationalism, and even of its later and revolutionary potentials.

There were others like Matswa in the 1930s, though few so well remembered. They were the makers of the first organized strike actions of any magnitude among 'urbanized' wage-workers. The Northern Rhodesia Copperbelt saw a major strike of African miners in 1935, and another in 1940; Mombasa had its first large strike in 1939. There were many such strikes, notably in Sierra Leone. In all these, the struggle for self-defence within the colonial model, the social struggle, began to join with the struggle for political concessions, the national struggle.

We shall see that the Second World War did much to encourage this convergence, thanks to its lessons in European reality, its inherent anti-racism, and the experience gained by Africans at home or abroad. The development can perhaps be epitomized in a letter of 1943 which appeared in two Nyasaland newspapers and in the *Bantu Mirror* of South Africa. Written by James Frederick Sangala, another man of the stamp of Thuku and Matswa, this letter called for a new association of Africans, saying that 'the time is ripe for the Africans of this country to strive for unity so as to obtain the greater development of the peoples and country of Nyasaland.' The way was open for the national congresses of Central Africa a decade later.

Barely a sketch of the sources and development of North African nationalism is possible here. More complex than elsewhere, earlier in their influence, drawing much from Middle Eastern Muslim innovators such as Jamal al-Din al-Asadabi (1838–97), better known as al-Afghani, these nationalist movements also drew, in their theory and approach to the masses, on concepts specifically Muslim. Prominent among these was *asabiyya*, which we may interpret as 'community solidarity' among Muslims. Another, closely related, was that of *al Jamia al Wataniyya*, which means something like 'the ancestor-blessed community', and in which we may see the Muslim development of still older concepts of community enshrined in the founding charters of pre-Muslim cultures.

The actual development of nationalist ideas was the work of the educated men of Islam. More numerous than those of Christianity, and with a greater sense of indigenous legitimacy, their thought evolved on divergent lines. 'Traditionalists' sought inspiration in a dream of restoring the moral and political supremacy of the Rightly-Guided Caliphate of the earliest years of Islam. 'Westernizers', on the other hand, believed that liberation must come through learning and applying the secrets of European power, notably of European nationalism. This divergence would continue, and would deepen.

None of these 'Westernizing' ideas appears to have meant anything to rural peoples until the 1940s. But the 1920s see the earliest signs of their serious impact on the now steadily growing populations of towns. This happens in Egypt, where a working-class consciousness begins to appear in this period. It happens in the Maghrib. Trade unions struggle into clandestine life; and a trades union congress is actually held in Tunisia as early as 1920. But the bourgeois nationalists then on the scene generally disown the social struggle as a threat to their own supremacy in the future.

For Algeria the convergence of social with national occurs first among immigrants in France, thanks chiefly to the daily education provided by French racism towards these immigrants, but also to the example offered by French working-class protest. This convergence begins to shift to the towns of Algeria in the 1930s. Morocco begins to display a comparable urban phenomenon, comparably tentative and as yet very weak, with widespread agitations which follow the famous *dahir* of 1930, a French administrative device rightly seen as a means of undermining the unity of Islam, and therefore as a blow to Moroccan identity and culture.* In Libya the process of proletarianization is scarcely begun, while the ravages of

---

*A logical evolution of Lyautey's policies of divide-and-rule, this *dahir* (or administrative decree) placed Berber courts of appeal and customary tribunals beyond the jurisdiction of the Muslim courts which applied the *sharia*, and their judges (*qadis*). It 'confirmed and stressed the difference between Berber custom . . . and Muslim law', and, by thus obstructing Berber assimilation to Islam in its Arab and Arabic essence, provided 'the real impetus to Arab nationalism in Morocco, a nationalism which eventually embraced Berbers as well'. D. M. Hart, in E. Gellner and Ch. Micaud (eds), *Arabs and Berbers*, Duckworth, 1973, p. 39.

Fascist Italy's reconquering campaigns are still deeply felt throughout the 1930s.

In all these countries, save perhaps in Libya, the great depression was the 'revolutionary mole' that burrowed the chief tunnels of convergence between the many and the few. The Second World War was to make those tunnels larger, and push them to the surface.

17

'USELESS VISIONARIES, DETESTABLE CLERKS'

Of all those protests and prophets in the bush, distant uprisings and desperate resentments beyond the horizons of the coastland, the few who first and for long preached a nationalist message knew little and cared less. At least until the radicalizing influences of the great depression, a more or less total alienation of ideas and beliefs barricaded the Western-educated groups from any political alliance with the large majority of Africans, and even from any political sympathy with their grievances.

This was understandable. The men who brought the nationalist message, often in the guise of Pan-Negroism, were Transatlantics: black Americans and West Indians for whom emancipation, necessarily in their position, had to begin by proving that educated black men were as good as educated white men. They accepted the missionary view that civilization must be brought into Africa from outside; but the task of regenerating the sadly decadent continent from which their ancestors had come as slaves should rightly and above all be theirs. They became, accordingly, the pioneers of progress by the imported model.

The 'back to Africa' emancipationists in the northern American states of the 1850s had framed their programme: 'Africa, to become regenerated, must have a national character ...' The Liberian colonists shaped it further. Their African roots long since lost in the fearful dislocations of slavery, they were very sure that all in Africa was savage barbarism save what might now be rescued by themselves. Characteristic of this attitude was the New Yorker Alexander Crummell (1819-98), whose grandfather had been a chief in Sierra Leone around the end of the eighteenth century. Translated to leadership in Liberia, Crummell took it for granted that the black colonists' mission must be to exercise 'the genius of free government' over 'this seat of ancient despotism and bloody superstition'. How otherwise were the colonists to succour 'a vast population of degraded subjects'? Meeting the criticism that 'our native population' might have a right to live as they thought best, Crummell replied in 1870 with the full doctrine of the Europeans. 'Both our position and our circumstances,' he declared in Monrovia, 'make us the guardians, the protectors, and the teachers of our heathen tribes.'[7] Even down to the use of the possessive 'our', it was just what the new imperialists were saying.

Immigrant West Indians reinforced the same missionary thesis. They argued that nationhood was necessary to progress and regeneration, that this must come by way of European political teaching, and that European domination was therefore an unavoidable and even beneficial stage on the road to that nationhood. This view was expressed in one way by Edward Wilmot Blyden (1832–1912), born in the Caribbean island of St Thomas and in time, after some hard struggles with white racism, a writer of distinction and a Liberian diplomat. 'Easily the most learned and articulate champion of the Negro race in his own time,' says Lynch, Blyden 'believed that European political overlordship was temporary, and that discrimination was merely part of the price that Africans had to pay to have their continent brought onto the world stage.'[8] Others put it differently. An issue of the *African Times* of 1880 saw 'the educated élite more or less under the influence of the Christian faith, more or less imbued with Christian principles', as the 'indispensable vanguard of the great army of civilization that must be projected upon the ignorant barbarism of heathen Africa'. But all thought that 'heathen Africa' could not possibly 'save itself'.*

* 'Westernizing' Africans were not of course alone in such attitudes; in one way or another, they emerged in all colonial situations of that period, notably in India, where the nationalist movement had origins in a comparable belief that colonial rule could provide a model for progress impossible by way of indigenous culture; and in India, too, this gave rise to a comparable alienation between the few and the many. Only Japan appears to have achieved a synthesis between ancestral and modernizing thought; but Japan, precisely, never lost her independence.

This acceptance of the colonial and Christian belief in the worthlessness or wickedness of Africa's cultures and communities has to be seen in its historical context. The best of those who spoke for it were men of vision and courage. They believed in humanity, rose far above the racist provincialism of the colonialists, spoke for a future in which all should be free to develop their talents and potentialities. Yet their alienation from indigenous culture was bound to push them towards practical approval of the colonial system. No doubt unavoidably, they saw Africa's future in terms of the civilization from which they came, and at whose hands they suffered a most unjust denial. Formed in a solid bourgeois tradition, then the only useful one available, they tried to make the most of it.

This initial alienation in the import of nationalist ideas, with Pan-Negroist ideas a frequent extension, was buttressed by a second, above all in British West Africa where there was still some free ground for political discussion. This second alienation derived from the cultural abyss which separated the educated but indigenous Africans, in certain coastal towns, from the 'illiterate masses' who surrounded them. Insofar as they were not the offspring of Transatlantics, these thinkers and writers were often the children or grandchildren of 'recaptives', the name given in the early nineteenth century to tens of thousands of enslaved West Africans, often from Nigeria, whom the British Navy had rescued from slave ships and put ashore as free people at Freetown in Sierra Leone. Here and in some other coastal places they established a 'creole society' which felt itself, and really was, widely apart from the indigenous inhabitants. In the essence of the matter, they too were colonists; as such, they embraced the same ideas as the Transatlantics. They agreed that colonial enterprise was benevolent, provided only that they should have a hand in it. Was it not their forefathers' contemporaries in Nigeria and elsewhere who had sold their parents into slavery? And wasn't it the British Navy which had set their parents free in the name of Christianity and civilization? Enterprising, energetic, often displaying great intellectual capacities, the best of these men, such as the medical doctor James Africanus Horton (1835–83), set about answering Blyden's demand that they should 'show the world' their right to equality with Europeans: 'by seeking after those attributes which give dignity to a state; by cultivating those virtues which shed lustre upon individuals and communities . . .': in short, by seconding the great enclosure that could lead on to nationalism and all that nationalism could give or guarantee.

Many of these Sierra Leonean descendants of 'recaptives', chiefly of Yoruba origin and known as Aku or Saro, returned to the land of their fathers or at least to Lagos Island in the course of the nineteenth century. Here at Lagos or at one or two inland towns not yet enclosed by the British, notably Abeokuta, they settled as the missionaries and 'natural leaders' of a Christian and eventually nationalist future. So it was, in the words of Ayandele, that 'the banished slaves and their offspring (became) the cornerstone of the Nigerian edifice' which the future was to build. They were little appreciated by those whom they proposed to lead, finding that 'their rejection by indigenous society was total and irrevocable'.[9] But they were not deterred. They believed that they held the keys to the future. And the future would prove that in this, at least, they were undoubtedly right.

Progress equalled acceptance of the European model in all its Christian and paternal teachings, and therefore a corresponding rejection of all that appertained to the 'savage backlands' of the African model. The same theme appeared wherever individuals managed to achieve a Western education. At least four of South Africa's early spokesmen for the rights of Africans – J. L. Dube, Sol Plaatje, P. Isaka Seme and D. D. T. Jabavu – were educated in Negro American colleges. So too, later on, were Central Africans such as John Chilembwe and Hastings Kamuzu Banda of Nyasaland (Malawi), the one an early and tragic voice in the call for independence, and the other eventually the first president of Malawi. Their 'home situation' was a great deal harder and more hostile than that of their West African contemporaries; but they held as firmly to the same vision of civilization *versus* barbarism.

We shall look at the situation of élites in the other chief area of their formation, the French empire, a little further on.* Mean-

*See Chapter 18.

while, far away in Angola during the 1890s, another product of the same alienation, José de Fontes Pereira, brought down settler wrath upon his head by advocating British colonial rule instead of Portuguese because Portugal, as he scarifyingly explained, was incapable of doing the civilizing job that needed to be done for the *preto boçal*, the brutish black of the bush. There were many others who argued in a comparable cause: if one's local colonial rule proved incapable, one's duty was to find another.

In British West Africa, where they were most numerous and in the long run most influential, the Western-educated few emerged chiefly from the relatively privileged society of creole Freetown. These had possessed mission schools since the first founding of the colony in 1787. By the 1850s Sierra Leone had forty-two primary schools with 6,000 pupils; 1854 saw the first creole lawyer; between 1858 and 1901 no fewer than twenty-five creoles qualified as medical doctors, many more as clergymen, more again as school teachers. Some stayed at home; others emigrated; all played some part in the preaching of the European model. Cape Coast in the Gold Coast (Ghana) became another centre of Westernizing ideas, though here the educated few were of local origin.

The style and savour of these often extraordinary men, whether or not of Sierra Leonean provenance, is well illustrated by the educated men of Lagos.

Fully adjusted to the British annexation of 1861, the Lagos worthies flourished in a scintillating display of talent, presiding, protesting, addressing, resolving in a gala of verbal virtuosity. Hindsight has sometimes found them absurd, pathetic, even contemptible in their readiness to lick the imperial boot, or seen them as pawns of dependence rather than as pioneers of independence. But hindsight has its own axe to grind, and the best of these men were more than that, occasionally much more. They need also to be seen as they saw themselves and as their many admirers saw them. The late L. C. Gwam, archivist of the Nigerian University of Ibadan, composed their biographies in the 1960s, but from right inside their own tradition.

There was the Honourable Alexander Sapara Williams

(1855–1915), barrister of the Middle Temple since 1879, Commander of the Order of St Michael and St George (1915), unofficial member of the Lagos Legislative Council (1901–13), member of the race-course board of management, trustee of the Glover Memorial Hall, spokesman for the Lagos agricultural show, vice-president of the Lagos auxiliary of the Aborigines Protection Society, vice-chairman of the livestock committee, Wesleyan lay preacher, and a great deal more beside. Who is going to say that Sapara Williams counted for nothing? Gwam tells us that he possessed 'all the qualities and qualifications that delighted, and still delight, the Lagos public about their political heroes. He was a successful lawyer. He was gifted by nature with dignity and poise. He was handsome, oratorical and rhetorical; he was sociable and accessible; he was a debater of no mean order; and he could be demagogic when he chose.'

And who is going to look down his nose at Dr Henry Rawlinson Carr (1863–1945), senior inspector of schools, Commissioner for the colony of Lagos (1910–24), 'book collector, matchless educationist, orator, musician, distinguished civil servant, Negro patriot and nationalist, lawyer, philosopher, saint and scholar'? Did he not advocate and practise monogamy because he believed that it accorded with 'the principle of the dignity of man'; Christianity because 'the practice of religion was the highest expression of man'; education because 'it was the vital force in the making of the individual and a nation'? All this may sound a little like a resolution of mutual self-esteem at the Pickwick Club. Perhaps: but the true 'period' of these élites was precisely mid-Victorian. They believed themselves at the forefront of ideological progress; in fact they were half a century behind the times.

They took themselves very seriously because they knew that only intense work and application could enable them to make careers. But who is going to accuse them of lacking humour and a taste for the spice of life? How otherwise appreciate the Honourable John Augustus Otonba Payne (1839–1906), civil servant, historian, churchman, accumulator of landed property, and a gift to his grateful fellow-citizens of Lagos for his 'leading part in organizing those Concerts, Musical Shows, Banquets, At Homes, Debates, Grand

Balls, Picnics, Regattas, Athletics, etc., which have since remained a powerful element in the social life of Lagos'? Was he, too, not a member of the sacred racecourse board, a trustee of the venerable Glover Hall? Did he not go so far as to organize a visit by Dr Edward Wilmot Blyden, in the piping times of '91, and did he not supervise, before Dr Blyden's lecture to a Muslim audience on 'The Greatness of Common Things', a banquet 'at an improvised Pavilion erected at Balogun Square, in an enclosure fenced in with corrugated iron sheets, constructed with palm branches and decorated with flags which were tastefully arranged, and with a Band in attendance'; and was it not the fact that the Honourable Otonba Payne there 'proposed the health of His Excellency Captain G. C. Denton, and replied humorously for the ladies whose toast was proposed by Mr Nash Hamilton Williams, Barrister at Law'? In 1891 the military enclosure was just getting into its stride, up-country in Nigeria and in many other places; but the Honourable Otonba Payne and his friends could have no reason for seeing anything wrong with that.

Some of these men wrote enormously for their public, small and colonial though it was. By 1900 no fewer than thirty-four newspapers had seen the light in Sierra Leone, nineteen in the Gold Coast, and seven in Nigeria; and all but a handful of these had been or still were owned and launched and edited by Africans. Remarkable journalistic talents were revealed: by none more notably, perhaps, than by John Payne Jackson (1847–1915), originally a Liberian of black American parentage who had settled in Lagos, and his still more redoubtable son, Thomas Horatio Jackson (1879–1936), a veritable titan of the Lagos press. The former's career was unhappily reduced 'by a frequent liability to the pains and penalties of *delirium tremens*' – what distinguished journalist will fail to sympathize? – but his son carried fire and brimstone into the days of tightening imperialist discrimination.

And with them, but especially with Thomas Horatio, the tone of political talk began to be a little different from before. Both Jacksons reacted to the growing racism of the 1900s and 1910s by excoriating British arrogance, greed, irresponsibility and collapse into the sin of pride. Thomas Horatio signalled Lugard's departure from the seat of Nigerian power, in 1920, by pointing out in his *Lagos Weekly Record* that 'we have lived under the cramped condition of a military dictatorship when the law from being a means of protection had become an instrument of crime and oppression in the hands of unscrupulous officials . . . The last administration (Lugard's) had made the very name of white man stink in the nostrils of the native.'[10]

Long before, in 1885, a governor-general of Angola had described such men as Jackson as 'useless visionaries and detestable clerks'.[11] But they had something real to say, and they knew how to say it, more often than not, with sting and savour.

Standing between a white civilization which would not have them but which they deeply admired, and a black civilization which would not have them either but which they in any case despised, these sometimes outstanding men were caught in a trap from which their most brilliant arguments could not release them. They had welcomed to Africa the European model of the nation-state, preached its virtues, expounded endlessly upon its necessity to Africa's salvation: provided, of course, that the mid-Victorian promise was to hold good, and the model was to pass under their control and government. Now they found that nothing like this was going to happen, and were left protesting to each other.

Other equivocations weakened their claim to be taken seriously. Their intense conservatism was one of these. All their programmes and flaming editorials spoke for the need to build a new community for Africa, a modern and nationalist community capable of displacing the communities of the past, and of standing equal in the world with the communities of Europe and North America. This was the revolutionary aspect of their vision that history would confirm fifty years later. Yet at no point were these prophets able to offer, or even to see the need to offer, any realistic analysis of the colonial system or of the kind of community which might derive from it. The economics of the new imperialism, let alone the long-term implications of introducing a nationalism based on economic systems which did not exist in Africa, were generally beyond the realm of their speculation. They swallowed the bait of the civilizing colonial mission and with it they swallowed the hook, the line, and the sinker.

This derived from the logic of their thought; it derived also from their belief in middle-class values. No matter what rhetoric they might unfold on behalf of a liberated Africa, they could favour nothing that smacked of plebeian agitation. Anything so subversive could only rock and perhaps sink the fragile boat of respectable argument, often very much a lawyer's argument, in which they were trying to navigate the storms of colonial subjection. In 1897, for example, the Lagos educator Dr Henry Rawlinson Carr was on a visit to England. Shrewdly concerned to understand the English, if that were possible, he made personal visits. One such visit was to the well-known strike-leader John Burns, who had already travelled to the Niger mission and formed there a warm admiration for Bishop Samuel Crowther. Carr's notes on the meeting happily survive; they show the two men as miles apart.

In that same year of 1897 the first major colonial strike erupted in Lagos. Labourers wanted more than ninepence a day, a miserable wage even in those times (though raised to a shilling, as it happens, only in 1937). They got small sympathy from the makers of Lagos opinion. Even Jackson's relatively radical *Lagos Weekly Record*, while arguing that employers would do well to pay a higher wage, observed that 'strikes were unknown in this part of the world, and it is infinitely more to the advantage of the Colony that this condition of things should be preserved, than that the people should be driven into learning how to combine for their own protection and interest.'[12]

With few exceptions – the Gambian E. F. Small was one of them – the great tidal waves of revolution in Europe during and immediately after the First World War passed over the heads of the few without teaching them a thing, or even without their noticing what had happened. Whenever they did notice they found the spectacle abhorrent, for their acceptance of the class structure of the European model was as complete as their belief that they themselves belonged to the ruling class, even if colonial power was too stupid to understand the fact. And this remained their view not only in West

Africa where settler racism took little effect, but even in South Africa where it all-pervasively did.

There is the case of Professor D. D. T. Jabavu. Though completely African in origins and social background, Jabavu was one of a small but important minority of blacks who were able, thanks to the relative liberalism of Cape Colony and its missionary belief in higher education for a few non-whites, to achieve academic honours and make good use of them. Journalist and politician, he led many protests against discrimination. But he was really another Lagos worthy who believed that the civilizing mission must be paid its price by Africans. Prudently conservative, though well able to be 'demagogic when he chose', Jabavu was soon under attack by the more radical wing of the protest movement of those days. Sol Plaatje was among Africans who accused him of feeding 'his masters', the ruling white party, 'upon flap-doodle, fabricating the mess out of imaginary native votes of confidence for his masters' delectation'.[13] Yet Jabavu was a spokesman of wide prestige, and many later Africans in South Africa followed in his tradition.

Jabavu believed that black collaboration with white supremacy would eventually lead to white acceptance of equality with blacks. He was consequently against all forms of agitation which might be frightening to whites. 'There has sprung into life a large number of Natives from the better educated class,' Jabavu told a Natal missionary conference in 1920, 'who have seized the opportunity of the general state of dissatisfaction to stir up the populace to desperate acts.' Personally he did not blame the populace, for they were 'landless, voteless, helots; pariahs, social outcasts in their fatherland with no future in any path of life'. Of all the blessings of this world they saw that the white man had everything, and they had nothing.

But their subversive leaders were dangerous. 'Armed with rallying catch phrases and a copious Socialistic vocabulary, they play as easily as on a piano upon the hearts of the illiterate minelabourers.' That was bad enough. Worse was that the Socialism they preached was not 'the harmless commonsense system advocated' in Britain by Labour leaders such as Philip Snowden and Ramsay Macdonald. It was the 'atheistic and revolutionist doctrines of Count Henri Saint Simon' reflected in England by Robert Blatchford, Charles Bradlaugh and J. M. Robertson.[14] Three years earlier the October Revolution had trampled on Tsarism and hammered at the gates of Western Europe: but of Marx, Engels, Lenin and that revolution, Jabavu appeared not even to have heard. In this, too, he was perfectly characteristic of the educated few.

Having sponsored the European model for Africa, the early élites tried hard to make it fit within a colonial system now set for a very long run. After the 1900s they found this ever more difficult. Discrimination against educated Africans was already a fact of everyday life by the 1890s; it grew rapidly more acute. We may look ahead a little here, for this deepening discrimination became a central influence.

What happened in the relatively favoured Gold Coast happened still more sharply elsewhere. Thanks largely to the educated group in the town of Cape Coast, the nineteenth-century tradition was that Africans should have senior posts in an administration which, according to imperial policy, they would eventually inherit. After about 1900, on the contrary, they were practically excluded from government except as lowly clerks. In 1926 a governor of excellent intentions, Frederick Gordon Guggisberg, sought to reverse this. He provided in his estimates for twenty-eight Africans to occupy senior posts along with 481 British (or 'expatriates' as they were later to be called). The African senior quota was to be seventy-six in 1930, 148 in 1935, and 229 by 1945, with a corresponding reduction in senior European staff. Nothing like this happened. Between 1926 and 1946 there was a small increase in African senior postings, but the European staff was almost doubled. The colonial system might not be altogether a system of outdoor relief for the English upper classes, since British officials were seldom of such elevated social origin; but it certainly begat its own system of patronage, and Africans, however well qualified, had to stand at the end of that queue.

The case was general, and it drove the educated few into their first serious questionings about the British model they had so vigorously accepted. They continued to accept the model as being the only alternative to 'savage barbarism', but they began to agitate more sharply for a share in its operation. This necessarily brought them closer to the culture and aspirations of the many; but not much. An African Christian resentment against European missionary control formed one aspect of this shift in stance.

Little stimulus to any such resentment was present so long as European missionaries would accept African clergymen as their equals. Notable among its kind, or at least among its Protestant kind, the British Church Missionary Society (CMS) had long done that with impressive results. Outstanding men had emerged from its ranks, above all Bishop Samuel Crowther (1806–91), a Yoruba enslaved in his youth, 'recaptured' by the British navy and set free in Sierra Leone, where he graduated with honours at the CMS Fourah Bay College. For years Crowther laboured in the interior of the Niger Delta with encouragement from distant CMS governors in London. But the new imperialism of the 1880s, based as it was on the operative principle that peoples subjected by force were peoples rightly subjected because of their 'natural inferiority' to whites, now turned its influence against Crowther and the whole concept of African Christian leadership.

While British consuls and traders were busy appropriating the leadership of African trade, new missionaries from England began doing the same in the leadership of missions. A 'deep racist feeling' of contempt for Africans won the upper hand, as Ajayi and Webster tell us; and it was not long before this began to provoke breakaways into African-led churches. With CMS and other missionaries now an arm of British nationalism, the Ethiopian message of these churches, the earliest of which was formed in Nigeria in 1888, still held to the Christian vision of a universalist community; but facing missionary racism this should be one, now, in which Africans could 'stand up and face the world'. No one expressed this better than another eminent son of Sierra Leonean parentage, the Nigerian Bishop James Johnson (1836–1917), who was not himself a breakaway.

Tireless in his Niger mission, James Johnson's vision took

him right over the heads of the European missionaries of his later years. Recapturing the glories of North African Christianity in Roman times, Africa should rise once more, 'her tears wiped off her eyes, her scores of cathedrals and bishops restored, her Christian colleges re-established'.[15] All should participate, all should be embraced. A universal faith should found a universal community in Africa, and this in turn, he prophesied in 1906, would remove 'differences of nationality, language, customs and tribal feuds and warfare', and promote a 'oneness and common interest'.

That was a prophecy which still echoes down the years; but to win his revelation of a new 'city of God', of a 'regeneration' going far beyond all question of race or caste or natural ambition, Johnson had by-passed more than the missionaries. He had by-passed the ancestors as well. They took their revenge. In the 1910s his Niger mission had to face a different challenge, coming not from racist missionaries but from an illiterate canoe-maker, Garrick Braide, who declared himself a prophet. Within three months Braide reduced Bishop Johnson's flock by half their total.

It was another lesson in the dangers of alienation. Johnson believed that England should become Africa's model. But those who followed Garrick Braide, Ijọ peasants and fishermen to whom it seemed that Bishop Johnson's orders were no less foreign to themselves than the orders of the Europeans, preferred their own model. The times being sadly out of joint, this taught that there would have to be atonement. So Braide dispensed with Johnson's clerical prayers, and compelled the sick to 'make confessions of their sin and to undergo penance' while he prayed for their recovery. 'Crowds upon crowds came to greet' Braide, the bishop himself reported sadly. Chiefs and masters of the country 'crawled along the ground to where he sat', and whenever Braide was on the march, 'every one that passes by falls on his knees . . .' Again one sees how essentially irrelevant to the multitude were the élitist ideas of those years, even when, as with Bishop Johnson, they were quite without self-seeking.

Disillusioned with the chances of progress by way of Christianity, others turned to secular politics, linking this now with an attempt, however difficult, to accommodate a defence of 'African values' with a continued belief in African barbarism. They set two large trends in motion. One was early forms of nationalist organization. The other was that literary partnership of 'Africanity' with 'Westernization' which became the Négritude whose characteristic spokesman was to be the first president of an independent Senegal, Léopold Sédar Senghor.

Of the second of these trends, the example may be cited of the Gold Coaster Sol Solomon, who Africanized his name as Samuel Richard Brew Attoh Ahuma (1864–1921), and became the principal of a secondary school founded by African initiative in 1906, the first school of its kind to receive a government grant. Nationalist and journalist, he was one of those who tried to square the ideological circle. 'Let us help one another,' he wrote in 1911, 'to find a way out of Darkest Africa . . . We must emerge from the savage backwoods and come into the open where nations are made.'[16] Yet the 'savage backwoods' were precisely the creator of the African values he sought so valiantly to defend. Others made the same hard effort to promote with one hand what they rejected with the other. Out of it, eventually, was to come that uneasy 'populism' of the late 1930s and 1940s, which was to marry, though briefly, the national cause of the élites to the social cause of the masses.

Secular politics, on the other hand, continued with the attempt to share control of the European model as transferred to Africa in the form of the colonial system. This is where one may see that however marginal the influence of the early élites may have been, it nonetheless exercised a profound historical importance. That influence established the world of the European nation-state as the manifest destiny of the colonial state, just as the colonial system itself would do the same in other and less obvious ways, so that decolonization, when it came, was bound and fettered within the terms of this nationalism.

The 'populist' tradition in British West Africa probably begins with Herbert Macaulay (1864–1946), Lagos civil engineer, journalist, artistic dilettante, lover of musical evenings, inexhaustible polemicist, 'his great black bow tie paralleling the flamboyant wings of his enormous white moustache', whom the fiery tribunes of the

1930s and after, such as Nnamdi Azikiwe, would celebrate as 'father of the nation'. Determined advocate of the Pax Britannica and all its works (save in many of its more obvious injustices, against which he fulminated with effect), Macaulay was another who tried to square the circle. His thought was a further display of the conflict between the European model and the 'African values' it rejected while claiming to protect.

The outcome can seem derisory. 'What actually unites a nation,' declared Macaulay in 1932, 'is the cult of a certain idea [which can unify] every citizen in the interest of the common weal ... Every man looks for something of that nature in his life to identify himself with.' Once more, we have the call to build a community which can realize unity and progress out of the supposed vacuum of Africa's 'savage backwoods'. Meanwhile, said Macaulay, the position of the élites who must build this community was difficult, because history 'has thrust us into the position in which we must lead dual lives'. Convention required conformity with European culture, but development needed the drive to be got from indigenous culture. What could you do about that? Macaulay recommended a sartorial synthesis, 'the wearing of English dress for business and of native dress for pleasure purposes'.[17] It was not much, perhaps; but the majority of the élites were to think it useful, and for long into the future.

Secular politics led to new initiatives impelled by the influences of the First World War. There came a new feeling that if West Africans were good enough to fight and die for the British cause of freedom, then they were good enough to live for their own. In 1920 there was formed a federal organization, with sections in Nigeria, Gold Coast, Sierra Leone, and The Gambia. The declared policy of this National Congress of British West Africa was 'to aid in the development of the political institutions of British West Africa under the Union Jack': to achieve, in other words, something like a West African Dominion of the British Empire.

With the Gold Coaster J. H. Casely Hayford as its president, the Congress gathered representatives of all those who now believed that political argument should take the place of Christian moralizing. The National Congress lived through the 1920s, but was soon the victim of its own internal contradiction. On one hand, for example, the Congress called for a federal union of self-governing territories. On the other hand, its members' chief aim was to extend their representation on British colonial legislative councils where, as non-voting members, a few were already present. Understandably, this middle-class forum ran directly on the rocks of conflicting nation-state ambitions. Of its thirty or so most active members, fifteen were lawyers and eight were merchants.

By the middle '20s, moreover, its Pan-Negroist overtones were meeting with a new critique from nationalists who now began to think that Transatlantic influences could be an obstacle to local progress. Among those who voiced this critique was a founder of the Gold Coast section of the Congress, Kobina Sekyi (1892–1956). He came to believe that the black American claim to lead Africa, as then expressed in its extreme form by the Jamaican Marcus Garvey (1887–1940), was both offensive and ridiculous; and he said as much in a pamphlet of 1925. The salvation of Africans could be materially assisted by the Africans in America, he agreed, 'but must be controlled and directed from African Africa as thoroughly African African'.[18] Pan-Negroism would have to become Pan-Africanism. Here was another thought that would run into the future.

Summing up these men of the 1930s, the Gambian historian Ayodele Langley expressed in 1972 what was by that time an increasingly common view. He saw them as 'cautious reformists': essentially, as 'co-operationists with exceedingly limited political objectives ... whose interests generally coincided with, and were in fact protected by, the foreign rulers they were agitating against'.[19] They sought to harmonize the colonial system with their own interests, and were therefore incapable of reaching a mass audience, or even of wishing to reach one. Revolution scared them stiff. Mass agitation appalled them by its implications. On all this the evidence is inescapable and conclusive: so far as these 'co-operationists' were concerned, the colonial system in every basic attribute should and would continue until, at some more or less remote point in a benign future, it could pass into their guardianship.

That was to happen in the 1960s. But the road to this result was still a long one. Meanwhile the 1930s produced an extension of existing ideas. No new ideas came to this scene, save here and there with distant echoes of the Russian Revolution and its consequences. What counted were immediate influences. One of these was the sheer wear and tear of colonial discrimination. Another consisted in the hardships of the great depression. Both inspired a sharper reaction and a new desire to find the mass audience which could drive through the hesitations and defeats of the 'old men' of the 1920s and before. So did a third influence. This was the Italian Fascist aggression of 1935 against Ethiopia, coupled with the spectacle of British and French connivance.

This aggression worked strongly for the unfolding of a less timid reformism. Here, after all, was the very object and end-result of the nationalist model, a Christian state which was also a nation state, having to defend itself against a perfectly gratuitous and brutal invasion, and this at the very moment when the educated few were beginning to think about ways and means of securing control of the system. But the impact went beyond the few.

Said the *Gold Coast Spectator* in 1935: 'The Gold Coast man, down to the schoolboy, knows that he has everything in common with the Ethiopians';[20] and the claim to 'mass response' was probably not an exaggeration. Long afterwards the Mozambican leader Eduardo Mondlane, then a village schoolboy in southern Mozambique, was to recall how deeply his community was stirred by news of the invasion. And in 1938 an English observer who also deserves to be remembered for her part in early nationalist strivings, Nancy Cunard, was almost certainly right in claiming that the colonial theme came into the centre of wide attention as never before. There was probably no part of Africa that did not hear about the invasion without a sense of outrage.

After 1930, in any case, the 'old respectables' of the National Congress were followed by men who were ready to pursue the politics of protest with a new determination, even if barely with new ideas about the future that they wanted. Of such was I. T. D. Wallace-Johnson in Sierra Leone, and, after 1935, Nnamdi Azikiwe in the Gold Coast and his native Nigeria. Others were closer to the 'old respectables' but talked a stronger and less patient language. They included the Gold Coaster J. B. Danquah and William Ofori Attah, H. O. Davies and Ernest Ikoli in Nigeria, and more of the same calibre elsewhere. With them, new organizations appeared. One of these was Wallace-Johnson's West African Youth League. Another was the Mambii party in the Gold Coast. A third was the Nigerian Youth Movement. In 1938 the latter issued a charter calling for 'a complete take-over of the Government into the hands of the indigenous people of our country'.

   The note thus struck was a new one in colonial Africa: only the nationalists of Algeria, Madagascar and Cameroun had so far made this outright call for an untrammelled independence. And yet the Nigerian Youth Movement, like other nationalist organizations of the time, merely extended the constitutional reformism of earlier years. Still without a serious analysis of the underlying nature of the colonial system, whether in its economic or cultural dimensions, they called for a 'complete take-over' of that system in its territorial fragments. They wanted power without questioning the elements from which that power was built. Their reformism extended only to reforming the nationality of the controllers: let British rule depart, and little else of substance need evidently change. Colonial government now began to toy with this idea and, after a while, to understand its usefulness.

   Exactly when the British began thinking seriously of withdrawing their political control from a system whose structural substance could then be conserved by African successors has remained a matter of controversy: in no systematic way, probably, before the end of the 1940s. Yet influential persons already had the idea, at least for West Africa, some time late in the 1930s. In 1939, for example, two of these with access to the inner councils of government, Lord Hailey and Professor Sir Reginald Coupland, began discussing the desirability of constitutional concessions. Coupland thought that Nigeria and the Gold Coast 'would be the most fruitful field in which to start some movement towards self-government'.[21]

   Colonial governors were seldom so advanced. Their job,

in any case, was to maintain the *status quo*. 'We are cursed with some professional agitators and an anti-Government, anti-imperialistic and anti-European press,' Gold Coast Governor Sir Arnold Hodson told the Colonial Secretary in London in 1936, but otherwise he had never seen a colony which was more contented. In seeing this he saw a lot less than was really there, as colonial governors usually did; for 1937 brought a major protest, the Gold Coast 'cocoa hold-up' aimed at improving European buying prices. Yet the local situation would still seem well in hand.

Onwards from the great slump, however, one's impression is that a situation began to shape itself in the minds of leading officials wherein they ought to begin to look for reliable African successors. Pointedly in West Africa, though elsewhere a mere shadow across the colonial future, politics were on the scene. Convenient chiefs and dependable headmen might no longer be enough: suitable politicians could also become necessary, so as eventually to man the administrative 'scaffolding' raised by colonial wisdom. But how could one be sure who was suitable? The problem of distinguishing 'good boys' from 'bad boys' was not, of course, a new one: it had always stood high on the list of political officials' duties, and colonial police archives show in detail that the duty was pursued. Now, after 1930, it began to be pursued with a new question in mind: how to tell the difference between 'good boys' and 'communists', between the probably suitable and the certainly unsuitable, with the 'communist' label generally attached to all who appeared to harbour any sort of radicalism.

The trouble for the political and police officials was that they themselves understood no politics except those of colonial rule. More, they did not understand the educated élites, whom they invariably distrusted and usually despised. Applying their simple categories of 'loyalty' or 'communism', they were often foolish; but they were also, and logically from their point of view, incurably racist.

In 1936 the younger Casely Hayford, a talented lawyer of liberal nationalist opinions, was appointed as a district magistrate of the Gold Coast after considerable official opposition, such posts being regarded as a European preserve. One of those who was gravely shocked was the colonial inspector-general of police. But 'what apparently disturbed them more than anything else,' comments Shaloff, who has read the official correspondence, 'were the allegedly subversive activities of Casely Hayford's wife, whom [the colonial attorney-general] described as a Polish Jewess of definite "Red" sympathies.'[22] The description speaks for itself, but Mrs Hayford's real subversion was, of course, that she had married a black man.

After the Gambian nationalist E. F. Small had attended a meeting of a section of the Comintern in Moscow in 1930, he made other such contacts in Western Europe, including one with the West Indian George Padmore, then working with the African section of the Comintern. Small was thereupon much pursued by the Gambian colonial police as a 'link-subversive'. Yet Small's views proved really no different from those of his 'colonial bourgeois' fellow-nationalists in Bathurst (Banjul).

Fears of communism or of whatever was thought to be such were shared by the educated men, and still more emphatically once they saw what happened to those among them who fell under suspicion. None of them was revolutionary: all, on the contrary, were staunch constitutionalists, and most asked only for gradual concessions within the framework of the empire. White discrimination often stung them into strong words; and since they were very good at the use of words these often took effect upon officials as being the worst thing that officials could think of, which was 'communism'. The misunderstanding was general, and it continued.

Only in South Africa, save for stray exceptions, did the ideas of anti-racism now begin to coalesce with those of revolution, and the primacy of 'explanation by colour' to give way, a little at least, to a willingness to look at the 'explanation by class'. Even so, the movement in that direction was small and tentative. The deepening thrust of white oppression, and the ever-growing solidarity against black workers of white workers with white employers, saw to that. The 'colour nature' of the South African system continued to hold the centre of the stage, but the 'class nature' of that system was at least examined.

In 1931 the vote was extended to white women, but of course denied to non-white women in the Cape, where some voting rights for non-white men still existed. A lady from the Cape Coloured community,* Cissie Gool, spoke for others beside herself. 'I am slowly going Red,' she told a non-white conference: 'I fear that I shall be blacklisted as a revolutionary.' And in 1935 her brother-in-law, Dr G. H. Gool, made history at the launching of a new organization designed to promote unity among moderates and radicals, the All-African Convention. This Convention, he urged, should go beyond the tinkerings of reformism. It should 'lay the foundations of a national liberation movement to fight against all the repressive laws of South Africa.'[23]

Little would come of that for twenty years or more. Yet the 1930s, whether in South Africa or West Africa, began to see at least a preliminary effort by educated men and women to reach an audience among the many. What this portended was to appear after the Second World War.

*In South African parlance, Coloured means of mixed African and European or Asian origin. For the early and very general cohabitation of South African whites with blacks, see an introductory review by W. M. French in *Race and Class*, vol. XXIII, No. 1, 1976.

IN THE FRENCH CONTEXT

The story of the politics of protest in French West Africa goes according to the same underlying themes as in British West Africa. In a thousand local variants the masses continue their self-defence against the coercions of the system. Here too they embark on desperate religious movements of messianic hope. They launch new brotherhoods of mutual aid. They rise in brave and bitterly repressed revolts; and in the towns they begin to reach towards their first experiments in trade union resistance. The last of these, after 1945, will briefly become a major factor on the scene.

But the educated few, the *lettrés*, know nothing of all this or ignore what they know. As in British West Africa they accept the lesson that Africa has no civilization, that civilization must come from outside, and that the colonial system is its necessary agent. Their numbers are in any case very small. Even by the end of the 1930s, less than five per cent of all school-age children will be in primary schools, while the merest handful can hope for a secondary education. Among the latter the luckiest go to the William Ponty lycée in Senegal. This emerges from a largely language-training school for the sons of chiefs established in 1904: unlike the British, the French are obsessed with the spreading of their language. Between 1918 and 1945 William Ponty trains nearly 2,000 graduates. About a third are medical auxiliaries; others go into the lower grades of the colonial service; the youngest among them will provide the post-1945 leaders of nationalism.

Only in the 'four communes' of Dakar, St Louis, Rufisque, and Gorée Island is there more than a handful of *assimilés*, Africans or Afro-Europeans with the rights of French citizenship;* and these are

*See page 98.

content with their privileged situation. Logically, Blaise Diagne becomes their political spokesman in 1914 as a deputy to the French parliament. Though of humble social origin, he is entirely within the tradition of élitist collaboration. His convenience to the French system is complete. During the First World War he becomes the French army's chief recruiting officer in West Africa. In 1923 he makes a pact with dominant French commercial interests: they will give him their electoral support, while he will defend their interests in parliament. In 1930 he speaks in defence of forced labour at a session of the International Labour Office. It is a pathway of collaboration which others will follow after him.

Yet there were great differences of form, if not of content, between the French and British systems. Where the British model supposed nation-building in Africa as the gateway to equality of rights, the French model called for assimilation to the nation already built, the French nation sacred and eternal, guarantee of all virtues, source of all culture worth the name and mother of every admissible ambition. While British African élites began to press for constitutional concessions towards territorial self-rule, French African élites had to push for citizens' rights within the concept of a 'greater France': for the application in practice of grand republican principles which banished, in theory, all discrimination. This led to a notably different style of political self-expression. In Nigeria, for example, the Lagos worthies and their kind tended to have their feet firmly on the ground of local practicalities. In the French context, their contemporaries were as likely to be high in the skies of philosophical dispute.

Any pushing for citizens' rights proved in any case extremely difficult until after the Second World War, and achieved nothing. French administration was more strictly authoritarian than the British, and had an even greater determination to treat all political protest as subversion directed by the Comintern and therefore worthy of the strongest repressive sanction. Dahomey managed to have a few ephemeral news-sheets by 1920s, but only in 1935 did the Ivory Coast achieve its first African newspaper, decades after the neighbouring Gold Coast. In Lagos an editor like Thomas Horatio

Jackson could get away with very sharp language; in French West Africa that sort of uncompromising spokesman, among whom the most notable, perhaps, was the Dahomeyan Louis Hunkanrin (1887–1964), was silenced by deportation. In 1935 a newspaper correspondent of the Dahomeyan capital, Cotonou, writes that 'Dahomey must belong to the Dahomeyans and not to a band of imperialist pillagers'; but he writes it in the *Cri des Nègres* of Paris.[24]

The silence was deeper still in the four equatorial colonies of Middle Congo, Oubangui-Chari, Chad and Gabon, where the régime of the concession companies, ending in 1930, left behind it deeply ravaged populations who were still subject to heavy exactions in forced labour. But the former German colony of Cameroun presented a somewhat different picture, for the League Mandate under which France ruled Cameroun, since Germany's defeat of 1918, supposed 'trusteeship' for an eventual and therefore national independence. The idea of nationalism accordingly began earlier here. Able to say what could not be said in Africa, the Paris *Cri des Nègres* was reflecting this as early as 1934, writing that Cameroun 'demands its independence, and an end to a mandate which has done the country no good'.[25] Later, Camerounian nationalists, along with those of Algeria and Madagascar, were to be the first to organize for independence in the French territories.

Madagascar was also a somewhat special case. Colonial doctrine still supposed assimilation to a 'greater France', but Madagascar is an island, and already had a long history of self-identity. Early calls for an outright independence sounded here as well. Again in 1934, for example, *La Patrie Malgache* of Tananarive bids racist French settlers, 'you who despise us by your actions and your writings' but are 'incapable of civilizing us or improving our condition', to go back 'beyond the Equator to your own country. The Malagasies have had enough of you. They want to civilize their own country as Japan has done. That is why they demand independence for Madagascar.'[26] It was the bourgeois nation-state formula under a guise different from anything that the Danquahs and Azikiwes were evolving in the same period of the early and middle 1930s; but the meaning was the same.

Generally, however, assimilation appeared as the only way forward, and France, but especially Paris, became the chief arena for politically-minded men. Here, directly under the lantern, life was safer. There could be more opportunities; there were certainly more freedoms. Much political activity developed among small groups and organizations with large names but few members and still less cash. There was some good polemical journalism. Several memorable personalities emerged. Yet here, too, the available audience was very narrow. An official count of 1926 showed only 1,813 tropical Africans as being resident in France; few of these belonged to the educated group. A count of 1932 showed only 21 black African students in French universities, though 19 Malagasies and 695 Indo-Chinese.

The politics of African protest followed three chief trends in Paris during these inter-war years. Sometimes these moved together, but more often they moved apart, and now and then in opposite directions.

One was the work of Antillais (West Indian) intellectuals, who played much the same role in the French context as the Trans-atlantics and 'Sierra Leoneans' in the British. Divided from any sympathy with or understanding of African realities by the dual alienation of being Transatlantics and Western-educated men who despised what little they knew of African culture, they called for unity around the twin ideas of 'Negro solidarity' and 'French civilization', caring nothing that these concepts were in practical opposition to each other. Prominent among them was the deputy of Guadeloupe, Maurice Satineau, whose ideas were no different from those of Blaise Diagne, the collaborationist deputy of the 'four communes' of Senegal. To him, as to Diagne, colonization was 'a human necessity' in the present state of things, since 'the autonomy of the colonies can neither help nor hasten the development of backward races.'[27]

Much more important, because much more attuned to African realities, was a second trend of those years. This flowed from the Russian revolution of October 1917. In 1920 the second congress of the Comintern declared that proletarian revolution would overthrow colonial power as well as capitalism. Emerging then, the French Communist party at once made itself a spokesman for anti-colonial independence. Various organizations were formed in Paris. Important among these was the Union Intercoloniale and its newspaper, *Le Paria*, and later, during the 1930s, the French section of the multi-national League Against Imperialism. Fraternal aid was offered to Africans in Paris. Attempts were made to infiltrate anti-colonial pamphlets and persons into the colonies. International congresses gave Africans a chance to meet a wide circle of protesters.

Yet with this trend, as with that of the Transatlantic intellectuals, there was an in-built though different equivocation. Whether in one phase of policy or another, Comintern doctrine took it for granted that revolution must begin in Europe, because this was where the working classes stood in strength; and these European working classes would in due course lead colonized peoples to their own revolution. This meant in practice that the interests of colonized peoples were necessarily subordinate to those of the European working classes. And this in turn meant a political subordination to whatever the French Communist party might decide were the interests of the French working class, or, rather, whatever the Comintern in Moscow or Stalin personally might dictate. It was not long before radical Africans in Paris were finding this unbearable. In 1931 the left-wing *Cri des Nègres*, organ of the staunchly anti-colonialist Union des Travailleurs Nègres, could even note that the appearance of black delegates at the sixth congress of the French trades union congress (CGT) was 'a big step forward'. Police repression of course continued against all who were thought to have communist connections, but aside from this discouragement it appears that dissatisfaction with Communist policy continued to grow among black Africans, as it certainly did among immigrant Algerians.[28] But the communists' unrelenting call for colonial independence probably compensated to some extent for doctrinal human errors.

There were other and different influences deriving from French politics. As with Labour party Fabians and Liberals in Britain, French liberals and social-democrats befriended Africans and sympathized with their problems. But these other influences were probably of small importance save on the personal level, since none of them was willing to tackle the root of the colonial problem, which was how to get rid of the colonial system.

A third major trend, or collection of trends, was represented by more or less autonomous thought and action among Africans themselves. Whether in one or other of their often conflicting organizations, such as the *Ligue pour la Défense de la Race Nègre*, formed initially as a committee in 1926 by the ex-soldier Lamine Senghor, they agitated against colonial injustices and tried, often ingeniously, to spread their ideas in the colonies. Split by personal feuds, jealousies and distrusts, harried by a chronic want of cash, heavily infiltrated by agents of the police, they could do little more than mark time. None of their leaders survived into the politics of decolonization. But several, including the Dahomeyan Kodjo Tovalou Huénou, the Senegalese Lamine Senghor, and the Sudanese (Malian) Tiémoko Garan Kouyaté, can be properly regarded as among the forerunners of nationalism in west and equatorial Africa.

Ideologically, they had much to contend with. On one side they had to deal with the Antillais assumption that a 'greater France' would bring light and happiness for all, for they could neither believe this nor stomach its conservative paternalism. On the other hand they were faced with the different paternalism of the communists, and they could not stomach that either. Above all, while somehow finding a practical route ahead, they had to conduct their struggle against the colonial system in a period when agitation inside the colonies was savagely repressed. The coalition government of left-wing parties known as the *Front Populaire* gave them fresh hope in 1936, but this hope, like the *Front Populaire* itself, was very brief.

They were able to make little or no contribution to ideological development. Yet some formulations of Tiémoko Kouyaté's of 1935 are worth noting. He thought that 'colonial nationalism is explicable only as a form of resistance to oppression. The day that colonial oppression disappears, whether economic or political, the retreat of colonial peoples into themselves will lose its justification. Colonialism is therefore condemned to die. But so is nationalism.' Later decades were to prove him entirely wrong; and yet it may still come to seem, in the perspective of the 1990s or beyond, that Kouyaté's argument retains its force.

Having moved from left to centre in political opinions, Kouyaté worked this formulation into a programme for action. According to a note made by a police agent, still in 1935, he proposed 'a federal régime with France as the guide-nation'. Each colony should become an autonomous and independent but federated state, with its own chamber of deputies modelled on that of France. The régime of *indigénat* (whereby all but a handful of Africans were excluded from citizenship) should be suppressed. All natives should be given French nationality and Dominion citizenship. The economy should be one of *libre-échangisme* (free enterprise).[29] Though unnoticed at the time – and Kouyaté himself was killed in occupied France[30] – this programme was in fact the post-war 'neo-colonial' formula *à part entière*. After vast upheavals the leaders of the Fourth French Republic, and then of the Fifth, would take it to their bosom twenty and more years later.

The origins of modern nationalism in the Maghrib of Tunisia, Algeria, Morocco, each of them within the French colonial system under one or other form of enclosure, harshest of all in Algeria, are earlier in time and more complex than anywhere else save in South Africa; but these origins responded to the same underlying search that appeared in all colonies. Variously expressed by scholars or 'simple folk' who felt themselves lost in the moral ruin of a hallowed past, this search was for the restoration of community. Nationalist ideas duly emerged, but in circumstances often different from elsewhere. The largest source of such difference, culturally, was the all-pervading presence here of Islam with its memories of a glorious past, its sense of weight and presence in the world, and its promise of a universal brotherhood within the faith.

Nationalist ideas came into the Maghrib from the Middle East by way of Egypt. They emerged in reaction against Ottoman overlordship and then against European imperialism, and were deeply marked by the pre-colonial concept which equated unity with the community of the believers. One of their characteristic forms was therefore Salafism, the cult of the 'pious ancestors', with its ambiguity of looking back and looking forward. Given this ambiguity, the invention of a practical nationalism proved difficult.

These ideas of restoration and modernization, going uneasily together, accompanied the rise of local bourgeoisies and in time produced a Muslim version of acceptance of the European model. In 1925 the memorable Sheikh Abd al-Hamid ben Badis spoke for this in writing that 'the Algerian people is weak and insufficiently evolved. It feels a vital need to come within the protecting wing of a strong and civilized nation which will enable it to progress towards civilization and development.'[31] It is the formula that all the local bourgeoisies followed during this period.

Radical influences came in from France but, again for a long time, barely touched the rural masses or the new proletarians of the towns and settler plantations. In 1920 the staunch old anticolonial aristocrat Vigné d'Octon could assert that there was not a single Arab from Tunisia to Morocco 'who does not know of the great Russian Revolution, and who, when facing the Orient, does not beg his God to make the reign of justice triumph, together with the Republic of the Soviets, over the land of Islam and the world'.[32] The evidence suggests that news of the October Revolution and its consequences reached more widely over North Africa than further south, but that Vigné d'Octon's claim was much overstated.

The French Protectorates in Tunisia and Morocco allowed a certain if narrowing space for the existence of a commercial and professional bourgeoisie. In Tunisia these bourgeois or pettybourgeois took the stage as early as 1920 with the formation of a Liberal Constitutional party, the Hizb al-Hurr al-Dasturi: in French, the *Destour*. Its polite call for parliamentary rights went unanswered save for a few minimal reforms. With the pressures of the great depression, younger men took the lead. In 1934 they formed a new and less moderate constitutional party, the Néo-Destour whose principal leader, Habib Bourguiba, was not arrested until 1938.

Convergence between the national struggle of the educated few and the social struggle of the many began to appear in the middle 1930s, partly under the impact of the great depression and partly through the determination of the Néo-Destour to seek that wider audience which the old Destour had always shunned. The brief euphoria of the *Front Populaire* in Paris seemed to promise a break in colonial rigidities. Political prisoners began to be set free. There came a dress rehearsal for the alliance between the many and the few that would end the protectorate twenty years later. Tunisian workers had formed their own trade union organization in 1924 in reaction against local racism among white workers. This survived, though against much repression, and Tunis saw a general strike in 1937, coupled with wide resistance to colonial rules and regulations. The following year brought repression, bloodshed, new arrests. With an interval for the Second World War, the scene was set for the 1950s.

Morocco follows much the same path. No parties are formed, but proto-parties aiming at reform begin to emerge in 1933: the Action du Peuple, in fact very much an élitist affair, is launched. The next year sees Muhammed ben Yussef acclaimed as king in the ancient trading city of Fez, and the Fez bourgeoisie affirms that he has given his support to the cause of Moroccan independence. With the effects of the great depression cutting ever more severely into daily life, these nationalists now begin, in Gallisot's words, to see 'the potential that they can exploit within the social question'. They are helped in this by widespread indignation at the 'Berber' *dahir*, promulgated in 1933, which is taken as another blow at Moroccan self-identity and Muslim unity.* Conditions make 1937 a 'terrible year' of hunger [33] and, for the time being, make a highpoint in convergence between bourgeois nationalists and urban masses.

But this process of convergence is clearest of all in the Algerian case, though not at first in Algeria. There the bourgeoisie is entirely French, save for a marginal presence of big Algerian land-owners whose acceptance of the ben Badis formula for collaboration is practically complete. This Algerian bourgeois resistance, insofar as it exists at all, is only in terms of the defence of Islam: in 1935 ben Badis himself becomes the leader of the *Association des Oulémas*

*See note on p. 163.

who are the direct descendants, here, of the 'pious ancestors'. They press for more Koranic schools, argue vainly for colonial acceptance of Arabic as an official language along with French.

The real action is not here, but over the Mediterranean in France. There the echoes of the October Revolution are easier to catch. As early as 1924 the ever-watchful police receive an agent's report on a Paris public meeting of about 100 people at which its liberal chairman, Pierre Mille, is vigorously barracked as the voice of the Ministry of Colonies. Someone called Hadj Ali, one of those 'forgotten men' of history who are nonetheless remembered, shouts to a speaker that: 'It's our complete independence we want. We've had enough of your sympathy, we want to be the masters in our own home'; and this is received with vehement cries of 'Long Live the Revolution.'[34] The idea grows as immigrants meet French domestic racism. Even by 1926 there are more than 18,000 registered Algerian workers in France; the great depression will largely swell their numbers, and continued settler exploitation of Algerian land and labour will continue to swell them after that. In 1926 there is launched in Paris the *Étoile Nord-Africaine* on a firmly anti-assimilationist programme. Under the forceful leadership of Messali Hadj (1898– 1974), by any measure the most influential Algerian political figure of these years, the *Étoile* makes its mark: by 1929 the police fear that it may have as many as 4,000 members. Algerian nationalism is born in the most classical form: by reaction to a foreign but dominating nationalism.

Messali and the *Étoile* take their own road. Helped into existence by the French Communist Party, they break with that party in 1933, once again on the grounds that French Communists see the colonial problem through their own French nationalist spectacles. 'The Algerians,' declares Messali, at least according to a police report, 'want independence and not communist guardian-ship'[35]; and there is substance in this quarrel, for the French communists remain true to the Eurocentrism of Comintern doctrine. They see rightly that the only organized working class in Algeria is European, and look to those Europeans to lead the Algerians to revolution. But they fail to see that in backing those Europeans they are also backing their settler racism and chauvinism. The quarrel will last, and will become bitter.

In 1937 the *Front Populaire* government in Paris fails with its promise of change, and agrees to a request by the Governor-General of Algeria for banning of the *Étoile*. Messali and others at once form a new party, at Nanterre near Paris, called the *Parti du Peuple Algérien* (PPA). It has a somewhat less firmly radical programme: 'neither assimilation nor separation [from France], but emancipation'. With this slight tactical retreat, Messali feels able to carry his campaign into Algeria. There is much organizational activity; convergence continues. In 1939, some 4,000 people demonstrate for the PPA in the streets of Algiers. Three days before the outbreak of the Second World War, the PPA is dissolved by government. The cause of Algerian independence is now, in fact, beyond all power of repression. But that is what years of bloodshed and resistance will still have to prove.

PART

THE DRIVE FOR NATIONHOOD:
1940 TO ABOUT 1960

(We) respect the right of all peoples to choose the form of government under which they will live.

> President Roosevelt and Prime Minister Churchill:
> The Atlantic Charter, 1941

Only an insignificant minority have any political awareness . . .
It must be realized now and for all time that this articulate
minority are destined to rule the country.

> Chief Obafemi Awolowo, 1947

19

'FREEDOM NOTHING BUT FREEDOM...'

The Second World War was decisive among many combinations of pressure that now began to make for political change in colonial Africa. After 1945 the colonial Powers could still resist or delay 'decolonization' (a word that belongs to the 1960s); they could not stop it. Thrusting into the play of élitist politics, multitudes of ordinary people made sure of that.

'We all overseas soldiers are coming back home with new ideas,' writes a Nigerian volunteer, Pte 82602 Theo Ayoola, from India in 1945 to a now very prudent Herbert Macaulay. In a few words this voice from afar sets forth the programme upon which new movements in every region of Africa will campaign for independence, raise the banners of nationalism and, at the same time, consciously or not, accept without further question or inquiry the whole bag and baggage of the European nation-state. 'We have been told what we fought for,' Pte Ayoola writes to Macaulay. 'That is "freedom". We want freedom nothing but freedom...' Plenty of his mates, by 1945, had got the same idea.[1]

They found themselves in a very different world. In May 1940 Hitler's tanks had won their battle for France; and French capitulation placed the northern half of France under direct German military rule, while central and southern France was given puppet independence under a régime formed by the aged Marshal Pétain at the town of Vichy. Henceforward the French were divided between those loyal to Vichy or merely quiescent and those, at first very few, who were determined to continue the war. Up to 1942, Vichy had the support of all French colonial administrations in North and West Africa and Madagascar, but not in the French equatorial colonies; the latter became a base for Free French forces under the command of General Charles de Gaulle, then operating from London. Late in 1942, when the British were flinging the Germans and Italians out of north-east Africa and the Americans landing in north-west Africa, all the French administrations joined or were taken over by the Free French.

In December 1941 the Japanese had continued their bid for Asian supremacy by bombing the US battle fleet at its chief Hawaian base in the Pacific. The USA then declared war on the Axis (Germany, Italy, Japan). This eventually ensured the defeat of the Axis in the West, as of Japan in the Far East, and opened the way for US super-power. Meanwhile, in June 1941, the Germans had invaded the USSR but were held before Moscow. In great battles during 1942–5 the Soviet Army eventually destroyed the bulk of the German army, guaranteed Anglo-American victory in the West, and opened the way for Soviet super-power.

Militarily, Africans suffered a good deal. By the time that Hitler's tanks pierced into France in May 1940, the French high command had brought in some 80,000 African troops, most of whom were conscripts. Their casualties were high; for example, 24,270 Tirailleurs were reported 'missing' at the June armistice, as well as 4,350 Malagasies.[2] But at least the fighting, though not the misery of the prison camps, was soon over.

Recruitment in the four British West African colonies reached 169,000 men by 1943, mobilized chiefly on a voluntary basis (though also with the help of various 'indirect pressures'). These fought in East Africa against Fascist Italy and afterwards in Burma against Japan. Facing a big Italian force in Somalia and Ethiopia, the British similarly recruited heavily in Tanganyika, Kenya and Uganda, while several other colonies, such as Nyasaland and the two Rhodesias, sent contingents to this East African army, as did the South African army. These East African campaigns were rapidly successful, but fighting in North Africa or Asia continued, and in Asia until 1945. Most African casualties were evidently suffered in Burma.[3]

The further consequences were contradictory. Politically, the war shook the old imperialist monopolies to their roots, save in the marginal cases of the Portuguese and Spanish systems.[4] The new

American super-power could have no interest in restoring foreign empires; nor, from different arguments, could the potential Soviet super-power. On the economic side, conversely, the circumstances of the war went far to complete and reinforce those very structures of colonial extraction which previous decades had installed.

British West African producers more than doubled the total value of their exports between 1938 and 1946. But this rise in production was accompanied by a higher rate of extraction than before, partly through the device of marketing boards which held down prices paid to African producers for the benefit of sterling balances accumulated in London. The whole system, in other words, enormously expanded. Effects were much the same elsewhere. Blockaded until 1942 by the British, Vichy French administrations in North and West Africa drove their peoples to substitute for imports, and, after 1942, to maximize exports. All this they did with much coercion and with little mercy.[5]

The Belgian Congo displayed the same picture. In 1945 the anthropologist Father J. van Wing, S.J., was speaking to a general case when he told the Belgian Royal Colonial Institute that 'for five years our populations were subjected to an extremely intense and varied war effort. The whole black population was mobilized to produce as much as possible as fast as possible, in order to export what the Allies wanted and to substitute for imports.'[6] This was done, as van Wing also remarked, by keeping wages and prices paid to Africans 'so low that only coercion enabled us to reach the end of the war without much damage' to the system. In the neighbouring Belgian territory of Rwanda-Urundi, again according to van Wing, war exactions were worsened by a two-year drought which claimed 'at least 60,000 victims'.

With all this the tale of sufferings went beyond any possible computation. They too rocked the system's political stability, as quite a few thoughtful colonial officials noted then or later. Every feature of dislocation stamped into the African scene by the great depression was enlarged and sharpened: the impoverishment of rural populations, the flight to urban slums and shanty-towns, the dismantlement of traditional communities, the general sense that life had run itself into a terrible insecurity where poverty alone could reign. Back in 1931 the former French colonial minister Albert Sarraut had declared that there was no point in disguising the truth: 'everywhere, colonialism is in open crisis.' Fourteen years later the circumstances were different; but they told the same truth, and now with an unanswerable eloquence. Social crisis penetrated every aspect of daily life.

A new consciousness responded to these trials and exactions. Yet at this stage it was not able to perceive the connection between social crisis and the system's economic expansion. It reacted against the first while generally ignoring the second, save here and there in terms of a new trade union militancy. No doubt this could not have been otherwise, for the knowledge and understanding necessary to analysis were not yet present, or, if present, were not utilized. What men responded to were the great emotive themes set going by the war: the spectacle of a powerful non-white nationalism in the shape of Japan or the militant campaigns of the Indian National Congress; the anti-Nazi propaganda of the Allies that was also, and unavoidably as the democratizing pressures of the war continued, an anti-racist propaganda; and, perhaps most of all, the stirring promise of the Atlantic Charter drawn up in August 1941 by Roosevelt and Churchill. 'Freedom nothing but freedom' was the call that seized the imagination alike of the many and the few. Let freedom come, and everything would change.

The Atlantic Charter declared that all peoples should have the right to choose their form of government when the war was won. Telling the House of Commons a month later that he had not become the king's first minister in order to preside over the dissolution of the British empire, Churchill sought to make the promise of the Charter apply only to countries occupied by the Axis. No, insisted Roosevelt, it 'applied to all humanity'.[7] Africans certainly thought so.

At least upon the literate, the impact was large and universal. 'The effect of the Atlantic Charter on the educated fraction of elected Algerians,' recalls the Algerian nationalist Mohamed Harbi, 'was very deep. Recognition of the right of peoples to liberty and self-determination gave to nationalism the sanction of the great

Powers.'[8] Meeting in December 1941 at the other end of the continent, an annual conference of the African National Congress of South Africa made the Charter the subject of its first resolution, giving its president (Dr A. B. Xuma), 'power to appoint a committee to go into the question of the Atlantic Charter and to draft the Bill of Rights to be presented to the Peace Conference at the end of the Present War'.[9]

Elsewhere the effect varied with the ideas of the literate, but even the most cautious were generally enthused by the Charter's promise. At least they should be able to look forward to some form of self-government within the British Commonwealth – a favourite theme among vocal Nigerians at that time – or to a large extension of citizenship rights within the French Republic. The most advanced nationalists went further, even though they were still very few outside the ranks of independence parties in Madagascar and the Maghrib, or of the Somali Youth League founded in 1943. These men could say little while the war lasted. But they spoke up strongly when the peace came. An editorial of April 1946 in the Malagasy nationalist newspaper, *La Nation Malgache*, sets their tone: 'We know very well that the colonialism and racism which some persons claim to reject is still alive within them. But such people must understand that the era of colonialist conquest and domination is ended. We are now in a new era, to whose existence . . . the Atlantic Charter and the United Nations are the historic witnesses.'

Such was the atmosphere in which the war concluded. A ferment stirred. Everyone chose his own target. There might be no deep analysis, but there was plenty of vivid prose. As long as a year before Pte Ayoola was informing Macaulay of what 'we all overseas soldiers' wanted, another soldier sent his version of the Twenty-Third Psalm to the *African Morning Post* of Accra:

> The European Merchant is my shepherd,
> And I am in want;
> He maketh me to lie down in cocoa farms;
> He leadeth me beside the waters of great need . . .[10]

Nationalism, first and foremost, should mean a better life.

On their side the colonial policy makers were convinced that all could be substantially restored by a gradual shift of décor. Wartime debate in the House of Commons recalled the venerable theme of Britain's trusteeship of native peoples, spoke warmly of a duty to 'teach the Africans the principles of democracy', but saw all this in terms of an extreme slowness. The Free French were even more conservative. In 1944 de Gaulle gave forth his much-trumpeted Brazzaville Declaration on colonial progress after the war. Its words were large, their substance small. Any question of an eventual African independence was rejected. There might be free Frenchmen; evidently there were to be no free Africans.

Events would show that all these policy-makers, even the least blinkered, were behind the times. They failed to reckon with the force of emancipatory ideas now at work. They equally failed to grasp what was beginning to be understood in the USA: that direct political control might by no means be necessary, any longer, to the continued survival or expansion of those forms of colonial extraction which the war itself had done so much to enlarge. This was to be a lesson more generally learned in the 1950s, when the social and political crisis induced by the great depression and the productive 'effort' of the war years would start to receive its partial and ambiguous solution. In the 1960s, by then beginning to see the link between 'under-development' and the realities of colonialist economy, Africans would label this solution by a new name, 'neo-colonialism': meaning the perpetuation of the same underlying system by means of an indirect and generally economic control, but under conditions of political independence.[11]

20

AFTER THE SECOND WORLD WAR:
THE SYSTEM EXPANDED

Historical facts, Marc Bloch affirmed, are in their essence psychological facts. History, in other words, is not a calculating machine. It unfolds in the mind and the imagination, and takes body in the multifarious responses of a people's culture, itself the infinitely subtle mediation of material realities, of underpinning economic facts, of gritty objectivities. African cultural responses after 1945 were as varied as one might expect from so many peoples and perceived interests. But they were above all inspired by a vivid hope of change, scarcely present before, certainly never before felt with any such intensity or wide appeal; and they were spoken for by men and women whose hearts beat to a brave music. These were the responses that moved African history into a new course. But there remains an obvious need for us, reverting to Braudel's metaphor, to look at the shaping circumstances and track the contours of the river-bed within which this new course was obliged to move.

As things turned out, the Second World War enabled the principal colonial powers to escape from their economic stagnation of the 1930s, whether through the full employment of war service and production or by expansive policies adapted to post-war needs. This ended the long depression of the colonial economies. Further, by bringing the USA into an unchallengeable leadership of the Western world, the war did much to shake the conservatism of British approaches. Then again, the war years had shown what African productivity could do for colonial powers in trouble, and it was now seen that this productivity might be harnessed to the long haul for 'recovery'. Thus predicated by about 1946, a continued export boom was duly triggered by the increasing demand for raw materials, not least by US stockpiling, that followed upon the outbreak of a new war in Korea. These expansive trends carried the colonial system to maturity, in the major empires, as part of a capitalism now increasingly organized within trans-national corporate structures. They went far to resolve a large contradiction of the period between the world wars: essentially, between high rates of profit and low rates of investment.

As we have seen, the old Leopoldian lesson now came to be widely applied: that you must risk a sprat to catch a mackerel, or that private investment aimed at a high rate of profit could become significantly more fruitful only in the wake of public investment content with a low rate of profit. Which is not to suggest, of course, that private profit had previously failed to arrive. Many colonial companies had gone to the bad, but many others had made money. A few had made very big money. Between 1939 and 1943, to offer only one example from the war years, dividends paid by Ashanti Goldfields stood annually at eighty per cent of issued capital after many years of comparably golden reward that was unreduced by any local income tax. For major mining and produce companies, it was not a rare example.[12]

The experience of the war, as well as the demand for new materials such as uranium, encouraged a belief that African resources could restore a shattered Western Europe. This conviction was inseparable from ideas, current in US policy, which presumed that US and Western security depended on winning a 'cold war' against Soviet power or influence. The African connection was explained in 1948 by the late John Foster Dulles, afterwards a most influential Secretary of State. 'Mr Dulles has for some time,' reported the London *Sunday Times* on 4 July of that year, 'been advocating United States financial and technical aid in developing the African colonies ... Africa, he has said, could make Western Europe completely independent of Eastern European resources, and that should be the aim.' But Africa could help to do the same for the USA, then about to oblige the British to sell a share in Congo uranium to an American group associated with the Rockefeller combine, as well as greatly enlarging American interests elsewhere in the African raw materials field. In any case it became accepted that the aim of maximizing colonial exports could be realized only by modernizing harbours and other basic needs in better communication, and that, for these purposes, private enterprise would have to rely on tax-payers' investment.

After about 1946, accordingly, we enter the era of 'aid for development' with all its panoply of illusions on one side and calculations on the other. The illusions were handsomely told, the calculations perhaps less so. 'Great Britain and her colonies,' announced a British Labour programme of 1949 at a time when that party was in power, 'have gone into partnership to liquidate ignorance, poverty and disease.' The reality was rather different. It came in the shape of an Overseas Food Corporation or an extension from the Colonial Development and Welfare programmes of a somewhat earlier time, their economic results being very small. This Corporation embarked on trying to produce peanuts in Tanganyika and poultry in The Gambia, and other things elsewhere, with the primary object of extracting more food from colonies already short of food for themselves. Each of the Corporation's major projects was a crashing failure, in the peanuts case with a net loss of some £36 million; but this was just as well for the colonial peoples concerned.

These ill-fated ventures failed to stem the flow of grandiose promises, heard again at full strength during 1951 in the quickly abortive 'Colombo Plan'; but they cut down British 'aid for development' to more careful injections of infrastructural investment. The French proceeded ambitiously: in France, after all, there was a much greater need, or rather a much more obvious need, to rebuild an outmoded economy. Transformed now into 'members' of the French Union, a fantasy truly French though in no sense a union, the colonies could now play their part in reconstructing 'greater France'. For this, however, they would need capital. A law of April 1946 provided for a ten-year plan of French public expenditure.

This led to an investment fund for 'economic and social development' financed through official organs. The fund was initially presented as satisfying 'the needs of the native populations', and aiding in 'the development of the French Union economy'. A retreat from post-war progressiveness soon modified even this very 'metropolitan' statement of likely gains. In 1951 the central objective was redefined as being 'to increase agricultural and industrial production in the perspective of a European community'. French being above all others the language of elegant ambiguity, this could mean one of a number of things or several at the same time. It turned out to mean that the fund should do for France, though on a larger scale, what devices such as the Overseas Food Corporation were supposed to do for Britain. Large sums were found: for French West Africa, some 270 billion francs (at contemporary values) between 1947 and 1952, with the French taxpayer meeting rather more than half the total. The same process continued through the 1950s. Colonial exports were considerably boosted. As the 1960s would duly reveal, these colonies were drawn ever more completely into the French economic system. The old 'economy of trade' had given way to a new 'economy of extraction'.

Similar ideas were current in the USA. Here they were often expressed in terms of the 'development' of colonies hitherto abandoned to barbarous or beastly Europeans; what these had failed to achieve, through incompetence or greed, Uncle Sam would generously make good. Other Americans, putting the same idea differently, held that US know-how could promote a capitalist 'take off' in Africa. The question seldom asked was who would control this if it should happen. When asked, however, the answer could be disturbing to the liberal America that came out of the war. In 1947 a then prominent publicist, James Burnham, called for the building of 'an American empire which will be, if not literally world-wide in formal boundaries, capable of exercising decisive world control'.

'This policy,' countered the equally prominent liberal publicist Walter Lippmann, 'can be implemented only by recruiting, subsidizing and supporting a heterogeneous array of satellites, clients, dependents (sic), and puppets,' requiring 'continual and complicated intervention by the United States in the affairs of all the members of the coalition which we are proposing to organize, to lead and to use'.[13] The full force of that forecast was to be demonstrated in Asia. Meanwhile, in Africa, things began slowly with programmes of US public spending, at any rate in British Africa where the door was wide open and opportunities attractive. Great financial endowments, most notably the Ford Foundation, soon became the unofficial arm of a policy generally directed towards promoting the ideas and techniques of American-style enterprise and its appropriate value-system. Under 'Point Four' and similar programmes, large sums were invested in various forms.

These American efforts had a practically universal success among all those in Africa who belonged to any kind of modernizing élite. This was partly an intelligent opportunism, since the United States could and did offer an exciting alternative to the dismally constrictive traditions of Western Europe. Partly it owed its prestige to the high hopes that Africans then vested in the United Nations, an organization of anti-colonial pressure, as they believed, in which the USA had a clearly dominant voice. But the USA had another and larger power of attraction: its government was clearly without any wish to secure territorial possession of any part of Africa.

At no point did the USA now seek to obtain territory in Africa, as the victorious European powers had sedulously done in 1919, any more than the USA sought to acquire territory in Europe or Asia. Far from that, US policy was found ready to encourage the reduction of European imperialist power, and even to welcome the spokesmen of African nationalism. There was, of course, a condition for this encouragement and welcome: that the nationalists should be entirely loyal to 'Western values', or, expressed more bluntly, the interests of an overall capitalist system now dominated by the USA. But there could be little objection to that, since very few of the spokesmen of nationalism wished to be loyal to anything else.

The drive and inventiveness of American enterprise also counted for much, as did its relatively overwhelming power after the wartime bleeding of Britain and France and the temporary ruin of Germany. All this induced a higher stage of monopolist growth, variously to become known as multi-national or transnational capitalism, which could have little tolerance for the old-style monopolies of Western European supremacy. There came the rapid development of vast corporations whose heart and centre remained in the USA but whose limbs and branches ran out through many countries. These could operate under a variety of national labels, and secure a wide scope for subsidiary industrial or commercial enterprise.

This many-sided drive for the primacy of American conceptions about Africa's future carried all before it from about the middle 1950s, and was barely troubled by any serious critique. Such African radicals who surfaced were firmly silenced by British or French or other colonial action, or later on by local governing groups for whom a 'Western destiny' had long appeared the only way ahead. This period of 'decolonization' thus became the decade of US ideological hegemony. Transnational capitalism had evolved its own techniques of indirect rule; and the European model acquired, as it were, a large American extension.

Chiefly in British Africa, this arrival of the USA brought fresh support to nationalists whose immediate concern, understandably enough, was to 'get out from under' the direct colonial incubus. But other influences were already on the scene.

The soldiers brought back their own ideas. With public broadcasting systems now making their bow, people who had stayed at home could listen to the promises of the Atlantic Charter and all that they seemed to mean, while the great military victories of the Russians continued to give forth their reverberating echo. Among those who listened and heard were young people leaving schools which were still few in number, but were more than before.

In French West Africa, for example, the number of primary-school pupils in 1935 was about 63,000; by 1945 it was more than 94,000. By 1948 there were perhaps four times as many West African pupils in French colonial secondary schools than ten years earlier. Comparable increases occurred in British West Africa, or still larger ones in the Gold Coast and in southern Nigeria; while the North African educational figures similarly showed a steep rise. Even in the rest of colonial Africa, including settler Africa, there was some improvement in totals. The education thus provided was generally primitive and paternalist, being still in line with an insistence on the automatic superiority of everything European; but at least it could forge some elementary tools for understanding the world of 1945 and after.

Onwards from 1946 the rise became faster, whether in response to African demand or because the colonial powers now favoured an expansion of literacy as part of their plans for modernizing their systems. Thus between 1946 and 1956 the rate of aggregate enrolments to primary and secondary schools (of various kinds) was less than twenty per cent in two territories and less than sixty per cent in two others, but over 100 per cent in most of the territories for which figures were available. Once again West Africa was to the fore, with a quantitative increase in the French territories of more than 300 per cent overall and a correspondingly large expansion in British West Africa. By 1958, for example, it was thought that nearly ten per cent of all Nigerian youth of school age was attending some kind of school. In West Africa, if not yet elsewhere, the nationalists were now addressing a very much bigger audience of literates.

These nationalists could meanwhile draw upon a bigger pool of recruits. In North Africa (Maghrib with Libya and Egypt), the number of students in higher education increased from 40,468 in 1950–51 to 122,570 ten years later. In tropical Africa the same figures were 2,270 students in 1950–51 and 13,620 in 1960. Many more students got to Europe. The total number of colonial students in British universities in 1939 was only about 400. By 1955 there were nearly 3,000, about a third Nigerians, a tenth Gold Coasters, and an eighth East and Central Africans. In that year, with another marked trend, about 400 Nigerians and some others were studying in the USA, while a few went to Holland, Germany and elsewhere, though not in any number, for another few years, to the Soviet Union and other Communist countries. Overall, the number of students in overseas higher education for the whole of tropical Africa in 1961–2 stood at 12,863, while the comparable figure for the five North African countries was 11,017.

There were important local variations. Belgian policy greatly expanded primary education, but remained hostile to permitting any African to study in Europe. Portuguese and Italian policy allowed a trickle of black students into their country's universities, but only at the price of their accepting a more or less complete alienation from African loyalties. In the Portuguese case, as the 1970s would prove, this was to backfire and help to bring about the very emancipation that it sought to avoid.

Rural exodus was everywhere a structural feature of these years. A steady rise in population growth, probably due to a reduction in the rate of infantile or child mortality and dating, as it would seem from very incomplete evidence, to soon after the Second World War, undoubtedly played some part in this. But whatever the demographic truth may have been, this rise in population growth took place against the background of a deepening rural impoverishment, itself caused chiefly by a shortage of food, associated with the boom in export crops. In this respect the pressures of the Second World War capped those of the great depression. Towns grew enormously, or rather they spawned slums and shanty-suburbs where peasants became proletarians* at a rate which alarmed all who saw it but which nothing seemed able to reduce. Chiefly, the towns grew like this because peasants had become too hungry to stay at home.

There came a general dismantlement of African communities. Ancestral charters and their solidarity might survive de-ruralization, for they answered to urgent psychological and material needs. But more and more they were distorted or degraded by the dislocation of kinship loyalty in cities, the uses of cash (when any could be found), and all those pressures of urban life which insisted, often now with a weary hopelessness, that the old certitudes were gone and would not return.

After 1945 the towns expanded very rapidly. Léopoldville (Kinshasa) had 221,000 inhabitants in 1950, but 389,000 in 1958. Luanda, capital of Angola, grew from 61,000 people in 1940 to 220,000 in 1960; Nairobi from 108,000 in 1944 to 250,000 in 1960; Dakar from 185,000 in 1948 to 383,000 in 1960; Abidjan, capital of

*A useful term, but again one to be employed with caution: this was not Europe, nor were these proletarians the product of any industrial revolution. I use it in its Oxford Dictionary sense as applying to 'one who is without capital or regular employment'.

Ivory Coast, from 48,000 in 1948 to 180,000 in 1960. Africa ceased to be so overwhelmingly rural a continent.

At the same time it would be a gross misuse of language to say that Africa's de-ruralized multitudes became 'urbanized' in any usual meaning of the word. They were peasants conglomerated into peripheral slums with next to no municipal water, light, or other services, and left to survive as they could. In 1954 the present writer made a rough survey of the municipal water supply in the *senzala* or 'African quarter' of Lobito in Angola: it came to one water-tap for an average of 1,200 persons in a population of about 20,000. The case was unlikely to have been exceptional. There was no urbanization in the sense of a planned transition from one way of life to another. All that happened was that these populations were subtracted – or sub-tracted themselves – from the African economy of their countries and became, in their hundreds of thousands, an addition to the reservoir of cheap labour available in the colonial economy. But in doing so they lost the roots of their old way of life. Their need for a new community became often a desperate one.

This undermining of a whole way of life was demon-strated very sharply in the settler territories. In 1903, for example, some 31 per cent of Southern Rhodesian cash earnings were in the form of wages, earned under the pressure of one or other settler-imposed coercion. Yet by the early 1930s the proportion paid in wages had risen to 80 per cent. In 1903 most of the food grown for sale in Southern Rhodesia was grown by African farmers. By 1930 official figures showed that the proportions were reversed: Euro-peans were now growing and selling about three-quarters of all local food. A farming people had simply been deprived of its heritage.

At one end of Africa, in Algeria, a similar process of dis-possession had induced the 'urbanizing' between 1936 and 1948 of about a million people, while the exodus of migrant workers to France, beginning twenty years earlier, became massive after 1948. At the other end, in South Africa, the proportion of 'urbanized' Africans was only 13 per cent in 1904, but 17.3 per cent in 1936 and 31.8 per cent in 1960, a rise all the more eloquent of rural pauper-ization in view of South African segregationist policies. 'While the native may come voluntarily out of his own area, for a limited period every year, to work with a white employer,' Smuts had reiterated in 1929, restating laws and practices long in force, 'he will leave his wife and children behind in their native home.'[14] The choice was between rural hardship at home or denial of any normal life in the white area. And since the first was more painful even than the second, the numbers of the 'urbanized' continued to grow.

The white economy, as in Southern Rhodesia or Algeria, effectively smothered the African economy. By 1950 about 57 per cent of all Africans in South Africa were in the 'white area', working with white employers, while the remaining 43 per cent were packed and piled into the 'native reserves'. Overcrowded and overstocked, fearfully eroded, these reserves could offer no more than an ugly caricature of the pre-colonial rural economy. Many of their inhabitants had no land or cattle, nor any hope of either. From viable farming communities these populations had become transferred into continual hunger at the worst or humiliated penury at the best. They clung bravely to their cultures, but the basis for their cultures had practically disappeared. As Marcello Caetano said approvingly of the Portuguese system in 1954, they were 'useful auxiliaries' in an economy organized or to be organized by whites; often enough, they were not even that.

In the non-settler territories, or rather in the more fertile among them, de-ruralization of African producers provided a lesser influence on events than a much greater African involvement in the production of export crops such as cocoa and cotton. Confirming African responses to oversea demand of earlier times, but carrying this process further, African farmers and entrepreneurs achieved a predominant role in their field of production. This did not turn them into the masters of the economic pattern within which they worked, for the pattern remained colonial; and these producers continued to be the 'useful auxiliaries' of overseas buyers and suppliers. We may note for later comment, however, that their involvement in a new export boom also brought its political consequences.

For these were the men (and sometimes the women) for whom the winning of a better share in the profits of the whole pattern now became, and very understandably, a major aim. Increasingly, wherever their numbers multiplied, they filled the middle and upper ranks of the nationalist movements, and became, ever more clearly, the commercial tail that wagged the political dog. Necessarily, their object was not to change the system by getting national independence, save in its political overlay, but to convert the system to their own advantage. With this in mind, they now played an often leading part as pioneers of a 'neo-colonialism' of whose desirability, however, the imperialist governments had yet to become sure.

There were many individual examples, but one may suffice. The Gold Coast became the first of the tropical colonies to win a national independence; and the many remarkable events which led to that result in 1957 began effectively in 1948. It began with a consumers' boycott of European or Lebanese stores. But the man who set that boycott going was not a politician or even a nationalist, save in retrospect: he was Nii Bonne, an entrepreneur originally from Sierra Leone.

How much did mass militancy contribute to nationalism after 1945 and in the 1950s? The Private Ayoolas and their kind certainly helped to create an atmosphere of expected change. So did the rapid rate of de-ruralization that now gave the nationalists a wide audience on the very doorsteps of colonial authority. Again, in many indirect ways, so did the deepening social crisis with which colonial power had somehow to cope and with which, in the end, colonial power preferred to cope by quitting the scene of local decision. Yet to nationalism itself, whether in its modes, ideas, or intentions, the 'urbanized' multitudes contributed relatively little, while the still ruralized multitudes contributed still less.

One reason for this was fragility or absence of political organization. A much greater reason, however, was that what really interested the multitudes was in no sense the drive for nationhood, very much an affair of petty-bourgeois or intermediate strata,* but

*In the difficulty of describing the various components of African society, 'intermediate strata' may be useful. I employ it as meaning urban Africans who were neither proletarian (see footnote on p. 212) nor relatively

the struggle against the social crisis in its immediate sense of hunger or joblessness, against the consequences of colonial capitalism, against the miseries of everyday life. In this struggle for self-defence, the 1930s had already seen combined action by dockers, railwaymen and other wage-earners in work-places which provided some permanency and fellowship: in Mombasa, for example, as early as 1934, in Dar es-Salaam in 1939, with others elsewhere. These men formed organizations of their own. They eventually converged on nationalism, as we shall see, but only as and when the nationalists wished or were able to persuade them that the drive for nationhood could be useful to the drive against poverty.

Trade unions were legalized in French Africa by the brief Popular Front government in 1937. Under Labour Party pressure the British colonial authorities gradually followed, but with particular care to impose their own ideas about what trade unions should be or could do. Militancy by self-organized groups of workers had in any case strengthened during the war and the years after it. There were more strikes, and some of them were very big, and several – as a general strike in Tanganyika proved in 1947 – were successful. Yet with few exceptions, organized workers' militancy played a minor role in the development of political ideas and action. Why this was so is important to an understanding of the nationalist situation.

Peasants flocked to urban slums and settled into a kind of unemployment that was really under-employment subsidized by kinsmen or by a host of small economic activities such as crafts and street-corner trade, petty crime, and so on. They were in any case difficult to organize even if skilled organizers had been present. Most came from communities in which long-accepted inequality, often severe, was softened by a general provision for social mobility along the scale of income or status; and this cultural trait discouraged militancy which invariably arose, in the colonial situation, only where denial of mobility was directly deployed and personally felt. The latter circumstance explains why mass militancy became consciously

---

privileged 'bourgeois' beneficiaries of colonial systems. Their employments were such as to make colonial discrimination especially obvious and personal, while they lacked the status compensations of their 'bourgeois' betters.

nationalist in the settler territories more easily than elsewhere, and also why, in those territories, the lower and then the higher ranks of nationalism were manned by intermediate strata whose status did bring them directly against race discrimination.

This lack of militancy could surprise outsiders. Peter Lloyd, for example, speaks of 'the European radical who looks to the urban workers and the poor to provide, variously, the leadership, the support or the spark for revolution. Yet those who have lived in these shanty towns' – he was writing of Nigeria – 'report neither the active radicalism nor the abject apathy and violence associated with the sub-culture of poverty.'[15] The European radical in question had obviously thought rather little about the possible origins of revolutionary thought and action, but the point is still a good one. Reformist nationalism could be no kind of 'revolt of the masses'.

Many workers who joined trade unions were often led into wastage of effort, another discouragement to militancy. Nigeria had about 182,000 wage-workers in 1939, but some twenty-five 'trade union centres' or 'federations' by 1943: and splits remained endemic as trade union bosses manoeuvred against each other or made off with the funds. Only in tightly-organized industries such as mining and railways did early forms of class consciousness begin to give shape and discipline to wage-earners' resentment. Some of these moved into the directly political arena.

Colonial administrations still sharply feared the growth of trade union militancy, and did their best to prevent or repress it. 'It is the government's aim to insulate trade unions . . . from politics,' commented a Uganda administrative document of 1960, but applicable to earlier years and to all territories, 'and there is some pride in having been successful until now.'[16] It was little to boast about, given the elementary nature of the 'national-social' convergence in the 1950s, but the success also had another source. This was the split in the hitherto united world trade union movement, in 1949, when the 'moderates' (forming the ICFTU) broke away from the 'radicals' (forming the WFTU): in Europe an aspect of the 'cold war', in Africa a means of isolating, as 'communists', all those ready to push their action into the politics of anti-colonial protest. The consequences

were widely felt and were reinforced by funds of largely US provenance that were now made available to the ICFTU for 'scholar-
ships' and other forms of polite and less polite corruption. Thereafter
the 'radicals' were in the wilderness for many years, while the
'moderates' thrust politics carefully behind them.

But didn't the nationalists, striving for political independence, resent this loss of a valuable ally? Generally, not in the least.
Most of the new nationalists were little less fearful of trade union
militancy, which might well escape their control, than the colonial
officials with whom they now foresaw a coming agreement. They
were ready to organize the masses for demagogy and demonstration,
but understandably preferred that the masses should not organize
themselves: after all, they were men for whom the inheritance of the
colonial state had become equivalent to possession of the national
state whose masters they might soon be. At any rate for the years
after 1950, Robin Cohen's conclusion on Nigeria can be widely
applied: 'The politicians neither needed the support of the labour
movement against colonial power, nor was co-operation with the
radical elements in the unions feasible after 1950.'[17]

Before 1950, however, there were notable acts of union
militancy that gave fresh force to the nationalist push. Lagos saw a
major stoppage in 1945. Grass-roots initiative led in 1947 to the
longest strike so far recorded in Africa, that of French West African
railwaymen. Their pre-strike message to the governor-general
showed how far things had come since ten years earlier: 'Open your
prisons, make ready your machine guns and cannon. Nevertheless, at
midnight on 10 October, if our demands are not met, we declare the
general strike.' Nineteen thousand men answered the call, and most
held out for 160 days. They were not shot back to work, and gained
most of their demands.[18] Nigeria, Sierra Leone and some other
colonies also saw impressive stoppages.

Workers' protest converged on political protest, and therefore on nationalism, more easily and rapidly in the territories of
white settlement. There, at least after 1950 and notably in Kenya and
Northern Rhodesia, trade unions became organic components of
nationalist movements until, of course, the winning of independence

removed their value to the nationalist leaders. There was much repressive violence. In Northern Rhodesia police bullets had killed only six Africans and wounded twenty-two during the disorders of a copper-mining stoppage in 1935; in 1940, during a bigger stoppage, the police killed seventeen and wounded sixty-nine. In 1946 the South African government shot back to work the greatest African strike in the country's turbulent history, when 100,000 African goldmine workers stopped in support of a demand for ten shillings a day (then about $2.50). The depth of feelings then expressed was another forecast of the shape of things to come: 'When I think of how we left our homes in the Reserves,' a miners' delegate told a mass meeting called to decide upon strike action, 'our children naked and starving, we have nothing more to say. Every man must agree to strike on 1 August. It is better to die here than to go back with empty hands.'[19] In the event, South African 'native' mining wages were not improved until 1973.

In Tanganyika a little later a strike of dockers was destroyed by troops and naval ratings who eventually killed one striker and wounded seven more. In 1950 the Kenya government replied to a general strike against starvation wages – and that is how an East Africa Royal Commission would portray those wages five years later – as well as against the imprisonment of trade union leaders. Mass arrests followed, and the strike was eventually broken after a show of force with armoured cars. The list could be continued.

Workers' pressure remained a critical part of anti-colonial struggle in British settler Africa till independence transferred the colonial state to its nationalist legatees. In Tanganyika, Shivji tells us, workers' strikes in the late 1950s played a crucial role in the struggle for independence. In the three years (1958–60) just before independence, there were 561 strikes involving 239,803 workers; and Kenya history displayed the same militancy. Thereafter the needs of the nation-state opposed African government to militancy inspired by the social struggle. But the militancy continued: for example, with 364 strikes in Tanganyika between 1961–4.[20] The politics might change, but not the economics. Less directly after independence,

African workers remained as 'productive elements' organized or to be organized within the economic structures installed by colonial rule. But that is part of a later story.

Other innovations shift the river-bed of history in this period. Transport improves as the post-war export boom gets into its stride and money for its infrastructure comes to hand. Roads are a little less bad. A rare bus service went through the Moroccan Anti-Atlas in 1935; now many ply in many countries. Produce and people go to town increasingly in trucks; driven to extinction, these trucks and 'mammy wagons' will litter the colonial trails. More passengers go by railway. In 1938 the French West African railways registered 330 million passenger-kilometres; in 1958 they registered 552 millions. This is the outcome of changing habits rather than of better railways, for the number of passenger wagons on the French West African railways actually decreases in this same period. But more people travel, though scarcely by air until the 1960s.

Other communications improve. There is a regular airmail from Freetown as early as 1938: by 1949 the Ivory Coast is linked telegraphically with France. Other colonies make similar innovations. Many more newspapers are edited by Africans and read by Africans. Radio becomes commonplace. Even telephones fitfully appear.

A new world is in the wings, a modern world, a technological world.

21

NEW PACE-MAKERS

In this 'new world' that began to open after 1945 the leaders of African nationalism, though often with great difficulty, were able to take the political initiative from one colonial power after another. The decade of the 1950s became the great period of campaigns for regained independence. Those who already sought the nation-state were confirmed in their strategy. Those who had thought that progress must be made through assimilation to the community of a European nation found that no such progress could be possible; and they too became nationalists. The nation-state on the European model became a universal aim. No alternative was thinkable.*

Having accepted this, the leaders of opinion set about their intricate task. If the colonial incubus now showed a few signs of being ready to be shifted off the scene, there was not the slightest evidence that it would go without being shoved. The pushing proved always hard and sometimes dangerous. No few leaders suffered privation, persecution, or imprisonment; large numbers of rank-and-file militants paid a stiff price for the gains eventually made. Opinion in later decades would tend to overlook this effort and its cost, and think the outcome a failure by reformists who should have been revolutionaries. Very few thought so at the time. Even those

---

*By nation-state on the European model I mean, as before, the structures and institutions, whether cultural, political or economic, projected into Africa by the experience and achievement of the bourgeois nation-state of Europe, above all of France and Britain. I ask the reader to bear with this perhaps necessary simplification of a complex 'transfer'; I intend it in no narrowly dogmatic sense.

who did think so accepted the 'bourgeois nation-state' as an almost certainly unavoidable transition.

Radical analysis was not so entirely absent as during the 1930s, but still was barely on the scene. Found among individuals here and there, its political weight was small or insignificant. In 1951, for example, the *Convention People's Party* (CPP) of Gold Coast won internal autonomy at the price of accepting continued British control within the structures of the colonial state. Should the CPP have refused this compromise, and pressed onwards to a revolutionary struggle for entirely different structures? Nearly all its leaders thought that they should not, and certainly they carried mass acclaim.

To nearly everyone, in that situation, half a cake seemed more than a promise of the whole cake in the near future. In 1951 Kwame Nkrumah himself might warn of the dangers of this compromise and, later on, wonder if after all he hadn't made the wrong choice; but he barely hesitated at the time. In 1952 a veteran Gold Coast radical and former worker in the Comintern, Bankole Awooner Renner, told me that the compromise had transferred the initiative 'from the hands of the oppressed to the hands of the oppressors'. But he spoke in a vacuum. The later ideas of liberation within structures entirely different from those of the colonial state were strongly present during the 1950s, it appears, only in one nationalist movement with a mass support, that of the *Union des Populations du Cameroun* (UPC); and this occurred, as will be seen, in circumstances where power went elsewhere.

For the majority of nationalists, the attempt to win nation-states on the European model was not only a stratagem, but a necessary end in itself. Even when they were not traders or would-be capitalists, they were persons for whom respectability was conservatism; and this again meant more than conformity with colonial norms. It derived from their relatively privileged position, but it also came from the heritage of ideas which had long taught that progress, even civilization itself, must come from Britain or France. Machinery and modern science had to do that, as everyone could see: so why not political institutions, codes of law, forms of democracy, modes of economic life? The pace-makers of nationalism meant to Africanize these imports of ideas and institutions; but they were sure that they must import them, for there was no other way to build a nation.

Who were these pace-makers? They were the spokesmen of the 1930s and their political descendants, but labelling is again difficult. Not all the Western-educated few were nationalists, at least in any active way; and not all the most active nationalists were graduates of universities or even of secondary schools. Their range of jobs defines them better.

In the tropical zones, West Africa had larger numbers of such persons than other regions, and British West Africa, with a far bigger population than French West Africa, had most of all. A list of Africans engaged in 'élite occupations' in Gold Coast, shortly before 1950, shows 10,305 in thirteen professions. A third of these were civil servants, though not in senior postings; another third were teachers, though not in higher education; some 140 were traders operating mostly in the shadow of European companies; while about 1,300 were cocoa brokers or buyers in the same situation. These formed what the British now began to think of as the local 'middle class' to whom, in God's good time, power might be gradually conceded.

Among them were 114 lawyers, 38 doctors, 32 journalists and 435 clergymen; and these composed what may be called the political class, the 'top élites' from which most of the pace-makers came. Fewer than a thousand persons in a population of some four and a half millions thus comprised the immediate political arena in confrontation with colonial power. Yet in this respect the Gold Coast was a highly favoured colony. Nigeria at the outset of the 1950s probably had a population of some forty millions, or nearly ten times that of the Gold Coast; but Nigeria had only 150 lawyers, 160 doctors, and 786 clergymen.

Elsewhere the numbers were sparse indeed. If the prestigious William Ponty lycée of Dakar had produced for French West Africa some 2,000 graduates by 1945, many were schoolteachers and only a handful were members of any 'top élite'. French Equatoria had many fewer. Britain's east and central African colonies had practically no graduates in higher education, and therefore very few doctors, lawyers, or comparable professionals; and there the pace-makers had to come from lowlier strata. South Africa had many Western-educated Africans trained in colleges and universities founded in a less illiberal past. But South Africa after 1948 was ruled by an Afrikaner National Party concerned to stifle all African aspirations and destroy all African politics. Only in North Africa were relatively large numbers of highly literate persons able to make their influence felt.

As politicians, the new pace-makers took over the assumptions of their forerunners, some of whom, like Nnamdi Azikiwe and Lamine Guéye in West Africa, were still their veteran spokesmen. They developed these assumptions and gave them doctrine. The first tenet of this doctrine was that the colonial state would become the nation-state within existing frontiers. The second was that this nation-state should derive its institutions from the European power whose control they meant to escape. The third was that these institutions were to be theirs to command as a right and destiny, in some words of the Nigerian Obafemi Awolowo's in 1946, 'for all time'.[21]

The rest should take care of itself. The proposed nation-states would almost all have many different ethnic groups. Yet the potential evolution of these 'submerged nationalities' – or forbidden nationalities, as their equivalents had been called in the Austro-Hungarian empire of Europe – would somehow merge and disappear into a parliamentary future. Ostensibly, at least, the superior claims of the nation-state – of the *état marché* in a later critique of Yves Person's [22] – would carry all before them. There was generally no attempt at coming to grips with underlying economic realities. Any questioning of the sacred rights of 'free enterprise' became in any case, for these pace-makers, an exercise in subversion of their own cause. They held it in horror.

Progress along these lines in West Africa was less difficult or dangerous under the British than the French. Though sorely impoverished, the British came out of the war as victors with a confidence and mood of tolerance which a demoralized and divided

France could not then have. British politicians were still quite slow in perceiving that a new form of Indirect Rule, no longer as between colonial power and subject people but between European nation and African daughter-nation, could now be possible and advantageous; but in understanding this they were soon jostled along by the USA.

Imperial government in London admitted an eventual West African independence to the agenda of the possible as early as 1943, and advanced it up the list after an electoral victory by the Labour Party in 1945. A convenient structure was to hand. This was the British Commonwealth, now soon enlarged from the 'old Dominions' of white civilization through the accession of India and Ceylon (Sri Lanka). Aside from questions of sentiment, the interests of the Commonwealth were cemented by an economic network of investment and exchange. From the standpoint of British finance, British West African colonies could very well add black dominions to white and brown ones. The flags would change; the assets would remain in London.

This was probably the extent of official foresight after 1945. There is no convincing evidence of any long-considered plan for decolonization in West Africa, much less elsewhere. It was rather that political concessions were seen as desirable, though at a rhythm slow enough to ensure continued control over many years ahead. Having occupied large countries by the hit-and-miss enclosures of the late nineteenth century, the British were now ready to withdraw from them if in course of time – probably a very long time – they could find convenient successors. There was talk of the development of African 'middle classes' capable of guaranteeing progress and democracy on the principles, of course, of parliamentary capitalism.

All basic policy documents appear to have assumed an essential continuity of government, though with power passing from an autocratic colonial administration to a parliament elected on the British system. As between the two major parties, Labour and Conservative, the only perceptible divergence lay in timing. With political initiative in the hands of West African nationalists, the Labour Party were for giving way slowly, the Conservatives for indefinite delay. On the principles of system both were agreed with the majority of the nationalists: the ex-colonies should assume that they could 'build capitalism'.

As in Africa, questioning voices on the left went unheard. Was this recipe for 'bourgeois nationalism' the right way ahead, at least for a Labour Party whose elected representatives still liked to sing the Red Flag? An editorialist in the leftward *New Statesman & Nation* found occasion as early as 1950 to remark that black nationalism might prove no more desirable than white nationalism. If transfer of political power were to mean that 'African self-government ... must tramp the same weary trail towards a genuine democracy which the White peoples have tramped, and are tramping still, then the end of White supremacy will have proved as selfish and as unconstructive as the beginning.' This being so, the one great enterprise upon which colonial power could now embark in Africa would be 'to ensure that self-government and independence are achieved for these territories under certain social – and, in the end, Socialist – safeguards'.[23] That was another case of talking in a vacuum. Not for twenty years would there be any acute analysis of the modes and systems within which decolonization took place, and of the possible alternatives.

Progress was harder in French Africa, where reconstruction of the metropolitan economy went together with a renewed determination to maintain the colonies as parts of *la plus grande France*, and where authoritarian methods had a tougher hold. Progress proved most difficult of all in the settler colonies, whether British or French, for in each of these the whites organized themselves to grasp the benefits of any decolonization for themselves. Yet once the process had begun in British West Africa it became hard to stop elsewhere, though years of armed struggle were to be sometimes necessary to nationalist success.

The great task, as the nationalists saw it, was to strike off the fetters of an imposed inferiority by removing the colonial incubus. Pushing, they met with resistance. Looking for a stronger leverage, they called for mass support. The consequences of the

Second World War produced this for them. The nationalist parties became mass movements.

But here is another term that can mislead. The new parties mobilized the clamour in the streets. They became movements with mass support or mass acclaim. They did not become movements of mass participation. The distinction is important.*

The new pace-makers embraced nationalism as the key to their problem of winning power. But they knew that they must show the colonial rulers that they did not stand alone as, generally, their forerunners of the 1930s had stood alone. They had to use mass support. This was what we may call the 'national struggle'. But the interests of the masses to whom they now applied were not directed, one should repeat, to the winning of political power in any direct and nationalist sense, but to the improvement of wages, the elimination of arbitrary decrees, the restoration of land taken by whites, and the lessening of poverty. This is what we may call the 'social struggle'. When the nationalists came to the masses and said that all their woes were the result of colonial rule, and would disappear with the disappearance of colonial rule, multitudes of people were ready to listen to the good news and follow these leaders in the hope that something useful might ensue. They became nationalists, as it were, by association; but the association, more often than not, remained a fragile one.

This convergence of the 1950s between struggle for nationhood, the 'national struggle', and struggle for social gains, the 'social struggle', thus occurred as a mutual opportunism. The nationalists needed the masses, and the masses needed the nationalists, but for purposes by no means necessarily identical. The nationalists became 'aware of their chance to exploit the social question', as

*A party or movement with mass support is one in which a self-chosen leadership can rely upon a wide audience of followers who are prepared to demonstrate or otherwise act in support of its leadership, but who are otherwise uninvolved in the leadership's policies, plans or intentions. A party or movement with mass participation is one with mass support which becomes organically involved in political life, and is organized and organizes itself for political discussion, activism and control within the movement's life and programme.

Gallisot remarked of the (Moroccan) Istiqlal, while the multitudes likewise came to see, along the lines of Pte Ayoola's letter to Herbert Macaulay, that they could have a use for literate or clever spokesmen who could argue with officials and employers.

The old gap between the few and the many was thereupon reproduced in a new scenario. The new nationalists, now with a clear vocation to grow into a subsidiary bourgeoisie, found a skilled leadership. All these stood on one side of the gap; on the other, meanwhile, there remained an inchoate quantity of supporters for whom that vocation could have little meaning, or little that promised them any good. There was a bridge across the gap. But this was built of hopes and aspirations which might seem to be the same for both but were really not the same, and were even sharply opposed; and so the bridge remained always liable to collapse into mutual distrust or worse.

This was most obviously the case with parties led by men of higher education or correspondingly privileged status, and least obviously, though still generally, in settler colonies where leadership came from intermediate strata whose everyday lives were closer to the multitudes or even identical with the multitudes. Only when colonial repression provoked a choice between mass action and defeat did these parties, movements, or congresses briefly become the focal points of widespread activism. Generally, the conditions under which parties of mass support could develop into parties of mass participation were not yet present.

Afterwards, when the bridge across the gap had crashed into what became a chasm, and the leaders of independence stood towards the majority of rural and urban people in much the same posture of repressive control as the colonial régimes had stood towards them, there would be recrimination. One may question if this was realistic. Were the ideas of the nationalists, for example, so clearly indicative of 'total ideological barrenness' as latter-day critics afterwards affirmed? It became easy to think so. Yet the judgement implies a political culture which those years did not provide.

With a few uninfluential exceptions, the nationalists made

the choice that seemed most likely to succeed; and it did succeed. However innovating their best spokesmen wished to be, all were trapped in the implications of their choice. Their chosen strategy had led them into every sort of compromise with colonial powers (and with the USA), and these were determined to guarantee the continuity of underlying structures. Beyond that, their own ideology was in line with their choice. Far from being 'barren', this ideology accepted the complex orthodoxy of the would-be bourgeois nation-state in wholesale and in detail. For it argued that a privileged leadership, potentially a ruling middle class, should direct an economy of private capitalism and of state capitalism; should promote a culture in which the ineffable verities of Oxbridge and the Sorbonne (or of Harvard Business School) were to alight on newer domes and towers where they would set the tone for all who aspired to wisdom; and, generally, should preside over a society whose values, however 'Africanized', would repeat the experience of their European predecessors.

This being so, their duty was not to fill in the gap or widen the bridge across it, but to make sure that they became strong and numerous enough to dominate the crossing. With no gap, and no close guard upon the bridge, there could be no middle class, or none that would be capable of holding power and deciding the future. On the contrary, there would be egalitarian confusion as the many invaded the privileges of the few; worse still, there might even be revolution. So it must be wise to call on mass support with a prudent eye to its dangers, now or later, while ensuring that the politics of confrontation with colonial power stayed safely in the hands of a political class of strictly limited numbers. Their prudence and its consequences called forth a corresponding prudence among the many, and this is what explains the atmosphere of doubt in villages and urban slums when independence came. The multitudes applauded, often with displays of vivid satisfaction at the ending of colonial rule, but doubt rang often in their cheers. Wasn't somebody, perhaps, being taken for a ride?

Yet for all those who were not in villages and urban slums, and sometimes for some who were, this decade of the 1950s was a time of continuing and unprecedented optimism. The incubus was shifting, could surely be removed; and with it there would go, there was already going, that whole fog of frustration and humiliation which the colonial systems had spread within their walls. Often against huge obstruction, the nationalists marched to new and happy tunes that were now heard from Africa, for the first time in history, across the wide world that awaited their arrival.

The following four chapters tell the story of this march into the political kingdom of their desire, and broadly trace the route along which the ideas of the 1930s and earlier became crowned with success.

22

WINNING THE POLITICAL KINGDOM:
IN BRITISH WEST AFRICA

British West Africa set the pace for the tropical regions. These four colonies had long been able to develop relatively large 'political classes' whose ideas about nationalism and African equality with other peoples looked back to a distinguished heritage. Memories were still alive of a nineteenth-century white presence which had offered a fruitful partnership before the onset of imperialism. A man of African descent had governed Sierra Leone, and eighteen out of forty-two senior posts in Sierra Leone government were held by Creoles as late as 1892. Nigeria, Gold Coast, The Gambia could each add to that same distant tale.

Nearly a century of confident political journalism lay behind the post-war newspapers of these nationalists, and much of it could still bear quotation. In contrast with their francophone contemporaries, these 'top élites' were scarcely distracted by the charades of Assimilation. If Oxbridge and the Inns of Court, or now the Royal Military Academy at Sandhurst, continued to set the tone for them, at least they were not supposed to become Englishmen, and so were spared the hypocrisies of behaving as such.

British policy, moreover, had long assumed that political power might one day pass to suitable successors in these four colonies. Cautious colonial constitutions had installed legislative councils where hand-picked Africans were allowed to discuss affairs, though not of course decide them. Colonial governors might still think it presumptuous for these 'detestable clerks' to demand self-government; they could not say it was illegitimate or unexpected. There was no British settler immigration to muddy the doctrine of trusteeship, and while Lebanese immigrants offered plenty of commercial competition they stayed out of politics. There could be no room here for the East and Central African colonial disputes over which community's interests should be paramount; once imperial interests were satisfied, those of Africans were what remained.

Gold Coast made the earliest break-through. The consequences of the Second World War rendered this possible; but the political skill of a single man, the visionary and yet practical Kwame Nkrumah, greatly speeded up the process. British authority, expecting to move very slowly, produced in 1946 a new constitution which gave a slight though perceptible nudge to the hopes of the local political class. This, it was thought officially, should prove enough for the years ahead. But the new constitution was practically a dead letter by 1948, and altogether so a year later. The accepted leaders of nationalism, however, were not those who killed it.

These leaders, and notably J. B. Danquah, had seen that the times were ripe for their political advance, and found the 1946 constitution far too meagre. In 1947 they launched an organization designed to obtain more; this was the *United Gold Coast Convention* (UGCC). Their intentions were to agitate for unequivocal British concessions which should carry Gold Coast towards independence within the Commonwealth, but not to go outside the comfortable limits of established argument. A passionate and often brilliant advocate as well as a man of chiefly heritage, Danquah was nothing of a tribune. He and his friends shared high status in colonial society and nourished no smallest wish to mingle their lot with that of the plebs. But they saw that some use would have to be made of the clamour in the streets, and looked around for ways in which they could safely 'reach the masses'. They needed a political organizer to do this for them, but under their control. They found Nkrumah.

Then in London and rising thirty-eight, Nkrumah was a 'man of the Thirties' with a certain difference. Like Azikiwe before him, he had spent many years in the United States, mostly in universities. Very much a reformist rather than a revolutionary in his political attitudes, he had nonetheless glimpsed alternatives, partly under the influence of the outstanding West Indian marxist and anti-Stalinist thinker, C. L. R. James. Moving to London in 1945, Nkrumah had continued to mix with leftist friends, and was now much influenced by the Pan-Africanist George Padmore, another West Indian with a strongly radical background, but who had now broken with the Comintern. Nkrumah had also won the reputation of a good organizer from his work for the Pan-African Congress held in Manchester in 1945.

Far away in Gold Coast, Danquah was recommended to employ Nkrumah, and wrote asking him to come home. Nkrumah accepted with hesitation, wondering if the UGCC's manifest conservatism might not prove a trap, but duly came, arriving in Accra at the end of 1947. The UGCC leaders looked him over and approved; Africans who were radical in England, as they knew, generally put a great deal of water in their wine when home again. Nkrumah began to form UGCC branches. He worked out a plan for mass organization which provided for an initial campaign of mass political education with the active aid of trade unions, ex-servicemen's, and other popular organizations; and then for 'constant demonstrations throughout the country'. This was using a lot less water than the UGCC notables could have wished, but they did not yet dissent.

They soon had cause for great alarm. Nii Bonne organized his boycott of European shops, and with intense success. Emotions began to run high, and then boiled over. On 28 February 1948, a notable date in the modern African calendar, an ex-servicemen's delegation marched to the Governor's castle to present a petition concerned with pensions and employment. Police barred its way. There were protests. A white police officer took a rifle from one of his men and killed an ex-sergeant among the demonstrators; others were then wounded. In itself, no doubt, this was a very small colonial event; but widespread rioting by huge crowds of people immediately followed, continuing for days and spreading beyond the capital. The police alleged a conspiracy, even a communist plot. This was ridiculous, but the Governor arrested the six chief leaders of the UGCC, none of whom was remotely concerned with any of these disturbances, and only one of whom, Nkrumah, had the least attachment to any left-wing thought.

They were quickly released, but turned at once against Nkrumah, fearing any further fracas from his possible or presumed radicalism. They could not quite brace themselves to sack him, but asked him to go back to London. He refused and formed in June 1949 a breakaway from the UGCC, the *Convention People's Party* (CPP). Mass support rallied to the CPP, and proved this by a widely followed general strike in 1950; and the CPP proceeded to win a general election at the outset of 1951. Whereupon Nkrumah, then a political prisoner, was invited to the Governor's castle and offered the leadership of a CPP government with internal autonomy. He and his fellow leaders of the CPP at once accepted.

This was not yet self-government, since all crucial powers stayed with the Governor, but it was certainly a long step towards it. In the atmosphere and circumstances of those days, it was widely seen as a major gain, and as a proof to all tropical Africans that real progress against colonial rule was possible. In the event, another six years of often difficult experience were required in order to achieve political sovereignty, by which time other colonies in West Africa were moving in the same direction; but the break-through of 1951 deserved its name. In 1957, Gold Coast Colony and Protectorate became a sovereign Dominion, and in 1960 a Republic. The nationalists called their new state Ghana as a symbol of the renewal of Africa's own history, reflecting as this did the ancient Ghana of the Western Sudan a thousand years earlier.

Events in Nigeria kept abreast in their own way. In this huge colony, with its teeming populations, matters were bound to be more complex.

The whole northerly part of Nigeria had been fenced around by its British officials as an area of Indirect Rule where, by definition, the ideas of nationalism should be allowed no footing. While these northern two-thirds of the country had been amalgamated for overall convenience with the southern third in 1914, they were practically treated as a separate entity, and a constitution of 1922 had excluded them from the first cautious steps towards African political representation then being introduced into the legislative councils of the south. This meant that the northern peoples – Hausa, Fulani, many others – had no access to modern politics. A comment of M. G. Smith's may apply to all the thirty-eight emirate states in the north. 'The government of Zaira emirate in 1950', he found, could be described as 'an autocracy inefficiently supervised by the British'.²⁴

All the same, nationalism found its way into the towns of the north, and 1950 saw the foundation in Kano of a modernizing group called the *Northern Elements Progressive Union* (NEPU) under the lead of the very cultivated Aminu Kano. They had a hard life at the hands of the local autocrats, whether emirate or British, but their lead was important. Responding reluctantly to the pressure of the times, especially from the south, the emirs formed their own organization a year later, the *Northern People's Congress* (NPC), and set about destroying NEPU as though it were the vanguard of a revolution. For years ahead, the NPC would continue to run the north on strictly authoritarian lines.

The south was then composed of two regions, created for administrative convenience in 1939. These were the Western, where the population was almost entirely Yoruba of varying internal loyalties, and the Eastern, where the majority was Igbo together with minority ethnic groups in the Delta. The Yoruba and Igbo were certainly nations in the traditional sense, while the minorities were more or less 'submerged' nationalities, although no more so than peoples in the north. But in neither of these southern regions had the British made any great effort to suffocate political thought; and so it was here in the south that nationalism first took hold and scored gains. Their numerous 'political classes' moved into nationalist politics as the continuation of pre-nationalist politics by other means, and new political movements quickly grew from a complexity of internal loyalties, clan groupings, town chiefdoms, ancestral societies and cultural associations.

Drawing adherents primarily from the Eastern Region, Igbo in majority, Nnamdi Azikiwe had formed the *National Council of Nigeria and Cameroons* (NCNC, the Cameroons being the British Protectorate of the northern part of the former German Kamerun) as early as 1944, and now proceeded to mobilize popular acclaim and mass support. Reacting to the 'Igbo threat' of Azikiwe's vigorous demagogy, the Yoruba lawyer Obafemi Awolowo launched the *Action Group* (AG) in 1950 with support from Yoruba in the

Western Region. These were the principal parties. They had much the same approach to nationalism, but differed in their structure. While the NCNC reflected the non-chiefly egalitarianism of Igbo tradition, the AG became a symbiosis of modernizing ideas with those of the immemorial rankings and chiefly grades of a notably aristocratic culture.

These three organizations, with the NPC making a third, faced each other with a rivalry inherent to the nature of their leadership. If an eventually independent Nigeria was to stay as one country – and most of them felt that it probably should – which regional leadership or coalition would dominate? Which would call the tune, which gather the lion's share to itself? The British now set about proving, however unintentionally, that 'bourgeois nationalism' cannot solve, save by force, the 'national question' that arises in a colony of different nationalities. In 1951 they introduced a constitution which confirmed an overall Nigerian unity, but transformed the regional legislative councils, hitherto no more than colonial décor, into regional legislatures with regional executives. These were still advisory in most of their attributes, but were clearly intended as the future heirs of independence.

This was a temptation for each of the three regional leaderships or 'top élites' – those of the Northern emirs, of the Yoruba chiefs and politicians in the West, and of the Igbo and other tribunes in the East – to assert not only a regional primacy, which they had already, but to do this in such a way as to advance their separate regional interests and, if possible, dominate the emergent federation. Each accordingly set about reinforcing its regional power, and took what small scope there was for winning adherents in other regions, while the two southern parties continued to press for independence. To this the British responded in 1954 with another constitution. This recognized the division of a federal Nigeria into what, *de facto*, became three colonial states. Pushing on, the NCNC and AG were now able to win internal autonomy for the Eastern and Western Regions, although the northern emirs were ready to follow only in 1959.

An independent Nigeria thus emerged in 1960 as a federation of three regions each led by a leadership which could make no real claim to represent an all-Nigerian nationalism. Representation in the federal assembly being based on voting numbers, the Northern Region put the NPC into a more or less permanent control of the federal government, since it had a majority of voters. This ensured a highly conservative control by the aristocratic Sardauna of Sokoto, Sir Ahmadu Bello, through the grave but ambiguous prime minister, Tafawa Balewa, and his like; but it naturally satisfied nobody else. Each 'political class' could and did monopolize the fruits of regional power, but federal power appeared to have passed indefinitely into northern hands. The 'submerged nationalities', meanwhile, were left out in the cold. A new region was formed in the Mid-West, but could scarcely relieve a situation that was clearly heading for trouble.

No doubt unavoidably in this system, each political class merely went with the tide of its personal or group ambitions. One divisive constitution after another was accepted as a means of pushing further claims. Many 'programmes' were published; none of them addressed itself to basic issues of social or economic transformation. Much was said about unity; still more was done to ensure that unity would not follow. 'So far,' observed the Sardauna of Sokoto on the morrow of independence, 'none of the "political" parties have produced programmes markedly different from each other.' The reason, he rightly thought, was easy to see. 'In the old days, when the British were the "government", all parties concentrated on demanding self-government to the exclusion of all else.' Their occupation was to attack colonial rule, 'and it was not particularly difficult and did not demand any real thought'.[25] The struggle for independence had become a dog-fight for the spoils.

Yet once again it would be wrong to accuse these 'political classes' of having no ideology. In the south they had fully accepted the ideology of parliamentary capitalism, and applied themselves to realizing it with a famous ingenuity and vigour. The northern leaders moved more slowly, but there too it became possible to see that modernization need not mean an end to chiefly hierarchies; and here the 'political class' was rapidly augmented by a military élite for an army still manned, as in the British tradition, largely by recruits from the north. Down below, true enough, the voting masses were soon showing signs of resentment at what they quickly saw as little more than a change of masters, but the new masters, now installed, treated such resentments as problems for the police rather than as problems of politics. Parts of Nigeria were in uproar even by 1962. An understanding that the 'national question' could be solved only by way of solving the 'social question' was not to appear for a long way ahead, and after many fierce upheavals.

Sierra Leone proceeded by its own pattern. This was complicated by the historical divide between the Creole society of Freetown and environs, and the nine-tenths of the whole population who lived in the 'protectorate' or, as it was often called, the 'tribal interior'. The former were thoroughly westernized by many generations; well versed in the ideas of nationalism, they had long been citizens of the Western world. The latter, with some important exceptions, were still enclosed within their own African history. The problem was to reach a synthesis that could weld the two together. Colonial rule in the past had naturally shown no interest in promoting this difficult process; it set about doing so now.

A constitution of 1947 provided for an unofficial majority in the territorial legislature. This was weighted in favour of the 'tribal interior', or rather in favour of its small political group of chiefs and Western-educated men. The Creole leaders disliked this, but protested in vain. Another constitution of 1951 then gave Sierra Leone a unitary constitution, obliterating the institutional division between Colony and Protectorate, and awarding internal political office to whichever leadership proved able to secure a majority of votes in a general election. The Protectorate-based *Sierra Leone People's Party* (SLPP) won the following election under the lead of a former physician, Sir Milton Margai. With this shrewd if devious man the Creole groups proceeded to a compromise which proved successful in winning concessions from the British in 1953 and after. In 1960 Margai was able to form a wide-based coalition called the *United National Front*. This held together well enough for the British to concede independence in 1961. The 'political class' was now left to confront the unresolved tensions of their heritage. These were many, and a variety of *coups* would duly follow.

The Gambia, with some 300,000 inhabitants compared with Sierra Leone's more than two million, had a somewhat parallel situation. Its modernizing groups were concentrated largely in Bathurst (Banjul), the administrative capital near the river's mouth. Three parties emerged here in the 1950s, drawing their chief support from the Wolof of the capital and its environs. A party of the 'tribal interior' emerged in 1960, the *People's Progressive Party* (PPP) led by Dawda Jawara with mainly Mandinka support. The British providing no obstacles, these groups achieved internal self-government in 1963. In 1965 a coalition between the PPP and one of the Bathurst parties led by P. S. Njie brought the country to independence in that year.

IN FRENCH AFRICA:
THE DUAL STRUGGLE

The political situation in French territories after 1945 reflected themes common to other European empires, but combined these in an often harsh duality. With significantly large populations only in the Maghrib,* francophone Africans had to wage their campaigns against Paris, but also against French settler groupings which could usually count on the active support of influential politicians in France. Unlike Britain in West Africa, this colonial power was for a long time after 1945 determined to retain its colonies within the metropolitan political as well as economic system. Its post-war mood was hurt and sensitive, moreover, and much inclined to reach for the repressive rifle.

French Africa's route to advancement was therefore rough and devious. Depressingly often the record of this period is one of administrative 'vigour' ranging from stubborn reaction against any sign of change, often by Gaullist officials whose ideas were indistinguishable from those of colonial officials of the 1930s or of Vichy, to fearful military massacres and years of colonial warfare. Liberalizing trends in France held the balance after 1945, but soon became and remained a minority in the National Assembly. Governors who saw that change was desirable and even necessary, men such as Brunet or Latrille, were briskly removed in favour of governors who saw nothing of the kind. Through right-wing French extremism of

*Compared with about 40 million in Nigeria and some 7 million in the other three British West African territories, there were about 16 million in the eight West African territories governed from Dakar, together with the French 'mandate' of Togo, while French Equatoria's four territories had some 4 million, with another 4 million in the French 'mandate' of Cameroun. These are approximate figures for 1945.

one kind or another, the hand of assassination struck down repeatedly those it most hated: the Tunisian Ferhat Hached as early as 1952, for example, the Camerounian Félix Moumié as late as 1960.

After the Western allies had driven the Nazis out of France, destroying the Vichy régime in the process, a new Republic, the Fourth, had to be built. Defeating a conservatism tarnished by collaboration with the German occupation, general elections produced a constituent assembly which agreed, in April 1946, upon a single-chamber legislature and tentative steps towards a new deal for the colonies. But the same year brought second thoughts to a middle-class electorate recovering from the post-war 'mortgage' of a radicalism induced by the wartime resistance of the left. A referendum rejected this first constitution by about $10\frac{1}{2}$ to $9\frac{1}{2}$ million votes, although overseas voters, many of whom were assimilated Africans, naturally accepted it by about 344,000 to 311,000.

A second constitution was approved in October 1946 by just over 9 million to just over 8 million votes, while overseas voters marked their understanding of the retreat from liberalism in their rejection of this revised constitution by about 335,000 to 238,000 votes. The 'French Union' proclaimed by the first constitution – neither a commonwealth nor exactly an empire – remained in place. Yet the cornerstone of its colonial principles was no longer the free consent of a widening overseas electorate, but, in Morgenthau's words, 'domination by France'.[26] Generally, there now followed a period of reaction in Africa and military reassertion in Indo-China. It was within this Fourth Republic, and eventually against it, that nationalism in French Africa developed from the ideas of assimilation to those of independence.

This development followed comparable lines in most of the French territories: modernizing groups accepted the lessons of nationalism and strove for the nation-state. A few had done this in the 1930s or even the 1920s, notably in Madagascar and the Maghrib, but the acceptance now became general. The nationalist pioneers looked round for mass support and often found it: wide populations, though chiefly urban at this juncture, had become confusedly aware of the possibility of useful change. Temporarily joined in populist campaigns, the national and the social struggles were able to gain some memorable victories. These settled accounts with colonial rule. Unavoidably, they left the few and the many to settle accounts with each other. That would be a different matter.

Again, as in earlier years, events in the Maghrib were influenced by those of Egypt. During the Second World War the Egyptian middle class had made some gains, not least in 1942 when the British occupying power, then fighting for its life against Axis armies in North Africa, forced King Farouk to accept a Wafdist government as a means of deflating anti-British feeling. But operative convergence between the 'national' and the 'social' came only in the wake of the war when new nationalist trends, drawing fresh strength from Westernizing ideas as well as from Muslim loyalties in the Salafist tradition, found leaders who were ready to fight both the British and the local bourgeoisie of landowners, bankers, and budding industrialists. In 1952 a military *coup* that was largely the work of young army officers, among whose nationalist motives was resentment at Egypt's defeat by Israel, swept the monarch and his tottering régime from power; and in 1953 they declared a republic. A year later the leader of the young officers, Gamal Abdel Nasser, became president on a programme of national but by no means radical renewal.

Two years later again, the USA and Britain went back on arrangements to finance a major dam on the upper Nile, being by now convinced that they must overturn the Nasserist régime if they possibly could. Responding to this, Nasser expropriated the assets of the Suez Canal company. Invasion by Israel, backed militarily by France and Britain, followed in October 1956. But the 1950s were no longer the 1930s, and this ill-judged enterprise came unstuck; the invading forces were politically obliged to withdraw. In this situation Nasser embarked on a more radical phase of policy that promised to go beyond populism* and seek far-ranging changes

*By 'populism' is meant an opportunist convergence of the leading nationalist strata with the social concerns and aims of the masses. Necessarily demagogic, populism was a temporary alliance of the few and the many

of socio-economic structure. The old bourgeoisie was duly destroyed; but a new ruling stratum, petty-bourgeois and bureaucratic, and greatly enlarged by the State capitalism of the Nasserist system, won ground. Thus the conflict between the 'national' and the 'social' aspects of emancipation, always inherent in populism, was tackled but not resolved. This conflict would surface repeatedly in later years, and would result, increasingly after Nasser's death in 1970, in wide oscillations of policy.

Throughout this period, but especially in the critical early 1950s, Cairo provided a sympathetic base for the nationalists of the Maghrib, and also gave them a little material support. These faced the Paris–settler duality in its full rigour. But the duality worked in Tunisia and Morocco differently from in Algeria. Partly, this was by reason of a variable between settler-population sizes: around 1945 there were about 250,000 Europeans in Tunisia, perhaps 300,000 in Morocco, but much more than a million in Algeria. Partly, the variable derived from the fact that Tunisia and Morocco were recognized as protectorates with some eventual claim to a life of their own, while Algeria north of the Sahara had long been governed as an integral segment of France, and so, in practice, entirely in the interests of local Europeans.

Up to 1942, Tunisia's Vichy administration continued the repressions of 1938–9. After British and American victory in North Africa there followed an uneasy interregnum, but Tunisian politics gradually began again, and the leader of the Néo-Destour and its 'political class', Habib Bourguiba, was able after many adventures to take a new lead in 1949. Mass support for the nationalist aims of the Néo-Destour meanwhile improved after Ferhat Hached's formation in 1945 of a federation of Tunisian trade unions. These proved militant, and challenged persecution. A major strike in 1947 cost thirty-two killed and some 200 wounded at the hands of a régime still bent on repression. At this point the Bey of Tunis reinforced the leverage

for the primary purposes of the few. After these purposes were achieved, the alliance just as necessarily broke down in favour of the further advancement of the few. Which did not, of course, prevent the few from continuing to use the demagogy of 'African Socialism' and similar fantasies.

of the Néo-Destour by making common cause with it. Tougher repression resumed in 1952 when the Néo-Destour was banned, its leaders were arrested, and a general strike was answered by violent measures and the calling of army reinforcements from France.

This was where the people of Vietnam, and not for the last time in recent history, began to interpose their influence on behalf of anti-colonial causes in Africa. Begun effectively in 1946,* France's war against the Vietnamese revolutionary nationalist movement, the Vietminh, was going badly, so badly that Paris now wavered in Tunisia, offered some partial reforms, found them rejected, and played with offering more: but always with a hand prepared to hit out hard at any nationalist initiative. In this uncertain situation the social struggle now brought its decisive contribution. Onwards from 1952 groups of peasant guerrillas formed in the hills. By 1954 some 70,000 French troops were tied down by peasant insurrection. Electing their officers, drawing recruits from ex-servicemen or 'social bandits' or young townsmen, these guerrilla bands began to shape a revolutionary army.

A somewhat familiar situation now evolved: in different circumstances, as we shall see, it appeared almost at the same moment in Kenya. Bereft of their petty-bourgeois leaders, either in prison or in clandestinity, the guerrilla leaders 'at the base', fighting a social as well as national struggle, began to build their own radical politics of anti-colonialism. This placed Bourguiba and his friends in another difficulty besides prison: for them, the rise of peasant revolutionaries (or, at least, of peasant radicals) might strengthen their hand in negotiation with France, but it might also deprive them of a monopoly of power in the state that emerged. As it was, things moved too fast for any further development on the left.

Clear heads in Paris saw Bourguiba's problem; after all, it was their own as well. In March 1954 they transferred Bourguiba from prison to detention and enabled him, if with obstacles, to become active again. In May came the French army débâcle of Dien

*One may date this from the French aggression in Haiphong of November in that year. For a handy précis, see G. Chaffard, *Les Carnets Secrets de la Décolonisation*, Calmann-Levy, Paris, 1965–7, 2 vols: vol. 1, p. 64.

Bien-Phu at the hands of the Vietminh. In July Bourguiba was set free, and a month later the Néo-Destour re-legalized. Large concessions to independence, and perhaps independence itself, seemed certain. The peasant guerrillas accepted an offer of amnesty; by December 1954, more than 2,500 had laid down their arms.

Insurrection was over, but the Néo-Destour had still to reap the gains of this resistance 'at the base'. In April 1955 Paris at last conceded internal autonomy. Predictably, there followed a split within the Néo-Destourian leadership between the majority, led by Bourguiba, and a radical minority led by Salah ben Yussef, forecasting the endemic conflict which would emerge, after independence, between the 'national' and the 'social' aspects of this long anticolonial campaign. But Bourguiba now had independence in his pocket, and this was conceded to him and his majority grouping within the Néo-Destour in March 1956.

In Morocco the idea of a national independence as distinct from a reform of French administration acquired body with the development of the Istiqlal, in December 1943, out of the cautious committees formed by the Fez bourgeoisie and its allies in 1937. Small in numbers and limited in their political ambition, these groups had little experience of populist politics, and were in any case much influenced towards prudence by the conservative Salafism of its then outstanding Moroccan ideologist, Allal al-Fassi. Yet the 1930s had begun to prove to them that they could achieve nothing without the evidence of mass support. And then, as elsewhere, the Second World War opened new perspectives. Trade unions were enabled to come alive with a new vigour. New stirrings moved the rural zones. Still cautiously, the leaders of the Istiqlal responded.

Like the Néo-Destour in Tunisia, they won recognition from their fount of traditional legitimacy, Sultan Mohamed V, whose position, however, was and would remain far stronger and less dependent on nationalism than that of the Bey of Tunis. For their part, the diverse governments of the Fourth Republic – between 1946 and 1958 there were no fewer than twelve French colonial ministers – answered nationalist strivings with a monotonous identity of policy: they manoeuvred, but chiefly they repressed.

Seeking to decapitate political resistance, they deposed Mohamed V in August 1953 and replaced him by a puppet. This had the opposite effect: resistance stiffened, and threatened to become violent in the towns.

That might have been contained. But at this juncture, early in 1955, a rural army that was very much a people's army took the field. With the arrival of this army of liberation, as it called itself, the French were now at war in all three countries of the Maghrib. Then came Dien Bien-Phu, and, as in Tunisia, Paris began to pull back. Mohamed V was restored to his throne and negotiations with the political class, initially with the Istiqlal, at once followed. France conceded independence on 2 March 1956, eighteen days before the same concession to Tunisia.

Much the same pattern of events was repeated in Algeria, but with many great variations and with an enormous violence. All this would shake every segment of Algerian society to its roots, and penetrate into every level of life. Eventually it would threaten France itself with a right-wing dictatorship, and in any case it tore down the feeble façades of the Fourth Republic as well as ending French domination of Algeria. In this epic conflict no human quality was absent, whether for evil or for good. Courage had to march alongside betrayal, and hope to live with horror; nothing was spared.

Pre-1939 ideas and agitations had re-emerged in 1943, as in the rest of the Maghrib. They were bound to be cautious, for the Allies had still to win the war, even though Vichyist authority gave way to a Free French leadership formed in the crucible of Gaullist nationalism. Concessions to Algerian sentiment might be unavoidable, but they should be little more than an exercise in the recovery of 'greater France'.

March 1944 saw the launching of a new Algerian movement called the Friends of the Manifesto, responding now in clear nationalist terms to this restated nationalism of the French. The 'formation of an Algerian nation' should be made 'familiar and desirable' as a popular programme; Algeria should become an autonomous republic federated to a restored but no longer imperialist

France. The surviving PPA went further, arguing that only a complete Algerian sovereignty could be enough. To such ideas, in no small measure the fruit of a sense that the war had 'changed everything', the Free French leader Charles de Gaulle, now at the head of a provisional French government, replied with an offer of trifling reforms, while the local European population, being in any case far more Fascist than Free French, got ready to fight for its colonial birthright.

Clashes ensued, and on 1 May 1945 the police fired on demonstrators, killing three in Algiers and one in Oran. 8 May, marking Allied victory in Europe, brought matters to a head. While great crowds of Algerians chanted slogans such as *Long Live Independent Algeria*, police opened fire at Guélm and Sétif. There was widespread disorder, and on 10 May General Duval undertook a major repression. Thousands were arrested; many were killed. Officially, 103 Europeans lost their lives and 1,500 Algerians. But the Army itself put the total of Algerians killed at 8,000, while the PPA claimed that the total was 45,000. The true figure was certainly very large.

The pattern of the future was clear for all to see. But it took shape slowly after this bloodbath. There followed nine years of alternating agitation and repression, with the politicians of the Fourth Republic ever more committed to keeping Algeria as a settler preserve within the French departmental system, and with the nationalists divided on what tactics they could best adopt. This division looked like a split between reformists and revolutionaries, but it was rather, in Harbi's view, a case of political divisions among 'petty bourgeois' groups whose local loyalties and attachments varied with time and place. A small minority were in favour of an armed struggle which they now thought unavoidable. These men began to organize secretly in 1952. Led by Ahmed ben Bella, they were ready to begin two years later.

In November 1954 they launched their rising in the eastern mountains of the Aurès with 300 Italian rifles bought in Libya seven years earlier and stored against eventual need, some grenades, a few revolvers, but a military leadership which had gone through the battles of Italy in 1943–4, where Ben Bella and others had fought in the Free French army. It spread rather slowly, but by 1956 had engulfed most of northern Algeria. Struggling to contain it, the Fourth Republic committed an army eventually some half a million strong.

By 1960 the fighters of the Algerian Front of National Liberation (FLN), which had emerged from the rising as a broad coalition of political trends, were reinforced by strong external bases in Tunisia and Morocco, and had fought this huge French army to a stalemate. General de Gaulle, now president of a Fifth Republic which had followed upon the collapse of the Fourth, got ready to negotiate a peace that would make Algeria independent. Many dramas followed. French generals in Algeria rebelled but were overcome, while quasi-fascist groups in France continued a campaign of urban bombing. Stubbornly courageous, de Gaulle held firm. In May 1961 the French army ceased fire. Algeria became independent in July 1962. At least a quarter of a million Algerians had died for this.

Without pushing the parallel to any dogmatism, one may note that convergence between the two aspects of the struggle for emancipation had operated much as in Tunisia and Morocco, but with several large differences aside from the fearful violence of the Algerian war. In Morocco and Tunisia the nationalists had reached their goal in alliance with trade unions and with guerrillas. All three elements had retained their separate identity, group-interest, and sense of specific purpose. In Algeria, by contrast, every major element that led towards success became temporarily unified within the FLN under the tremendous pressures of colonial warfare. This unity was reinforced by the fact that the Algerian bourgeoisie, such as it was, stood aside in neutrality or else backed the French, so that leadership remained largely with men of the intermediate strata, many of whom were close to the masses.

These factors, much influenced again by the 'levelling' effect of settler domination on Algerian society, gave the FLN an insistently populist and sometimes even revolutionary tone and temper; and this deepened as the war evoked an ever widening participation. Out of this would emerge an Algeria which appeared, for a while, to have resolved the two aspects of the struggle into a synthesis that would fully politicize the social aspect and give it primacy. A 'socialist' Algeria seemed to stand in sharp contrast to the 'neo-colonialist' outcome in Tunisia and Morocco. This was a good deal less than the truth, and yet Algeria, even while promoting a strongly bureaucratic structure within a framework of state capitalism, retained interesting aspects of innovation. These would count in the future.

The large island of Madagascar had produced by the 1930s, among its modernizing thinkers, a strong sentiment in favour of a national future. The end of the Second World War saw this embodied in a number of new parties or movements which reflected class divisions rather less embryonic than on the mainland. Of these the most important were the Mouvement Démocratique pour le Renouveau Malgache (MRDM), speaking chiefly for intermediate strata, and the Parti des Désinhérités de Madagascar (PADESM), based on plantation workers, while two or three small groupings spoke for the bourgeoisie of Tananarive and other towns.

The policy of Paris vacillated for much the same reasons as elsewhere. French generals were above all concerned for their army's battered prestige; even when they were not of right-wing opinions, this led them into right-wing positions wherever French colonial supremacy came under local nationalist pressure. Colonialist staffs were ex-Vichyist or at least rigidly conservative. Many Fourth Republic politicians spoke warmly of the implications of the French Union proclaimed in 1946, but generally preferred to let things slide. In these circumstances the running tended to be made by vociferous minorities: above all, by settler minorities.

The settlers in Madagascar were relatively few: in the late 1940s, perhaps 40,000 with recent origins in France and another 20,000 'poor whites' from Réunion. But they made up for any lack of numbers by the vigour of their racism. The diatribes of their newspaper, *Tana-Journal*, were probably characteristic of their opinions, in this case on the colonial reforms of 1946: 'The demagogy of our Government has turned these savages into French citizens, into electors: how disgraceful!'[27]

These settlers rapidly inflamed the atmosphere of conflict that existed in any case between Malagasy claims and the hesitations of Paris. In 1947 Madagascar saw a virtual repetition of the rising protest and all-out repression of Algeria in 1945, but on a still more violent scale. In February 1946 the two Malagasy deputies elected to the French National Assembly had proposed that their island should become a free state within the French Union. They asked for this again in April, while at home the MRDM continued to gather mass support in favour of the same end. In August they pressed for a referendum on the island's future. In September the colonial minister, Marius Moutet, responded with a cable to the high commissioner, ordering the latter to 'fight the MRDM by every means' at his disposal.[28] Many arrests followed.

Increasing resistance faced growing intimidation early in 1947. Insurrection began in March. This was widely popular, and with all the elements that were to appear in comparable situations elsewhere, whether colonial or neo-colonial: in the Maghrib, in East Africa, in the Portuguese colonies, in the ex-Belgian Congo. With the partial help of the educated few, nationalist ideas mingled with the advice of diviners speaking for ancestral charters. Large numbers of people grasped whatever weapons they could find. Peasant rebels took large areas out of French control, and lost them only after a military repression of quite extraordinary severity. The blockade of dissident areas and ensuing hunger killed many more than the troops shot down, but the troops shot down several thousand. No agreed figure of Malagasy dead has ever appeared, for while contemporary reports put the total at between 80,000 and 90,000, mostly by hunger, later estimates were much smaller. But they were still large.[29] In 1948, according to official records, nearly 6,000 political prisoners were held by the French.

Only in 1956 was the state of siege lifted and an amnesty proclaimed, and not until 1957 were the last political prisoners set free. But the MRDM and its leaders were among the casualties. French policy could now select whomever it found convenient to govern an autonomous colony within the limits of a new law of devolution of 1956 and its executive decrees of 1957. In 1960, with a

political class now well tailored to French interests, a formally independent government at last emerged. It would remain so tailored
until late in 1972, when new moves for independence began.

Repression in the 'black African' colonies of West Africa
and Equatoria was mild in comparison with the Maghrib and Madagascar. Here the pressures for change were less powerful, but also less
well aligned. Three phases can be distinguished between 1945 and
1960.

The first phase ran from 1945 to 1951. It opened with
considerable gains which the French retreat from the first to the
second constitution could reduce but not annul: the abolition of
forced labour and much of the 'subject status' (indigénat) on which
that labour was based;* the creation of territorial assemblies, weak in
influence and yet an improvement on the purely authoritarian
practices of the past; the opening to Africans of many new opportunities for higher education; and, not least, the election to the
French National Assembly of a score of African deputies.

All this, if within narrow limits, established the legitimacy
of African politics. Colonial interests did their best to subvert this
legitimacy, but could only partially succeed thanks to the strength of
French left-wing sympathies. Anti-colonial politics, moreover, began
to win mass support. A vigorous populism became possible. While
African 'sections' of French parties such as the SFIO (Socialists)
remained little more than a means of mobilizing the assimilated few,
a party of a new type emerged in Ivory Coast. This was the Parti
Démocratique de la Côte d'Ivoire (PDCI).

Led by the formidable Félix Houphouët-Boigny, an
administrator as well as a wealthy planter and physician, the PDCI
campaigned against settler discrimination, colonial repression, and
administrative stagnation. Embarking in 1946 on a grass-roots'
campaign of political agitation, the PDCI had much success, and
became, with differences, the somewhat earlier equivalent of the
CPP in the Gold Coast next door.

*Gains associated especially with the Senegalese deputy, Lamine
Guèye.

In October 1946, inspired partly by the PDCI and partly by a new vision of unity and struggle, 800 African delegates of territorial parties and sections met at Bamako, capital of the Soudan (afterwards Mali), and formed the multi-territorial Rassemblement Démocratique Africain (RDA), by any measure the most important of the post-war movements in these French colonies. For the first time on any scale, African political opinion turned strongly against assimilation. A year later the veteran colonial minister, Albert Sarraut, might preside over the first session of the Assembly of the French Union with the benign assurance that a 'vast community' would now 'absorb the old configurations of the Empire within the new image of Union'. But this was not at all the opinion of the RDA and its sections.

They agreed with Pierre Cot, a prominent spokesman of the French left, when, six months before Sarraut's bromide, Cot had said that the new constitution of France 'must be a supple one, open to all choices of further development', and that 'the objective is independence.' Their founding documents are eloquent on that point. 'Rejecting assimilation,' declared the RDA at Bamako, 'we ask within the French Union for an association to which we freely consent, founded on an equality of rights and duties.'

Their deputies in the French National Assembly, being too few to form an independent group such as the business of that Assembly required, accordingly affiliated themselves to the very large group of deputies elected on the ticket of the French Communist Party. Their reason for so doing, of course, was not that they themselves were Communists – Houphouët himself, as his later politics would show, was resolutely a man of the right – but because the Communists, unlike any other French party, were prepared to give them necessary facilities without questioning their principles. Yet in 1947, with the 'cold war' becoming icy, the Communists were edged out of a coalition with the Socialists (SFIO) and Popular Republicans (MRP) whose leadership had moved from left to centre; and the RDA, together with the Communists, found themselves in permanent opposition.

This was matched by repression in Africa. In 1949 Governor Péchoux was instructed to destroy the PDCI in Ivory Coast and went about his work. Only a few dozen Africans were killed, very moderate for the Fourth Republic, but arrests went into hundreds. Other sections of the RDA fared variously, with some advances in Guinée but reverses elsewhere. The parties of compromise with assimilation, notably those affiliated to the SFIO or MRP or a new Gaullist party which had now become active, were content to temporize. Compared with 1946, the overall position was one of standstill.

In 1951 Houphouët-Boigny decided to strike a bargain with the then colonial minister, the Socialist François Mitterrand. In exchange for a prospect of internal autonomy he abandoned the RDA's parliamentary affiliation with the Communists, turned against those who, like the Soudanese Gabriel d'Arboussier, thought it better tactics to reject this move, and a year later entered the government of France as a minister of state. One may compare this compromise with that of the CPP and Nkrumah, in Gold Coast, with the British in the same year.

A second phase opened. Beginning with this mutual reconciliation between a powerful trend in African nationalism and the immediate demands of Paris, this second phase continued until 1958. These were the years immediately after French defeat in Vietnam, and the conceding of Moroccan and Tunisian independence. In West and Equatorial French Africa, two trends predominated. One, merely opportunist, was for an internal autonomy which could eventually become a separate territorial independence within the French Union or outside it. The other, very lively at the time but eventually defeated, was for the internal autonomy of all the territories, but within two autonomous federations, one of eight territories for West Africa, and another of four territories for Equatoria. These two federations might be inside the French Union or not, according to the way things should fall out.

The leaders of this second trend were the radicals of the RDA: its former secretary-general d'Arboussier (of mixed Soudanese origin); the trade unionist Sékou Touré, leader of the Parti Démocrate de Guinée (PDG); Djibo Bakary, leader of the Sawaba

(Freedom) Party of Niger (but affiliated to Léopold Senghor's inter-territorial alliance, the Parti du Regroupement Africain [PRA], not to the RDA); and Barthélemy Boganda in Oubangui-Chari (Central African Republic). These and others held that the transformation of the two colonial 'federations' into a dozen separate states, most of them financially crippled and politically feeble, was tantamount to an act of 'balkanization' from which the ex-colonial power must emerge as the principal beneficiary. To the concept now gaining ground in Paris, that twelve 'associated states' should be added individually to the French Republic, they opposed the idea of con-federation: of two African federations, West and Equatorial, joined with France on a footing of equality of rights, and big enough to make this claim effective.

They were defeated. In 1956 the Socialist Marius Moutet brought in an enabling law providing that a first instalment of power should be devolved to African governments in each of the twelve territories, leaving finance, law and order, and military and police affairs with the representatives of France. Against this the 'confederalists' argued in vain, and against them, too, the number of political Africans who now sensed gains immediately ahead became rapidly larger. In that direction Houphouët led the way. Ivory Coast was the best endowed of the twelve territories, and would have had to pay a relatively high contribution to the support of a 'confederal' solution. Houphouët could see no good reason for doing that.

But the enabling law's executive decrees required time for application, and in 1958 the Fourth Republic crashed into the gulf opened by its failures in Algeria. Taking power in a new Republic, the Fifth, de Gaulle initiated a third phase. This was brief but decisive. With the black African tide now running strongly for independence, de Gaulle set himself to ensure the future. In a characteristic ma-noeuvre, he offered a referendum designed to leap-frog the more radical leaders and leave them in isolation or bring them to heel. Each territory was offered a choice between two options: to 'as-sociate' with France, or to become fully independent. In the second case, however, all French assistance would be annulled.

A majority of territorial national leaders wished for the

second choice, but felt too weak to take it. Even those who did not feel too weak, notably Sékou Touré in Guinée and Djibo Bakary in Niger, again tried before crossing their Rubicon to win French agreement to a confederal solution. If de Gaulle would agree to that, then they would agree to enter the 'French Community' offered by de Gaulle to those who should reject independence. But de Gaulle would not agree.

Guinée accordingly voted 'no' to the French Community, which meant 'yes' to independence, by a huge and undoubtedly honest majority of some 95 per cent. But in Niger, where Sawaba had been unable to follow the PDG of Guinée in undermining the influence of pro-French chiefs or 'chiefs', and where French administration, for that reason, was able to deploy its secret funds to good effect, the vote for independence was officially a minority of 102,687 to 372,383, with 62 per cent of abstentions. Officially: one may speculate on the true figures. In the oasis region of Agadès, for example, the administration is said to have registered 30,000 voters among nomads who could be expected to vote as their chiefs directed them; but in that season of transhumance, comments Chaffard, 'apart from a few thousand urban electors, there cannot have been more than five or six thousand nomads in the constituency.'[30]

One out of twelve had been able to choose freedom, yet the outcome could only be provisional for the eleven which had not. Once a single territory had achieved independence, the rest were bound to follow. Paris was soon ready for this, having by now well identified its convenient successors and shown its teeth to those who, like Touré and Bakary, had proved inconvenient. In 1960, each of the remaining eleven became a separate nation-state. And with an average population of some three million people, each was fast held within the enclosure of the French financial and commercial system.

As in British Africa, this was victory for nationalism at a price. Yet the price was higher here because the emergent 'nations' were smaller, weaker, less capable of autonomous development. It would be overstating the truth to say that this was assimilation under another name, save perhaps in Senegal; but the emergent 'middle class' proved unusually subservient. One may characterize the

process of their accession to power by generalizing a comment of
Martin Staniland's about the Ivory Coast: decolonization here 'consisted of a bargain between a seriously weakened colonial autocracy
and the local "inheritance élite".'[31] The one withdrew its claim to
any further autocracy, the other its aspiration to any real sovereignty.

France had two other territories in a different category.
These were the UN trusteeships of Togo and Cameroun. Politics
in Togo shaped the same course as in the rest of French West Africa,
though ahead of its neighbours. Togo became an 'associated state' of
the French Union and achieved internal self-rule in 1958, acceding to
independence in 1960.

Cameroun also became independent in 1960, but against
the background of a dramatic and original political experience. This
arose within the duality of a nationalist campaign at grips both with
Paris and local settlers, and took its rise from a miniature repetition of
Algeria in 1945 and Madagascar in 1947. Out of that brusque contest
there emerged the first of tropical Africa's revolutionary nationalist
parties, and, opposing it, the stiffest of the early post-colonial dictatorships.

Pre-war calls for Camerounian independence were re-
doubled after 1945, drawing confidence from the Atlantic Charter
and the United Nations. Surely the era of 'trusteeships' could now be
ended? Paris did not think so, and was encouraged in not thinking
so by the reactionary vehemence of settlers, as well as by the convenient flippancy of old-style African politicos such as Prince Manga
Bell of Duala, an eccentric and indeed extraordinary figure whose
notions of the good life had been learned at the school of pages in
Potsdam, during the period of German Kamerun.

Bell's port-city of Duala was the scene of the first post-war
moves. Duala had much changed during the war, doubling in size
with the arrival of impoverished peasants. The number of European
residents in Cameroun had also increased in 1945 to about 4,000, half
of them inhabiting Duala. In September of that year African railway
workers at Duala struck for a better wage. The local Chamber of
Commerce, a settler stronghold much inflamed by rumours of

stronger action to come, was at once up in arms. Perhaps literally: the evidence suggests that these Europeans, already preparing to launch a strong political representation in Paris, had found a pretext for smashing the newly-formed trade unions.

What seems to have happened was that groups of African 'unemployed' drawn from recent rural migrants were provoked into attacking trade unionists, including those on strike. These disorders were at once enlarged by settlers armed with guns. In Richard Joseph's summary of these events, based on official or other testimony, 'what ensued as the whites roamed about Duala can only be described as a massacre.' A French administrator declared that these settlers shot 'natives, men, women and children, on sight', killing between sixty and eighty persons.[32]

Thus engaged in Duala and spreading elsewhere, mass protest soon found its embodiment in a nationalist party, the Union des Populations du Cameroun (UPC), founded in 1948 under trade unionist inspiration and led from the first by an ex-union organizer, Reuben Um Nyobé. Adhering at once to the RDA, then in its early radical phase, the UPC had unusually close links with the social struggle, being in this respect like one or two other sections of the RDA, notably the PDG in Guinée. Um Nyobé himself was one of the most remarkable of all the post-war personalities of African nationalism, and one of the very few who appears to have seen, from the start, that winning power could be only the easier half of the battle for a genuine emancipation. But he and the UPC faced unusually tough obstacles.

From 1948 until 1955 the UPC was able to conduct a legal campaign against increasing obstruction. Colonial administration went through the familiar manoeuvres of promoting convenient Africans, stonewalling at the United Nations and the rest, but was ready by 1954 for sterner measures. These were signalled by the arrival of Governor Pré, who, like Péchoux in Ivory Coast five years earlier, set about wrecking the chief force of popular nationalism. UPC meetings were banned and UPC leaders harassed; anti-UPC 'guerrillas' even began to molest local UPC committees. None of this sufficiently answering, the UPC was declared illegal.

Insurrection followed. How far Um Nyobé himself believed the moment for this well chosen is a question that may never be resolved, but there is at least some evidence that he thought it premature. As it was, he crossed his Rubicon and marched with unrelenting courage towards the formation of a revolutionary movement. Guerrilla units took shape in those southern areas where local loyalties especially favoured the UPC. There, in the forest, 'liberated zones' were established under the control of newly-formed village committees. Justice was applied by 'people's courts'. The administration of everyday life, from the registry of marriages to that of contracts and labour regulations, became the task of local executives. As the later history of nationalism would show, most clearly of all in the Portuguese colonies, all this betokened the rise of a modernizing movement of a new type, a nationalist movement based on mass participation rather than mass support, and, as such, the earliest of its kind.

The French proved too strong for it. They played two cards, each of them formidable. One was military repression against a movement not yet fully developed and bereft of outside aid. The other was the deployment in nationalist politics of convenient local allies, in this case drawn mostly from the Muslim north, where colonial power had absorbed autocratic sultanates. Fighting the UPC in the south, the French promoted these northern conservatives. In 1958 Um Nyobé was killed by a military patrol; and although the insurrection continued for years after that, it never managed to expand from the few zones in which it had begun. Meanwhile Cameroun moved to internal autonomy, and from there to a political independence under the lead of the man whom France had chosen, the northerner Ahmadu Ahidjo. The movement of mass participation had failed, and dictatorship took over.

24

FROM EAST TO SOUTH AFRICA: THE SETTLER FACTOR

Confronting nationalism, most of these territories displayed the duality of French Africa: colonial policy on one hand, local settlers on the other. The course of post-war African politics had to be far more difficult than in British West Africa.

There were two large exceptions, and a few partial ones. No white settlers of any political importance – no settlers, that is, of British origin – lived in the Anglo-Egyptian Sudan, while British rule here (the condominium with Egypt being a verbal formality) was concerned with little more than control of the upper reaches of the Nile Valley, considered as strategically necessary to British control of Egypt. Once British power evacuated Egypt, effectively in 1956, there was no sufficient reason for not leaving the Sudan. With a corresponding Egyptian renunciation of rights under the condominium, British evacuation occurred peacefully in 1956. The 'scaffolding' of administrative unity erected by a British rule modelled in some degree on practices in British India was then filled by Sudanese personnel; and government passed amiably into the hands of Sudanese notables who, together with those in the administration, formed the Sudanese political class. Rivalries within this class were for a while contained. The British Protectorate of Northern Somaliland similarly lost its strategic value to British imperial designs, and had much less commercial value than the Sudan. Again with no British settlers, it was evacuated without incident in 1960 and joined to the former Italian colony of Somalia.

The partial exceptions to the 'settler category' were Uganda, where a small community of British were never able to gain a dominant local influence, and Zanzibar, where the role of dominant white minority was played by a small Afro-Arab landowning group with strong ancestral attachments to southern Arabia. Besides these, three small territories in or around the periphery of South Africa were exempt from local settler control. These were the 'High Commission Territories' of Basutoland (Lesotho), Bechuana-land (Botswana), and Swaziland; in the last, however, white resi-dents from South Africa possessed land and exercised some influence.

Aside from South Africa, the settler minorities of largest influence and local power were in Kenya and Southern Rhodesia. Those of Kenya, nearly all of whom were British, while their spokesmen sometimes derived from the English aristocracy or upper class,* set the tone for less numerous and confident white minorities in Tanganyika and Uganda. Those of Southern Rhodesia, including many Afrikaners, tended to do the same for their fellows in Northern Rhodesia and Nyasaland.

All these minorities continued to believe that they lived in a sea of savagery; however small and dreary their own cultures,† the politics of nationalism could only be about themselves. 'We know what Native opinion is worth,' Leopold Moore had said of Northern Rhodesia in 1939: 'There is not one intelligent Native in this country. Their opinion is worth nothing at all.'[33] It remained the universal white conviction save for a handful of isolated liberals and several persecuted left-wingers. To have taken Africans seriously as people, after all, would have been to threaten the very basis of settler life, which was its claim on all land and labour that settlers might require.

'Native policy' was necessarily a form of paternalism. Most whites thought this should be stern and heavy-handed; a few argued for a little tolerance. One recalls the member of the Southern Rhodesia legislature who referred his colleagues, in a speech of 1944, to a book of 'political economy' where 'it was worked out ex-tremely well logically, that the finest thing for the backward races was a long term of benevolent serfdom': only to add, in sorrowing

---

*'Officers to Kenya, NCOs to Rhodesia' had become the emigrant password in the 1920s.

†See, for example, the 'Martha Quest' novels of Doris Lessing, or the parliamentary records of any of their legislative assemblies in any year.

reflection on the poverty of human nature, that in his view they had yet to progress far enough to make a benevolent serfdom possible. This being the unhappy case, a little charity could be sensible self-interest. 'I do not think,' he told his fellow legislators, 'that hon. members have any idea of the effect it will have on the efficiency of the natives if they are decently treated.'³⁴ But there was no curiosity, it seems, to find out what that effect might be.

Small wonder, then, that all ideas about useful political change came to be concentrated, among Africans, in the word freedom; and that the Swahili word for freedom, *uhuru*, or equivalents such as *kwacha* in other languages, should stand for whole programmes of national emancipation. Beyond that, many insights can be had from looking at the linguistic translations and transformations of modernizing political terms.³⁵ It says much for the formative atmosphere of East African nationalism, for example, that African politics should be regularly equated with in-built and unavoidable dissent. Among the Nyakusa, for example, it appears that the word 'politician' in these years was currently rendered as 'a man who works against the government'. In Swahili, again during the 1950s, African politics could be widely understood as 'the disturbance of local and central government by refusing to obey the law, pay poll tax ... (or) striking for higher wages'.³⁶ Generally, the larger languages had no difficulty in finding exact or effective equivalents. 'Seek ye first the political kingdom,' exhorted Nkrumah in 1957. *Utafuteni kwanza uhuru*, 'go first for freedom', echoed the Swahili slogan of a year later. Generally, there was no lack of facility in translation.

Leadership, as noted earlier, came from intermediate strata who were usually close to the multitudes. Colonial and settler bars on secondary or higher education (operated simply by not allocating funds), and on access to skilled jobs, meant that the relatively large Western-educated groups of British West Africa were absent here. The roots of nationalism accordingly stood deeply in the social struggle, as Harry Thuku's had done in the 1920s and others since; and the national struggle, for a long time, was only the frail flower that budded from those roots. The 'political kingdom' was *uhuru*, the freedom from injustice and oppression, far more than any raising of a national flag. So that the process of convergence noted in West Africa was displayed here by an initial unity of ideas and aims. Only with independence did this give way to a process of divergence as the few made good their power and privilege against the many.

Though the settlers were a violent lot, given to use of the 'strong hand' at the slightest provocation, African belief in the possibilities of peaceful change remained a dominant one: *siasi ni nguvu*, politics is not force. This was indeed the reverse of settler belief: for the settlers, politics precisely had to be force. How otherwise had they obtained their birthright, or conserved it? They proceeded on this belief until, in the end, they raised a counter-violence they could no longer contain.

In Kenya, all protest against the system was declared illegal in 1940. Leaders of the Kikuyu, Kamba and Teita groups, assembled round the Kikuyu Central Association (KCA) formed in the 1920s, were interned, while the persistent Mombasa trade unionists had been toughly handled a year before. The white minority seemed bound, now, to have things all their own way, provided only that their leaders could show skill and tolerance. But this was a condition emphasized still more strongly in the atmosphere of 1945. 'By the end of the war, and Kenyatta's return,' the Kenya nationalist Oginga Odinga would recall years later, 'large parts of the country were in a state of ferment. Land was still the issue. The KCA had never died ...'[37]

In spite of settler influence, colonial policy introduced a few cautious reforms. African politics became possible again. A Kenya African Union (KAU) emerged. It acquired a new leader in Jomo Kenyatta, veteran of the early 1930s who now came home after years in England. There he had studied anthropology and written a notable book, *Facing Mount Kenya*, practically unique in those years as an inside account of African ancestral institutions. But Kenyatta at once led into the strategy of nationalism, which he also thoroughly understood.

From now onwards a trial of strength between mass-supported nationalism and the white minority was in the making, but under a singular equivocation. There emerged a sense of all-Kenya nationalism, of freedom for many different peoples never previously organized to think of themselves as forming a unity of nationalities; but the driving control, more and more, was that of Kikuyu national-ism as a distinctive entity and force. This was partly because the Kikuyu formed the biggest nationality in Kenya. They had also undergone a more direct and painful expropriation of land and local freedom than other nationalities. Thirdly, their homeland included the expanding city of Nairobi, colonial and now industrial capital built on the long-standing hegemony interests exercised by Kenya's white minority over the whole of British East Africa. The Kikuyu had unusual access to the meaning of racist discrimination on one side, and to modernizing influences on the other.

This in-built trial of force might still have been a largely peaceful one. But the white leaders, now running hard for a complete sovereignty of their own nationality over the future nation, made sure that it was not. Their characteristic notion was that a continued repression of African political spokesmen would be sufficient to their purpose, since they took it for an obvious truth that these spokesmen were demagogues without a mass following or agents of a foreign power, most probably Moscow. Only cut down these rootless agitators, and the mob would quietly go home. When this proved wrong, and the peasants rebelled even after the imprisonment of all their foremost spokesmen, the whites looked round for other explanations and found almost any except the one they could not bring themselves to admit: that the peasants had rebelled because they found the system unbearably unjust.

Armed resistance took shape in despair of any peaceful evolution. Characteristically for colonial situations, it occurred precisely in zones of maximum discrimination: in Nairobi and the 'white highlands' of settler expropriation. The so-called 'Mau Mau' war which followed colonial declaration of emergency in October 1952 was long and grim. When it ended in October 1956, effectively with the capture of Dedan Kimathi, it had cost the British taxpayer £60 million with the commitment of some 50,000 troops and police, had killed some 10,000 Africans and impounded 90,000 others in concentration camps under sometimes appalling conditions, and by 1956 had forced 1,077,501 Kikuyu and Embu into 'designated villages' under strict security guard.* Formally defeated, the rebellion nonetheless put an end to any further prospect of settler rule.

'Mau Mau' has something of a place of its own along the spectrum of nationalist ideology. It was a modernizing movement in that these urban workers and peasants fought for national independence. But they had to do this without their nationalist leaders, all of whom were under arrest or in exile. Moreover, although Kenyatta and four others were duly sentenced in 1953 for organizing the rebellion, the balance of the evidence suggests that these and other leaders had no hand in promoting armed revolt. Their position seems rather to have been that of the Néo-Destourian leaders, of Tunisia, in the presence of peasant insurrection at the same moment in time: they could not denounce the insurrection without committing political suicide and to some extent they could welcome its pressures on the colonial power, but they wished neither to lead it nor to be in any way compromised by it. They wished only to profit from it.

With their leaders out of the running, thousands of Kikuyu took to the hills 'either to fight or to seek refuge from the terror spread about the countryside by Government forces' after the declaration of emergency. There, as four of Kenya's later spokesmen commented in 1966, these men and women 'had to fend for themselves, and create new cadres'.[38] They formed a 'Land and Freedom Army', created a 'Kenya Parliament', and, rather like the UPC in southern Cameroun, began to construct a new administration of their own. All this was done by men of small or no literacy, Karari Njama being apparently the only fully literate man among them.

By 1956 the British army was closing in on them. They held out under very harsh conditions, but gradually the modernizing elements gave way to a retreat into ancestral beliefs, and these, with the continuing pressures of violence, became increasingly self-

*Among the killed were some 30 whites and 1,700 Kikuyu 'loyalists'.

destructive. Disbandment followed defeat. But in a larger sense the rebellion had not failed, for it had proved to London that the old Kenya system must go. The settlers tried to obstruct progress, but their failure was greater than the failure of the rebellion. In 1960 a constitutional conference met in London. Addressing it, Colonial Secretary Iain Macleod explained that its object was to found 'a nation based on parliamentary institutions on the Westminster model, and enjoying responsible self-government'. Three years later, upon this model, a Kenya with majority rule became independent with Kenyatta as president. This Kenya would rapidly evolve an acute divergence between the few and the many. But the origins of this divergence, or some of them, may be dated to the non-participation of the nationalist leadership in the rebellion of 1952–6.

These events in Kenya ensured corresponding changes in the rest of British East Africa. Tanganyika and Uganda were equipped with the same model, achieving political independence respectively in 1961 and 1962. Each had produced mass-supported movements that now inherited power. Of these the most impressive was the Tanganyika African National Union (TANU) formed in 1954 under the leadership of a far-seeing thinker, Julius Nyerere, with its origins in the cultural associations of the pre-war period. The neighbouring island of Zanzibar (with Pemba) became independent in 1963, and was almost at once the scene of a widely popular revolt against its small Afro-Arab landowning group. A union between Tanganyika and Zanzibar, each retaining its autonomy, was made in 1964; the resultant amalgam was named Tanzania.

In central-southern Africa the settler minorities seemed for a long time after 1945 to have everything going for them. In fact, as a later history would show, they had already made the wrong decisions from their own standpoint. In 1923 the Southern Rhodesian minority, then totalling some 34,000, had voted by 8,774 to 5,998 to become a self-governing British colony rather than join South Africa as a province of that country, although it is also true that South Africa did not want to have them. This vote ensured them full power in Southern Rhodesia, and it came to be assumed that this must always continue. In 1924 the Northern Rhodesian settlers voted by 1,414 to 317 against amalgamating their territory with Southern Rhodesia; they too believed that they were bound to do better on their own.

Opinions changed in the 1930s, partly because British imperial policy held out no hope of an eventual sovereignty for a settler-run Northern Rhodesia or Nyasaland, and partly because dominant mining interests now saw advantage in amalgamation. A pre-war campaign for territorial amalgamation failed to win results in 1939, however; and the world war stopped further agitation. This began again after 1945 and was crowned with success in 1953, when London agreed to a Central African Federation composed of the three territories, but with the Colonial Office continuing to run Northern Rhodesia and Nyasaland. The British aim, or at least that of the ruling Conservative Party and the Colonial Office, was to give this settler-dominated Federation full independence as a Dominion; and the settlers, mistakenly once more, believed that this was what would happen.

African opinion watched with growing distrust and dissent. Loosely organized 'congress' type movements took shape from the 'pre-nationalist' stirrings of the 1930s. As in East Africa, these were led by men who were close to the interests of the masses. Looking for effective strategies, they learned what lessons were available, and were helped in this by a handful of white radicals, prominent among whom in Northern Rhodesia was the civil engineer Simon Zukas, and, a little later, the ex-administrator Thomas Fox Pitt. The early 1950s saw the emergence of a determined leadership composed of men such as Kenneth Kaunda in Northern Rhodesia and Chipembere and Chiume in Nyasaland, while Nyasaland nationalism also had the considerable benefit, in London, of the physician (and later president) Hastings Kamuzu Banda. They had a hard time; but those in Southern Rhodesia, living under uninhibited settler rule, had a harder one.

These new leaders, gathering mass support, made progress in the two northern colonies. They found, as had others elsewhere, a friendship and support in radical circles in Britain, including a small but formidable fraction of the British Labour Party. Gradually, too, they found an audience among a number of Conservatives who, learning from the experience of settler intransigence in Kenya, now began to think, with Colonial Secretary Macleod, that the wisdom of the future advised large allowances for an African progress acceptable to British interests. Various pressures brought success, including a new Conservative preoccupation with advancing Britain's position in Europe rather than in 'the empire', although this success was not achieved easily or without phases of repression and counter-attack. But moving along a constitutional road now opened by London, the Malawi African National Congress achieved independence for Nyasaland in 1964, while its corresponding movement in Northern Rhodesia achieved independence for Zambia a few months later.

The goose of Central African Federation had continued to cackle, but was cooked as soon as its two northern territories were clearly on their way to independence. The settler-controlled Federation necessarily collapsed. This came about in 1963 with the secession of Nyasaland under Banda's energetic control. There remained Southern Rhodesia, governed at all points since 1923 by its settler minority: if on a different and in some respects less rigorous pattern than South Africa's, segregation and discrimination ruled in all fields of life.

From the Union in 1910 until 1948, South Africa was ruled by a succession of all-white governments pledged to legal and customary discrimination against Africans and Asians, and in slightly less degree against the Coloured (mixed origin) community of the Cape. Building this discrimination on the Land Act of 1913 and other laws of expropriation, these governments were usually dominated by the English-speaking minority, and often led by the veteran Afrikaner statesman, Jan Smuts. They retained some tincture, notably in the judiciary, of the old 'Cape liberalism' of British colonial times.

Commercial and industrial interests, chiefly in English-speaking hands, began to argue after 1945 that there might be some ground for easing the more acute forms of discrimination. Their capitalism, flourishing on extremely cheap African labour and on inflows of British capital attracted by consequently high dividends, had more than doubled its manufacturing output during the Second World War. It should continue to do so, but there might now be a case for raising the level of colour bars so as to ensure more skilled workers. At the same time a number of official inquiries confirmed what all critics had long since known, and did so in very convincing detail: South Africa was a country of gross injustice and crushing non-white poverty.

Tentative though they were, all ideas of minimal reform were swept from the scene in 1948, when a general election handed government to the extreme racist Afrikaner National Party under D. F. Malan.* His party came to power on a programme which supposed that the logic of the 'separate development' of the Smuts era should be carried to its end. This was *apartheid*, which called for the eventually complete physical separation of white and non-white communities, and more practically, meanwhile, for a much more severe apparatus of legal and customary discrimination. Following this programme, South Africa during the 1950s became a state of rigid Afrikaner dictatorship with no concern for appearances. Colour bars were reinforced, pass laws multiplied, punishments for infringement made still harsher (so that, on average during the 1950s, about one-tenth of the whole African population passed every year through imprisonment). Forms of slave labour reappeared in the countryside. All types of organizational self-defence among urban Africans were stamped out of existence.

With no support from the white community, save from members of a small and much harassed Communist Party and a few stray liberals – since the English-speaking United Party, though disliking parliamentary opposition, found *apartheid* only a sharper but quite acceptable version of the system it had itself installed – the non-white organizations responded as they could. Their legal attempts at resisting the gangrene of *apartheid* culminated in 1952 with a passive 'defiance campaign against unjust laws'. This united the African National Congress with the Indian National Congress and with

*More correctly, this was the Purified National Party formed by a pre-war breakaway from the 'old Nationalists'.

representatives of the Coloured community and achieved mass support, only to be crushed by new draconian laws and penalties.

From then onward there was nothing left for the non-white organizations, many of them now illegal, save quiescence or revolt. But with the ratio of whites to non-whites standing overall at about one to five, and with the whites in possession of an over-whelming police power and will to use it, revolt was hard to organize and harder still to begin. Provoked by an iron repression, revolt nonetheless occurred repeatedly in the stricken countryside: for example, at Marico in 1957, then in Sekukuneland and Zululand, and, most impressively and stubbornly, in the Transkei during 1960. All these risings, big or small, were smashed by troops and police, and with no redress of grievances.

In the cities, meanwhile, tensions among Africans sharpened into the demoralization of drugs and violent crime, or a host of acts of reasonable defiance which ended in shooting by the police. The most dramatic of these assaults occurred at Sharpeville, in 1960, when police shot into a peaceful crowd of protesters, killing sixty-seven and wounding 180, most of whom, characteristically, were hit in the back while running away. Noticed throughout the world, this little massacre shook the confidence of foreign investors for a while. But these soon recovered, and were now joined by many more, often now from the United States. Feeling itself in full command at home, its economy in the midst of a new boom, its gold more valuable than ever, white South Africa now began to see its future as the domina-ting influence throughout the sub-continent from the Cape to the Congo.

Yet clandestine attempts continued to be made by radicals, mostly black but some white, to plan for an armed resistance which could challenge this unrelenting system. They were repeatedly be-trayed by informers, notably at Rivonia in 1963, when the most determined of their leaders, including Nelson Mandela and Bram Fischer, were tracked down and jailed for life. The further organ-ization of resistance was then transferred abroad to Tanzania and some other African countries. There, through the rest of the 1960s, men were trained in irregular warfare, and efforts made to infiltrate them into South Africa. But the fate of these attempts showed that only a major shift in African opinion within the country, betokening a new will to resist no matter what the cost, would now be able to influence the future. That shift, as we shall see, would not appear until the middle of the 1970s.

25

IN THE LESSER EMPIRES

Though modelled on the dictatorships of Mussolini in Italy and Hitler in Germany, the régimes of Salazar in Portugal and Franco in Spain were unable to do much for their patrons during the Second World War. Their geographical positions made them far too vulnerable to reprisals from the Western Allies although Franco, being in this respect somewhat better off than Salazar, sent a division of his army to fight with the Germans in their invasion of the USSR. In return for this neutrality, very partial though it was, they conserved their empires. Belgium conserved hers, of course, since she was a victim of German invasion. A defeated Italy forfeited her colonies.

Ethiopia's deliverance was assured in 1941 by a British army with a considerable African component, and this did rather more than reinstal the pre-1935 situation. The restored emperor Haile Selassie and the system of patronage and clientism on which his empire rested were able to strengthen their earlier positions; and in certain important ways the years after 1945 saw a completion of the centralizing controls initiated under Menelik late in the nineteenth century. Though in theory a modernizing autocracy, Ethiopia was based more firmly than before on its 'traditional' foundations.

Thanks to bargaining between the victorious powers, this empire retained the Ogaden in spite of its clearly Somali character, and regained Eritrea (hitherto an Italian colony) as a federated state and then, in 1962, as a subjected province. With substantial finance and technical aid from abroad, increasingly from the USA, the system was able to absorb its internal conflicts until early in the 1970s. There were many small rebellions and one attempted *coup* against the emperor, while the students of Addis Ababa University nourished a continuing trend of radical thought; but there was no political development until 1974, when a revolutionary process began.[39]

Libya came under British and French military occupation, soon with the addition of a major US airbase; and its future was settled only after a bewildering series of great-power manoeuvres, chiefly between the Western powers as a group and the USSR now striving for influence in the African arena. Independence was granted in 1951 to a régime of contained rivalry between the Sanusi hierarchy headed by King Idris and an urban nationalism led by intermediate strata in the towns. The instability inherent to this compromise between the 'traditional' and the 'modernizing' elements in Libyan nationalism became acute after 1955, when oil was found in large quantities, and was partially resolved by the removal of the kingship in 1969, at which point power was taken by young officers under Mu'ammar Gadafi. Though populist in nature, this régime developed features aiming at democratization after 1975.

Modern Somali nationalism began in 1943 with the foundation of the Somali Youth League. This looked back to the early Somali states of the fifteenth century; drew inspiration from the state-forming ideas of the anti-colonial hero, Sayid Mohamed Abdille Hasan (d. 1920); and aspired to the unification of the five Somali segments split between the Italian colony of Somalia, British Somaliland, French Djibouti, the Ogaden in Ethiopia, and the British-held Northern Frontier Territory adjacent to Kenya, all containing a total of perhaps four million people in 1945.

Somali unification was all the more logical and desirable in that Somalis formed the entire, or almost the entire, population of all these territories save in Djibouti, which they shared with Afars, a closely related people. A British proposal to the Peace Conference of 1946 made unification momentarily attainable. This would have assembled the four major segments (but not Djibouti) under a British trusteeship with an eventual prospect of independence within the British Commonwealth. The proposal failed chiefly through Soviet objection, entered on the grounds that the Western Powers would not assent to a Soviet trusteeship over Libya. The Somali nation had to remain geographically divided as before.

The Italians also asked for trusteeship over Libya. Denied this, they were compensated with a ten-year trusteeship over their former colony of Somalia, beginning in 1950. Partial unification of the Somalis came in 1960, when British Somaliland was added to Somalia and both formed an independent republic. In July of that year the leader of the Somali Youth League, Ali Shirmake, became his country's first prime minister. He had just taken an Italian degree in political science; but if philosophers ought to be kings, it soon emerged that political scientists might have less to be said for them.

The Belgian Congo had stayed with Belgium and, as we have seen, provided a gruelling 'war effort' in forced labour or its virtual equivalent. With some relaxations of severity but no change in pattern, this 'effort' continued after 1945. It was criticized by Belgian radicals, and also by others. 'We are developing the economy of the Congo,' a prominent Catholic expert told the Royal Colonial Institute in 1951, 'to the detriment of its peoples. We must put a brake on the appetite for gain.'[40] No brake was applied. A highly centralized administration, accustomed to regard Africans as 'adult children', marched firmly with a narrowly monopolist system of economic extraction: by the middle 50s, 3.17 per cent of employers had 51.15 per cent of the wage-earning labour force. All seemed 'well in hand'. As late as 1955 a much-publicized unofficial forecast suggested that Congolese independence could be fixed for 1985. Predominant Belgian opinion thought this daring if not utopian.

The development of modernizing political strategies proved extremely difficult in circumstances which debarred all Africans from any experience outside the Congo, or even, with a few small Protestant exceptions, to any education outside the strictly paternalist teachings of Catholic missionary schools; and in this respect the African situation was worse even than that of the Portuguese colonies. After 1948, a system of 'civic merit cards' provided that every Congolese over twenty-one could show 'by his good conduct and habits that he sincerely desires to attain a more advanced degree of civilization': of assimilation, that is, to Belgian culture and colonial values. This was useful as an opening to small-scale privilege and could help towards some understanding of comparative realities; but the scope was very small. Writing in 1957, the future nationalist leader Patrice Lumumba claimed that only 884 such cards had been issued by the end of 1955.[41] Law and order, meanwhile, was in the hands of a *Force Publique* long utilized for 'pacification'; but even within this body of African mercenaries the officers, by 1960, included no Africans. Self-help and cultural associations were permitted for the first time in 1955, but were tied closely to colonial leading strings.

While nationalism remained little more than a slogan meaningful to very few, mass protest within ancestral charters possessed a vivid and continuing history from the earliest days of the Leopoldian adventure. The many nationalities of the Congo Basin had long striven to defend their interests within the ideology of those charters or, after about 1920, increasingly by a synthesis of these with millennial and other Christian reinterpretations. It was therefore natural that the strategy of nationalism, promoted in the 1950s by primary school-masters, administrative clerks, small traders and their like, should become grafted into 'traditional' systems of thought and loyalty. The notion of a Congolese nation might be a chimera, but the notion soon won ground that a coalition of nationalities, organized in as many parties or movements and dubbed 'a nation', could possibly push for substantial gains against the colonial system. This was an advance, although, as events would show, one within narrow limits.

The going proved rough. But early in 1959 the Belgians suddenly shifted their ground. The proximate cause was a serious clash in the colonial capital, Léopoldville (Kinshasa). Police and *Force Publique* opened fire on angry crowds, killing forty-nine and wounding others. Accustomed to thinking of Congolese disturbances as no more than muffled noises in the bush, barely heard and soon suppressed, home opinion was sorely disturbed. But the probably decisive motive in Belgium's shift of policy was of another order. It appears that Brussels now calculated that a very rapid transfer of political power to inexperienced men and conflicting parties could be the best way of prolonging the underlying colonial structure for a long time ahead.

Brussels now behaved, at any rate, as though it believed this. Almost at once the Belgian government offered a more or less immediate independence. There followed a year of confused and mounting agitation by a cluster of groupings, most of them based on as many different nationalities or regional loyalties. These achieved a unity of tactics sufficient to demand an African government qualified to declare independence, if it wished, by January 1961. Brussels replied by advancing the date. In January 1960 a constitutional conference ended with an agreement on independence in the following June.

Independence came, and, as tension after tension erupted through the frailties of a régime without unity or roots, chaos came with it. Only one political movement now showed itself as possessing the vocation and the actual or potential support, rising above the rival leaderships of regions or nationalities, that could be capable of welding a Congolese national framework. This was the *Mouvement National* led by Lumumba. Becoming Prime Minister, Lumumba strove to find and keep his feet in a rising tumult of contention and violence, the latter set going by a mutiny of the rank and file of the *Force Publique*. But his rivals and his enemies, whether foreign or domestic, proved too much for him.

On the day of independence, for example, the civil service on which Lumumba and his government had to rely consisted of 9,801 Belgians and 11,803 Africans. Of the latter, 11,000 were barely literate clerks in grade five, while 800 were in grade four; of the remaining three persons, none was in grade one. Many of the Belgian officials at once went home to Europe, while most of those who stayed were unwilling or unable to transfer their skills, let alone explain their files.* Even if they had remained and loyally served the new state, disintegration was unavoidable. The mineral-rich Katanga province seceded under Moise Tshombe on 1 July and the South Kasai under Albert Kalondji on 8 August.

Lumumba as prime minister and Kasavubu as president

*It appears that Brussels advised Belgian officials in Katanga to stay put, secession there being on the way, while the rest were told that it would be first come first served in the rush to find new jobs in Belgium.

asked for UN military and other aid against the secessionists, chiefly those of Katanga. This arrived in a number of contingents, including units from Ghana, Nigeria and Ethiopia, but with highly equivocal results. For by now the prize of dominant influence over these vast and immensely rich regions had become an international interest, with the USA leading the game. Finding that the UN was content merely to hold the ring, Lumumba proceeded to ask for aid from the USSR and other countries in the Soviet bloc. He was at once labelled as a Communist, and in September the central government was seized by a young US protégé, Joseph Mobutu. Antoine Gizenga, loyal to Lumumba, reacted by forming a separate government at Stanleyville (Lubumbashi). In December Lumumba attempted to reach Stanleyville but was seized on the way by Mobutu and in January 1961 sent to the secessionists in Katanga, who at once murdered him. Years of instability and violence were to follow.

The Belgians left their trusteeship territory of Ruanda-Urundi, lying along the eastern flank of the Congo, with other in-built tensions. Consisting of two historically separate kingdoms, Ruanda-Urundi became the independent states of Rwanda and Burundi in 1962. In each, colonial rule had confirmed by forms of indirect administration the generally exploitative domination of a Tutsi minority, of about fifteen per cent, over a Hutu majority of about eighty-four per cent, the remaining one per cent being Twa (Pygmies). Independence enabled the Hutu majority in Rwanda to end their inferiority by primarily peaceful means; and the outcome, though here and there with regional violence, proved relatively stable. In Burundi, making an eventually fearful contrast, the Hutu were unable after independence to gain headway against Tutsi rule, and worsened their position by ill-judged attempts at doing so. In 1972 a Hutu insurrection of great violence was followed by a Tutsi war of Hutu extermination. It appears that some 80,000 Hutu, or even more, were killed within a few weeks. Nationalism had resolved nothing here, save by death.

In 1945 there were about fourteen million Africans in the Portuguese colonies of Angola, Guinea-Bissau, Mozambique and

São Tomé with Principe, as well as about a quarter of a million in the quasi-colonial Cape Verde Islands.* Though with a numerically tiny exception for assimilated persons (see below), all were subject to a régime of *indígenato* ('native status') applied by a particularly backward colonial system. Suffocatingly provincial in its cultural fascism, this system was reinforced by a notably primitive form of Catholic missionary control over such education as there was. This was little. A sociological investigation as late as 1970–71, in those parts of Angola then little touched by the politics of liberation,† found in their samples that only 22.7 per cent of family-heads in zones of cultivation could name the country's capital, and only 5.9 per cent in stock-raising zones. Asked 'What is Lisbon?', those who knew the right answer were respectively 9 and 1.7 per cent.[42] Save for a small fraction living in towns, 'Portugal's wards' remained within their own cultures, or within what survived of these, and far outside the boundaries of modernizing protest.

Two factors opened a breach to the outside world. One derived from the Portuguese claim not to apply a racist policy. The claim was a singularly feeble one. In principle, Africans could 'enter Portuguese civilization' by assimilation. By 1950, according to the official census of that year, the proportion of *assimilados* to the whole population of Angola was 0.75 per cent; less even than this in Mozambique; and less again in Guinea-Bissau.‡ Yet these small

*The inhabitants of the Cape Verdes were not subject to the regime of *indígenato*; formally, they were all Portuguese citizens. In practice, however, they were subject to a colonial discrimination little different from that applied to the inhabitants of the mainland territories.

†See Chapter 30.

‡The exact 1950 figures for Angola were 30,089 *assimilados* in a total population of 4,036,687, and for Mozambique 4,349 *assimilados* in a total population of 5,731,317; no exact figure was given for Guinea-Bissau, but the proportion of *assimilados* there appears to have been about 0.3 per cent. And while it is true that the number of non-whites living in the equivalent of assimilated status was larger than the number who had registered for that status, it is also true that a notable proportion of all *assimilados* had a white father, who could often ease the full force of discrimination. The number of *assimilados* of purely African origin was certainly far smaller than the registered totals.

assimilated groups were important in the development of political ideas.

A handful of them, greatly privileged, could enter colonial secondary schools established for white settlers' children, and a handful of this handful could reach university in Portugal. Among the latter, after 1945, were the later leader of the Angolan liberation movement, Agostinho Neto, who became a physician in the intervals of political imprisonment, and the Guinea-Bissau leader, Amílcar Cabral, who became an agronomist. Their numbers were a little enlarged by Cape Verdian students in Portugal, including the later veteran of the liberation war and Cape Verdian prime minister, Pedro Pires. Here in Portugal they lived in contact with Portuguese democrats, some of them communists and others not, who worked clandestinely for an end to the dictatorship, and who opposed Portuguese colonialism. From these experiences they derived the strongly radical, analytical and marxist strand of thought in the movements of liberation which the best of them were afterwards to lead. It is probably right to say that a practical and effective marxism appeared in Africa primarily and even initially through them.

A second factor breached the 'wall of silence' round these colonies. This had its origin in *assimilados* living in the colonies but in contact there with Portuguese radicals, notably in Angola. Their realism led these young men and women, like their companions in Lisbon, to see that they must somehow overcome the wide distance that divided them, as the pioneers of nationalism, from the multitudes whom José de Fontes Pereira and the 'men of the '90s' had long before dismissed as the 'brutish blacks' of the bush. Viriato da Cruz in Luanda (Angola), and others in Lourenço Marques (Maputo, Mozambique) were among those who now argued that their duty was to 'discover' their own countries, their own peoples, and in this way overcome their own alienation. They reversed the old Transatlantic prescription, that civilization must come from outside Africa, and displaced it by a programme, at first a very imprecise one, that accepted Africa's own civilization but would act to modernize it.

When the two strands of thought began to come together, around 1955, tentative nationalist movements took shape. The beginning here was in Bissau, of course secretly, with the foundation in September 1956 of the African Party for the Independence of Guiné and Cape Verde (PAIGC) by six men under the lead of Amílcar Cabral. The People's Movement of Angolan Liberation (MPLA), again with Cabral's initial membership, followed in December. A similar trend, not yet crystallized into a nationalist movement, emerged in Mozambique. These were insignificant groupings as yet, but they held the future in their hands.

Alarmed by political changes in colonies next door to their own, the agents of the Salazar régime struck back by strengthening their repression. This became severe in 1958, severer still in 1959, worse again in 1960. Nationalist militants who remained alive or out of prison faced an unavoidable choice. All concessions being refused, they could subside and shut up ; or they could prepare to fight.

Little needs to be said about the politics of the Spanish colonies in this period. Their populations in the Western Sahara and equatorial Guinea (the mainland enclave of Rio Muni with the island of Fernando Poo) were small or very sparse. Their development into modern politics began in the 1950s but remained largely for the future.

PART

BUT WHOSE NATION?
THE SEARCH RENEWED

Pó seco, tudo tarda que tarda dentro de iago, icata bida lagato.

Leave a log in the water as long as you like: it'll never be a crocodile.

Peasant opinion, Guinea-Bissau, traditional

And other spirits there are standing apart
Upon the forehead of the age to come;
These, these will give the world another heart,
And other pulses. Hear ye not the hum
Of mighty workings?
Listen awhile, ye nations, and be dumb.

John Keats, 1817

THE GAINS OF INDEPENDENCE

'This idea of a Gold Coast nation,' opined an editorialist of the *Gold Coast Leader* as long before its proclamation as 1928, 'is a fundamental one.' Looking round the scene of their successes as these came one by one to hand, the nationalists found powerful reasons to agree. The successes were obviously not complete, but who had thought they could be? With whatever reservations, the strategy of nationalism on the accepted model had proved its unique value. Hurried along by the currents of ten or fifteen years of hazardous campaigning, those nationalists who were still living had managed to keep their heads above water, and were swimming hard. If they had entered nothing like heaven, the political kingdom so long denied them was theirs at last. For quite a few, it was much even to have survived. For most, it was good to be alive.

The coming of independence could in those days seem a climactic moment dividing the past from an altogether different future when all things would be possible. For this optimism there was an all-pervasive reason, a psychological fact that was surely a large historical fact. Hidden away in the mesh of interwoven interests among administrative files now partially open to inspection, controls were still retained by the withdrawing colonial powers. But the most blatant control was gone or could now be removed. This was the rule that all things must be ordered as though whites were naturally and inherently superior to blacks: the cultural bludgeon of colonial government. Now the bludgeon had no local hand to wield it,[1] and with this there came a profound sense of cultural rebirth.

Different groups arrived at their emancipation with varying enthusiasm. Some were tired, asking only for the comforts of the promised land, thinking that 'independence meant the end of the struggle', as Oginga Odinga said about nationalist supporters in Kenya in 1963, and that 'all would now be in order'.[2] Others suspected that the destination they had reached was not the one they had set out to find, and were at once for pressing further; but they were few. Most were well enough content, sensing that the future must in some way or other be better than the past.

Cries of excitement varied in strength and sincerity, but the overall impression one retains of those sunsets when the imperial flags came down, and the banners of nationhood climbed to mast-heads lit with flares and fireworks, stays firm and clear. Independence spelt renewal, the flinging down of racist barriers, the fraught emotion of swaying crowds, dancing, drumming, for whom their own ideas, beliefs, and abilities could now be clothed in a new respect and value.

This may be seen as the chief achievement of the 'political classes'. They had asserted the right of Africans to stand level with other peoples in all ways cultural or psychological. They had struck down the old spectre of a 'natural' inferiority, and banished the haunting fear that racist teachings, so grimly argued over so many decades, might after all contain a truth. Such cultural enlargements are never simple or immediate; but the first step was taken, the doorway to equality was open. There came the beginnings of a major development in the thinking of Africans, or at least of literate Africans, about their continent and its humanity in the scale of world achievement. There came a vivid consciousness of having grasped destiny by the hand so that Africa's history could begin again.

Other feelings soon appeared among the multitudes; not at first, however. Peasants might retain a rural scepticism, wage-workers note that pay levels stayed as before, minor chiefs question if the nation-state could possibly serve their interests as well as the colonial state (nearly all major chiefs had long been sure that it could not). But these tended to be second thoughts, and it is likely that the great majority shared to some extent in the joy of the nationalists. New songs, new dances, new cultural societies, new festivals sprang into being. The radio bulletins became exciting, interesting, even personally important; so did the gossip from the capital, the political talk on the veranda. Everyday life gave fresh dimensions to itself.

The literate, especially the writers, began to speak in voices of their own. Many of them, one feels, shared the perceptions of a poem of 1957 – broadcast, characteristically, on his country's new national radio – by the Ghanaian Albert Kayper Mensah:

> ... And as I walked, I saw a Lazarus
> Emerge from a tomb, his dead-clothes o'er his shoulder.
> His powerful body freed from bandages,
> A rising flame of life, from the night of death.
> Uncertain yet how long the ravages,
> The germs, and the million killing ways of earth
> Will spare his new-found Life, his radiant grace.
> And as he walked past me, I saw my face.[3]

The tone might be apocalyptic, but so were the times. There were many initiatives, new explorations, responses to cultural challenge. Novelists appeared, even if there were few at home to read them; but now as never before they could reach out to a wide audience, an international audience. With a sometimes brilliant talent, they set about doing this from Somalia to Senegal and from Nigeria to Kenya. Dramatists and cinéastes, radio playwrights and producers, all these made their bow; while poets and calypsonians struck out themes of cultural release. African publishing took a little longer to appear, yet now, at least, great European houses dropped their concentration on the white market in Africa and began, from early in the 1960s, to serve the black.[4]

Literacy and book-learning being the key to modernization, all the nationalist movements had called for more and better education. In settler colonies the need was almost total, whether to supply institutions of post-primary schooling or (but this was a universal need) to decolonize the content of what was taught. Even in Nigeria, where some secondary schools and a higher college of education had long existed, colonial racism had frowned on any plan to produce 'intellectuals', and denied senior postings even to those who had gone to Britain for the 'golden fleece' of a university degree, and duly come back with it. To maintain the white man's control it had been vital to maintain the white man's prestige, and so the education of the black man, Ade Ajayi has said, had to be controlled 'not only through the prejudices of the white teacher and the white text-book author, but also sometimes by actual directives of the administrations in laws said to be designed for the interests of the black man'.[5]

Nigeria, like some other relatively favoured colonies, was fortunate in having a basis for higher education. Its university college of Ibadan had produced 190 first degrees in 1948–9 when the college achieved the status of a university; forty of these were in the arts, twenty-nine in medicine, 121 in science. Independence brought expansion. In 1958–9 the Ibadan total rose to 1,005 degrees. With higher degrees now added, and including diplomas comparable to first degrees, the total in 1968–9 stood at 3,661, and other Nigerian universities were now in the field. Few of the new states could do half as well. But all began trying to catch up, and the production of 'high-level manpower' became a large priority. Senior bureaucracies could expand, and educational modernization reach into new disciplines. This enlargement went right down the scale to the primary level, and now with many decolonized textbooks.

The cultural gains of independence had a wider impact. Undermined in Africa, the mythologies of 'natural white superiority' were weakened even in Europe and America where they had first appeared. New antidotes were applied to old racist poisons, whose virulence was challenged by a growing body of scientific reassessment. Until now there had been little effort to question the tradition of Hegel's famous lectures of 1830–31, affirming that the Negro exhibited 'the natural man in his completely wild and untamed state', and that Africa was 'no historical part of the world', being able to show 'neither movement nor development'. Now this changed.

The study of Africa became a serious discipline in many universities: better still, a dozen disciplines, whether of history, archaeology, linguistics, sociology, politics, music, or the natural sciences. With a good tradition of social anthropology to back them, British historians had given a lead in the 1950s; now this was followed rapidly in the United States, France, the USSR, and elsewhere. All this helped to open doors for escape from racist enclosures. By as early as 1967, only a decade after the first tropical independence, Europe and North America had some three or four dozen universities where African history was being regularly taught. Research students preparing for university posts in one or other aspect of African culture were being enrolled from countries as remote from Africa as Canada and India, Japan and Uzbekistan, while many more were in similar preparation in African universities. 'If we include those now in training,' Roland Oliver estimated for that same year of 1967 in respect only of African history and closely related disciplines such as archaeology, 'there must today be getting on for a thousand people around the world who are actively engaged in extending the frontiers of knowledge in one or another part of this subject.'[6] In the wake of Africa's political independence the world probably acquired more accurate and detailed knowledge of Africa in ten years than in all preceding time. This enlightenment had its liberating feed-back into the more general ideas of daily life.

The kind of thinking that emerged in the 1960s was not yet capable in a systematic way of questioning the accepted structures of the nation-state in Africa, nor was there, at least until after 1965, any sufficiently pressing reasons for doing so; that would be the task of the 1970s. On the contrary, the model in its educational dimensions greatly discouraged this sort of scepticism. Gains in this field were achieved at the cost of a severely élitist ideology and practice, and of a timid orthodoxy always concerned to stultify any critique of 'established Western values', especially if this should come from the left, and above all if it should be marxist. Yet these gains were still a useful springboard for further advance.

Whatever doubts were present, it was everywhere accepted that real progress could be made only when Africans had regained political responsibility. For this elementary need, no price could then appear excessive. If there was little questioning of the underlying assumptions of this independence, this was more than élitist orthodoxy: it was also that acceptance of these assumptions had proved to be the only way ahead. Doubts were therefore marginal. For this was a tide that must be taken at the flood, or else leave those who would not travel on it beached in impotence and isolation.

Running fast, the tide carried men to places hitherto unthinkable. Prime Ministers in ex-British territories joined their colleagues from the old world and the new in Commonwealth conferences which at least displayed a new equality accepted by all. Others in ex-French territories were received in Paris with a blandishment and blare of trumpets which, whatever they really signified, still had their value in this forging of the necessary international symbols of a manifest equality. The United Nations welcomed a panoply of African spokesmen whose arrival had been barely so much as guessed at by the optimistic when the UN was founded.

Political Africa became an integral part of the forum of world affairs, and even now, while dozens of sovereign and often extremely separated states were taking shape, there were some contrary gestures towards the Pan-African unity which had fired the vision of the Transatlantic prophets long before. Nkrumah had led the way, in April 1958, with the assembling at Accra of the heads of state of the eight countries then independent; and out of this and other such initiatives there eventually came, in 1963, an Organization of African Unity (OAU) for all the new states. Being an organization only of governments or rather of heads of state and nominees, the OAU necessarily became a lesser United Nations, and could never begin to realize the more euphoric aims, written into its charter, of governing Africa with a single legislature, executive and so on.* But this minimal OAU was still much better than nothing; and the gains, once more, proved larger than the institutional price that had to be paid for them.

Heads of state or their deputies met periodically for policy reviews. These meetings soon declined into verbal futility and presidential bombast, while the very real differences of policy that now existed between groups of these states made it hard or impossible to get anything done. Yet there evolved a principle of common

*The point was well put at the time by H. M. Basner in the *Ghanaian Times* of 30 May 1963: 'Thirty-one signatures on a piece of paper cannot unite a continent . . . The inspiration and organisation means provided by [the OAU Charter] will become a reality only if the masses of Africa are mobilised into action.' An outstanding South African radical, Basner died in exile in 1977.

attitude, and sometimes even of common action, never conceivable before. The OAU secured a wide agreement on certain basic issues concerned with organic cooperation, with the further decolonization of the continent, and with the settlement of inter-state disputes. Even by 1970 the list of frontier conflicts resolved by OAU mediation was a useful one. Such settlements were seldom definitive because they could not be; the states and their international attachments saw to that. But they oiled the wheels of an abrasive post-colonial diplomacy, reduced warfare, won time for more fruitful approaches. In 1964 there came the foundation of an African Development Bank with a subscribed capital of £80 million, another pointer to something better in the future.

Gestures towards unity were made at regional levels. Ghana and Guinea declared their Union in 1959, Senegal and Soudan joined briefly, as Mali, a year later. Some East African governments tried for an organic federation. All shipwrecked on the jagged separatisms of the nation-states now in presence. The 'inheritance élites' had not become their countries' first ministers in order to preside over the liquidation of their new domestic empires. Nor had they done so in order to expose themselves to blasts of criticism by the many at 'the base'. Interterritorial conferences of delegates of voters, as distinct from representatives of governments, might have eased the way towards organic unities: the interests of the voters in different states, generally, were not in structural competition as were those of the various ruling groups. But the model presumed an unquestioned primacy for the ruling groups; and there were no more gatherings such as that of the RDA at Bamako in 1946, or of the pre-independence parties in East Africa late in the 1950s, or Nkrumah's assembly in December 1958 of the delegates of sixty-two nationalist parties or movements. All the same, the idea of an eventual unity remained alive, and the best of the nationalists continued to hope for a time when progress between peoples, rather than negotiation between governments, might become possible.

Much else was stimulating. In their varying degrees of rank, the nationalists took possession of their kingdom and enjoyed it.

The lucky few enjoyed it enormously, uproariously, above all extravagantly. But even the not-so-lucky had a share in the fun: for a while, for a year or so. And the fun at this stage, after all the boredom and the silence of the colonial years, was scarcely something to begrudge. Behind it, too, there emerged a sentiment of being in the train of an 'immense legitimacy', for had not the weak prevailed against the strong, the poor against the rich, the 'wretched of the earth' against the privileged and powerful? This sentiment might be briefly deserved, but it was very real at the time and had its creative value.*

The force of this particular sentiment obviously varied. Remote communities could have little or no sense of significant or helpful change. An isolated nationality such as the Karimojong, living far off the modernizing track, their ancestral charter barely fractured by peripheral colonial rule, suddenly found themselves transferred into the nation-state of Uganda; it might as well have been that of Kenya, Sudan, or Congo. They would wait to rejoice, or to mourn; and there were many such.

Elsewhere the sentiment of a regained justice was evidently weak wherever independence came in such a manner as seeming most plainly to exclude the many from its benefits. In his presidential speech at Kenya's independence, for example, Kenyatta spent no words in celebrating the forest fighters of the Emergency, or all those humble folk who had suffered or died in the desperate struggle which opened the way to independence. In such cases, the concept of the nation-state as successor and inheritor of ancestral communities capable of giving these a new and valid form and content in membership of the modern world, was necessarily hard and even impossible to see.

In tropical zones the sentiment of right triumphing over wrong, and of the historical legitimacy and indeed necessity of the bourgeois nation-state as the embodiment of a new community, a

---

*I take this term, 'immense legitimacy', from a writer who used it in very convincing circumstances: Comandante Jika (Gilberto Teixeira da Silva): *Reflexões sobre a Luta de Libertação Nacional*, Luanda, August 1976 (but written in 1969–71). It could be widely applied.

new society, was probably strongest in West Africa. There, for decades, the pioneers of nationalism had traced this very pathway to renewal, and there, more than in most regions, the consciousness of a long and successful history of state-formation on a centralizing pattern was frequently alive, whether in the Sudanese interior or among major peoples of the seaboard.

It is hard to be sure. But in recovering what nationalists felt at the time there is a reasonable parallel with the record of what other nationalists had felt a few decades earlier, in another time of decolonization, when the 'submerged nationalities' of the Austro-Hungarian empire and its peers inside Europe had achieved their political kingdom. Very few of those Czech and Slovak nationalists, or Croat and Slovene or similarly liberated neighbours appear to have grasped, in 1919, the further implications of the model they had taken for their own. Yet all could still find good reasons, even unanswerable reasons, for believing that their new condition was bound to be vastly preferable to their old; and so it was, as indeed one's own memories repeatedly confirm, with the thinking of the great majority of African nationalists in 1960.

In both cases, Eastern European and African, the ideologies in play were strikingly alike, just as the consequences would be alike. All the way along that prestigious struggle against the old empires within Europe, proceeding through heroic years, there were men of talent, courage, high intelligence, names to conjure with: from the distant times of Kosciuszko to those of Masaryk, Pilsudski, Pasić, many more. They too could be demagogic when they chose, and use the clamour in the streets if diplomatic levers failed. They too reached their political kingdom and built their nation-states, claiming that by this solving of the national problem they would then solve the social problem which lay all around them, the problem of poverty and backwardness and strife. But when they had solved their national problem, as they thought, they found that solving of the social problem was altogether beyond their strength; and soon there came a thunderous crashing of bridges between leaders and led, with bitter conflicts and the iron-handed dictatorships of Horthy, Živković and their like, as well as a furious 'tribalism' while enclosed nationalities one by one rejected the frameworks into which they were built, and Croats cried out against Serbs, Slovaks against Czechs, Macedonians against Bulgars, and so on down the line. Political systems gave way to purely administrative systems, and stiff bureaucracies ruled the day.

Did these breakdowns derive from some inferiority of human nature? Were they caused by 'lack of honest politicians', or because there was 'no ideology'? Such explanations were often made, but missed the point. For example, 'it would be absurd to suggest,' as Seton-Watson remarked of these Eastern European countries, 'that contempt for the public, pompous laziness, love of formality and fear of responsibility were the monopoly of Balkan bureaucracy.'[7] It would be just as useless to refer such phenomena to a 'social pathology' inherent to some special kind of human nature.[8] However perverse, corrupt, and liable to drive men mad these phenomena might be, they manifestly derived from the material and ideological structures within which they appeared.

The economic parallel holds equally well. The leaders of the new European states found that the gains of their bourgeois model were mortgaged not only to unresolved rivalries between the 'inheritance élites' of enclosed nationalities, denying that the new nation-states had solved even their national problem, but also and more painfully to a 'neo-colonial' subjection to the post-1919 Powers, above all to the Germany of Hitler's Third Reich. Within this subjection, the gulf between the many poor and the few beneficiaries among these peoples widened and could only widen into new strife and uproar. Wading through violence and deceit, 'strong men' tried to hold their states together while revolutionaries rotted in gaol and reformers spoke in vain; and nothing that was done could make the model work as the pioneers had promised. Even so, it still appears unlikely that many thought the price of independence from the old empires larger than the gains of escape. There could be no going back; somehow, instead, there must be another way forward.

However different the context, the nationalists of the new African states were in a comparable position, facing comparable problems and contradictions, making comparable gains just as their peoples had to pay a comparable price. As writers, tribunes, visionaries, men of action, these Africans were not outshone, even though they had generally to work in languages not their own. Often they were brilliant; seldom were they pedestrian. Their successes were of the same order; so, in the outcome, were their setbacks. This was as true in the field of politics or economics as in the character of their bureaucracies. If within different idioms, it was true in the dimensions of their bourgeois ideology, of their belief in the model they had chosen. Even their African Socialism, surrogate of the real thing adopted as a badge of populist appeal, can find its earlier parallel in the socialism of such men as Pilsudski.

Like circumstances tend to produce like results. In Africa as in Eastern Europe the bridges crashed and 'strong men' walked in solitary power while corruption spread like a disease, and force took the place of fellowship and violence of persuasion. Once again it was shown that this way of solving the national problem could not solve the social problem; that the colonial state turned nation-state could not be usefully reformed, but must be revolutionized; and that only this kind of revolution, only a clear priority to the solving of the social problem by whatever means the future might reveal, would be able to fulfil the promises of national freedom.

WRESTLING WITH THE IMPORTED MODEL: ANGER AND FRUSTRATION

The gains of independence were real and many, giving history a new life and content, and continuing to accrue or even to develop in later years. When recalled from within the African scene, these were years of an intricate unfolding of ideas and initiatives that grappled with new opportunities, exploited new responsibilities, wrestled with realities which were also new in the sense that colonial power had previously concealed them. They were also years of paying the price for independence on the imported model.*

Beginning once more to work out its own indigenous processes, Africa's history revealed its own particularities. Unresolved tensions of the colonial period, sources of a myriad resentments settled by 'pacification', were now relaunched within the infra-African arena. Jagged edges in the relations of a mosaic of communities and nationalities, overlaid by colonial rule, came thrusting to the surface. Regrouped within the nation-state that was still the colonial state, old and less old troubles and ambitions shook and rattled at its feeble institutions, broke through its constitutional defences, trampled on its frail procedures and made nonsense of its preaching certitudes. There was much anger. There was even more frustration.

The resulting dislocations became large, riotous, and at times hugely destructive, disgracing old reputations, overturning new parliaments, erupting into malice and revenge, and bringing into power persons who ranged from one extreme to the other of the moral spectrum. Some were brigands, bandits, executioners. Others were grave and responsible administrators, civilian or military, who laid a firm hand upon the levers of power and tried to save the state

*For further discussion, see Chapter 28.

within the principles and orthodoxies that they knew. A handful
were idealists, innovators, even revolutionaries. Many had talent,
courage, persistence, and many had no apparent virtue; but all were
lashed by the same tempest.

Yet what is really interesting in this period after independence is not the political failure of the adopted model, since this
was a failure, as could afterwards be seen, that was written into the
situation. The historical interest lies elsewhere: in the working out
of confrontation between the colonial heritage and the pre-colonial
heritage, now that the second is free to challenge the first; and,
along with that, the resultant development of ideas concerned with
searching for a different model. These are the fields of theory and
practice within which this history plays out its ongoing and decisive
themes into the 1980s and beyond.

Must the whole of the pre-colonial heritage be scrapped
except in folklore and sentiment, as a number of prestigious nationalists had long since argued, thinking that civilization had to come
from outside Africa? Those who still thought like this – or those, at
least, who were prepared to say so in public – soon found themselves
shoved off-stage; with regained prestige and confidence, the pre-
colonial heritage soon ensured as much. Contrariwise, should not the
imported model be now displaced by a return to pre-colonial values,
beliefs, institutions? Several had said this too; and now there were
some who tried their hand at this kind of restoration, going into
disastrous wars against injustice with bodies washed immune to
bullets, marching vainly towards a millennium of ancestral reinstate-
ment. Or could one find a creative synthesis between old and new,
between 'traditional' and 'modern', by tinkering with each until
somehow they would weld? Much of the history of these years is
concerned with efforts at reaching a viable synthesis between old and
new, not by changing the structures of the imported model but by
reshaping and relaunching them. Later on, other efforts become
increasingly rooted in the conviction that the imported model can
not be reformed in any fruitful way; and these embark on
revolution.

Interwoven in confusion or sharply opposed, these trends

of thought and action give the post-independence period its restless dynamism and questing ideological thrust. A familiar contemporary impression that Africans had suddenly acquired the means of harmonious progress, guaranteed by parliamentary systems and 'established Western values', and had then as suddenly thrown them away or mislaid them by incompetence or graft, leaving only a sterile chaos, was wide of the truth. There is plenty of chaos and sterility of thought accompanied by clamorous uproars, incredible disasters, sad defeats. Frustration can often make it seem that even the smallest improvement in the quality of life has gone out of reach. The warlords and the bandits do indeed rampage in more than one national caravanserai of buffoonery or Papa-Doclike gloom, brandishing their clubs and filling up their cemeteries. The get-rich-quick brigades do indeed march through other carnivals of pseudo-parliamentary charade, chanting hymns to Négritude plus ten per cent and calling in their police whenever honesty may threaten to appear. Yet through all this crookery and in spite of it, burrowing often out of sight, persisting even in a desert of discouragement, the search for new and valid forms of community such as can relay but enlarge and modernize the communities of the past, somehow continues on its way.

The evidence of this search could occasionally be seen at the time. At other junctures the search was far from obvious, was indirect, was inconsistent with itself, partial in clarity, uncertain of conviction, prefatory to fresh confusions. How could a true unity of minds and energies be forged, old wounds healed, new wounds prevented: and all this within a continent aggressively enclosed by competing international pressures and a host of conscious or unconscious local agents of those outside pressures? No simple answers were found in these years, or, if any were, none proved effective.

It follows that any attempt to classify the newly-independent states, more than forty in number by 1970, into neat categories according to type of régime or to some fixed standing along an available spread of ideological options, must be fairly useless. The attempt was often made, as a mountain of written commentary is there to show, but it came to little good. Country Y was said to be safe and sound, or suffering and wretched, within this or that 'system', only to prove by an unforeseen upheaval that it was nothing of the kind. Country Z was reported in good shape, only to demonstrate precisely the reverse. Some régimes were labelled 'military' and therefore 'bad' (or, alternatively, 'good') as though the highly varied nature and ideas of these generals and colonels, majors and captains, and eventually sergeants and corporals, were really of no significance. A rough and ready division into simple categories may be possible, as we shall see on p. 329 below; but before analysing the reasons for anger and frustration it may be well to have a summary conspectus of the breakdown.

That the price for political independence on the given model might be a high one was a suspicion that soon became a certainty. Of the early upheavals which proved important, many were concerned with serious issues of strife between competing interests. A few were acts of merely personal ambition; and the number of these increased for a while as barrack-room paranoia became a disease to be reckoned with. But generally, between 1956 and perhaps 1965, the upsets were the outcome of a new freedom of action among or between interest-groups or nationalities hitherto repressed or favoured by colonial rule, with each, now that the colonial lid was off, seeking to advance or protect its sectional claims and concerns. In thus elbowing and manoeuvring for shares in the strictly privileged cake of the colonial state turned nation-state, the rival 'inheritance élites' were bound to come to blows: not only with each other, of course, but also with those who aspired to join the feast. This could be reasonably deplored only by critics who thought the model unacceptable. But since the model was as yet barely questioned, there was much lamentation on the subject of 'dishonest politicians', rather as though any politicians, in this situation, could have acted differently and still remained effective.

External influences were many and of different kinds. Mostly they were indirect. Paris kept a close hold on its former colonies, save for Guinea, by way of military agreements and financial controls. London was also concerned to safeguard the model and its economic understructures, but in less direct ways. Washington's influence was paramount in the ex-Belgian Congo and in the ex-British territories, with London willing enough to play the same game but often reduced to a secondary influence in its old empire. Federal German and other Western-type influences arrived somewhat later. On the other side, the influence of the USSR and other states in the Soviet bloc began in a small way with trade-and-aid agreements early in the 1960s, when their study of Africa became a serious and soon a large discipline. There is no evidence for the 1960s that this 'Eastern influence' had any immediate political consequences, however, or even any immediate political intentions other than to assure 'presence'. An increasing number of Africans began to study in universities in the Soviet bloc, but by no means often with ideological consequences favourable to revolution. The period of direct ideological competition, as between the ideas of capitalism and those of non-capitalism or anti-capitalism, opened only in the 70s.

Several régimes proved stable. This usually occurred wherever independence was accompanied by a more or less far-reaching reorganization of colonial or para-colonial structures. Such was the case in Egypt, where the Nasserist régime displaced the old bourgeois parties, notably the Wafd, by a petty-bourgeois bureaucracy in control of a state with populist policies. Installed in 1958, the régime of the PDG in Guinea under the innovating but increasingly personal rule of Touré was able to withstand several externally mounted conspiracies and much recalcitrance at home. There were several stable régimes of a more orthodox type. Tunisia's Bourguibist system was among these.

Generally, however, the régimes installed at independence became rapidly subject to upsets and uproars. Striving to contain these, the multi-party parliamentary systems gave way increasingly, whether in theory or practice, to one-party systems. Most of these one-party systems at this stage, perhaps all of them, decayed into no-party systems as their ruling elements became fully bureaucratized. Politics came to an end; mere administration took its place, reproducing colonial autocracy as the new 'beneficiaries' took the place of the old governors. This happened de jure, as in Ghana, or more often de facto, as in Ivory Coast and Kenya.

All this occurred against a background of minority or majority pressures. Ruling groups disputed for possible gains, and consumed an ever-growing proportion of revenue. 'As for the cost of the presidential and ministerial establishments,' a comment on Gabon remarked a few years after independence, 'with all their more or less useless journeyings back and forth, it is probably higher in proportion to the national income of Gabon than the cost to France of the court of Louis XVI' on the eve of the French Revolution.[9] Such 'establishments' incessantly improved their incomes by self-awarded decree, access to bribes, or the perversion of export–import controls, with foreign contract-hunters playing an eager role.

Discontent grew apace. With populations now expanding at a rate of more than two per cent a year, and orthodox policies insisting on the maximization of exports, food produced for home consumption became scarcer and therefore dearer. Rural incomes appear generally to have fallen steadily or at best remained stagnant at their previously low level. Urban or other wage levels reflected the same trend. Thus the Nigerian index of real wages, with a base of 100 in 1939, stood at 144 in 1965, but at 112 in 1970; and in that year an official commission found that Nigeria had 'intolerable suffering at the bottom of the income scale, because of the rise in the cost of living', while this suffering was rendered 'even more intolerable by manifestations of affluence and wasteful expenditure' which could not be explained on the basis of visible and legitimate means of income.[10]

Some economies grew in size, but the growth merely emphasized these trends of widening indigence and even of acute poverty. Ghana's cocoa production, to offer one such example among many, surpassed all previous records; but so, at the same time, did Ghana's indebtedness to foreign lenders. 'Aid for development' accentuated a growth that could be crippling in its consequences. Flocks and herds in the Sudanese Sahel, for another example among many, were enlarged by a multiplication of water-points without any rational plan of long-term conservation and ecological balance; when severe drought struck in the early 70s, death by thirst or hunger followed. 'Aid for development' also added to the burden of indebtedness to foreign lenders. Annual debt service became a major budget item, another foreign milking of the revenues available for distribution at home.

Democratic politics being for the most part reduced to general elections for parties entirely possessed or run by the 'inheritance élites', nothing but one or other form of dictatorship could contain the resultant rivalries and resentments. Some of these dictatorships remained civilian in appearance. But wherever the civilian 'élites' could not defend their state within its established structures and 'Western values', then the military 'élites' must evidently do it for them. Populist convergence by the few with the many being now at an end, since the 'élites' had made their bargain and got their nation, military take-over as a means of protecting the interests of the few against the claims of the many became frequent. Later, in the 1970s, military take-overs were more complex in their motivations, and were sometimes another aspect of the renewed search for a stable and progressive community. Broadly, the 1960s were a time of reaction, the 1970s one of new experiment.

A list of all these institutional upsets would be tedious; and brief descriptions would often over-simplify local complexities to the point of uselessness. Mostly they were concerned with rivalries between one or other group of 'inheritance élites', some already on the scene, or others newly formed in the post-independence years. Many of the upsets were triggered by eruptions of mass discontent, whether in virtual insurrection or long-simmering disorder. In rare cases, as with UPC in Cameroun or with the Communist Party of the Sudan, mass discontent found revolutionary leadership; much more often, it remained within 'traditional' forms of political thought and action. Several upsets of régime, notably in Zaire, had strong origins in foreign interference.

Many of these upsets were made without bloodshed, or with very little. The Sudan led off with a peaceful military take-over within little more than two years of independence, and shifts of power became endemic after 1964, leading eventually to a mass killing of Sudanese communists and their supporters. Difficulties here were long enlarged by a generally complete failure to satisfy the legitimate aspirations of the non-Muslim peoples of the southern Sudan, and by the prolonged guerrilla war with which these peoples responded to what they saw as northern colonialism. Zaire, the ex-Belgian Congo, fared very badly after the destruction of the Lumumbists; and regional dissidence against the political dictatorship then installed, or afterwards against the military dictatorship of Mobutu, continued with large-scale risings in 1964–6. These were crushed, but widespread dissidence persisted through the 1970s.

Many of the smaller francophone states passed from one ephemeral régime to another, once again with the military playing an increasing role in an effort to defend the established systems. Here too the pre-colonial inheritance wrestled against the colonial with consequences that were sometimes bizarre, and the emergence of personalities who were still more so. Taking over the Central African Republic (ex-Oubangui-Chari), General Bedel Bokassa ruled as an old-style potentate whose similarity to the 'Emperor Jones' was strikingly confirmed in 1976, when Bokassa announced that he had become an emperor himself. More and more often, the grave history of bourgeois nationalism repeated itself as lurid farce; unhappily, the farce was often now a bloody one. Rather less often, the British inheritance led to tragic dramas of the same kind, as when General Idi Amin destroyed in 1971 the innovating régime led by Milton Obote in Uganda.

The *coup* period really begins in 1966. The motivations, too, became more complex. In Algeria the régime headed by Ahmed Ben Bella was bloodlessly displaced in 1965 by an army take-over under Colonel Houari Boumédienne, but here the motivations were of a serious and structural order, though partly derived from rivalries within the FLN which had won the anti-colonial war. Algeria, in contrast with its neighbour Morocco, became a field of interesting experiment.

Major upsets occurred in 1966. In January, middle-rank officers assassinated some of the leaders of the Nigerian federation, calling for an entirely different federation cleansed of corruption. This was widely popular, but its political legacy and its trail of bloodshed were bitterly avenged. Other take-overs followed. After much violence and disorder these led to a civil war in 1967 when the leading 'inheritance élite' in the Eastern Region declared a separate republic of Biafra which continued fighting with various forms of external aid until the end of 1969. A generous peace was made by the military régime under General Yakubu Gowon, who now declared a new Federation of twelve states (formally initiated in 1967), later increased to nineteen.

With good administration, this Nigerian administrative devolution went a long way towards a shrewd recognition of the identity of constituent nationalities, but could in itself do little about the underlying problems of social disarray. Any solution of these would have to derive from political rather than administrative choices. Recognizing this, the Gowon régime promised to return the country to civilian politics. Tripped by its own frailties, this régime was displaced in 1975 by another army group, under Brigadier Murtala Mohamed, who undertook to step back eventually in favour of civilian politics. A man of outstanding capacity, Mohamed was assassinated in an especially disgraceful, though otherwise happily abortive, *coup* early in 1976, but the promise was confirmed by his friend and successor, Lt-Gen. Olusegun Obasanjo. Constitutional committees were set to work, and had produced their initial reports before the end of 1977, with civilian rule promised for 1979.

The military in Ghana overthrew the Nkrumah régime in February 1966 with a good deal of violence, reacting ostensibly against its authoritarian nature, and ruled on a policy of reaction until 1969 when it retired in favour of a parliamentary régime under Kofi Busia. This proved once again what Nkrumah thought the years 1957–60 had already proved: that the parliamentary model would not work. Busia's régime duly reopened the door to 'tribal' politics between contending groups, plunged the country still further into debt, became widely disliked, and was evicted without the slightest need for violence in 1972 by a new military régime under Colonel Ignatius Acheampong. This was soon beset by sharpening economic and other crises. Sierra Leone embarked on a series of upsets in 1967, but with no ideological innovation. In 1968 a leftist régime in Mali was destroyed by a rightist military *coup*. In 1969 the

Libyan army ousted the Sanusi monarchy; and the Somali army removed its country's parliamentary façade.

By 1970 there were nineteen states under one or other kind of military régime, with more on the way. They were beginning to be fairly diverse in their nature and intentions. In 1976, as already noted, General Bokassa of the Central African Republic donned the purple; but in Dahomey (renamed Benin), by contrast, a military régime imposed in 1972 after a long series of civilian *coups* and counter-*coups* embarked, under Major Mathieu Kérékou, on what undertook to be the building of an entirely different model derived from a revolutionary politics of liberation.* The Somali military régime had meanwhile moved in the same direction, as had also the military régime led by Marien Ngouabi in the Congo People's Republic (formerly Congo-Brazzaville).†

The list of upsets could be lengthened, but some further inquiry into their underlying causes is likely to be more helpful.

*For the politics of liberation, see especially Chs 29 and 30.

†Ngouabi was assassinated by 'moderates' in 1977, at a time when several anti-radical conspiracies were under way in different countries, but the régime itself did not fall.

28

WRESTLING WITH THE IMPORTED MODEL: UNDERLYING CAUSES

Striving for independence, the anti-colonial movements and their leaders had become nationalists, but nationalists without nations.* Taking over the colonial state, they remained after independence in much the same condition in spite of all the sympathetic magic of flags and anthems, ceremonial artillery, police outriders on monster motor-bikes, and oratorical flapdoodle: the nations remained to be built. New governments laboured at this. They tried to enclose the spokesmen of constituent ethnic groups within a shell of unified national effort, and they appealed to the enthusiasm of the masses. But the spokesmen tended to prefer their own ethnic shells, while the rural and urban multitudes, queuing up for immediate benefits offered by the nationalist promise, clearly thought flag-wagging a poor substitute. Doubts about the real intentions of the leaderships soon shaded into dissent, and dissent into hostility.

In the circumstances of this emancipation, much of this was nobody's fault: any transformation of the colonial state would need time. Many members of the new ruling groups proved honest, efficient, hard-working; and, as we have seen, they achieved gains unthinkable under colonial rule. The best of these men and women needed to fear no comparisons with their contemporaries outside Africa. They were the unsung heroes of the attempt to build nations on a capitalist pattern, battling to reduce graft or irresponsibility and to apply the law as the law was meant to be applied. Their trouble was that the given pattern could not meet its expectations. Many

*This was only in part true of single-nationality states such as Somalia; but these were few and, even with these, a nationalist consciousness had still to be generally aroused.

of them, as there is much to show, became rapidly aware of this in-built failure of institutions.

Nationalism had proposed two roads to progress: the escape from foreign rule, and beyond this the betterment of life for the many by an all-round modernization. The escape without the betterment would therefore spell betrayal of the nationalist promise, but now it appeared that the nationalists were bound to live with this betrayal. The given pattern insisted on the promotion of a property-owning middle-class. That being so, modernization was going to be possible only at the price of a reduction such as the prophets of the past had not envisaged. The new men in power still laboured at the work for which they had been trained. But they found themselves pushed increasingly into a colonialist posture towards all who were outside their ranks but who, in theory, were supposed to benefit from their labours.

As time went by, the less responsible among the 'inheritance élites' gave up any further effort to resist the tide of privilege, and turned to their personal interests. The best continued to swim against the tide. They criticized dishonesty, rejected the easy choices of this 'neo-colonialism', lost their jobs, went abroad. Some were stowed away in prisons; others were murdered to close their mouths. All this was especially obvious in states where the coming of independence had most plainly put the many outside the ring of beneficiaries. Kenya provided a case in point.

The process of decay was not of course immediate or complete. Kenya remained the scene of some very robust party politics until about 1970, and conserved a parliament after that, even though, by now, this parliament was expected to act as a rubber-stamping instrument of the ruling group's decisions, while the party of government (KANU) was largely reduced to a petrified bureaucracy. Critics remained; but they fared hard.

Early in the 1970s one of these critics was a prominent Kikuyu businessman and politician, Josiah Mwangi Kariuki. He was vocal and courageous. 'Since Kenya became independent in 1963,' he dared to say in 1975, 'we have moved away from the state which we intended to create.' Kenya had become 'like a tree growing very tall very quickly, but it is going to fall because it does not have deep roots, is not firmly rooted in the people and in society'.[11] Roundly contemptuous of the get-rich-quick activities of the politicians in power – and of these, now, President Kenyatta was widely held to be the wealthiest – Kariuki said much more to the same effect. A lot of people loved him for it, but the régime did not.

One day in 1975 Kariuki was found dead and mutilated in the bush. This was not the first murder of a prominent Kenya politician, but the first time that a Kikuyu had suffered in this way. Appointed to inquire into the murder, a parliamentary select committee returned damaging evidence to implicate the government's special police. The committee accused the police of undertaking a 'determined cover-up exercise', and described the murdered man as a hero whose philosophy of a fair distribution of wealth had made him the enemy of many persons. Which persons? A report in The Times[12] indicated a common opinion when it spoke of 'a growing discontent with the way in which President Kenyatta is consolidating the wealth and power of a small clique composed of his own family and his closest supporters'. Although the committee named the head of the para-military General Service unit of the police as the last person known to have been with Kariuki,[13] no satisfactory proceedings followed its report. Other leading critics were then arrested.

The Times' report on these arrests is worth quoting for its evidence of the kind of 'multi-party democracy' that now reigned in Kenya. An MP called Martin Shikuku said in a debate that 'there were some people who were "trying to kill parliamentary democracy in the manner that KANU had been killed"': after, that is, the opposition had been silenced some years earlier. 'Loyal MPs protested and Mr (Jean Marie) Seroney, who was acting as chairman of the debate, was asked to rule Mr Shikuku's remarks "out of order". This he refused to do, saying that Mr Shikuku was only stating the obvious.'[14] A few days later 'plainclothes policemen entered the Nairobi Parliament building and arrested Mr Seroney and Mr Shikuku at gunpoint. The next day it was announced that they had been detained under the Preservation of Public Security Regulations.' They could be held indefinitely without trial.

Mockery of the law, outrageous trampling on the decencies of everyday life: all this became as common to many of the new states as in other continents where the times were out of joint. Yet these forms of decay could not be attached to the ruling groups *as a class*. One perhaps needs to insist on this if only because the shorthand of terminological definitions can risk an absurd dogmatism. At best, these beneficiaries represented the embryo of a potential class: in the meantime, they were a disparate collection of persons acting within the arena of a complex opportunism, and, for many if not for most of them, their eventual choices were no more crystallized than their class consciousness. The cases of Kariuki and Messrs Shikuku and Seroney illustrate this point, as indeed had that of Pio Pinto, an earlier victim of political gangsterism in Kenya. Such men knew very well that the nation could not be built against the multitude, even if they had yet to discover how to build it with the multitude.

The picture so far sketched, of putative nations run by power oligarchies concerned above all with their own advancement or defence while the majority of inhabitants, probably more than nine-tenths, continued to live in deepening rural poverty or in urban slums where the anxieties of today promised to become worse tomorrow, obviously calls for some larger dimensions. To give it this perspective, let us look briefly at the structures of the states which had now appeared, and at the interplay between these structures and the limitations of the imported model.

What manner of unified community could be offered by the new state? How did its components fit or fail to fit together as a nation?

With some exceptions, the states emerging from colonial rule were predominantly rural in population, with between 90 and 95 per cent of people living in villages or nomad settlements. These rural people might be labelled as a 'class' of cultivators and stock-raisers, but in fact they were united neither in their social consciousness nor in any nationalist ideology. At most they formed a collection of communities amalgamated by the hazards of colonial frontier delimitation. Many communities had joined the nationalists in the hope of anti-colonial improvement, but an ancestral charter of separate self-identification still held wide sway in each of them.

Yet their mode of production was no longer the independent system within which ancestral charters had taken shape. It had been changing for a long time into a different mode, a colonial mode.* This had acquired two combined aspects, each greatly enlarged in the years after political independence. The first evolved in export enclaves continuously expanded by the effects of the Second World War and its post-war boom. Here the situation was such that production for an external market, externally controlled, had increasingly introduced elements of a subordinate or auxiliary capitalism, strong enough to weaken ancestral charters although not to displace them.

Outside these enclaves there were very large 'support' zones whose value, within the colonial mode, was to act as providers of cheap labour and, where possible, of cheap food as well: in any case, they provided food for the families of men who left on migrant labour, and these men, in the export zones, could be and often were paid wages calculated to support a single man on his own. Here there was no introduction of the elements of capitalism; on the other hand, the loss of their labour to export zones persistently undermined their pre-colonial viability, self-confidence, and sense of community, but once again without supplying any alternative. Thus the ancestrally defined and chartered community was doubly dismantled: by new elements of capitalism within the export zones, and by social and economic decay within the 'support' zones. This process is vividly illustrated by the figures for labour migration.

Migrants now reached numbers far larger than in fully colonial times. But the nature and spread of migrations remained much the same: it was simply that the colonial mode, having expanded, called for more workers. As before, the main flows were from territories of semi-autonomous rural production for local needs into territories of plantation and mining. Four regional patterns held firm. In West Africa the seasonal but permanent flow was chiefly from Volta, Togo and northern Dahomey (Benin) into Ghana, and

*See especially Ch. 20.

from Volta and Niger into Ivory Coast. In Central Africa the magnet was Zaire (ex-Belgian Congo) with migrants from Rwanda, Burundi, and Angola. In East Africa, other migrants from Rwanda and Burundi and the southern Sudan sought work in Kenya, Tanzania, Uganda and Malawi, while Sudanese skilled workers could be found in many other countries as well. In southern Africa migrants from Malawi, Mozambique, Botswana and Lesotho went away for work to South Africa, Rhodesia and Zambia.*

These flows had become vital to the export zones which, without them, would have run into depression for want of labour or been forced into more advanced methods of production. As it was, they underpinned a labour-intensive economy at otherwise untenably low levels of wages and living conditions. By the 1960s, moreover, they had become almost as vital to the 'support' zones, since rising population appears to have gone together with an indubitable economic decay. The whole system, in short, had acquired its own dynamism. The flows became stable and continuous; they also grew in size. Figures for 1970, for example, show that 15.2 per cent of the population of Ghana was composed of Africans of foreign origin, while the comparable figure for Ivory Coast was almost 45 per cent.

The facts destroy any notion that these flows owed their impetus to any supposed appeal of 'city lights' or desire to earn the blessings of 'high mass consumption'. No doubt some migrants went for such reasons. But few of them ever came within sight of 'city lights'. Of those who went to Ghana, about 77 per cent became farm labourers, another 5 per cent mine-workers, while 10 per cent found work in a variety of handicrafts; and the proportion of farm labourers among migrants in Ivory Coast was probably higher still. Very large numbers of migrants from central and southern Africa worked on white South African farms. Another huge contingent provided indispensable mining labour; no fewer than 382,000 in the peak year

*These flows take no account of refugees. By 1970 about 500,000 Rwandans had sought refuge in Uganda, and nearly 850,000 in Zaire. Upwards of one million Angolans appear to have fled into Zaire and Zambia from the Portuguese colonial war of 1961–74, and smaller number of Mozambicans for the same reason into Tanzania and Zaire.

of 1962, of whom 152,000 derived from South African 'Native Reserves', 75,000 from Lesotho, Botswana and Swaziland, 85,000 from Mozambique, and 72,000 from other states.[15] These did indeed catch sight of 'city lights', but from the enclosure of mining compounds and the scope of pitifully small payment. All the others continued to do much the same work as they had done at home, and for wages which made any access to 'high mass consumption' quite impossible.

The years of colonial and post-colonial 'development' – growth, that is, of the colonial mode of extraction – merely continued these trends. There was no general 'development' of migrant skills or of capacity to master new economic opportunities. On the contrary, there was retrogression. In 1946–50 the proportion of migrants of Voltan origin who worked abroad in plantations was 51 per cent, with 27 per cent listed as working in 'industry'. But in 1970 the comparable proportions had become 70 per cent and 21 per cent. Real wages stagnated or fell. The true reasons for migration, very clearly, have to be sought outside the subjectivities of 'village boredom'. If more and more peasants preferred to leave their homes for ever lengthening periods, their motives lay rather in a worse impoverishment at home, and in a corresponding despair.

Within the 'developed' zones the evidence is harder to summarize. Cocoa production in Ghana, for example, continually if erratically rose in volume, drawing more and more entrepreneurs and land-speculating operators into a business where wages, thanks largely to immigration, could be held down or depressed. But cocoa prices also fluctuated for the entrepreneurs, and if savings grew in size the use of savings seems barely to have changed. The elements of capitalism in these zones did not accumulate, by all the signs, into anything resembling the 'take-off' into a capitalist system.

The case seems to have been general. An inquiry into conditions in Hausaland (northern Nigeria) during the early 1970s indicated that this important zone of peanut production for export had barely changed in economic profile since the beginning of the century. Some aspects of life had improved; others had evidently worsened. 'On the one hand there are many countrymen who finance their pilgrimage by air to Mecca; on the other hand there continues to be a very great incidence of highly impoverished households, even where conditions are such that land is not scarce and there is a ready cash demand for any food crops that may be produced.'[16]

While social and economic inequalities probably became more acute during the colonial period, or remained no less acute than before, we may generally conclude that this Africa of the new states had developed no rural stratifications such as could underpin the emergence of capitalist systems, even in those zones of export maximization where the elements of capitalism were sometimes strong. For many rural majorities, in consequence, the ideology of nationalism on the capitalist pattern had to appear in a socio-economic vacuum, and as something perfectly artificial or extraneous to the world they knew.

Between five and ten per cent of populations, and in a few cases considerably more, were more or less permanently urbanized. Yet even with these urban-dwellers the horizontal divisions of a class consciousness capable of fitting into the ideology of bourgeois nationalism were largely absent or elusive. Though in fragmentary or distorted forms, the ancestral charters held sway here as well, and not only at 'the base'. Leading nationalists could still be found consulting oracles; university graduates could still want to know what ancestors might advise.

The spin-off from long export booms within the colonial mode of extraction certainly had some consequences in class formation. But these, too, were often less mature than they might seem. The figures for 'unemployment' illustrate this. Numbers of unemployed generally became much higher after independence, partly because there was more information, partly because there were more 'urbanized'. Did these large urban masses therefore constitute the further growth of a working class, or even of a proletariat save in the limited sense of being people without any property? Were they even 'unemployed'? In fact, the bundling together as 'unemployed' of all persons not registered in wage employment was a statistical absurdity peculiar to the 'neo-colonial' situation. There being no unemployment relief, huge numbers of 'unemployed' were officially surviving on precisely nothing.

Seldom developing any consciousness of forming a social class, the 'urbanized' masses continued to defend themselves within what remained to them of their traditional cultures. Migrants brought kinship ties with them, and kinship ties could open the way to an unofficial means of subsistence, however erratic, fluctuating, and always liable to personal disaster, that was somehow capable of sustaining life in vast peripheral slums. Such 'informal economic activity' was intricate, ranging from small-time handicraft to the exchange of minute quantities of food or other goods; or an ingenious diversity of services such as errand-running, backyard beer brewing, the operation of kinship clubs and mutual-aid societies; or the dispensing of oracular wisdom, magic, fortune-telling, together with odd 'employments' on the fringe of the official economy in shops, garages, even factories; along with prostitution, petty crime and general brigandage against the official economy. Very large numbers of the 'unemployed' were better described as 'under-employed'.

Whether employed or not, such workers undoubtedly formed or were in the course of forming a new social class in Africa, a working class. But this was a working class which, generally, had yet to become conscious of itself *as a class*.

Rather than a consciousness of distinctive class at this stage, there evolved in this catch-as-catch-can conglomeration of needs and energies a certain stability of warfare between the many have-nothings and the few have-somethings. Given the strong tradition of social mobility which migrants often brought with them, a day-to-day opportunism ruled this warfare. Those who could exact a wage-paid job did so; others hoped to do so on another day; most 'got by' in a situation that offered no prospect of improvement; while a few, as the politics of liberation would show, became mobilizable by a leadership bent on serious change and capable of proving that it meant what it said. But for the great majority of these proletarians, as in the rural areas, nationalism on the capitalist pattern could have no meaningful message, or none that they could welcome. For them, this nationalism belonged to people with safely salaried jobs, private houses, motor-cars, and other forms of conspicuous wealth.

With all the latter, something like recognizable forms of class consciousness were now perceptible. Though their expectations naturally differed, and hence their understanding of what nationalism could or should mean, they provided the active membership of the new nation. Numerically they were few; proportionately to total populations, perhaps only a few per cent of each.

Here and there a working class could be descried, at least in its early form. Algeria by the 1960s, with a third of the whole population resident in towns, had some 120,000 wage-workers who had been or could be organized in trade unions. In the same period the greatest of the tropical states, Nigeria, was said to have an active labour force amounting to 25 million: of these, 70 per cent were in agriculture and allied rural pursuits, 15 per cent in commerce, 9 per cent in small trade or handicrafts, while just over 6 per cent were classified as wage-earners. The total of the latter, mostly urban, was said to have increased from above 180,000 in 1938 to some two million in 1970; by then, perhaps some 600,000 Nigerians, or about one per cent of the total population, worked for wages in enterprises employing more than ten persons. Here, manifestly, was something more than the embryo of a working class; and yet, once again, the term could mislead in failing to allow for the cultural 'overhang' of ancestral beliefs, divisions, and expectations. These wage-earners lived, moreover, among a much larger number of like-minded persons who were often differentiated from them only by not having found a wage. Culturally, they were less a working class than an employed sector of the unemployed.

Above the 'lowest classes', though not very far above, there began the 'have-somethings' to whom workers in safe jobs often tended to belong. The 'have-somethings' in their various levels or gradations are also hard to specify, as limping terms such as 'intermediate strata' or 'petty bourgeoisie' have already proved to readers of this book. Broadly, they were persons with a more or less regular income from private enterprise or those who managed to insert themselves into the service of the new state. These were the groups who had provided the regular troops of the nationalist move-ments, chiefly because they had known the direct experience of racist discrimination within the colonial systems, and because they meant to 'occupy' these systems once the foreign occupants were removed.

The topmost ranks of the intermediate strata* of have-somethings merged with the 'political classes' proper, who provided the officers of the nationalist movements. Town-dwelling pro-fessionals or unusually successful businessmen, they included rural or urban chiefs who had fitted themselves into a local party-political structure and so were now able, after independence, to influence or control the local route to benefits. Often enough, at least in West and North Africa, these were persons able to live on a comfortable foot-ing in everyday life, while their talents and experience ensured that they became the prime occupants of the ex-colonial state.

The withdrawing colonial powers rightly saw these 'top élites' as the natural inheritors of structures convenient to 'established Western values'. They themselves were well aware of this; mean-while, being practical men and women, they put their savings into property and personal consumption as well as the support of their kinsmen, and looked around for more. Their politics became the pursuit of personal power, and power the means of personal accumu-lation. The new nation, after all, was their oyster. What Colin Leys found in Kenya in 1970 became generally the case: 'most politicians were in business.' They were much criticized for this, but quite unfairly, since they were only doing what the imported model assumed they would and should do: which was to grow into a fully-fledged middle-class, a property-owning bourgeoisie, capable of building an indigenous capitalist system and of imposing on that system its appropriate ideology.

Yet even here, as it were at the very heart and centre of nationalism, there stood a disabling equivocation. Kenya politicians might go into business, and business might boom, but the business remained part of a foreign capitalism. Kenya output expanded by about 50 per cent between 1963 and 1970, with a doubling of the annual total of investment, but 'virtually all the expansion that

*See note, p. 215.

occurred was foreign-owned and controlled.' The consequence was not to promote an indigenous middle-class capable of standing on its own feet, but a group of national though subordinate intermediaries. 'The real result of African businessmen's political activities and of the [Kenya] government's policies,' Leys concluded, 'was to foster the emergence of a small protected stratum of African capital-owners, a distinctive type of "auxiliary bourgeoisie".'[17]

It continued to be argued, however, that time would make good this weakness, and that ruthless policies of 'building capitalism' would eventually result in the emergence of genuinely national middle classes, and, with that, of genuinely national capitalist systems. Perhaps this could be possible or at least conceivable wherever large units possessed comparatively large domestic markets, such as was the case with Nigeria, even though sceptics might point to the fact that such exceptions had proved extremely difficult or downright impossible to bring about in the long history of 'neo-colonialism' in Asia and Latin America. If so, however, these exceptions would eventually produce the nation.

But for the great majority of the new states the aims of indigenous capitalism seemed perfectly beyond reach even in the perspective of many years ahead. There the effective accumulation continued to be made by foreign interests, or else by groups of local 'auxiliaries' whose scope for class development appeared minimal or entirely absent. Forms of exploitation could solidify into new initiatives, as with the expansion of the Mouride peanut landlords of Senegal or the emergence of a 'planter class' among Ivory Coast Africans. But the emergent bourgeoisie remained auxiliary insofar as it existed at all.

And so it came about that the new state systems were 'occupied' by small fractions of their inhabitants, all speaking in the name of national unity, while the great majority, peering into this national idea from outside, remained dubious and confused, and not much less alienated from the sources of power than during colonial times.

Over these realities, whether of weak stratification, alien

ideology, or economic subordination, the planners of the imported model passed with a blithely dismissive hand, content for the most part to argue that growth of the colonial economy, suitably re-clothed in African camouflage, was equivalent to the development of a new economy. Is this to overstress their insistence on the model's being shaped to a capitalist pattern? It would be hard to do that. One prestigious adviser after another enlarged upon this absolute necessity. Some wrapped their advice in nationalist language; others were less tactful. None explained the essence of what they meant more clearly than an American economic historian, Walt W. Rostow, whose *Stages of Economic Growth* provided the doctrine of 'inevitable capitalism' with its basic text. Published in the 'African year of independence', 1960, this went through seventeen impressions by 1968, and has a place in the history of these years.[18]

Rostow's argument, briefly, was that all societies every-where fall into five categories of economic progression: 'the tra-ditional society, the pre-conditions for take-off [into sustained growth], the take-off [itself], the drive for maturity, and the age of high mass-consumption'. Irrespective of all diversities of history, structure, class-formation and the rest, this progression must necess-arily be towards capitalism, whether private or state or the two com-bined, and the end result must always be the same. This result would be a copy of the system and culture of the USA in its own post-1945 'age of high mass-consumption'.

In order to reach this happy destiny, a backward society must acquire 'a new élite, a new leadership'. Equipped with an 'appropriate value system', this élite of future capitalists would assemble the capital necessary to 'take off', or to what Europeans in Europe have called industrial revolution; would become a dominant middle class and thus impose its value system on its whole society; and would then advance as surely as the moon-led tide toward the blessed shores of plenitude for all.

No news was likely to be more welcome to the new ruling groups. They had already accepted the political lessons of the capitalist model, notably those of parliamentary democracy on the pattern of Westminster or the Palais Bourbon, for this had been vital to their stratagems of escape from colonial rule. Now they were more than ready to accept the economic lessons, which, in any case, fitted with their perception of what was right and good as well as with their new interests as occupants of the state. 'In substance,' explained a Nigerian economic historian in 1973, 'the philosophy behind the economic history of Nigeria is based on "Competitive Capitalism" '; [19] if he meant competitive commercialism, he was surely right. Far from having no ideology, the majority of these nationalists possessed a subtle understanding of 'private enterprise'. They believed in its virtues, understood its requirements, and thought its critics unrealistic or merely envious.

The economic lessons took a little more time to be accepted in new states with an initially weak traders' component and a less consciously élitist leadership. This was notably the case in East and Central Africa. Here the nationalists had often issued from an actual identity of interests between intermediate strata and masses. Divergence between the few and the many called for a positive act of cleavage by the few, rather than, as in West Africa, for a mere return to an earlier cleavage. So that here, when ruling groups accepted the doctrine according to Rostow and divergence was well in play, there came a proliferation of official myths designed to obscure this digging of a gulf between the few and the many, this building of defences by the few against the many. With that, we have the proclamation of 'African Socialism' in a Kenya whose ruling group was most emphatically committed to an African capitalism. Or, in another relevant case, there is the promulgation in Zambia of an 'African Humanism' by another ruling group of the same mind. Such deception, occasionally self-deception, flourished in several variants.

Nation-building had been taken to mean the creation of unity among all segments of the population. Now it transpired that this nation-building meant something quite different. It meant, first and foremost, the self-promotion of ruling groups into full class status as a dominant bourgeoisie; meanwhile, those many who were still 'outside the nation' in all but a geographical sense would have to stay outside, awaiting the moment when they could be admitted to its benefits according to their eventual class rankings. Given this duty, the ruling groups did not fail for want of trying. They trod faithfully in the footsteps of the British, French and other budding bourgeoisies of the eighteenth and early nineteenth centuries. They went into politics and they went into business. They embarked on 'primitive accumulation' with energy and skill. They carved up the spoils of independence with all the eagerness and rancour of Whigs and Tories. *Enrichissez-vous!*, Guizot had exhorted the businessmen of mid-nineteenth century France. Their African successors stayed for no second bidding.

Politics became a catch-as-catch-can between contending groups, often mobilized on an ethnic basis. Parties became vehicles for ramming one's way to personal gains. Principles gave way to the demands of 'primitive accumulation'. Forms of graft and crookery grew into an ingenuity and shamelessness scarcely seen since the eighteenth-century years of Robert Walpole and his friends. Parliamentary rules collapsed under the strain. Parliamentary systems became ridiculous. Governments got to be widely hated. When the soldiers stepped in they were often moved by a need to preserve the most elementary forms of unity in these states.

Is this, again, an overstating of the evidence? Scarcely. In May 1972, for example, a military *coup* put an end to the eminently 'neo-colonial' régime of Philippe Tsiranana in Madagascar. What had gone wrong with Madagascar, these soldiers said, was a national economy which the nation could not control, being geared to that of France or other foreign interests: an economy which worked only for the benefit of the few, so that 'a widening gulf has opened between the rich and the poor, between the towns and the countryside'. What was further wrong was a system of education, copied from that of France, which was out of date and inappropriate to the country's needs: a system of education which achieved nothing save more joblessness and under-employment. Above all, there was 'a profound decay in the morality of public and business life'.[20]

Such recriminations were many. Overthrowing President Michel Micombero two years later, the spokesmen of an army takeover in Burundi declared that this much bloodstained country had become torn by the strife of 'multiple clans of egoist politicians greedy for personal power and material benefits to the detriment of the peasants, the workers, and the wage-earners'.[21] But whether these or other soldiers could do any better, unless they were to move in entirely new political directions, was what many now gravely doubted. The reasons why such doubts had arisen are better seen in the comparison of a few type-cases than in any catalogue of woes.

The Republic of Somalia formed in 1960 offered perhaps the clearest case of the impossibility of achieving an effective unity of consciousness and effort within the adopted pattern of the nation-state, for Somalia had an unusually 'simple' composition. Living in splendid but exacting solitudes that run for countless miles between the Indian Ocean and Ethiopia, their plains slowly rising through a camel-coloured wilderness to the gauntness of the Haud, Somalia's population of about 3 million were almost all Somalis, all adherents to an Islam of the same orthodoxy, all speaking the same language save for local variants of dialect, while some four-fifths of them followed, as nomads, a more or less identical way of life. The remainder were cultivators along the Juba and Shebelle rivers, or, as to somewhere between 5 and 10 per cent, were residents of towns. Ethnic simplicity of composition was qualified by the self-organization of Somalis, from a remote period, into five major clans (genuine tribes, in this case, as distinct from different nationalities), and several small ones. Yet the underlying cohesiveness of this society was retained by a universal consciousness of belonging to the same overall community, whether as nomads, cultivators, or townsmen.

Somali nationalists since the 1940s had enlarged on an old tradition of anti-colonial resistance by calling for the kind of unity, over and above clan divisions, such as could build a modern nation. Their great predecessor, the Sayid Mohamed who had fought against colonial rule for more than twenty years, had paved the way. Before the Sayid's innovating work, Somali nationalism must have long existed as the recognition of a common bond, but, says Andrzejewski, it 'was probably diffuse and comparable to German or Italian nationalism before unification – and hence the fascination which nineteenth-century European history has had for the Somali

Italian-educated élite'. The Sayid crystallized this notion of Somaliness, of *Somaalinnimo*, into something new. 'The novelty of the Sayid's movement,' Andrzejewski adds, 'was the ideal of creating an Islamic state which would give a political entity to the nation which had long been in existence. For he was well enough travelled to know what the colonial powers did to nations not recognized officially as sovereign states.'*

Taking up the Sayid's work in 1943, nationalists formed the Somali Youth League and eventually, in 1960, achieved their new political entity. But this was a very different creature from the Sayid's ideal. Its constitution was modelled on the Italian parliamentary democracy which had emerged from the defeat of Fascism. Its principal elective feature consisted in a complex form of proportional representation which allowed for the social divisions of Italian history and above all of Italian capitalism. Transferred to Somalia, this mode of representation necessarily reflected the divisions of Somali history. These were clan divisions. Party politics accordingly became clan politics, or, as Touval remarked of the resultant situation, political parties became based 'upon tribes or tribal alliances', while 'allocations of political spoils or civil service posts [were] carefully calculated to fit a tribal balance'.[22]

Yet this was only half the trouble. Tribal rivalries might still have worked themselves into modernizing forms of unity if the system had allowed any majority participation in its management. It allowed no such thing. Unavoidably, power fell into the hands of that very small fraction of Somalis who had mastered Italian and English, Somali not then being a written language, and who possessed other forms of privileged status. The democracy of the words of the constitution was turned upon its head. Effectively, the state consisted of the ruling one per cent of the population: the remaining ninety-nine per cent were in the position of clients, or, being far away across their nomadic plains, scarcely belonged to this state in any sense at all.

With politics reduced to a distribution of gains among an

*Personal communication. One may compare this ideal with those of the Mahdia in the Eastern Sudan and other movements of Muslim innovation in the Western Sudan somewhat earlier.

insignificantly small ruling group, the essential was to have a seat in parliament. The initial clan parties consequently fissured into sub-clan parties, extended-family parties, even one-man parties, each of which at once bartered its seats or seat against specific benefits, consisting often in cash paid by the new prime minister or in business concessions. What emerged was a system of organized irresponsibility and in-built corruption. Parliament became 'a sordid market place where deputies traded their votes for personal rewards' to the grow-ing disgust of the public.[23]

Only five parties were on the scene at independence. They contested 123 seats in the new legislature. But twenty-one parties fought the general election of 1964 with 973 candidates. On the morrow, however, it was found that the largest grouping, the now decadent Somali Youth League, disposed of 104 seats out of 123. No fewer than sixty-two parties with 1,002 candidates took the field in the elections of January 1969; yet the day afterwards the Somali Youth League was able to count on all the seats save one.

Presented as a multi-party system with the highest creden-tials, the constitution had led directly and indeed logically to a one-party system which was in fact a no-party system. Offered as the framework of a unified nation, it had transformed Somali unity into dozens of quarrelling and useless factions. Argued as the basis for a Somali capitalism, it had ended in a mere system of payola. Only between January and October 1969, Prime Minister Egal is credibly said to have paid out some half a million pounds to parliamentary clients from a treasury desperately short of cash. When the army moved in and stopped this carnival, not a single life had to be taken. That moment, on the contrary, was one of widespread satisfaction.

Other cases revealed the same decay in more complex forms. On the surface often appearing very different, they were in fact an elaboration of the Somali case.

Nigeria was one of these, and, by its size and scope, among the most instructive. Here it was not so much a case of divisions between tribes or clans, although these divisions existed, as between the organized spokesmen of nationalities, some of which were very large. Both aspects of the Somali experience, 'tribalism' and corruption, accordingly emerged with correspondingly greater force, and, as noted in the last chapter, with hugely eruptive fission. The federal assembly became an arena of competition for gains between regional representatives who were, in fact, the deputies of as many ruling groups within constituent nationalities. Each region, three in 1960, four soon afterwards, became as effectively independent of the others, as 'separatist', as the system would allow; and in this respect the system allowed a great deal. Each ruling group milked for its own purposes whatever public funds it could reach, but in doing so, of course, was again behaving as the given model really required; in order, that is, to produce a dominant middle class whose hegemony would impose an 'appropriate value system'.

The system broke down in 1966, irrecoverably in all its political aspects, but its weakness had long become flagrant. The well-known Nigerian who remarked in 1963 that 'one thing is clear in the minds of the young elements in our country: Nigeria is not being effectively governed', was already speaking for a wide conviction. 'Our government,' he went on, 'is a hydra-headed octopus that veers and backs, depending on the prevailing planets and political winds, and that oscillates and flounders and hopes, whatever happens, for the best. It is not purposive; it is not logical; it is not disciplined.'[24] Another Nigerian writer protested at about the same time against 'the appalling mismanagement of our public affairs, the lack of direction on the national level, the moral depravity of our society', and he too was speaking to no hostile audience.[25]

By the outset of 1966, just before the first federal régime of 1960 collapsed in bloodshed, a member of the federal assembly could say that 'this country is on fire', and only assert what everybody well understood.[26] And when the régime crashed a few days later, with the assassination of its prime minister and other leading figures, the event was met with strong public approval. Large numbers of people had passed from disliking their elected leaders into actively despising or even hating them. Many violent preludes to that *coup* of January 1966, notably in the Western Region during 1965, amply prove as much. The young officers shot down their venerable leaders as though it were an act of common justice.

This *coup*, as we saw in the last chapter, really solved nothing. Those who made it passed quickly from the scene and were replaced by more senior officers who, in turn, were removed a few months later by others. The regional divisions – above all, the nationality divisions – were now inflamed beyond bearing, and it seemed for a while that the federation must fall apart. Fears of an 'Igbo plot' to dominate the federation led to widespread slaughter of Igbo residents in the Hausa-Fulani north, and, in 1967, to the secession of the Eastern Region under its Igbo ruling group. This was overcome, but military rule had to continue throughout the federation if only because nothing else seemed able to hold the country together.

Knowing that they must find an alternative, even though, in a telling Nigerian phrase, oil revenues could meanwhile 'stop a lot of mouth', the successive military rulers looked for one. But within the given model of capitalism, which they all accepted, the problem still left them with a hazardous choice. If the return to politics was the return to parliamentary-party rule, how avoid the return to strife between rival segments of the 'new élite' that was to grow, according to the rules, into a bourgeoisie? Or how, if a return to politics was intended as another effort to 'build the nation', avert the renewed alienation of all those multitudes who, again according to the rules of building capitalism, could be admitted to no share in management save the periodical casting of votes? The alienations of the first federation (1960–66) had shown just how destructive popular dissidence could be. Yet return to a parliamentary system pledged to build capitalism meant that no major challenge to that objective would be permissible. In that case, the new parties would be like the old parties: all would have the same programme under regional or local-state variations of form. The centrifugal pressures must then work against the federation in just the same way, essentially, as before. These and other questions and conclusions found more than one anxious voice in the constitutional discussions of 1976 and after.

Yet this appeared to be a far healthier situation than in countries where the proponents of the given model intended to prolong it no matter what the consequences might be. Morocco was a case where questionings were no longer safe or even possible by the early 1970s. A régime of violence had survived at the cost of imposing silence.

The Moroccan background had some conditions that were generally typical. But a high rate of de-ruralization accompanied by rapid population growth had already led by 1960 to an unusually large proportion of 'urbanized': of perhaps 3 million people compared with 8 million remaining in the rural areas. This had gone together with a general impoverishment, hard to define in statistics but evident from massive 'unemployment' in the cities and a falling rate of food production outside them. It appears, for example, that the *per capita* production of cereals had fallen from 364 kgs in 1936 to 115 kgs in 1966, with no improvement on the horizon. Alienation from the political system was acute throughout the population, while tensions between rival groups within the system had become endemic, and were held in check only by repression.

Convergence between élites and masses barely continued after the independence which it had wrested from France. A parliamentary system on the model of the Palais Bourbon soon went to the wall. The history of the first fifteen years of independence, beginning in 1956, is one of singularly stiff handling of protest or revolt. It is also one in which the power of the monarchy was made absolute through a reduction of the political class into clients of the king (Mohamed V to 1961, afterwards Hasan), and, from about 1971, into tied subsidiaries of a royal dictatorship.

This was not smoothly achieved. The bulk of the urban bourgeoisie was well enough content to be the king's junior partner in circumstances which might give it the scope to grow in size, now that direct French domination was removed; but a minority adhered stubbornly to the politics of convergence. This was largely the work of Mehdi ben Barka, who led a minority out of the Istiqlal in 1959 to form a new party, *Union Nationale des Forces Populaires* (UNFP) and tried, in alliance with trade union and other mass organizations, to create what he described as a party 'based on a programme and an ideology', as distinct from a party of businessmen and clients.[27] Ben Barka was assassinated in 1965 as part of the monarchy's successful plan to complete its domination of the state. This plan allowed for the élites to grow, but only within the orbit of royal power. Meanwhile that power was guaranteed by giving its guardians of the army, police, and civilian bureaucracy a share in the spoils.

Royal expropriation relied upon two other supports. The French had already provided the first by their destruction of the ancient quasi-independence of the *bilad as-siba* – the Berber 'zone of dissidence'* – by its absorption in the colonial state after 'pacification' was completed in 1934. This meant that the monarchy could now control the whole of Morocco, by a system of patronage and coercion, in a manner not possible for pre-colonial kings. Secondly, the majority of the Istiqlal willingly confirmed its position as subsidiary ally. What emerged was another case of stability in stagnation. With the economy scarcely expanding, but with population increasing at upwards of three per cent a year or more, even this stability could be prolonged only by heavier repression. Just how tough this repression became was revealed in 1971 when even the king's most trusted janissaries were provoked into trying to kill him. Here, too, the promises of nationalism were sacrificed on the altar of minority dictatorship.

Other cases would lead to comparable conclusions. The given model had failed to work, or had become workable only by denying the liberation it had promised. Yet by this time, whether in one region or another and in varying degrees of clarity, the question of a possible alternative was being openly posed in a number of states where men were free to speak their minds, or else privately, as a mass of evidence could also show, in other states where they were not.

*But 'Berber', as distinct from 'Arab', means less in this context than it might suggest. All Moroccans are Muslim and nearly all, probably, descend from the same ethnic stocks.

29

NEW DEPARTURES: TOWARDS
AN AFRICAN MODEL

A memorable nationalist of the 1920s appealed for a programme of independence which should be thoroughly 'African African', and no copy of any other kind of programme. Half a century after Kobina Sekyi sent forth that call, it could still seem very up-to-date. How were these new nations to develop modes of self-organization that would be adequate to the modern world?

Evasive answers were no longer enough, as when another Ghanaian, a leader of that country's military régime in 1976, told *The Times*[28] that they had tried 'the Westminster pattern' under Busia in 1969–72 (as they had tried it under Nkrumah after 1957), but, because 'this had not proved a success', they were now looking for something different. 'The search would take a long time,' he said, and 'in the end it would be based on local realities and local experience.'

And in Ghana, he could have added, many seekers might be dead, for his country's jails now held political opponents under merciless conditions. Just because political stagnation and autocracy were spreading like a plague, thoughtful persons in many countries now began to argue that home-grown realities could be measured to a democratic system only by far-reaching changes of theory and practice. New ideas and programmes appeared. They were not, as it happened, quite the earliest embodiment of a belief that the 'Westminster pattern' could neither advance independence from the political into the socio-economic field, nor even give it reality in the purely political field. Nkrumah in Ghana had begun to turn away from the given model by about 1961, influenced partly by his experience of trying to work it between 1951 and 1957 as a subordinate, and then after 1957 as leader of an independent government;

partly by the sterility of a parliamentary opposition which rested its case, above all, on a regional separatism; and partly by ideas about the superiority of an eventual socialism. His own experiment, the one-party state which became a no-party state, ended in failure; but later events in Ghana continued to provide an ample demonstration that the failure of this alternative in no way removed the need to find another.

Sékou Touré and the PDG of Guinea had also tried to cut away from the given (French) model early in the 1960s, and with more durable results, although a gradual petrification of personal and bureaucratic rule had produced, by the early 1970s, another form of stagnant frustration. Here there were innovations in the cultural field, however, whose further influence might be dynamic. Modibo Kéita and the nationalists of Mali had moved in the same direction, though hampered by lack of an effective theory of structural change and an effective practice of realizing it; they were in any case re-moved from power in 1968.

Developments in the late 1960s introduced a more effective trend. Its point of departure was that power would always lead to a ruling-group dictatorship, and so into a deepening of the gulf between the few and the many, and thus onward to increasing strife, corruption or defeat, unless power could be derived from structures altogether different from those of the given model. In itself, this conviction was not particularly new in Africa. What was new were its ideas about a possible alternative.

Tentatively, if with much apparent confidence, a new politics began to emerge. This proposed that the leaders in power would have to turn their backs on élitist self-promotion: would have to abandon, that is, the project of becoming a ruling class, and there-fore the aims of trying to build capitalism. They should reorganize their parties and their policies so as to identify their own future, whether as a group or as individuals, with the interests of wage-earners and peasants. To adapt some words of Amílcar Cabral's of 1964 that became widely known, they should 'commit suicide' as a petty bourgeoisie bent on becoming a national bourgeoisie.[29] Putting it another way, ruling groups should sacrifice their specific hopes of gain to a new convergence with the masses, and thereby make the solving of the social problem in all its tensions and complexities the high road to unity and progress.

At the same time, this politics looked to a comparable movement of cultural convergence from the direction of the masses. Just as the ruling few must break with the colonial heritage, so must the many begin to win clear of handicaps imposed by the pre-colonial heritage. No one need be asked to abandon the shrines of the ancestors; but the ancestors must learn to speak the language of modern reality, or else accept retirement into cultural decay. The guidance of ancestral belief, in other words, must begin to make way for that of secular science. Usable survivals of the pre-colonial heritage, on the contrary, should be cherished and developed as part of the basis of a new kind of state.

The one aspect of this cultural change was obviously as difficult to realize as the other. But once both were in motion, it now began to be argued, the colonial heritage of autocracy could be over-come while the pre-colonial heritage, the history of centuries, could receive a new and once more creative content. The national synthesis of an all-embracing community, as viable in the context of the future as the old communities of the ancestors had been viable in the con-text of the past, would then become approachable. The many would have found their historical vocation as makers of the future; merged with the many, so would the few.

This new politics could be called the politics of mass participation. Increasingly, as it continued to unfold, it became known as the politics of liberation. Its development after 1966 occurred in many forms. Obstacles were still more numerous: on the one hand, the habits and interests of new bureaucracies, businessmen, property speculators, and all who hoped to join these by some lucky turn of fortune's wheel; on the other hand, a rural alienation from the sources of state power (a mass alienation, taking city-dwellers into account) that was often both acute and profound. Nothing was easy for this new politics and little, for a long time, proved anywhere successful. But the development persisted, bringing enlargement to the spectrum of political ideas.

*

A simple categorizing of régimes, relating to about 1970 or after, may be helpful at this juncture.

A first category now consisted of a few régimes with relatively strong economies. Their ruling groups could still add wealth and status to themselves, and, by continuing to grow, hope to become a middle class capable of building an indigenous capitalism. Some of these groups were now under military protection; others still managed with civilian equivalents. Examples were Nigeria, Ivory Coast and Liberia in West Africa, Kenya in East Africa, Tunisia in North Africa. Some of them, notably Nigeria, embarked on a constructive process of administrative reform, achieving resilience and flexibility; others merely hardened their arteries. None of them in this period produced any political innovation.

A second category was numerous. These were régimes with relatively weak economies in most or all of which the parliamentary model had decayed into an autocracy, but where, because of economic weakness, ruling groups had no thought of being able to grow into dominant middle classes. Often relying on foreign partners for their survival, these were bureaucratic dictatorships of a peculiarly crude type. A few became personalized tyrannies, as under the Emperor Bokassa or the Saviour Mobutu. They could be called warlord régimes, or piracies. They had no politics worth the name.

A third category, few in number, was also composed of régimes with weak economies, though with one or two potentially wealthy exceptions. These were the régimes that had turned away from the given model and its decadent derivatives, and were ready to experiment with democratic politics. It was among these that political development occurred.

Within this third category a further division needs to be made. Some among them were independent régimes within the 'neo-colonial' situation. Others were régimes-in-formation within territories which otherwise were still colonies. This chapter is concerned with the evolution of the first of these sub-divisions; the next chapter with that of the second.

An important case of political experiment was offered by

Tanzania after 1967.* Here, as in most other independent states, the gains of independence had been real, and these continued. Public health services improved. The schooling system expanded: from a production in 1961, for example, of 176 'high-school seniors' to 1,488 in 1971, and so on down the educational ladder. The economy also expanded, though on familiar colonial lines: little industrial development, but a threefold production of sugar in the first decade of independence, a twofold production of coffee, cotton, pyrethrum. National power capacity increased from 144 million kW. to 380 million in the same ten years.

This was growth within structures carried over from the colonial state, with a corresponding concentration of political and material power in a small ruling group. Elements of capitalism became stronger: for example, in the old producers' cooperatives of the colonial period, in some sectors of private enterprise, in the emergence of a para-statal sector, and even in a few rural areas such as Ismani in Iringa where, early in the 1970s, some 9 per cent of farming families had 53 per cent of land under cultivation, and owned 96 per cent of capital equipment. Yet these elements were far from forming a capitalist system. Meanwhile, the inequalities on which these elements rested became the focus of widening protest.

President since 1961 and a persistently innovating thinker, Julius Nyerere summed up in 1971 the situation as it had appeared in 1966, the year before political experiments began. 'There was a gradual realization that . . . the nation was drifting without any sense of direction.' Existing policy or lack of policy fed growing discouragement, a growing inequality between the few and the many, a growing resentment on the part of the many, and, on the part of the few, a growing tendency to fat living. 'The country was beginning to develop an economic and social élite whose prime concern was profit for themselves and their families, and not the needs of the majority for better basic living standards.'[30] Even the gains of independence deepened these ills within the state, for they gave rise to

*The scene of this experiment was the mainland of former Tanganyika, while a somewhat different history unfolded in Zanzibar (with Pemba).

expectations which the productive system could not satisfy. As elsewhere, this was painfully illustrated by the steady increase of jobless school-leavers.

Working from this kind of analysis, and in a situation where innovating change was less opposed than in Kenya, Nyerere launched the outlines of an alternative in 1967, embodied in a document known as the Arusha Declaration. There it was explained in vigorous and simple Swahili addressed to the whole political community – now a fairly wide one thanks to the grass-roots ramification of the ruling party, Tanganyika African National Union (TANU) – that unity and progress could not be achieved by capitalist forms of growth, but only by the development of alternative policies of self-reliance, democratic participation, and an eventual socialism. A moral homily as much as a political programme, Arusha stated the case for convergence by the few upon the many, aiming at the primacy of the many, in an impressive manner then entirely new.

Convergence by the many on the ideas of modernization was to be by way of development of traditional 'mutual aid', of *ujamaa*, into new forms of collective or cooperative self-organization. Later formulations of this 'policy of self-reliance' had an increasingly practical content. Notable among them was the 1971 *Mwongozo* (Guidelines of TANU) where a democratizing emphasis placed TANU objectives squarely within the politics of liberation. The main thrust now was to build a party of mass participation against the increasing power of a bureaucracy enlarged by the nationalization of banks and other foreign enterprises. Just how much this was required could be seen in the concentration of bureaucratic power: by 1971, for example, nine principal government secretaries were said to have accumulated 89 directorships and 26 chairmanships in the para-statal sector, or an average of 13 each.[31] Corresponding power-rivalries soon accompanied this concentration.

A long contest followed, showing just how difficult it was to promote systemic change within and against an established 'neo-colonial' culture and structure. Nationalizations obstructed the further growth of a commercial bourgeoisie; but they also multiplied the number of bureaucrats. Scattered peasantries were asked to reorganize themselves into self-help villages which the government was ready to equip with elementary social services, such as could not be given to isolated homesteads. But this process of mass participation in social change was increasingly 'expropriated' by being carried through by orders from above, and eventually by merely administrative action. Meanwhile relatively rich peasants set out to appropriate the *ujaama* (self-help) villages to their own ends, or otherwise undermine their collective work.

Wage-earners responded to the ideas and liberties proclaimed in *Mwongozo* with a strengthened social consciousness and will to common action in their self-defence. In 1971–3 alone there were 31 strikes involving some 22,700 workers whose demands went beyond a higher wage, and began to aim at the achievement of a democratic process. They stood by the Arusha projection of a state whose government would be 'elected and led by peasants and workers'. They belaboured managers and officials with Clause 15 of *Mwongozo* which said that 'there must be a deliberate effort to build equality between the leaders and those they lead', and forbade any leader to be 'arrogant, extravagant, contemptuous or oppressive'. Speeches and leaflets reflected the aspirations of an egalitarian democracy. 'We are ready to work night and day if allowed to take over this factory,' declared one placard. 'For twenty-one years now, from 1952 to 1973, there has been no improvement at the factory,' said another. A third said: 'This factory belongs to the workers. It is in Dar not in Persia.'[31a] Several factories were taken over by their workers. But all this was opposed by a heavy bureaucratic hand.

By the middle 70s it was clear that the whole experiment was under heavy attack by dominant groups of bureaucratic or 'petty bourgeois' strata who were unwilling to 'commit suicide' as a privileged class, and that an effective democratization, organized through TANU, had scarcely begun. Critics held that the proclaimed convergence here was little more than a belated example of the old-style populist convergence of the anti-colonial campaigns, or a means to prevent that very class struggle, by the many against the few, such as was now vital to any anti-capitalist alternative. Generally, these critics emphasized the fragility of a democratizing policy based on a party with mass support, but without an articulation into local initiatives and decisions capable of ensuring mass participation. As a one-party state Tanzania had not become a no-party state, but the dangers of this decay were widely discussed.

Those, on the contrary, who believed that the experiment had not failed, or need not fail, accused such critics of a pessimism deriving from European experience or schematic dogmatism. What in any case seemed clear was that the whole political community had moved into a new arena of debate and confrontation since 1967: Tanzania, compared with Kenya, could claim to have become a country of relative participation. Much was in motion, it was argued, whose outcome had yet to be measured.

Theoretically, perhaps, the central question lay in judging the potentials of the dominant strata, bureaucratic or otherwise. Their qualifications ensured that they ran the state. But was it so certain, in Africa's specific circumstances, that they would always come down on the 'pro-capitalist' side of a class contest with peasants and wage-earners? Was this their settled 'petty bourgeois' destiny, here in Africa where class stratifications were still blurred or even embryonic? Having installed themselves inside the 'neo-colonial' state, were they necessarily debarred from seeing its incapacity, and, through seeing this, accepting the need for a different state? In fact, the politics of liberation worked through these years in diverse and sometimes very original forms. To this central question, unexpected answers came to hand.

Somalia was the scene of some of these unexpected answers. By 1969 its régime installed on the Italian parliamentary model in 1960 was in more or less complete decay. *Afminsciar* and *mussoqmassoq*, emotive words denoting administrative folly and corruption, sectional or individual intrigue, waste, irresponsibility, and frustration, had become the badges of a decade of fruitless squabbling and stagnation. Yet there was nothing to suggest that the régime must collapse. No currents of popular revolt were on the scene. The nomads might be abandoned in their wilderness, the towns filled with refugees from rural hunger, the ranks of 'unemployed' swelled with school-leavers. Discontent might be flagrant, and the government deprived of all credence as a patriotic entity. But no practical alternative appeared remotely present. The generals and colonels who abolished the régime in October 1969 could very well have continued to preside over the mixture as before, and confirm the European reputation of their 'petty bourgeois' destiny.

They did not do this. On the contrary, they embarked on an 'African African programme', Somali in this case, aimed at creating national unity out of social unity and not, as the 'neo-colonial' programmes prescribed, the other way round. They were fortunate in possessing a leader, the army commander General Mohamed Siad Barre, whose authority – and indeed whose authenticity as a nomad's son in this country of nomads – was matched, as with Nyerere, by a mind of singular originality and moral strength. To their initial motives of an outraged patriotism Siad Barre added radical ideas of his own, culled partly from a study of modern Italy and partly from a wide experience, together with other radical ideas put forward by a small group of Somali intellectuals.

These ideas took shape slowly. An initial 13-point programme spoke in general terms of the need to build 'a society based on labour and on the principles of social justice'. This had revolutionary implications, but might still be populist verbiage. Having cleaned up the administration with a tough hand, in January 1972 the military government went a step further, declaring in a new 'charter' that 'socialism is the only philosophical system which can help to form a society based on labour and the principles of social justice.' Another kind of 'African socialism'? No: this was to be 'scientific socialism', a term now introduced so as to insist that a marxist analysis had here acquired a local content and application.

The central problem was seen as democratizing a state in which no organs of participation existed to lessen, let alone replace, a merely bureaucratic rule at every level. That could not be done by any capitalist programme possible in Somalia, as the previous decade had painfully proved. But the 'democratization of political power is the only way to interrupt the course of capitalism', in some words of the government's newspaper, *Stella d'Ottobre* (Somali still

being an unwritten language), 'and to develop our national productive forces, with the people becoming participants in the political
and economic management of the nation'.[32] What the few had
therefore to do, Siad affirmed, was to mobilize the many in such a
way as to enable these to face their own problems and, step by step,
assume responsibility. To this end they must 'break with previously
established values': those, that is, of the colonial heritage but also,
where necessary, of the pre-colonial heritage as well.

A first step was to give people command of the language
of politics and administration. This had therefore to become Somali.
By 1973 an effective script was evolved in a Latin-alphabetical form,
breaking with the strong Muslim tradition that if Somali were
written at all it must be written in an Arabic script.* Urban literacy
campaigns were completed by 1973, and in 1974-5 thousands of
secondary-school students and their teachers spent some seven
months in teaching the nomads how to read and write. All administration was now in Somali. Meanwhile the initial means of promoting
mass participation were under construction. A 'proto-party' was
formed in the shape of a 'political office' and its ramifications. This
had the dual task of interweaving itself with the bureaucratic system,
while promoting representative committees of local self-government.
In all settled localities there were installed, by 1975, a complex network of sector and sub-sector and lesser committees down to the
smallest unit of settlement.

This was not yet a working democracy, but it was certainly
the beginning of mass participation. Local powers were handed
progressively to these committees, while developing their elective
structure: by 1975, for example, I found that the city of Kismaayo
had some 1,200 local men and women in self-government committees for a population of about 50,000, and this proportion appeared
to be a general one.

Parallel developments among the nomads were built on
the literacy campaigns. Thanks to this approach, an extremely

*Many efforts had been made to write Somali in an Arabic script
but the latter proved inadequate to Somali, a Cushitic and not Semitic language.

severe drought in 1975 could be greatly alleviated by the opening of relief camps under 'proto-party' as well as bureaucratic control. Subsequently, it proved possible to persuade some 100,000 destitute nomads to join the areas of southern cultivation in new villages organized on a collective and cooperative basis. At the same time, perhaps more remarkably, another 20,000 destitute nomads agreed to abandon their age-old fish taboo, and form fishing cooperatives along the fish-rich seaboard. It appeared obvious that no bureaucratic régime on the old élitist pattern could ever have scored this memorable success, or even attempted it.

Yet this success, however demonstrative of a genuine self-reliance, could still mean that the new régime was different from the old in little more than being honestly devoted to the public good. If the aims of 1972 were to be achieved, military rule would have to go. More, military rule would have to be displaced by the organization of mass involvement in politics. This meant that the 'proto-party' would have to develop into a revolutionary party capable of governing on the principles of 1972: capable, that is, of working for mass participation from the level of local affairs to that of national affairs. This could only be a long and difficult work. Merely to instal a secular caste of 'holy men', preaching socialism but keeping fast hold on bureaucratic power, would clearly end in another form of dictatorship. On the other hand, the years 1960–70 had given any form of 'party politics' a very bad name.

The achievements of the new régime, notably against the 1975 drought, undoubtedly helped at this point. They had done much to induce a higher level of political awareness among a widening number of militants. In June 1976 the ruling military council felt able to dissolve itself into a Somali Revolutionary Socialist party formed at a congress of 3,000 militants, with Siad as secretary-general. With this, the Somali alternative was firmly installed on the basis of a programme derived from Somali realities and addressed to their potentials. But it was characteristic of Siad's style that this régime should sing itself few chants of praise. If a new Somali unity of aim and action within a new national community were now emerging from this priority on the democratization of political power, while the values of a new society were preparing to displace the broken values of the old, this was, to quote Siad in November 1976, 'with humility, patience, and above all the awareness of having launched a very long process, perhaps the work of an entire generation only to ensure its foundations'.[33] Such was the prospect of 1976.

The search for renewal, as distinct from further efforts at working or reforming the imported model, continued in many forms. Some of these were easily observed and reported, as in Tanzania and Somalia. But others we have to follow into distant and obscure places, hidden regions and secret rendezvous, and by way of the minds of men and women of whom the wide world knew precisely nothing.

These others have a central importance in the development of political ideas. For they most clearly reveal the link, often submerged or hard to trace, between old forms of self-defence in anti-colonial resistance, and new forms cast within the mould of modernizing but revolutionary ideas. Or they display, if you prefer, the elusive and uncertain interface between time-honoured ideologies of a primarily religious explanation of the world, or of politics, and new ideologies of a primarily secular conception.

It was along this interface between the teaching of ancestors and the teaching of revolutionaries that the politics of liberation had somehow to take its stand and hold its ground. This proved immensely difficult, perhaps the most intensely passionate enterprise in modern African history: in a large sense, certainly, the most decisive since the first days of primary decolonization. For the problem was never a simple one of straight confrontation between old and new, never a crude matter of mere displacement of the old by the new: but much more, and always in circumstances of enormous risk and hazard, physical exhaustion, mental loneliness, material obstruction, a problem of discovering how to make the new grow out of the old, how to achieve this development as an organic and therefore genuine prolongation of Africa's own history. The great successes, as we shall see, reveal all this in unrelenting tension. But the failures have also much to tell.

After 1961 the ex-Belgian Congo was governed, at least in theory, by politicians and soldiers who had taken part in the destruction of Lumumba and his *Mouvement National* or in the provincial secessions which had accompanied that destruction. Dissidence remained widespread, and found leaders. These were radicals and Lumumbists who had lost out to the right-wing or merely opportunist puppet figures of the 'Binza Group' in Léopold-ville. Prepared in 1963, half a dozen big rebellions erupted in 1964. The biggest were led by Pierre Mulele in Kwilu, and by Gaston Soumialot and others in Kivu and Maniéma. All ended in disaster. This disaster came primarily from the failure of modernizing ideas to get on top of the ancestral heritage.

Each displayed much the same ideological morphology. Mulele called for social revolution, while the others preached at least a 'new liberation', to be won through armed struggle. The most 'ideological' of these leaders, Mulele, took his precepts from China's communists or from the Vietminh or comparable sources. Many of his directives to volunteers, whether these were rural or 'urban', almost literally repeated the maxims of Mao Tse-tung. But those to whom he appealed, chiefly from the Pende nationality, held to their own ideas and continued to explain reality by their own beliefs. Among these beliefs was a conviction that Mulele's rebellion heralded a second and this time true independence, and would be followed by the complete removal of all whites and other oppressors, including those of the Léopoldville régime, with a return in triumph to the rule of the ancestors.

This transformation called for fighting, but victory was seen as being guaranteed by the magical power of Mulele's leader-ship, just as was immunity to death or wounds in battle. Only traitors could be killed by the weapons of the enemy, a comforting belief made the more so by a supporting explanation that was characteristic of the 'fail-safe' nature of religious charters: anyone so killed, it was held, must have been a traitor. Soon Mulele was fol-lowed as a being of indestructible power. Whether or not he could help himself, Mulele went along with this. A Congolese Faust, he called up spirits to his aid. Thinking to control them, he found that they controlled him. Facing bullets undeterred by magic, his followers went down in defeat.[34]

Many of the initial rebels in the eastern risings, led chiefly by Soumialot, appear to have operated outside the close confines of ancestral culture, and adhered, if vaguely, to a modernizing programme of political change. But they were soon swamped by youthful mobs (*simba*, *jeunesses*), often little more than children, for whom variants or distortions of ancestral belief became the only rules they would obey. Baptized into 'a new society, that of the *simba*',[35] these *jeunesses* flung themselves against the official army's battalions with sticks and stones, chants and charms. They were everywhere victorious so long as those battalions, as at first, believed that their adversaries were armed with a magic stronger than their own.

Reliance on ancestral belief deepened with walk-over victories, and the belief became ever more adapted to the circumstances in an armed struggle that was now a fanatical crusade more than any kind of socially motivated revolt. Increasingly, *simba* took their orders not from military commanders with a hold on reality, but from diviners and a specially recruited corps of 'doctors' who received fees on a graduated scale – small fees for *simba*, large for commanders – so as to administer the indispensable *dawa* or immunizing magic. With ancestral belief applied to blindly destructive purposes, the movement became drowned in superstition and fear. The effective enemy ceased to be defined by realistic analysis or study of the official army's tactics and intentions, but by the malevolence of witchcraft. At the order of diviners, witches were duly found and beaten to death or burned alive. A reign of terror beat upon people in captured towns and villages, and those outside this 'new society' were liable to physical abuse or death.

How far Soumialot and other leaders encouraged or failed to discourage this supremacy of *simba* beliefs and practices is not clear from available evidence. They certainly failed in any effort they may have made to secure control of it. Commanders in the field may initially have gone along with *simba* beliefs and practices as a means of winning their 'troops' to a realistic attitude. But the weight of evidence suggests that these commanders either held the same beliefs, or more or less willingly were swept into a full acceptance of them.

The end, again, was disaster. Towards the latter part of 1964 the Léopoldville army's troops began to perceive that well-aimed gunfire was superior to any charm. They had most of the guns in any case, but were helped in November by the landing of Belgian and US paratroops on Stanleyville, then the headquarters of the eastern risings, the object of these landings being to destroy the rebellions and to rescue hostages. After that the *simba* were finished off, sometimes with great carnage, by about 500 white mercenary troops. These, as Verhaegen says, had no military training and for the most part no courage, but made a reputation simply because they disbelieved in magic.* Though dissidence simmered on, the 'neo-colonial' structures of the Congo (Zaire) stood once more intact.

Did these disasters signal an unavoidable failure? Or was it rather that the right politics, and therefore the right leadership, were lacking? Even as the defeats in the Congo became complete, other movements in territories still fully colonial were engaged in other desperate battles. They did not fail. But they had to meet the same harrowing challenge.

*So poor a soldiery were they that even the Léopoldville army, once it had recovered its wits, was able to disperse them. Later, in Angola early in 1976, other bands of European mercenaries were dispersed still more easily by the army of the Republic of Angola with Cuban aid. See W. Burchett and D. Roebuck, *The Whores of War*, Penguin, 1977.

30

THE POLITICS OF LIBERATION

Late in 1963, as Mulele and Soumialot were preparing their ill-fated enterprises in the Kwilu forests and the hills of Kivu, far away in western Africa a different movement of anti-colonial insurrection was also facing defeat, and by the same internal adversary.

This movement was the PAIGC (Partido Africano de Independência da Guiné e Cabo Verde) formed during 1956 in the Portuguese territory of Guiné, lying between Senegal and (ex-French) Guinea, by Amílcar Cabral and five other men. Beginning from practically nothing, the PAIGC was to win throughout the world a great and well-deserved reputation as an effective movement of structural change. Its ideas were to prove far ahead of most political thinking in Africa, and, whether for hard-headed realism or depth of insight, would outmatch the Portuguese dictatorship at every significant point. Yet the PAIGC came now within a hair's-breadth of disaster at the hands of those very types of ancestral belief which ruined the movements of Mulele and Soumialot. That it could survive and win was to mark another large moment in Africa's modern history. The parallels with the Congo rebellions are vividly instructive, but the contrasts in principles and leadership are even more so.

Though very different from the Congolese leaderships in their abilities and background, Cabral and his comrades shared with them a situation much the same in many of its formative aspects. Their country was even more of a rural backwater than the rural Congo. Less than half of one per cent of its population was literate, but here in its rural areas illiteracy was practically total. The vast majority lived within ancestral cultures little modified by Islam, still less by Christianity, and scarcely at all by any modernizing outside influence.

Being unable to induce Lisbon into concessions to African advancement, the PAIGC began preparing for an armed struggle late in 1959. This meant securing a solid base in rural support and the beginnings of rural willingness to participate in war against the colonial power. Very difficult to achieve, the necessary degree of preparation required three years of political work. But in January 1963 the leaders of the PAIGC were ready to begin the fight, and had immediate success. Small groups of fighters attacked Portuguese police and army posts well inside the country, while the bulk of the Portuguese forces stood guard along the frontier against expected infiltration from outside. Several zones were quickly cleared of Portuguese control.

Each group of fighters then made a standing camp in the forest, taking in more volunteers as arms were captured or were trickled across the frontier from neighbouring Guinea. Tactical needs placed these forest bases, each with its own commander, fairly distant from one another. Although linked by couriers, each group was expected to operate more or less on its own, since combined operations had still to be a matter for the future.

After about March 1963 the colonial command counter-attacked in strength with troops and planes brought from Portugal, raiding and bombing the guerrilla bases. Life for the fighters turned difficult and dangerous. In June the rains began, and porterage through swamps and creeks became precarious. Food ran short. With next to no medical service or supplies, fevers and skin ailments were now painfully common. By autumn the movement was deep in trouble, but for reasons very different from any of these. Thirteen years later the PAIGC decided to reveal the full extent of these reasons, and the ways in which disaster was averted.[36]

Drawing on a detailed memory, Luiz Cabral enlarged on the resultant situation at the end of 1963, after nearly a year's guerrilla effort.* He recalled that the PAIGC at this time was heading for

---

*One of the six founders of the PAIGC, Luiz Cabral in 1963 was in charge of the crucial frontier zone of Quitáfine, as well as being a member of the central executive. Ten years later he became president of the independent Republic of Guinea-Bissau while remaining deputy to the secretary-

its ruin: abuse and crime against village people in guerrilla-held areas had led to something like a reign of terror:

> The people were in fear, and our struggle risked destruction at the very moment when our fighters had taken to arms. We found that abominable crimes were being committed in our name, and that people had begun to flee from some of our liberated zones. The best fled to other zones controlled by those of our comrades, Nino and others, who stood firm for the unity and aims of our party. But even these comrades were in danger of being killed by the ones who were committing crimes.[37]

What had happened?
Francisco Mendes*:

> These problems became acute after our militants began to receive arms from the exterior and to reinforce guerrilla bases during the second half of 1963. Such problems were worsened by long distances between bases, and poor communications. With fighting groups more or less autonomous, an overall control was hard to exercise. And most of our militants were young and inexperienced.

> At that point, many fighters began to exploit their new authority for personal reasons. They began to reject the overall authority and unity of our party, and to abuse the people, especially the women, in zones they controlled. Above all, they began to group themselves on a tribal basis, to build an autonomy on tribal affiliation and religious belief, to give priority in recruitment and the handing-out of arms to members of their own tribes or families, or through their tribal chiefs if they had any.

Other aspects of the situation that had overwhelmed Mulele and Soumialot one by one appeared. Mendes: 'These men also began to seek advice in old customs and beliefs about witchcraft,

---

general of the PAIGC, Aristides Pereira, who had succeeded Amílcar Cabral after the latter's assassination by agents of the Portuguese dictatorship in January 1973.

*Another formidable Bissau recruit to the PAIGC, Mendes (Chico Té) worked as a political initiator in the north of the country and then was principal commander in the north. In 1974 he became prime minister of Guinea-Bissau.

invoking the spirits of their ancestors or the spirits of the forest (*irãos*) with the help of charms and ceremonies, asking their diviners to find out if their actions could be successful. They became the victims of these beliefs. They made others the victims of them, too.' Just as in the Congo, the belief in bullet-immunizing charms became common, and, again as in the Congo, 'the belief that death or wounding in battle was brought to this or that militant by witchcraft. So that when the Portuguese attacked or bombed their bases, they rejected efficacious methods of self-defence, realist methods, and said instead that witches had eaten their men. There began a hunt for "witches", and some of those accused of witchcraft were shot and others were even burned alive.'

Bernardo Vieira (Nino), with Umaro Diallo as his second in command, was then in charge of crucial southern areas (Cubucaré, Tombali, Como).* Young men like Mendes – all three were in their early twenties – these two met this calamity at its most severe, no doubt because the peoples of the south, chiefly Balante and Nalu, had retained a strong hold on their ancestral cultures: in contrast with the north, where these problems were much less acute, few were Muslim.†

What they had most to fight against at first, Vieira and Diallo recalled, was 'tribalism – at that stage a worse enemy than the Portuguese. We had to mobilize our people and explain realities to them, the realities in which they lived: not big things like imperialism and colonialism, of which they'd never heard, but colonial taxes, forced labour, local oppression. That was how we could build unity in our struggle. We had steady success, but tribal conflicts and beliefs became the major obstacle.' Vieira: 'Each tribe had its own customs, modes of making sacrifice, beliefs. We were not as we are

*Other leading volunteers of the first hour, whose courage and intelligence proved decisive, Vieira became Commissioner for Defence of the Republic of Guinea-Bissau in 1974 and Diallo the army's chief of staff.

†Which is not to say that Muslims had no magical practices. On the contrary, Muslim 'marabouts' were the chief providers of magical charms. They seem to have done it as a business. 'We pointed out to our militants,' Mendes said, 'that those marabouts didn't even believe in their own charms, because they all fled to the frontier when the fighting began.'

not against religion, as such; and so we didn't want to interfere. The people really believed in their religion; besides, unnecessary clashes with witch-doctors (*feitiçeiros*) had to be avoided because these persons had great local prestige.'

But matters now reached a point where they had to interfere, both because of the principles of their politics and because they would otherwise lose control of the movement they had launched. This is where we reach the point of crucial difference from the Congolese movements. Nino, Mendes, Osvaldo and their like did indeed interfere.

Vieira:

For example, people believed in the witch-doctors when these said that if someone fell ill then it was because the old people wanted to kill that person.* Then the young men went out in groups to find the guilty witches. This happened in our zone, as the armed struggle got under way, and with very bad consequences. I remember once we were crossing a river, and a man fell in and drowned. The militants of that place – not the fighters under my command, but the village militants – came to me and said the old ones were responsible. They said they didn't know which old ones, and demanded my permission to go and kill the old ones [whom they could find]. I refused to let them. I refused. I tried to explain that the man had drowned because he had fallen into the river and could not be saved. They wouldn't have my explanation. They even went on a sort of strike against us, saying they would carry no more supplies. But I stood firm, and found other ways of carrying supplies. After that, gradually they listened.

But this loss of control to magical belief was widespread:

It happened in many places. In our zone, for example, there was a witch-doctor at Dar-Salaam [a crucial point of creek-crossing between the mainland and the 'island' of Como] who had a lot of persons seized and beaten. Umaro and I went there and set them free.

*Not, of course, a belief peculiar to Guinea-Bissau. The literature on witchcraft in Africa is large and often luminous. For my own résumé of the evidence, see *The Africans*, Longmans, 1969. (*The African Genius*, Atlantic, Boston, 1969.)

The local people were angry with us: they said that we wouldn't even allow them to 'wash' their village. Sometimes the witch-doctors accused persons of giving information to the enemy so that the enemy came and bombed them. They said that the witches brought the aircraft there. And the villagers killed these 'witches' and sometimes burned them alive. Or they seized all the goods and belongings of an accused person.

In this situation,

it came to a test. I decided to arrest a widely known witch-doctor, a woman called Kubai. She was going about everywhere in our zone, raising accusations, sowing fear; she was the chief witch-doctor in our zone. I arrested her and accused her of crimes, making her frightened. After a while she said she would tell the truth: that all her accusations were lies, lies she had learned to tell from her father. I even got her to say how many people she had caused to be killed. Then I called the villagers where we were, and she said all this in public, openly, before them all. And I called more people from other villages, and she told the truth to them as well. And people began to understand.

The evidence shows that it required great courage and determination to withstand the pressures of these beliefs and practices, but also, crucially, that it called for a fixed loyalty to the revolutionary teachings of Cabral, through whose school Vieira, Umaro and others like them had passed, as well as an unusual clarity of mind about the purposes of those teachings. Not everyone had these virtues. Vieira:

Some of our commanders let themselves be dominated by such beliefs, even if they didn't much believe in them. Some even killed 'witches' themselves. Umaro and I had to stand against all that, we had to cut through all that. Yet it was difficult to convince some of our comrades. Then it got to the point even where witch-doctors were learning commanders' military plans and deciding which actions should be made and which should not. Commanders began to refuse our orders. One in particular, near Bedanda (Cubucaré), even planned to ambush and kill me. Luckily, the local people heard about it and warned me. There were those among our comrades who wanted me to attack him. I preferred not to do that. I went to visit him in his base, but I couldn't persuade him. He'd become insupportable. He was already in open revolt.

It was now touch-and-go in these critically important southern zones. Characteristically deciding that the issue must be brought to a head, no matter what might follow, Amílcar Cabral decided to call a congress of all leading commanders and militants. Organized largely by Luiz Cabral and presided over by Amílcar, whose authority in the movement appears to have remained unquestioned even while some commanders were refusing obedience to executive orders, this congress aimed at a decisive showdown. Taking place on 13 to 17 February 1964, in the presence of some 200 persons, it certainly arrived at one.

Commanders and leading militants were assembled by many days of hard marching. The congress took place in a forest clearing near the small village of Cássaca in Quitáfine, a zone less subject to the witch-hunt 'reign of terror' than others in the south, and at a moment when tough fighting was in progress against a Portuguese offensive aimed at re-taking the nearby 'island' of Como. Only three commanders refused to attend. But most of the others, save for those remaining loyal to PAIGC policy, came as though they were independent potentates: 'just like tribal chiefs, each with his personal servants, followers, and guards' (Mendes). Each sat down separately around the clearing, each entourage obeying its own commander and nobody else. As well as these there were the commanders and militants loyal to the leadership, provided with a contingent of armed fighters under Osvaldo Vieira.* The question was: who would prevail?

The evidence suggests that nobody was sure of the answer when the congress opened. There is space here only for crucial points. Briefly summarizing, three factors proved decisive. These were the nature and unity of the leadership, the existence of such men as Pereira, Luiz Cabral, Mendes, Vieira, and the character and quality of Amílcar Cabral himself. Begun in an atmosphere of suspicion and hostility, the congress gradually thawed a little. All who had come, however recalcitrant some of them might be, still believed

---

*No relation of Bernardo Vieira's, but a leading commander in the north of the country. Volunteering in Bissau in 1959, he died of cancer in 1973.

that they were followers of Cabral; and all of them still faced the same enemy, while from across the sea-creeks, as a sufficient reminder of that, there came throughout those days the sound of gunfire from Como, where others of their units were engaged in a life-and-death fight to hold the island. Cabral steered the congress according to his plan, leading it to a crucial session which lasted from eight in the evening until near dawn the next day. In this session he turned to 'questioning all the civilian militants [who had also been invited to attend] from various zones. These spoke one by one of the barbarities which were being committed against the civilian population.' (Luiz Cabral)

As the night wore on, angry or bitter revelations built an atmosphere of shame and revulsion. Cabral waited until all had said their say, and then spoke at length. Mendes:

He said that he had not created the party to give any tribe or group an advantage over others, but for the liberation of our whole people. He said that the party had to be the instrument of a *national* unity. He said that this unity must be forged in our struggle against the colonialists. He spoke of the old resistances that had all failed – and why? Because then each people had fought for itself, and so the Portuguese could always win. Now was the time to resist with all our people fighting together against the same enemy.

About witchcraft, he said that this was indeed a reality in African belief, but that we must go beyond it.

Then he dwelt on the crimes and abuses, 'and condemned all who were guilty of them'. Towards dawn, as he wrestled with the conscience of the dissidents, there came a dramatic moment. One of the guilty affirmed: 'Very well, if you think I am to blame for these things, then disarm me and investigate.' Cabral replied: 'Yes, I agree. I order you to be disarmed.' All sources affirm that this was an agonizing moment of decision. But the man put down his weapon on the ground in front of him. Cabral said: 'Now I order the others to be disarmed.' And that worked, too: first the rank-and-file fighters in the entourages put down their arms, and at last their commanders. With the loyalists remaining under arms, the courage and clarity of this leadership had won.

Luiz Cabral: 'It was decided to arrest all who had done harm. Osvaldo (Vieira) and Constantino (Teixeira) were in charge of that. Afterwards we sent these men to different zones where later on they became reintegrated in our ranks; some of them today are even commanders. We had to execute only two men who were past saving, who were in open revolt, who had refused to attend', the third commander who had refused to attend being killed by a Portuguese bomb. This done, the PAIGC leaders launched the core of a regular army, both as an additional protection against any renewed disintegration of control and as a move towards mobile warfare. Beginning with 900 volunteers who then found they must go wherever they were told, this force suffered a desertion rate at the outset of between thirty and forty per cent, but grew strong enough, within four years, to have fought the Portuguese to a standstill. They established local courts under village leadership, and took other steps to ensure that their politics were empowered with sufficient strength to enable justice and tolerance to carry their cause to success.

No attacks were made on religion provided that it made no further threat to unity. Bernardo Vieira: 'Even to the end of the war (in 1974) our fighters wore *gri-gris* (amulets) if they wanted. They would even ask for leave to go to their villages and undergo the cure of the country: that is, receive the blessing of the ancestors. And we allowed this': with good reason, for once the diviners had understood the process now in play, the advice of the ancestors fell duly into line with it. 'They came back to us strengthened in their self-confidence. They fought better. They had more courage.'

I have dwelt on these details not so much for their intrinsic interest, though that is considerable, as because they define a moment in the development of ideas, absolutely decisive for any further progress, when the primacy of ancestral belief was made to give way to a fully secular interpretation of reality: when, as it were, the Balante and the Nalu sufficiently accepted that the world was round and revolved about the sun, and was not the centre of the universe, no matter how sincerely they might continue to 'go to church'.

From this time onward the movement launched by the PAIGC could and did increasingly operate as a firm unity of participation in the modernizing and socially revolutionary ideas and aims enunciated by its leadership. Whether one cares to see this as a development in religious thought, or, more meaningfully as it seems to me, as a critical 'break' between the religious and the scientific approaches to reality, it is clear that something of profound importance had occurred. From the clarity and courage of Cabral and those young men who had 'interfered' there evidently flowed, for the peoples who followed them, the onset of a new age. They had taken the full weight of an old history on their shoulders, and had thrust open the door to a new history.*

Here it was, in other words, that convergence of the many on the liberating ideas of the few was caused to meet the convergence of the few on the primacy and interests of the many. The programme of the PAIGC was thus confirmed, as elsewhere with its companion movements in Angola and Mozambique, in an effort 'to free and modernize our peoples by a dual revolution: against their traditional structures which can no longer serve them, and against colonial rule'.[38] With this, success became possible.

The success was continuous and in the end complete, as the bare facts are enough to show.[38a]

By 1968 the army of the PAIGC had effectively won the war on the mainland of Guiné. Incapable of recovering a strategic initiative, the armies of Portugal were held at their work there by fear of the consequences that a withdrawal from Guiné would have for Angola and Mozambique. They stopped fighting in April 1974 after the young officers' *coup* within the Portuguese army which,

*If in different circumstances, and with less drama, the same break-through also occurred with MPLA in Angola and Frelimo in Mozambique: see, e.g. my *In the Eye of the Storm: Angola's People*, Longmans, 1972, Penguin, 1974, introduction. The capacity to make this 'break' was indeed a central proof of these movements' having taken the essential step from merely anti-colonial politics to the politics of liberation. Other movements of the same type, or aspiring to be such, would have to meet the same test. In Benin (Dahomey), for example, the new régime of Kérékou engaged in 1975 in a 'vast battle against sorcerers, covens of witches, secret societies, food taboos', etc. (*Afrique-Asie*, Paris, 29 November 1975) deeply influenced by experience in the colonial wars and perhaps above all in Guiné, overthrew the dictatorship prolonged by Marcello Caetano from the time of Oliveira Salazar.[39] During 1972 the PAIGC held a general election in its liberated zones (then some two-thirds of the country), and proclaimed an independent state in September 1973. Independence was made complete in September 1974. In the Cape Verde Islands, linked culturally with Guiné since the sixteenth century, a general election in June 1975 gave an overwhelming victory to the PAIGC,[40] and the Cape Verde became a sovereign republic a month later.

Comparable policies led to the same decisive victory for the Mozambique Front of Liberation (FRELIMO). Formed in 1972 in Dar es-Salaam (Tanzania) as a coalition of several small nationalist groups of diverse ideas, under the strong leadership of Eduardo Mondlane, FRELIMO began its armed struggle in September 1974, having trained several hundred volunteers in guerrilla warfare in Algeria. Successes were achieved in the two northernmost provinces, Cabo Delgado and Niassa. But further progress was stalled until 1968–9 when a majority of the leadership, first under Mondlane and then (after Mondlane's assassination by agents of Portuguese inspiration in January 1969) under Samora Machel, successfully forged a policy of all-out revolutionary struggle against a minority in favour of compromise; opened new fronts; and installed the power of FRELIMO as far as the middle of Mozambique by the time of the April 1974 *coup* in Lisbon. As elsewhere, the post-*coup* Portuguese leadership of General António de Spínola tried to recover by negotiation what it had lost in war, but, as elsewhere, failed. Mozambique acquired an unconditional independence under FRELIMO in June 1975.

Angola's advance to the same end proved more difficult. The ideas and basic policies of the Angolan liberation movement, MPLA, were indeed no different from those of PAIGC or FRELIMO, but MPLA laboured under two especial handicaps. One of these was the continued and unbending hostility of the Zaire authorities of President Mobutu, who worked for an Angolan decolonization which should give him and through him his international backers (chiefly, as before, the USA), a predominant influence in an Angola detached from Portugal. This Zaire hostility meant, in practice, that the military effort of MPLA was largely held to the vast and semi-desert eastern districts far from the principal centres of population.

A second difficulty lay in the divisive activities of Mobutu's favoured movement led by Holden Roberto, the FNLA, and, after 1970, in the similarly divisive activities of UNITA under Jonas Savimbi, a movement largely created to oppose MPLA.[41] In terms of the development of ideas, Holden's FNLA could at best claim to be a movement of anti-colonial nationalism, though chiefly of the Kongo nationality on which it was almost exclusively based, while Savimbi's UNITA, though still more doubtfully, might also claim to be a movement of reformist compromise. Neither had any of the attributes of a movement of national liberation.

As things evolved after the Lisbon *coup* of April 1974, external opinion hostile to the politics of liberation ensured that the defeat of the Portuguese would be followed by a trial of strength between these two factions on one side, and MPLA on the other. The former were presented by this external opinion as 'anti-communist' while the MPLA was labelled as 'communist'. While holding the ring in 1975, the Portuguese tried to square a circle by promoting a 'transitional government' of all three movements. This led only to fighting and disruption. Initiated by FNLA, a 'second war of liberation' now brought fresh successes to MPLA which had asserted its primacy in twelve out of sixteen districts by September 1975 and was poised to secure the rest. In order to stop MPLA from winning, a large-scale invasion from the north was then mounted by Mobutu in Zaire with a mixed force of FNLA, disguised Zairean army, and white mercenary troops; when this proved not enough, there came another invasion from the south in October 1975, this time by some 6,000 white South African troops with armour and air support, again in cooperation with armed bands of FNLA and UNITA. By March 1976, MPLA forces had routed both invasions, partly with the aid of Soviet weaponry and partly with the support of a Cuban force which had begun to arrive, at MPLA invitation, in the wake of South African intervention. Proclaimed in November 1975, the republic of

Angola under MPLA government reached full sovereignty with the defeat of these invasions.

A propagandist view of all these events, that the movements of national liberation were agents or instruments of a Soviet imperialism, need not detain us here. Much aired at the time, this view was possible in the resultant African situation only for those who ignored the nature of the movements and their history. These owed much to Soviet aid in the military field (as the MPLA to Cuban military aid), but their evolution in the political field remained their own. This evolution showed strong influence from a marxist approach to reality: indeed, these movements may be said to have been the first in Africa to have fully indigenized a marxist analysis; and they were certainly bent on finding an alternative to the capitalist nation-state. But what their evolution really displayed was an African politics of mass participation in a mature phase. Their search for an alternative derived from the nature and application of that politics.

When they began, the pioneers of these movements were even more emphatically 'nationalists without nations' than any nationalists elsewhere. It might be possible in other colonies to think of building nations on the model of Britain, France, or Italy; in these colonies, the politics of Lisbon ensured that there could not be the smallest scope for building nations on the model of Portugal. No such option existed for the educated few. This being so, their merit lay in fully accepting the conclusions that must flow from this: either continued defeat, or an attempt, however difficult, to build nations on a different model. Whatever that might become, they saw that nothing could be achieved unless the educated few, or those among them with the courage and clarity to try it, were able to identify themselves with the interests and cultures of the many.

This was their unvaried beginning. They 'went to the people'. Those who survived the repression of the late 1950s and early 1960s continued with the launching of an armed struggle. By harsh experience, this soon confirmed their need for policies altogether different from a mere reform of the colonial state. Élitism here would get nowhere, for nothing useful could be done unless mass sympathy or support were transformed progressively into mass participation. Here no quantity of fine words would help. The peasants would fight, would accept the bitterness of such warfare and hold firm against the worst reprisals, only if they were sure that their own interests stood at the heart and centre of the struggle.

For the leaders, unavoidably, this meant accepting that the solving of the 'national question', the problem of building a national consciousness real enough to absorb each existing 'pre-national' consciousness or individualist divergence, must always depend on solving the 'social question', the problem of meeting the material and cultural needs of everyday life. Out of this necessary acceptance (and those who refused it were lost) there came the practice of their revolutionary theory: the immensely difficult promotion, in liberated zones, of a new socio-cultural system based on the democracy of village committees and the creation of elementary schools, clinics, trading networks, tribunals, and the rest. A new type of state could thus emerge in embryo even while the wars continued.

To that development the armies of colonial power opposed more than a decade of unrelenting warfare; and we have seen some of the obstacles thrown up by the pre-colonial heritage. The need to overcome both was the sense of Agostinho Neto's definition of 'dual revolution'.* Other leaders said the same thing in other words. 'When we took up arms to defeat the old order,' explained the Mozambican leader, Samora Machel, in 1974, 'we felt the obscure need to create a new society . . . in which all men free from all exploitation would cooperate for the progress of all. In the course of our struggle, in the tough fight we have had to wage against re-actionary elements, we came to understand our objective more clearly. We felt especially that the struggle to create new structures would fall within the creation of a new mentality . . .' This had to call for the reduction of individualism, for the liberation of women, for the building of attitudes of collective responsibility. It had to impose a break with the pre-colonial as well as the colonial heritage, for 'in order to lay the foundations of a prosperous and advanced economy, science has to overcome superstition . . .'[42]

*See p. 350.

With time and travail, the practice of this theory duly evoked its two-way effect. Many of Cabral's writings emphasize this. Coming chiefly from the towns, and usually with an inherited contempt for 'peasant simplicity' and 'peasant ideas', the leaders 'live day by day with various peasant groups in the heart of rural populations, and come to know the people better. They discover at the grass roots the richness of the people's cultural values ... acquire a clearer understanding of the economic realities of their country, as well as of the problems, hopes, and sufferings of the masses of the people.' Steadily, the leaders 'enrich their own culture, reinforce their ability to serve the movement by serving the people'.

Crossing the cultural divide between themselves and the many, the leaders then found that the many were ready to come to meet them. 'On their side, the working masses and especially the peasants, who are usually illiterate and have never moved outside the boundaries of their village or region, come into contact with other groups, lose the complexes which limited them in their relationship with other groups, whether ethnic or social, and perceive their crucial role in the whole struggle. They break the bonds of the village universe and integrate progressively with their country and with the world.'[43]

This was not to question the validity of Africa's own heritage, but to give that heritage a wide scope for development. The future would still be built upon the past, but in a new synthesis with the present. 'While we scrap colonial culture and the negative aspects of our own culture, whether in our character or environment, we have to create a new culture, also based on our traditions but respecting everything that the world today has conquered for the service of mankind.'[44]

This emergent synthesis was both the product of the politics of mass participation, as evinced in these wars of national liberation, and the essential means of their success. That is one central reason why these movements have to be seen as fully indigenous, no matter how much they may have owed to the initial stimulus of European revolutionary ideas, or, later on, to various forms of Soviet or other external aid. Logically, after independence, policies aimed at a further development of grass roots democracy along the lines of the wartime liberated zones. These assumed various forms of *poder popular*, 'people's power', according to different local circumstances in the new republics. Certainly, this mature politics of participation now faced a maze of new problems. Just as certainly, the authenticity of its success carried development of the ideas of nationalism still further into a new stage, opening new perspectives for reorganization and independence in ever stronger contrast with the 'neo-colonial' stage of the politics of populism. How widely this was felt to be the case, even by 1975, could be seen in the still embattled countries to the southward.

31

UNDER THE SOUTHERN CROSS

These developments in the politics of liberation had little or no effect on Rhodesia, Namibia or South Africa before 1974. Either from the enforced provincialism of their situation or from the scepticism of despair, or perhaps as much from a very characteristic doubt in colonized African minds as to whether 'other Africans' could do anything new or useful, the enclosed black populations gave little sign of understanding what was under way in the Portuguese territories.[45] On their side the white minority régimes had an even greater ignorance or indifference, in this respect following the judgement of the US National Security Council which, as late as 1970, insisted that all the white minority régimes were there to stay, including those of Portugal.[46]

After 1974, however, the effects of Portuguese defeat by the liberation movements exercised a growing influence throughout southern Africa. The politics of constitutional reform linked to protest by peaceful means began to make way for more effective and therefore more radical action. A new note was heard. A leading militant of the Zimbabwe People's Army (ZIPA), by this time waging a guerrilla war inside Rhodesia, spoke for this when he affirmed in October 1976 that: 'We are not fighting for economic or political reforms. We are fighting for the complete transformation of Zimbabwean society.'[47] A further extension of the politics of liberation would now unfold in these southern countries. But the route to that development, as well as its early consequences, proved long and dubious.

Anti-colonial protest in Southern Rhodesia* had won mass
*The 'Southern' was dropped with the independence in 1964 of

support many years earlier. Led by men who seldom belonged to any kind of élite, this took forms that remained close to the interests of the many, especially in the towns. Much concerned with the alleviation of everyday grievances arising out of white discrimination, protest organizations found a base in African trade unions and other urban associations.

Given that Rhodesia was still a colony in formal terms, and that neighbouring territories had made progress or seemed bound to make it by a peaceful pressure for concessions to African equality, the leaders of anti-colonial protest found it reasonable to think that the same means in Rhodesia could yield the same result. Joined in congress-type movements, they took it for granted that their chief purpose was not to aim at any 'complete transformation of Zimbabwean society', but to give Africans a share, eventually dominant, in the reform and benefit of the existing system.

Just how little reform might achieve was repeatedly shown by every aspect of daily life, whether in relation to pass laws, movement restrictions, labour colour-bars, discriminatory land apportionment, or other parts of an all-pervasively racist system. Yet the real potentials of reform were best illustrated perhaps by the schooling structure. In 1947, 81,821 African children were registered in the lowest school class, 'sub-Standard A'. But even this small fraction of the total African school-age population seldom got beyond the second lowest class, 'sub-Standard B'. In 1954 only 4,429 reached Standard IV; in 1956 only 1,889 were in the second year of post-primary education (Form II); and in 1960 no more than fifteen pupils of the more than 81,000 who had entered the schooling system in 1947 were able to complete the twelve-year gamut of classes which gave the qualifications of a secondary-school leaver. The upper levels improved early in the 1960s, and African secondary-school leavers began to trickle into the University of Rhodesia. Yet in 1965 the government was still spending £6.12 million on educating some 60,000 Europeans and £6.45 million on educating some 643,000 Africans: or about the same amounts for a white–black ratio of about

Northern Rhodesia (Zambia), while nationalists had already begun to call their country Zimbabwe after its ancient culture of that name.

one to ten in a population where blacks now outnumbered whites by about sixteen to one.

Hopes vested in reform were somewhat reinforced in 1961. The two northern colonies of the not yet defunct Central African Federation were now clearly moving towards black majority rule and independence. Reacting against this, Rhodesia's whites began to clamour for their own sovereignty. But with decolonization far advanced in most of Africa, London insisted on prior steps towards majority rule. After much elbowing this led to a new constitution, the first since that of 1923 had given the local whites a virtually complete sovereignty.* Stipulating a weirdly complex 'weighting' of votes between a white 'A' roll and a black 'B' roll, so composed as to ensure that the 'A' roll would remain on top, and justifiably described by the prominent African spokesman Joshua Nkomo as being 'drawn up by White men for White men', this very cautious step towards an eventual electoral majority for Africans was approved in a practically all-white referendum by 41,949 votes to 21,846, this being a 77 per cent poll of those eligible to vote. Characteristically, the decorative importance of chiefs was enhanced by the formation of a Council of Chiefs, even though most of the men in question were government-salaried nominees or persons of no traditional authority.

Hindsight would indicate that this constitution gave the whites all that they essentially needed in order to guarantee their political and economic control for all foreseeable time. But white provincialism once again triumphed: the timid concessions of this constitution merely inflamed white racism. A general election of December 1962 gave a majority to a new party of diehards, the Rhodesia Front. Its leader, Winston Field, was described by the London *Financial Times* as a 'right-wing tobacco farmer', which was putting it mildly in terms of political attitudes in Europe, but even Field was soon found 'too soft' by his electors. Meanwhile he introduced new measures of political repression and in 1963, when the Central African Federation died, put in a formal demand for Rhodesian

*'Reserved clauses' were written into the 1923 constitution, opposing racist discrimination against blacks, but remained a dead letter.

independence. A Conservative British government stalled uneasily, but eventually made its agreement conditional upon a more liberal constitution. Independence, it agreed with the Labour opposition, could be given only to a Rhodesia ruled by the majority of its whole population.

A substantial fraction of whites now began to think of taking what London would not give. Asked in January 1964 what would happen 'if we declared our independence', Field's deputy as prime minister, Ian Smith, replied that it 'might be a three-day wonder'. In June Smith ousted Field and in May 1965 won another white general election by a landslide over the 'moderates' of the old United Federal Party. Just over 2,000 Africans voted (on the 'B' roll); of these, 209 voted for Smith's Rhodesia Front. 'It seems to me,' Smith commented, 'that it is the real Rhodesian nation which has emerged.'[48] He was only saying what all settler spokesmen had always thought: the 'nation' could only be the whites, undiluted save by a few tame blacks.

What London had refused to Field it continued to refuse to Smith, and on 11 November 1965 Smith carried out the Rhodesia Front's long-announced plan, and declared Rhodesia independent by unilateral decision. This was rebellion against the British Crown, but the Crown took it very tamely, refusing to reassert its formal control by military means, although that might have been easy then, and contenting itself with economic sanctions. These were later widened by the United Nations, but were rendered ineffective by South Africa, Portugal and an array of sanctions-breaking business-men in many countries. The rebel régime easily survived.

This proof that constitutional pressures would yield no good stiffened African protest. But its style remained opportunist, confusedly demagogic, and given to rivalries and splits. Such frailties were increased by a political repression which now sent many of the established leaders into long years of prison or rural detention, while sporadic outbursts of police activity carted off hundreds, in the end thousands, of their followers. A crucial split in African political ranks had in fact already occurred between the Zimbabwe African People's Union (ZAPU) formed in December 1961 by the Bulawayo trade unionist Joshua Nkomo and chiefly Ndebele in composition, and a fraction, chiefly Shona, led by the Rev. Ndabaningi Sithole, which broke away and formed the Zimbabwe African National Union (ZANU) late in 1963.

Both of these organizations now turned to the tactics of armed struggle, though with ZANU in the lead, basing their actions on infiltration from Zambia. The first of these actions came in the middle of 1966. None was effective. By the end of 1968 some eighty-six captured raiders were under sentence of death in Rhodesia, although executions began only later. Nationalist politics were now in exile, where leaders continued to spar for supremacy in Lusaka, Zambia's capital, and elsewhere. Soon they were suffering from an acute form of that *dementia emigrantis* which commonly occurs in such cases.* Violent dissensions erupted between factions, leading to the demoralization of fighting men assembled at training and holding bases in Zambia. This misery culminated in 1975 with the murder in Lusaka, so far unexplained in any satisfactory way, of the leading ZANU proponent of armed struggle, the barrister Herbert Chitepo. By this time, Zimbabwean exile politics had become deeply enmeshed in wider issues, Zambia's president, Kenneth Kaunda, having decided that progress in Rhodesia might best be achieved through negotiations with Ian Smith's protector, Prime Minister John B. Vorster of South Africa.

Meanwhile, with Mozambique's accession to independence under FRELIMO in June 1975, the politics of liberation began to work its influence on young militants in the base camps. This influence widened as President Samora Machel applied economic sanctions to Rhodesia in line with UN policy, declared his government's full support for Zimbabwean liberation, opened his territory to Zimbabwean fighters, and, in 1976, began giving these guerrillas an active aid. Responding, these fighters turned their backs on their quarrelling politicians, and set their sights, in the word of Chidawa Chirimuta quoted at the outset of this chapter, on 'a complete

---

*I owe the name of this well-known disease to Professor Hugh Seton-Watson, who identified it among European political exiles during the Second World War.

transformation of society'. By late 1976, with thousands of fighters now inside Zimbabwe and scoring many small successes, an armed struggle stretched white forces to their probable limit of possible mobilization, and Smith was having to buy as many foreign mercenaries as he could find.

Learning from their miscalculation over the Portuguese territories, Washington and Pretoria saw that a continuation of this armed struggle was likely to produce an irreversible radicalization of African political opinion in Zimbabwe, and lead to a decolonization on the pattern of the Portuguese territories. Their only alternative was to press the Smith régime into political concessions. With Vorster uneasily consenting, such pressure was duly applied by the US government. Late in September 1976 Smith told his electorate that majority rule would have to come within two years. Smith and his allies now embarked upon a long rearguard action, testing Zimbabwean political leadership more severely even than before.

Other such tests emerged in Namibia (South-West Africa), where the political stagnation of half a century was again quickened by Portugal's eviction from Angola.

Although in theory a League of Nations Mandate after 1919 and a Trusteeship Territory of the United Nations since 1945, 'South West' had become a South African colony in all but name. Little save sporadic protest broke the silence until 1945, when the echoes of the Atlantic Charter and the Charter of the UN began to encourage spokesmen of several ethnic groups to petition the UN against racist government. Entered over many years, these petitions produced no changes but helped to build international support. In June 1971 the International Court of Justice finally advised the Security Council, on the latter's request for an opinion, that South Africa's administrative presence in Namibia was illegal, and, this being so, 'South Africa is under obligation to withdraw its administration from Namibia immediately, and thus put an end to its occupation of the territory.'

Though ignored by Pretoria, this prestigious opinion gave the African group at the UN a new field for pressure. They were able to make some tactical gains. A UN Council for Namibia was formed to assist an eventual transfer of power, and, in 1975, an Institute for Namibia was installed in Lusaka (capital of Zambia) with the object of providing practical training of Namibian personnel. But protracted exchanges between the UN secretary-general, Dr Kurt Waldheim, and the South African authority remained without result. A good deal more was evidently needed. This could only come from greater nationalist pressure.

Nationalist organizations had crystallized in 1959 with the formation of the South West Africa National Union (SWANU), and, more important, with the self-organization of the major constituent people, the Ovambo,* in an Ovamboland People's Organization (OPO) which then expanded, a year later, into the South West Africa's People's Organization (SWAPO), henceforth the chief spokesman on the African side. These organizations suffered the usual growing pains of new political enterprises and much persecution, but were able to win a growing support. This broadened into participation when SWAPO opened an armed struggle in 1966; and participation was taken further, early in the 70s, by strikes and demonstrations in Windhoek and other towns and mining centres. Their cause was greatly reinforced with the freeing of Angola in 1976, after which SWAPO could count on a firm ally in its rear, while, at the same time, Pretoria's methods of repression were somewhat hampered by the UN spotlight on the territory.

No longer unchallenged, Pretoria had already turned to manoeuvre. In 1974 a plan was devised for the division of Namibia into ten 'tribal homelands', and a conference of nominees met in September 1975. With the South African army's failure in Angola, another conference of nominees assembled in March 1976, and on 18 August Pretoria duly announced that the territory would be given an interim state government composed of approved 'tribal' and local white personnel, with formal 'independence' following in December 1978.

*A census of 1970 reported the Ovambo as numbering 352,640 out of a total African population of 671,601; Whites numbered 90,583 and Coloureds 28,512.

Mocked by SWAPO as a blatant deception, these manoeuvres failed to win any support at the UN, or even among Western Powers whose policies had thus far aimed at protecting South African control. But the manoeuvres continued. As in Zimbabwe, the key question now was the extent to which the opening of 'safety valves', designed to air 'convenient' African opinion, would be able to deflate the pressures for real change.

In South Africa itself, the 60s brought new strength to the *apartheid* system and its dominant ideas. No longer a fragment of the British imperial economy, South Africa had become an indigenous capitalism unique in this respect throughout the continent, and uniquely strong. The Sharpeville massacre of 1960 had briefly checked the inflow of Western capital, but by 1965 the long boom was once again expanding with money from abroad. Gross domestic product (in constant prices) more than doubled between 1960 and 1970, and grew to a quarter as much again by 1975. A traditional reliance on the export of minerals and farming produce disappeared, offering a clear sign that this had ceased to be a colonial economy: in 1970, for example, manufacturing output provided more than 27 per cent of GDP, compared with 11 per cent from mining, and 9.5 per cent from agriculture; while, still in the same year, some 1,530,000 persons were employed in manufacture compared with 600,000 in mining and just over two million in agriculture.

This economic system was further armoured by every weapon of political and social repression. Its bravest opponents had been killed or were in prison or driven into exile. Even so, it contained no element of compromise or tolerance. Revealing the weakness of their fanaticism that would afterwards become flagrant, its leaders had no thought of halting on their way.

'Re-grouping' of non-white population units continued at a rising pace, even though this imposed a new weight of suffering on uprooted communities. Theoretically, this was part of the overall 'plan' of entirely separating whites from non-whites. In practice, since the whites remained utterly dependent on non-white and above all black labour, the separation could be only on a local basis. In 1970 some seven million blacks remained in the Native Reserves, about 13 per cent of the territory, while more than eight million blacks were 're-grouped' in 'separate locations' within the 'white areas'. *Apartheid* had always supposed non-white inferiority; now it confirmed non-white helotry.*

Always non-citizens in white South African law, policy and attitude, these eight millions in the 'white areas' became foreigners in constitutional terms as well. They were to be citizens only of the Reserves (of the Bantustan 'homelands'), even though, for most of them, their forefathers had inhabited the 'white areas' long before the coming of the whites, and most of them had never so much as set foot in a Reserve.

The reshaping of the Native Reserves into ten 'Bantu Homelands' (Bantustans) was continued. This was officially presented as the advancing of their populations to 'self-government' and even to 'independence'. But Colin Bundy was surely nearer to the truth, in 1976, when he described the 'Bantustan' programme as 'a prerequisite of the South African cheap labour policy, a method of social control, and an attempt to foster and reward an African collaborating class in order to dominate more permanently the dispossessed majority'.[49]

Even by the time that the Purified National Party won power in 1948, the Reserves had become rural slums. Without industries or modern towns, ports or rail networks or any of the prerequisites of modernizing progress, they were grossly overstocked and overcrowded. What the Assistant Director of Agriculture of the Ciskei Reserve had said of his own area in that same year of 1948 could be said of them all: that 'over perhaps ten per cent of the total area, the incidence of soil erosion may be described as slight; over fifty per cent as bad; over the balance, as nothing less than terrifying.'[50] Here, long since, people lived by scratching the merest subsistence from small plots and a few thin cattle. Nothing got better

*SA population at 30 June 1974 (official estimates based on 1970 census): 17,745,000 Africans (71.2 per cent); 2,306,000 Coloureds (9.3 per cent); 709,000 Asians (2.8 per cent); 4,160,000 Whites (16.7 per cent): total 24,920,000.

here after 1948: rather the reverse. This same 12.4 per cent of land surface became still more forcibly crammed with Africans 're-grouped' from areas where their presence was unnecessary to whites. In the ten years 1960–70 no fewer than 1.6 million blacks were 'repatriated' from white areas into these zones of endemic hunger.

It was then said that these Reserves would be helped to build a political life of their own. In 1962 the Afrikaner prime minister, Hendrik Verwoerd, announced that the largest of them, the Transkei, was to have a limited form of local self-government under nominated and supervised chiefs and administrators. This began to be put into effect in 1963. Continuing, the programme became a propaganda exercise. By 1975 it was claimed that the 'Bantustans' were to become 'independent states'. The largest and 'most advanced', that of the Transkei designed as the homeland of some 3 million Xhosa, duly became 'independent' in October 1976. 'Westminster Moves to Umtata' (the Transkei capital), announced an unusually shameless South African advertisement in The Times[51]: 'We have moved your Parliamentary system to our country. Statute by statute.'

Not surprisingly, this 'independence' met with no recognition. All control over the economy, defence, security, foreign affairs remained with Pretoria, while the leading members of the Transkei opposition were in detention, trade unions were hamstrung, and the population was destitute. Yet there was a core of truth in the impudent claim to have moved Westminster to Umtata. Like other 'Bantustans' in course of formation, the Transkei was indeed a version, if still a crude and curious one, of the typical outcome of applying the imported model. Again in Bundy's analysis, 'the concentration of local power by South Africa in the hands of a successor élite, that élite's strong-arm tactics and petty corruption, and the gathering rush towards bureaucratic single-party rule', were all elements of the 'neo-colonial' condition that other and serious political independences had brought to birth. However distorted by the South African mirror, no small part of newly independent Africa could now see itself in the lineaments of this Transkei 'system': provided, of course, that it was willing to look.

Negatively, no doubt, the system would produce its own means of self-destruction by corruption and repression, as well as positively by the emergence of domestic opposition linked to the politics of liberation. Even its chosen leaders were driven as early as the first years of the 70s to a stance of demagogic hostility to *apartheid*, as was shown by many gestures made by some of them, notably by Buthelezi of the Kwa-Zulu 'homeland'. Yet Pretoria found reason to believe that it had reinforced itself, and this reinforcement was seen in terms of policy to meet the wider challenge of black political independence elsewhere. During the 1960s, Pretoria had developed a dual programme of response to independent Africa and the rest of the world. One aspect of this was economic and political, the other military.

The Afrikaner leadership, now in firm partnership with major investment corporations, had begun to think of a systematized economic hegemony over the whole southern sub-continent. Sure of its 'internal colony' of some 20 million non-whites, South African capitalism should develop its own 'neo-colonies' to the northward. There evolved the idea of a Southern African Common Market, in which South African economic control would absorb a wide range of black political sovereignties as far north as the Congo Basin.

Initial moves argued for a 'dialogue' with these neighbours. A willing partner was first found in the new president of Malawi, Hastings Kamuzu Banda; he sent three ministers to Pretoria in 1967 where they signed a commercial agreement, and much the same proved possible with President Tsiranana of Madagascar. White society was given the thrilling spectacle of black diplomats lodged in exclusive and expensive hotels where they were even dined by white hosts, something that the more stone-minded of Afrikaner politicians found a betrayal of their deepest beliefs. A dispute arose between *verligte* or 'enlightened' Afrikaner politicians, led by Prime Minister John Balthazar Vorster, and *verkrampte* or 'unbending' Afrikaner politicians; eventually, the latter broke away into a new and 're-purified' party of their own.

But the *verligte* carried the day for their vision of the future. This was on the pattern of the solar system. Inside South

Africa, around the sun of Pretoria, there would revolve the little planets of the 'Bantustans'. Not far beyond them, likewise in obedient orbit, there were the three small countries of Lesotho, Botswana and Swaziland, each firmly in the grip of the South African economy. Beyond these now, reaching into African space, there should be many other planets as far as the outermost pull of South African influence, probably the Zaire of the notably compliant President Mobutu. Between them all, these planets could provide every raw material that the highest conceivable development of South African capitalism could require.

But in case all this was not enough, and it should come to fighting against 'communists', identified as all principled opponents of *apartheid*, white South Africa's armed forces were enlarged and armed with sophisticated weapons of major warfare. The military budget rose from an equivalent of $62 million in 1960 to $168 million in 1962. In 1963 the UN sought to apply an arms embargo. This being ineffective, it was followed by further purchases of foreign equipment; in 1964 the military budget stood at $375 million. An arms industry sprang into being, operating chiefly on licences obtained from a variety of Western Powers; in 1972 the military budget climbed to $479 million, in 1973 to $691 million, and afterwards to more again.

Most of these foreign military purchases were made in France and Western Germany in complete denial of the UN embargo to which these and other suppliers were formally committed. France supplied Mirage fighters and various helicopters, armoured cars, and the means of building an arsenal of air-to-air and ground-to-air missiles. Also with France, the West Germans helped Pretoria with nuclear research to the point that it appeared that Pretoria might eventually be able to make its own nuclear weapons. Piaggio and Aeroitalia reconnaissance and other aircraft came from Italy. Optical instruments, computers, and other communications equipment came from the USA as well as from Western Germany, while the USA also sent South Africa $9.6 million worth of herbicides between 1969 and 1972, these being the 2.4-D and 2.45-T defoliants used in Vietnam. Britain largely observed the embargo, though continuing to supply spare parts and replacements for aircraft and other equipment sold earlier.

The diplomacy of 'dialogue' was thus accompanied by the carving of a big stick on the good old Prussian principle of 'Be my brother, or else . . .'[52] Yet this menace seemed notably weaker by the middle seventies. The 'dialogue' had ceased to prosper after 1971. Up until then President Houphouët-Boigny of Ivory Coast had led its African supporters with an assurance that the whites of South Africa, 'since they are Africans like ourselves and have a role of prime importance to play in the development of our continent, must advance beyond *apartheid* by eliminating the only reason for disunion between us';[53] but Houphouët, after all, was only the boss of a small country tied to French leading strings. Prime Minister Busia of Ghana welcomed South Africa 'into the council of the nations, into the brotherhood of man' in the hope that this would lead to a 'multi-racial régime'; but Busia was evicted in 1972 by other Ghanaians who thought differently on the matter. Even arch-conservatives such as Ahidjo in Cameroun and Mobutu in Zaire, in other circumstances Pretoria's natural partners, found this 'dialogue' more than they could safely stomach.

Big though the military stick undoubtedly was, the hand that held it was now seen to waver. Though designed in a secondary way to deal with any insurrectionary attempts that might develop inside South Africa, the big stick was primarily carved to compensate for Pretoria's weakness in white manpower. A corps of Coloured and Asian servicemen began to be raised in 1973 for ancillary duties; otherwise, the principle remained sacred (and no doubt necessarily so) that only whites could be trusted with guns. This meant that a military power manifestly built for external use could be employed only for short periods of devastation; a protracted war was beyond this system's strength.

With Portuguese collapse in 1974, the two great 'flank guards' of the Pretorian system were destroyed. Even so, Pretoria cared to oppose no armed intervention to FRELIMO's complete success in Mozambique, while Pretoria's brief attempt to oppose the MPLA's complete success in Angola ended in smarting defeat. On top of this, Pretoria's hold on Rhodesia was now threatened by the radicalization of Zimbabwean nationalism, and even its easy occupation of Namibia was under notice to quit. Reacting to an international isolation never felt before, Prime Minister Vorster told his electorate in a New Year's message of 1977 that South Africa might well have to face the future on its own.

Other troubles gathered at home, enhanced by defeat in Angola and a general downturn in the South African economy. It might be possible to stand off rural discontent in the 'Bantustans'. But the more than eight million blacks who remained as rightless non-citizens in the 'white areas' were another matter. Living under the harrow, they found its blade ever more painful. If the boom of the sixties had raised the colour bar a few notches so as to produce more skilled workers, wage differentials between whites and blacks by no means narrowed. Rather, they widened. In 1950 African earnings totalled 10.3 per cent of white earnings; in 1960, 16.8 per cent; in 1970, only 15.4 per cent. Something had to give.

The year 1973 saw major strikes against starvation wages in manufacturing. These wages were raised, even doubled, as were those in mining. But the average differential between white and non-white was still 4.7 to 1 in manufacturing after the wage raises, and 9.3 to 1 in mining. The economy grew, but any development into 'high mass consumption' was excluded. After 1970 this growth fell off and faltered into a severe inflation. A consumer price index based on 1970 ($=$100) stood at 123 in 1973 and 159 at the end of 1975 when the economy, according to Hubert Houghton, was 'really in decline'.[54] This decline could be reversed; but its impact on black living standards in the 'white areas' proved dramatic.

Yet the bulldozers of *apartheid* drove blindly on. In May 1976 the authorities of the Transvaal decreed that Afrikaans, the language of the ruling three-fifths of the white minority, should become a compulsory vehicle of instruction in African schools. In *apartheid* terms, this was a small and mild addition to African disabilities; but it proved one too many. Demonstrations of a massive size and courage scarcely ever seen before, or at least since the campaigns of passive resistance in 1952, erupted in the large Soweto township near Johannesburg. More, they were above all demonstrations by young men and women often still at school or at least of school age: with an heroic determination, the newest generation spoke their mind about the future of their country. They were met with the customary police bullets but were not put down. Officially, the police killed 174 Africans in Soweto, mostly by shooting into the back of retreating crowds; unofficially, they killed far more. More townships joined in widening defiance and disorder. Schools were burnt down, deserted, denied to white access. Protest spread southwards into the Cape province, where African demonstrators were joined by Coloureds. From one month to the next, onwards from May 1976, the silenced multitudes had found their voice, and the voice proved angry and unafraid.

More alarming for the *apartheid* régime, this was also a voice with a strong political note. Partly the note was that of the long banned and persecuted African National Congress, expressed in leaflets and slogans; partly it rang with a new hope inspired by African victories in Mozambique and Angola. If minority dictatorship could be destroyed in the Portuguese colonies, why not here at home as well? *Apartheid*'s walls of Jericho were assailed by something more potent than criticisms from afar. These walls stood intact, while the perspective of the 1980s suggested that any liberation must still lie far ahead. Yet this same perspective showed as clearly that the politics of liberation, moving southwards once again and cutting through the myths and delusions of a fruitless reformism, had found a new field of application. From now onwards the politics of liberation would dominate new thought in South Africa as well. Recognizing this, the white dictatorship responded, onwards from early 1977, with the persecuting, banning, or killing of a still wider range of its critics and opponents. But this was the reaction of an inherent weakness.

THE LIMITS OF NATIONALISM –
AND BEYOND?

I said at the beginning of this inquiry that the getting from the 1880s to the present day was like the scaling of a difficult and distant summit, and so it may now feel, perhaps, to those who have come with me as far as this. The summit, too, is only a temporary top, ceasing to be one even as we reach it. Yet the view from where we now stand is already long and large, reaching back through decades of a crowded evolution and pointing, with a nice temptation, at least a little way toward the future.

Thinking about the route we have found through an immensely rich experience, the author feels inclined to apologize for short-cuts and omissions. They were necessary. Yet how really give the history of this nationalism in its contrasts of personality, style, motivation and the rest without including several score biographies of the men and women who lived its full intensity in their characters and choices? How tell it 'as it really was' without sufficiently portraying Sa'adu Zungur, grave and unforgotten poet of Muslim innovation; or Mamadu Konaté, statesman of the Western Sudan; or Adegoku Adelabu, ebullient seeker after Nigerian destiny; or Tom Mboya, shrewd advocate of anti-colonial campaigning, cut down in Kenya savagely before his time? How convey the tragic grandeur of these years without the example of Déolinda de Almeida, pioneer of the emancipation of Angola, victim of a tyranny; or Eduardo Mondlane, founding father of a new Mozambique but victim of another tyranny; or Mehdi ben Barka, practical visionary of Moroccan progress, victim of still another tyranny; or Bram Fischer, unflinching spokesman of the free South Africa for which he gave his life in the jails of Pretoria; or so many others scarcely mentioned in these pages or not mentioned at all?

Or how really elucidate this nationalism without a much fuller account of the shifting posture of twentieth-century Africa within its enclosing economic systems? How transmit the resonance of its phases from the early vision of the nineteenth-century spokesmen to the practical installation of their ideas, and then to the emergence of the politics of personal protest and their later linkage with mass protest, and onward to a new harvest of post-reformist ideas, of revolutionary ideas, of the ideas of the politics of liberation: how do this, indeed, without recalling in their bitterness or nourished joy the tone and temper of innumerable private meeting or mass encounters, staunch victories or grim defeats in the forest of the night?

What were the projects in Um Nyobé's unforgotten satchel as he flung it from him in the moment of capture and death? How might not Lumumba have developed if he could have reached Stanleyville before the killers overtook him? What fresh plans for the future, what new thoughts about the relationship between party and state, between democracy and socialism, were in Cabral's mind when vile conspiracy killed him on the eve of victory? Whither might not Murtala Muhamed have taken his convictions but for the assassin's hand? And all those others who died in the strength of their youth and courage, but with names unknown to a wider world: how can we be sure of understanding them aright?

One can do one's best, and await correction. All speculation apart, a history of these hundred years could be written in a hundred ways. This way has followed a conviction about the nature of a century's historical truth. It has seen the great deciding fact along the pathway of experience as the quest for a new community, for a new truth and consciousness born out of the communities of the past, fruit of those old communities through all the reductive or enlarging influences of foreign rule and alien culture, but capable of going beyond their limits, of making good their deficiencies, of binding nationalities into nations, and claiming as of right, as Cabral said, 'everything that the world has conquered for the service of mankind'.

Viewed from where we stand now, nationalism appears in

all its ambiguous fertility. The early nationalists and their successors were justified in their strategy. They failed to see a lot of things, while other things they saw mistakenly, or partially, or even upside-down; but they saw the main target, and they saw it round and clear. Nationhood had to be the answer to the colonial problem: to the challenge of European racism and its material accompaniments. And nationhood had to be the answer to the pre-colonial problem: to the challenge of all that previous African development, beginning far back and full of merit, but capable of no further development without great changes within itself.

Nationhood won the day. But it had to come as a bastard birth or, rather, out of parents so ill-matched as to make the raising of the infant worse than chancy. Married to colonial attitudes, structures, values, the cultures of Africa brought forth a creature of self-contradiction that mocked the vision of the past. The few were set against the many. Nationalities were counter-posed to nations. Old inequalities from the pre-colonial heritage, whether between man and man or more painfully between man and woman, were enlarged by new inequalities from the colonial heritage; and the outcome was frustration or defeat. The nation-states of the late 1950s and early 1960s had to appear as the oppressors and exploiters of the many by the few.

Which is not to prophesy. It may be that the more powerful among these nation-states, perhaps one or two of them, will be able to build their ill-assorted systems into new unities and new democracies. It may be that new constitutions, as a Nigerian drafting committee proposed in 1976, will be able to guarantee a national ethic of honesty, selflessness and dedication within capitalist structures, and through a further growth of what exists. It may be that energy, intelligence and a solidly commercial tradition can still turn that trick. It may even be that organic federations within the framework of international capitalism will overcome existing frontiers, and, as pledged in West Africa's fifteen-state 'economic community' (ECOWAS) of 1976, eventually carry these countries out of their constrictive separatism and nationalist rivalry.

But the evidence is barely encouraging of any such results,

although not because of any lack of talent, and still less because honesty is far to seek. The societies of England and France were quite exceptionally dishonest in the decades of their early capitalist development, and we know from J. H. Plumb that in those days the 'aim of politics was not directed to liberties . . . nor to social justice, but to the pursuit of office',[55] because office meant power, privilege or perquisite, and was the vital key to success in a race that trampled losers underfoot. In due course the good bourgeois of England and France could rate himself a man of blameless honesty and purpose; and the future African bourgeois could expect to do as well.

The doubt about capitalism's possible future in Africa – about the future of the imported model, no matter how reformed – arises in no small measure from that 'in due course'. The old capitalist countries took a very long time to build their systems, and to build them they had to wade through decades of insurrection, repression, and war between each other. What African country, save one or two, will be able or willing to march that daunting road in the decades now ahead? With the gulf between the few and the many becoming ever deeper: with populations expanding at a rate that will double their size by the year 2000: with middle classes still to be built, and capital to build them ever harder to find or borrow? Even in Nigeria, abounding with commercial energies, there appeared to be some doubts. The 'Fundamental Objectives' set forth for Nigeria by a constitutional committee of 1976 laid it down that the economic system should not be operated in 'such a manner as to permit the concentration of wealth or the means of production and exchange in the hands of a few individuals or a group'.[56] But how do you put that together with building private or even state capitalism?

The future will say. Meanwhile the history of these years appeared strongly to suggest that the imported model in any of its variants had reached the limits of its usefulness, and that this nationalism, if world history were anything to go by, must now lead into worse strife or frustration.[57] This might have seemed a very dubious or merely 'ideological' conclusion a few years back. It seldom seems like that today, even if the conclusion be contested. For the 1970s lifted political discussion out of the cosily paternal orbit of 'estab-

lished Western values', just as the 1970s promoted a realistic analysis
of 'established Eastern values'. New departures, new experiments,
new achievements combined to induce a sturdy scepticism about any
kind of foreign model that might be recommended.

There came the development of programmes for constructive change aimed at building indigenous models; and some of
these, in the perspective of the 1980s, were manifestly within an
entirely new field of independent thought, having discarded the
various simulacra of other people's systems along with the rest of the
decorative verbiage of the 1960s. The tone now was sharper; it was
also clearer. What the new republics of the mid-70s adhered to was
in no way 'African socialism', or 'Arab socialism' or any other
ornamental substitute for the real thing: they adhered to 'scientific
socialism'. Hasty opinions might see this as consent to another
imported model; if so, they missed its meaning, which was that the
methodology of revolution had put down independent roots into the
realities of Africa's search for a new community, and acquired
indigenous content as well as form.

Always with possible exceptions, the evidence further suggested that this trend towards renewal, towards revolutionary ideas
and structures, was now in course of enlargement. Powerful and
independent states such as Nigeria might prefer to persevere on
familiar lines. Powerless or largely dependent states began to show
signs of thinking differently. New areas of experiment seemed on the
way. And then in states not yet independent, in Zimbabwe and
Namibia or even in South Africa, any worth-while progress except
along the lines of this trend towards the politics of liberation now
appeared hard to imagine.

The influence of this trend owed much to the failure of the
politics of reformism, of trying to build capitalism. It appeared in a
time, moreover, when capitalism had lost its spell-binding hegemony,
a loss that derived in the early 1970s, no doubt, greatly from defeat on
the battlefields of Vietnam. But the new trend claimed to do more
than fill a void; it posited virtues of its own. These were its capacity
to deal with two major sources of disintegration: the conflict between
the few and the many, and the closely related conflict between

enclosed nationalities and enclosing nation. Beyond all this, a new morality seemed very necessary.

To the old theory of nation-building the new trend opposed a different one. The old theory may be termed 'coagulation'. It supposed the continuing primacy of the 'national question' over the 'social question': the nation was to be built from the top, by agreement among ruling groups, and this agreement was to be imposed downwards level by level. The conflict between the few and the many was to be contained by one or other kind of force until the few had built themselves into a cultural and economic domination, into a position of class hegemony, when force could be reduced or set aside. The conflict between enclosed nationalities and enclosing nation was to be denied as the product of malicious tongues, or thrust aside as a backward 'tribalism': or again contained by force, allied to bargaining with the self-appointed élites of this or that constituent nationality if these should prove too strong for containment only by force. In the measure that this nationalism could succeed, the rich diversity of African culture was turned into a source of weakness.

As a somewhat extreme and yet relevant example, the Ethiopian empire had already shown what this sort of nation-building had to mean even after decades. 'Many years ago in Tigray,' an Ethiopian history recalled in 1976,

I was taught in Tigrigna. Our Tigray schools taught Geez, Amarigna and English, as subjects. So Tigrawat who went to school could command their own language and three other languages of value to them. Afterwards, without any discussion, consultation or popular consent, the Ethiopian ministry of education ordered that Amarigna had to be the medium of instruction, and that only English would be taught as a language-subject. Tigrigna, the mother tongue, and Geez, which are rich written Ethiopic languages, were dropped completely. Indeed, when the minister of education visited my school and heard the students outside class speaking in Tigrigna, he became very angry and ordered that we must not speak in Tigrigna but in Amarigna. Later, Eritrea too suffered from the same imperial policy. But this suppression of the culture of the Tigrigna-speaking people of northern Ethiopia, of Tigray and Eritrea, and that of people of southern Ethiopia such as the Galla, was a constant source of national conflict.[58]

With or without much force, or even with concessions to enclosed nationalities, it had to be commonly the same elsewhere; and what went for their cultures applied to other aspects of life. New forms of authoritarian rule, as we have seen, had to be devised to hold these nation-states together. All these forms were a sore reduction of the vision of freedom, yet nothing else was possible with this 'co-agulation theory'. You had simply to take all the 'bits' in presence and ram them together. Whenever the angry amalgam fell apart you had to reassemble it and ram again.

The new trend proposed a contrary theory, which may be called 're-formulation'. This argued, as all its examples revealed in their various ways, that no real nation can emerge from the amalgamation of disparate or conflicting nationality interests, but only by organizing all elements in presence on the basis of their specific social interests: by building the nation, that is, upwards from the bottom and not downwards from the top. Once this was undertaken, all elements in presence could be harmonized within the same overall system because their specific social interests were identical in kind or closely similar. That being so, the social question had to have primacy over the national question. You had to start from the real and immediate needs of the people 'at the base': their need for control over their own communities, their need for understanding how to use this control so as to improve life, their need for means to make this improvement possible.

Such basic social needs cut through every ethnic or regional dispute, or, with patience, could be made to do so. Therefore they provided a sure foundation on which to assemble an organic whole. As soon as each community possessed the means of controlling its local affairs and understanding its local interests, you had the means of attracting each community, no matter how small or remote or wrapped up in village business, into the wider community of a district, of a region, of a country: in a word, of a nation. An entire people would thus re-formulate its component attitudes to unity and common action.[59a]

The innovators of this new trend had acquired a clear definition of their model by the early 1970s. One of their clearest formulations was offered by the secretary-general of the PAIGC (of Guinea-Bissau and Cape Verde), Aristides Pereira, in a 20-year review of his party's experience. Their model, he explained in 1976, demanded that for every decision bearing on public life, 'participation at the base is guaranteed, level by level, through a democratic system of organization. This system presupposes, at the level of each [executive] committee, the existence alongside it of an assembly of delegates on the level below it; and this assembly elects and controls the executive committee in question.'[59] With a national party functioning inside this kind of framework, mass participation and therefore mass agreement, leading in turn to unity and common action, became transposable from level to level, upwards from village to district, district to region, region to central government. With due allowance for the frailties of human nature, a true consensus can emerge. The rich diversity of African culture is turned into a source of strength.

Gaining ground, this trend began to be present in every region of the continent. It could be seen openly at work in quite a few republics, as earlier pages have shown. It could be seen less openly but still insistently in others. It held the centre of the stage in areas of contest such as Eritrea, where by 1977 the Eritrean People's Liberation Force (EPLF) was clearly operating on the same principles as the movements which had won the day in the Portuguese colonies, as were also, by the slender evidence then available, some comparable movements elsewhere.[60] And the same trend towards the politics of liberation could be marked in the discussions of students and others in a score of countries where 'coagulation theory' and its coercions still held official sway.

This trend seemed likely to command the future. Its gains and its appeal were as manifest as its capacity to offer new and valid solutions. But this again is not to prophesy. No matter how effective this new trend now evidently was, several difficult problems raised new heights ahead: of how to promote democracy while pressing on with structural change; of how to divide party from state and yet ensure that policies should not flinch; of how to give power to the organisms of mass participation and still retain a revolutionary thrust. And the routes up their rock-face looked no simper than before.

Existing liberation movements had won their struggles, whether warlike or not, by placing the social question at the centre of their priorities. But they could not have done this successfully, or reaped the unifying gains of doing it, if they had been no more than loosely organized fronts or coalitions of persons and groups with different ideas, ideologies, and ambitions. Such movements would have quickly fallen apart, as the unsuccessful ones did indeed fall apart. But the successful movements were something more than fronts or coalitions, although they were also that. Each contained within itself an 'inner party' or core of tried leaders whose task was to ensure that the movement stayed true and firm to the principles of its theory and practice.

These 'cores' of a revolutionary nationalism got bigger as the campaigns went on. They took in new members from peasant or other volunteers. They were reinforced by fresh militants who had come to understand the nature of the liberation struggle, and how to win it. Yet each core remained, and for long had to remain, in large degree a self-perpetuating minority control. Risky, no doubt, yet unavoidable; and, as the facts showed, adequate to a long initial phase. But didn't this adequacy derive from the lucky fact that the successful movements were led by men and women of outstanding probity and devotion? The question misses the point, which is that the tasks in hand could not be accomplished without the leadership of out-standing men and women. Whenever such leaders failed to appear there were no liberation movements, or else there were disasters. One may put the same thing differently, and say that each movement got the leadership that its aims, principles, and practices enabled it to deserve.

Success in war, or comparable development where no wars were necessary, brought a new phase. The unproclaimed 'inner party' began to be at odds with a further unfolding of the democracy of mass participation. Still at the centre of policy, the continuing social struggle had now to be given its own permanent political identity and democratic instrument. Only this could enable mass participation, freed as it now was for the work of building a community at the national level, progressively to overtake and dispense with the act of substitution by which the initiating 'inner party' had launched the struggle in the name of a nation not then born. The revolutionary core had therefore to expand and democratize itself into a revolutionary national party within its national movement.

Late in the 1970s, each of the successful movements turned to this problem of promoting national parties pledged to revolutionary change. This called for the selection of a large number of militants capable in this new phase of serving the principles and safeguarding the practices, no matter at what personal sacrifice, of the phase now concluded. And this was where the onward path became slippery and steep, but again unavoidably, because it had to pass by way of the perils of forming a political bureaucracy which should not be allowed to decay into petrifaction and dictatorship. It had to ensure that this new party should be intermeshed with the structures of democratic control. All this was bound to be difficult and problematical, as world experience has everywhere confirmed. Perhaps it was most difficult of all in countries where no armed struggles had given their bitter but effective education.

Yet already, here and there, such difficulties were beginning to be firmly grasped. What, for example, should be the relationship between a revolutionary party and a new state which it had brought into existence so as to realize its revolutionary programme? There must remain, replied the thinkers of the PAIGC of Guinea-Bissau and Cape Verde, a clear distinction between the two. Their tasks were not the same. The party must persuade and influence and steer. But the state, above all embodied in assemblies and executives of democratic participation and in supporting mass organizations, must be the agent of its own development:

> The subordination of state to party is laid down in our constitutional texts; but this subordination must in no way

signify a confusion of the two entities, or substitution of the state by the party. Each has its own functions; and these, although complementary, are different and use different ways and methods. Any such confusion or identification is prejudicial to one or the other: it leads to inefficiency, it creates or extends bureaucratic petrifaction (*o burocratismo*) ... (Artistides Pereira, *Relatorio*, Bissau, November 1977).

Once more, the gains of independence gave new ground on which to wrestle with the problems of advance.

A further summit loomed ahead: much higher, still very distant, and yet ever more clearly there to be climbed. If the politics of this revolutionary nationalism could resolve conflict between nationalities, then its next great task must be to resolve conflict between nations. This would signal the move towards an organic unity between national peoples as distinct from mere agreements between national governments: a unity that would mark the supersession of the frontiers of colonial partition, the threshold of a new era, and the onset of a new history.

The glimmer of that distant peak came from far ahead; yet it could be argued that new generations would see it nearer and less impossible to climb, for this was already the process revealed by twentieth-century history. To adapt something said about youthful 'mischief-makers' in colonial Morocco, the nationalists of those years had proved able to 'judge and penetrate the mysteries of the Europeans, work with them, and eventually replace them'.[61] In the perspectives of the twenty-first century, new 'mischief-makers' would judge and penetrate other mysteries. It would be for them to find the harmonies of Africa that were dreamed of by the pioneers.

USEFUL DATES

These brief lists are a frame of reference and a supplement to dates in the text. The principle of their selection is not quite as arbitrary as it may seem: it is aimed at indicating what kind of things were going on at any particular moment. Very detailed lists of dates are in G. S. P. Freeman-Grenville, *Chronology of African History*, Oxford University Press, 1973.

Northern Africa means North Africa plus the Horn; Middle Africa means countries generally in the tropical zones; while Southern Africa means countries generally south of the Zambezi.

USEFUL DATES LIST ONE, Late C.19 to 1920

NORTHERN AFRICA	MIDDLE AFRICA	SOUTHERN AFRICA
1881–98 Period of the Mahdia in (Eastern) Sudan.	1876 King Leopold forms 'International African Institute'	1859 Earliest railway in S. Africa.
1881 French seize Bizerta; invade Tunis; impose protectorate (1883).	1882 French declare protectorate over (Moyen) Congo area.	1860 Earliest import of Indian indentured workers into South Africa.
1882 British and French fleets bombard Alexandria; immediate prelude to British domination of Egypt. Italy declares colony in Eritrea.	1884 Germany declares protectorates in Togo, Kamerun, S. W. Africa, German E. Africa. Spain declares protectorate in Western Sahara.	1867 Diamonds discovered in South Africa.
1895 Italy invades Ethiopia; defeated at Adowa (1896).	1884–5 Berlin conference makes rules for European aggressions in Africa.	1879 Zulu war of resistance (in Natal).
1896 British invade (E.) Sudan; take Dongola.	1885–1908 'Congo Free State' under personal rule of King Leopold.	1884 British declare protectorate in Basutoland. King Lobengula of Ndebele accepts British protectorate; gives mining rights to Cecil Rhodes (chartered Br. S.A. Coy).
	1885 British declare protectorate in Niger Districts.	1886 Witwatersrand goldfields opened.
	1886–8 French military expeditions into W. Sudan; these continue.	1885 British declare protectorate in Bechuanaland.
	1887 British deport King Ja Ja of Opobo to West Indies.	1889 De Beers Consolidated founded. British declare protectorate in Nyasaland.
		1890–97 Much railway building in South Africa.

1889 French declare protectorate in Ivory Coast.

1890 French exchange claim on N. Nigeria for British acceptance of French protectorate in Madagascar.

1890 BSA Coy raises British flag North of Limpopo (Southern Rhodesia fore-shadowed).

1892 French defeat King of Dahomey; declare protectorate.

1894 British declare protectorate in Uganda, and in the interior of Central Africa (Northern Rhodesia fore-shadowed).

1894 Against resistance, BSA Coy com-plete occupation of territory N. of Limpopo (S. Rhodesia).

1895 Britain declares protectorate of British East Africa (Kenya, Uganda, Zanzibar).

1895 French declare protectorate in Madagascar.

1896 British invade Asante; declare pro-tectorate; formally annexe in 1901. British declare protectorate in Sierra Leone.

1896–7 Shona and Ndebele resist British occupation.

1896–1905 Armed resistance to French occupation of Madagascar.

1897 British take Benin, Ilorin. Ashanti Goldfields Ltd founded.

1898 S. Leone rising against hut tax. Anglo–French settlement of Nigerian boundaries.

1896–1903 Dam on Nile built at Aswan.

1897–8 Inter-imperialist agreements on Somali boundaries; Ethiopians annex much Somali territory (1897–1900).

1898 British defeat army of Mahdi at battle of Omdurman.

1899 Anglo-Egyptian Condominium in (E.) Sudan: in fact, British.

NORTHERN AFRICA	MIDDLE AFRICA	SOUTHERN AFRICA
1900–1904 First British military expeditions against Somali resistance led by Sayid Mohamed. His resistance continues until 1920, ending only with his death.	1899 Northern Rhodesia proclaimed. 1900 British declare protectorate in N. Nigeria. 1901 Railway from Mombasa through E.A. reaches Lake Victoria (Nyanza). 1903–31 Benguela–Katanga railway built (90% British owned). 1904 French constitute AOF (Afrique Occidentale Fr.) with colonial capital at Dakar. 1905–7 S. Tanganyika peoples rise against Germans (Maji Maji).	1899–1902 British war against Afrikaner (Boer) Republics. 1899 Railway from S.A. reaches Salisbury (S. Rhodesia). Tanganyika Concessions Ltd formed. BSA Coy has protectorates N. of Zambezi (S. Rhodesia). 1904–7 Herero and Nama rise against Germans in S. W. Africa (Namibia).
1908 Egyptian National University (founded at Cairo). 1909 Anti-nationalist press censorship in Egypt.	1908 Belgian parliament takes over 'Congo Free State': as Belgian Congo. French constitute AEF (Afrique Equatoriale) Française with colonial capital at Brazzaville. 1910 British settlers in Kenya form political organization (Convention of Associations).	1910 Union of S. Africa formed (Cape, Natal, Orange F. S., Transvaal).

1911 French occupy Fez. Italy invades Tripolitania and Cyrenaica.
1912 French declare protectorate in Morocco.

1914 British declare protectorate in Egypt.
1917 Sanusi, undefeated in Libyan interior, make peace treaty with Allies.
1919 Renewed nationalist agitation in Egypt.

1920 Destour formed in Tunisia. Algerian Communist Party founded.

1914–18 First World War; fighting in many parts of Africa; many Africans conscripted.

1914–19 Lugard governor-general of Nigeria.

1919 Post-war peace conference launches League of Nations. German colonies transferred to British, French, and Belgians as Mandates.

1920 E. Africa Protectorate becomes Kenya Colony; Uganda and Zanzibar remain separate. In Kenya, Thuku forms Young Kikuyu Association.

1912 African National Congress formed in South Africa.
1913 Native Land Act in South Africa.

1915 South African troops enter German South-West Africa (Namibia); prelude to virtual annexation under cover (after 1918) of League Mandate.

1920 Whites in South Africa form coalition government under J. C. Smuts on renewed programme of racist discrimination.

NORTHERN AFRICA	MIDDLE AFRICA	SOUTHERN AFRICA
1921-6 Armed resistance to Spanish and French in Morocco led by Abd al-Krim.	1920 National Congress of British West Africa founded. Lever Bros acquire Niger Coy.	1920 Major strike by African mineworkers on Rand. First aircraft fly from London to Cape.
1922 Britain end protectorate in Egypt which becomes formally independent but with continuing British controls. Bey of Tunis threatens abdication in support of Destour.	1922 Enlarged colonial legislative council for Nigeria.	1922 White mineworkers' strike on Rand, martial law, much fighting. Referendum in S. Rhodesia: whites vote for colonial autonomy.
1923 Wafd wins Egyptian elections.	1924 British government takes over N. Rhodesia from Br. S. Africa Coy.	1923 S. Rhodesia becomes Crown Colony with full white autonomy.
1924 Trade union federation formed in Tunisia.	1925 New colonial constitution for Gold Coast.	1924 Hertzog government in South Africa; Labour Party allies with right-wing Afrikaners; end of white industrial action.
1927 Messali Hadj becomes leader of Etoile Nord-Africaine.	1926 Matswa forms *Amicale.*	1926 S. African African National Congress and Indian National Congress hold conference.
1928 Italy signs 20-year treaty of friendship with Ethiopia.	1925-31 Sir D. Cameron governor of Tanganyika.	1927 African strike in S. Rhodesia.
1930 'Berber *dahir*' in Morocco.	1928 Trade union founded at Bathurst (Banjul). N. Rhod. Copperbelt cleared of malaria, prelude to large-scale mining.	1930 Land Apportionment Act in S. Rhodesia.
	1929 Tanganyika African Association founded. Aba 'women's riots' in E. Nigeria.	

1932 Italians finally defeat Sanusi in Libya.
1934 Néo-Destour formed in Tunisia.
1935 Italy invades Ethiopia.
1936 British end military occupation of Egypt save for Suez Canal Zone, retain treaty right to keep 10,000 troops in Egypt for twenty years. Parti du Peuple Algérien founded.
1937 Moroccan nationalist Allal al-Fasi exiled to Gabon for nine years.
1938 In Sudan, Graduates General Congress formed.
1939 Civil disobedience in Tunisia. Bourguiba arrested. In Algeria Ferhat Abbas forms Union Populaire. Libya declared part of Italy.

1930 Africans in N. Rhodesia organize welfare societies.
1930 Congo–Océan railway completed between Pte Noire and Brazzaville.
1931 Benguela–Katanga railway opened. Diamonds discovered in Sierra Leone.
1934 Kenya Land Commission reports. In Senegal Lamine Guéye forms Parti Socialiste.
Gold Coast: Dr J. B. Danquah heads protest delegation to London.
1935 Major strike by African mine-workers on N. Rhodesian Copperbelt.
1937 Gold Coast cocoa hold-up. N. Rhodesia African Congress formed.
1938 French recruit 20,000 troops in AOF.
1939 Nigerian regiment raises 15 battalions.

1933 Rump of Nationalist party joins with S. African party to form United Party.
1934 D. F. Malan organizes Purified National Party on extreme racist ticket.
1936 New segregation laws in S. Africa; Hertzog is prime minister.
1939 Hertzog for neutrality in the Second World War, but S. Africa declares war on Germany with Smuts as prime minister.

USEFUL DATES   LIST THREE, 1940–70 (for Independence dates see List Four)

NORTHERN AFRICA	MIDDLE AFRICA	SOUTHERN AFRICA
1940–41 Major battles between British and Axis (Italian and German) forces in W. Egypt and Cyrenaica. Italy attacks Br. Somaliland (August 1940).	1940 French mobilize African troops in Fr. W. Africa (AOF).	1940 S. Africa has joined British against Axis, in spite of extremist Afrikaner support for Axis.
1941 British defeat Italians in E. Africa. Ethiopia liberated (May).	1941 Free French and British fail to take Dakar from sea. Uprising at Luluabourg in Belgian Congo.	
1942 British defeat Axis in W. Desert. Americans land in Maghrib.		1942 British land in Madagascar and instal Free French régime.
1943 End of Second World War in Africa. Somali Youth League formed.	1943 British African troops fighting Japanese in Burma. Nyasaland African Congress formed.	1943 S. African United Party under Smuts wins general election.
1944 Istiqlal demand Moroccan independence (January).	1944 NCNC formed in Nigeria. Free French government calls colonial policy conference at Brazzaville.	
1945 French repression of Algerian nationalists (May); major uprising follows, many thousand Algerians believed killed. Egyptian government vainly demands end of British military occupation. Arab League formed in Cairo.	1945 Major strike at Duala (Cameroun). African deputies elected to first post-war French national assembly.	1945 African railway strike in S. and N. Rhodesia.

1946 General strike in Cairo.
Messali Hadj forms MTLD in Algeria.

1948 Clashes between SYL and Italian colonials in Mogadishu.
Ethiopia resumes occupation of Ogaden.

1950 Britain returns Somalia to Italy as UN Mandate.

1951 Guerrilla war in Egypt against British forces in Suez Canal Zone.
Libya an independent kingdom.

1946 New constitution for Gold Coast gives an African unofficial majority in restricted legislature.
French abolish forced labour, extend citizenship to Africans.
RDA holds conference at Bamako in Soudan (Mali).
Jomo Kenyatta returns to Kenya.

1947 New constitution for Nigeria gives African majority in restricted legislature.
First African trade unions in N. Rhodesia.
East African High Commission formed.

1948 UPC formed in Cameroun.

1949 CPP formed in Gold Coast.

1950 Action Group and NEPU formed in Nigeria.
SLPP formed in Sierra Leone.

1951 New constitutions for Nigeria and The Gambia.
Gold Coast gets internal self-rule under Nkrumah.
NPC formed in Nigeria.

1946 Major strike of S. African mine-workers.

1948 National Party in South Africa led by D. F. Malan wins general election, on apartheid programme by 79 to 74 but polling fewer votes than opposing United Party.

1949 'Unofficials' conference in S. Rhodesia bids for settler-controlled federation of two Rhodesias and Nyasaland.

1950 S. African National Congress and Indian National Congress join in new anti-apartheid campaign. Police repression follows. New apartheid laws. Dutch Reformed Church comes out for repatriation of all Indians.

NORTHERN AFRICA	MIDDLE AFRICA	SOUTHERN AFRICA
1952 Anti-colonial agitations strengthen in Maghrib. King Farouk of Egypt forced to abdicate; Gen. Neguib in power; rise of new Egyptian nationalism.	1952 State of emergency in Kenya; arrest of nationalists; eve of 'Mau Mau' rising.	1952 Non-white political organizations in S. Africa launch passive resistance to apartheid; 'defiance campaign'.
1954 Gamal Abdel Nasser takes power in Egypt. Algerian nationalists begin war of independence (November 1954–62).	1954 CPP wins another election in Gold Coast, and Britain promises independence. Western and Eastern Nigerian regions receive internal self-government.	1953 S. African government employs emergency powers against passive resisters and brings in tougher apartheid measures. Central African Federation of two Rhodesias and Nyasaland begins (ends in 1963).
1955 Moroccan army of liberation attacks French forces. Sultan Mohamed V restored to throne. Armed resistance in S. Sudan, lasts until 1972.	1955 UPC banned in Cameroun. Togo promised independence. New constitution in Tanganyika. Emergency in Kenya approaches end.	1955 S. African Congress of the People adopts Freedom Charter. Strijdom is prime minister.
1956 Bourguiba president of Tunisia. Nasser becomes president of Egypt, nationalizes Canal, is invaded by Israel with Anglo-French military support. These invaders withdraw. War in Algeria continues with 450,000 French troops in the field. Oil struck in south Algeria. Sudan an independent republic.	1956 State of emergency on N. Rhodesian Copperbelt. Oil struck in Nigeria. French pass 'enabling act' for tropical colonies as prelude to their separate independences. PAIGC formed secretly in Guinea-Bissau, and MPLA in Angola.	1956 Welensky prime minister of C. African Federation. In S. Africa, more arrests of non-white leaders, now accused of 'treason'.

1957 Gold Coast becomes independent Ghana.
Constitutional advances in Nigeria.
SLPP wins election in Sierra Leone.

1957 In S. Africa, Africans legally banned from worship in white churches.
S. African government charges fail against 61 defendants in Johannesburg 'treason trial'.

1958 New 'treason trial' of 91 defendants at Pretoria.

1958 Gen. Abboud takes power in Sudan. Yaoundé Convention between European Economic Community and French-speaking states.

1958 President de Gaulle offers referendum on independence, but only Guinea PDG able to make and maintain rejection of further French tutelage. Um Nyobé killed in Cameroun. H. K. Banda returns to Nyasaland; campaigns against Central African Federation.

1959 Oil struck in Libya.

1959 Federation of Senegal, Soudan (Mali), Volta, Dahomey proclaimed; last two at once back out; Mali Federation of Senegal and Soudan briefly follows.
Northern region of Nigeria receives internal self-government.

1960 British Prime Minister Macmillan tells S. African whites that 'wind of change' is sweeping continent.
S. African police kill 67 Africans at Sharpeville and wound 180.
Nationalist leader Luthuli arrested for accusing S. African government of genocide.

1961 In Algeria, settlers and some French officers launch terrorist OAS (Organisation de l'Armée Secrète) against French concession to Algerian nationalists.

1960 Many independences (see List Four).
Interventions in Congo.
Lumumba murdered (January 1961).

1961 South African 'treason trial' ends with acquittals.
After referendum, South Africa becomes republic.

NORTHERN AFRICA	MIDDLE AFRICA	SOUTHERN AFRICA
1962 Algerians win independence.	1962 Mauritius gets internal self-rule. Kenya nationalist leaders reject secession to Somalia of Northern Frontier District although official commission finds overwhelming support for secession in NFD. Nyerere elected president of Tanganyika. Milton Obote forms UPC government in Uganda, prelude to independence. FRELIMO formed (in Dar es-Salaam) to fight against colonial rule in Mozambique.	1962 ZAPU banned in S. Rhodesia; Winston Field becomes prime minister.
1963 Frontier clashes between Algeria and Morocco.	1963 OAU formed in Addis Ababa. PAIGC launch armed resistance in Guinea-Bissau.	1963 C. African Federation dissolved. ZANU formed in S. Rhodesia, banned. In S Africa, Chief Matanzima head of (Bantustan) government of Transkei. More mass political trials with heavy sentences (on Mandela, Fischer, and others).
1964 Cairo conference of non-aligned countries. In Sudan, Field-Marshal Abboud assumes power, but civilian government formed and Abboud resigns. Renewed political activity.	1964 FRELIMO launches armed resistance in Mozambique. Beginning of revolts in Congo (Zaire) led by Mulele and Soumialot.	

1965 Mobutu becomes military dictator of Zaire.

In Algeria, military government under Boumédienne ousts Ben Bella government.

OCAM (*Organisation Commune Africaine et Malgache*) formed.

1966 Military coups in Nigeria, Ghana, C. Africa Republic, Volta, and others attempted elsewhere.

Beginning of guerrilla warfare to liberate Zimbabwe from racist rule.

1967 Military coup in Sierra Leone.

Abortive coup in Ghana. Coups in Togo and Dahomey.

Beginning of Nigerian civil war (to January 1970).

President Nyerere of Tanzania launches Arusha policy.

East African Community formed by Kenya, Uganda and Tanzania.

1968 In Sierra Leone, civilian government restored; Siaka Stevens prime minister.

1965 In Rhodesia, Rhodesian Front wins election, and, under government headed by Ian Smith, declares unilateral independence from Britain (11 November).

1966 Prime Minister Verwoerd assassinated in S. African House of Assembly; is followed as prime minister by J. B. Vorster.

NORTHERN AFRICA	MIDDLE AFRICA	SOUTHERN AFRICA
	1969 Military coup in Mali. Gen. Ankrah, Ghana military ruler, deposed on charges of corruption; is succeeded by Gen. Afrifa. Civilian rule restored in September under prime minister Busia (till January 1972). Army in Somalia takes power on radical reforming programme under Gen. Siad Barre (October).	
1970 Aswan High Dam in Egypt (United Arab Republic) goes into operation. Nasser dies in Cairo, is followed by Anwar al-Sadat.	1970 End of Nigerian civil war (January). The Gambia becomes a republic. Coup attempted in Togo. Portuguese launch commando raid on Conakry. Chinese begin construction of railway below Tanzanian Coast and central Zambia (completed in 1976).	1970 Prime Minister Vorster visits Malawi as official guest. Chief Buthalezi becomes head of Zulu Territorial Authority (Bantustan).

1969 Military coups in Sudan, Libya and Somalia.

USEFUL DATES LIST FOUR, National Independences

Already Independent

Ethiopia
Liberia
South Africa

The 1950s (chronologically)

Egypt, with process beginning in	1952
Sudan	1956
Morocco	1956
Tunisia	1956
Ghana (col. Gold Coast)	1957
Guinea	1958

The 1960s (alphabetically)

Algeria	1962
Botswana (col. Bechuanaland)	1966
Burundi (col. Urundi)	1962
Cameroun	1960
Central African Republic (col. Oubangui-Chari)	1960
Chad	1960
Congo (People's Republic of) (col. Moyen-Congo)	1960
Benin (Dahomey) (col. Dahomey)	1960
Equatorial Guinea (col. Spanish Guinea), Rio Muni and Fernando Poo	1968
Gabon	1960
Gambia, The	1965
Ivory Coast	1960
Kenya	1963
Lesotho (col. Basutoland)	1966
Madagascar	1960
Malawi (col. Nyasaland)	1964
Mali (col. Soudan)	1960
Mauritania	1960
Mauritius	1968
Niger	1960
Nigeria	1960
Rwanda (col. Ruanda)	1962

Senegal	1960
Sierra Leone	1961
Somalia (col. Italian Somalia *plus* British protectorate of Somaliland, excluding Somali territory in Kenya, Ethiopia and the [French] Territory of the Afars and Issas)	1960
Swaziland	1967
Tanzania (col. Tanganyika; united in 1964 with Zanzibar)	1961
Togo	1960
Uganda	1962
Upper Volta	1960
Zaire (col. Belgian Congo)	1960
Zambia	1964
Zanzibar (in union with Tanganyika, as Tanzania, since 1964)	1963

The 1970s (alphabetically)

Angola	1975
Cape Verde	1975
Comoros (save Mayotte Is.)	1975
Guinea–Bissau (completed in 1974)	1973
Mozambique	1975
Sahara Arab Republic (disputed)	1976
São Tomé (with Principe)	1975
Seychelles	1976

LIST FIVE, Population Totals of Countries in Africa

The following totals are those listed in the 1976-7 edition of *Africa South of the Sahara* (Europa Publications, London), and, for North Africa, in the 1977 edition of *Africa Guide* (Saffron Walden, England). Many are estimates, and serve to give little more than an order of magnitude, usually conservative. All are said to be growing at a rate of plus or minus 2.5 per cent a year.

Algeria	16,000,000	(1975)
Angola	5,669,504	(1970)*
Benin	3,029,000	(1974)
Botswana	709,000	(1973)
Burundi	3,600,000	(1973)
Cameroun	6,539,000	(1975)
Cape Verde	272,071	(1970)
Central African Republic	1,607,000	(1971)
Chad	3,949,000	(1974)
Comoros	294,800	(1973)
Congo People's Republic	1,300,020	(1974)
Egypt (United Arab Republic)	39,000,000	(1975)
Equatorial Guinea	245,989	(1960)
Ethiopia	27,239,000	(1974)
Fr. Terr. of Afars and Issas	200,000	(1973)
Gabon	950,009	(1970)
Gambia, The	494,279	(1973)
Ghana	8,545,561	(1970)
Guinea	5,143,284	(1972)
Guinea-Bissau	487,448	(1970)†
Ivory Coast	6,673,013	(1975)
Kenya	12,912,000	(1974)
Libyan Arab Republic	2,257,000	(1974)
Lesotho	969,634	(1966)‡
Liberia	1,501,400	(1974)
Madagascar	7,928,868	(1972)
Malawi	4,039,583	(1966)
Mali	5,376,000	(1973)
Mauritania	1,290,000	(1974)
Mauritius	845,755	(1974)

*Not counting some 450,000 refugees in Zaire and Zambia.

†Not counting some 90,000 refugees in Senegal, many of whom have since returned.

‡Including 117,273 absent working in South Africa.

Morocco	16,700,000	(1975)
Mozambique	8,233,978	(1970)*
Namibia	852,000	(1974)
Niger	4,476,000	(1974)
Nigeria	79,758,969	(1973)†
Reunion	467,675	(1974)
Rhodesia	6,420,000	(1975)
Rwanda	4,123,000	(1974)
St Helena	4,952	(1974)
São Tomé (with Principe)	76,430	(1972)
Senegal	4,315,000	(1974)
Seychelles	58,000	(1975)
Sierra Leone	3,000,426	(1974)
Somalia	2,941,000	(1972)
South Africa	24,936,000	(1974)
Sudan	14,171,732	(1973)
Swaziland	526,000	(1975)
Tanzania	14,758,000	(1974)‡
Togo	2,171,000	(1974)
Tunisia	5,570,000	(1975)
Uganda	10,461,500	(1972)
Upper Volta	5,541,000	(1972)
Western Sahara	74,902	(1974)
Zaire	24,165,770	(1974)
Zambia	4,695,000	(1974)

*Not including perhaps 80,000 refugees, mostly in Tanzania, many since returned.
†Officially repudiated as an over-estimate: the 1963 count gave 55,670,052.
‡Of whom 112,000 in Zanzibar and Pemba.

REFERENCES AND NOTES

Any comprehensive and elucidatory listing of the books and papers by very many hands whose insights I have drawn on for this book, and of other sources in books and papers, would have to be another book; and the economics of publishing, let alone the exhaustion of the author, exclude it here. Any short listing would be unsatisfactory because it would be unfair to authors not mentioned. So I ask all who may trace the influence of their work to allow me to thank them anonymously, but warmly.

It may be helpful, all the same, to mention a handful of general histories of modern Africa for readers who wish to add to their factual knowledge or consult other viewpoints. In English, the concluding volumes of the Cambridge *History of Africa*, ed. R. Oliver and J. D. Fage (the whole work totalling some two million words, in eight volumes, each with extensive bibliographies) are in a reference class of their own; for the same reasons of comprehensiveness, the concluding volumes of a projected UNESCO history of Africa may be expected to be the same. On a much less ambitious but still very useful scale, there is E. A. Ayandele, A. E. Afigbo, R. J. Gavin and J. D. Omer-Cooper, *The Making of Modern Africa*: vol. 1, *The 19th Century to the Partition*, vol. 2, *The Late 19th Century to the Present Day*, in the Longmans *Growth of African Civilisation* series, London, 1968, 1971. A very large quantity of facts is assembled in R. Hallett, *Africa since 1875: A Modern History*, Ann Arbor, University of Michigan, 1974.

In French one thinks at once of the notably useful histories of R. Cornevin, often in collaboration with M. Cornevin: for this period especially their *Histoire de l'Afrique des Origines à la 2e Guerre Mondiale*, and its pendant, *Histoire de l'Afrique contemporaine de la 2e Guerre Mondiale à nos Jours*, Payot, Paris, 1964, 1970; as well as R. Cornevin (but excluding North Africa), *L'Afrique Noire de 1919 à nos Jours*, Presses Universitaires, Paris, 1973. In 1975, besides, R. Cornevin published the first of a much more detailed series of surveys devoted to modern Africa, dealing in that volume with Southern Africa, British East and Central Africa, Belgian Africa, and German Africa, with another volume in preparation on remaining regions: *Histoire de l'Afrique*, tome 3, *Colonisation, Décolonisation, Independance*, Payot, Paris 1975. Admirably compendious but once again excluding North Africa, is H. Deschamps (ed.) *Histoire Générale de l'Afrique Noire*, tome 2, *De 1800 à nos Jours*, Presses Universitaires, Paris, 1971. Especially strong on analysis, but again excluding North Africa, is C. Coquéry-Vidrovitch and H. Moniot, *L'Afrique Noire de 1800 à nos Jours*, Presses Universitaires, Paris, 1974. A valuable overview is Y. Benot, *Idéologie des Indépendances africaines*, Maspero, 1969.

The references which follow here are limited to citations in the text, save for a few which add fact or comment; reference numbers for the latter are printed in bold type in the text.

PART ONE: p. 15 to p. 39

1. Marc Bloch, *Apologie pour l'Histoire* . . ., Colin, Paris, 1967, p. 10.
2. Fernand Braudel, *La Méditerranée* (2 vols), Colin, Paris, 1966, vol. 1, p. 13.
3. Ivor Wilks, *Asante in the Nineteenth Century*, Cambridge, 1975, p. 650.
4. For this and the above citation from the *Lagos Standard*, J. Ayodele Langley, *Pan-Africanism and Nationalism in West Africa, 1900–45: A Study in Ideology and Social Class*, Clarendon Press, 1972, p. 29.
5. Al-Hajj Umar of Kete Krachi (trans. B. G. Martin) in J. A. Braimah and J. Goody, *Salaga: The Struggle for Power*, Longman, 1967, p. 191.
6. General Lord Methuen, quoted in E. Holt, *The Boer War*, Putnam, 1958, p. 128.
7. Sol T. Plaatje, *The Boer War Diary*, J. L. Comaroff (ed.), Macmillan, 1973, p. 2.
8. In Obaro Ikime, 'The British Pacification of the Tiv, 1900–1908', *Journal of the Historical Society of Nigeria*, Vol. VII, No. 1, December 1973, p. 103.
9. C. S. Salmon, quoted in J. W. de Graft-Johnson, *Towards Nationhood in West Africa*, 1928, reprinted by Frank Cass, 1971, p. 80.
10. In J. F. Ade Ajayi, *Christian Missions in Nigeria 1841–1891: The Making of a New Élite*, Longman, 1965, p. 73.
11. R. T. Burton, *A Mission to Gelele, King of Dahome* (2 vols: vol. 2), London, 1864, pp. 200–201.
12. H. M. Hole, *Old Rhodesian Days*, Macmillan, 1928, p. 7.
13. J. T. Bent, *The Ruined Cities of Mashonaland*, Longman, 1892, p. 40.
14. J. A. Atanda, *The New Oyo Empire*, Longman, 1973, p. 255.
15. Kobina Sekyi, *The Blinkards* (1916), William Heinemann and Rex Collings (joint publication), 1974, pp. 40–41.
16. Quoted in A. C. Hill and M. Kilson, *Apropos of Africa*, Frank Cass, 1969, p. 31.
17. S. R. B. Attoh Ahuma, *The Gold Coast Nation and National Consciousness*, 1911, reprinted by Frank Cass, 1971, p. 11.

PART TWO: p. 43 to p. 71

1. See D. L. Wheeler, ' "Angola is Whose House?" Early Stirrings of Angolan Nationalism and Protest, 1822–1910', in *African Historical Studies*, Boston, vol. II, no. 1, 1969, p. 1.

2. V. L. Grottanelli, 'Sul Significato della Scultura Africana': Eng. text in *Africa*, October 1961.

3. F. van Langenhoven, *Consciences tribales et nationales en Afrique Noire*, Inst. Roy. Col. Belge, Brussels, 1960, p. 15.

4. J. Vansina, *Kingdoms of the Savanna*, University of Wisconsin Press, 1966, p. 14.

5. See, e.g., J. C. Caldwell, 'The Demographic Victory: Population Change, 1880–1935', in A. A. Boahen (ed.), *General History of Africa*, VII, Unesco, Paris, 1976; and papers and references in C. Fyfe (ed.), *African Demographic History*, Edinburgh University, 1977.

6. For an extensive discussion and bibliography, see B. Davidson, *The Africans: An Entry to Social and Cultural History*, Longman, 1969 (US edn, *The African Genius*, Atlantic-Little, Brown, Boston, 1969). The view explained here is based on the findings set forth in that book.

7. D. K. Fiawoo in C. Oppong (ed.), *Legon Family Research Papers*, no. 1, University of Ghana, 1974, p. 163.

8. Somalis, for example, explain to Europeans that their lineage is their 'address', defined by father's and grandfather's name after their given name, and thereby clearly 'placed' in the lineage systems – at least for other Somalis.

9. E. O. Ayisi, in Oppong, op. cit., pp. 68–74.

10. I. M. Lewis, *Islam in Tropical Africa*, Oxford University Press, 1966, Introduction.

11. E. Gellner, *Saints of the Atlas*, Weidenfeld and Nicolson, 1969, p. 15.

12. J. Waterbury, *North for the Trade: The Life and Times of a Berber Merchant*, University of California Press, 1972, p. 148.

12a. E. E. Evans-Pritchard, *The Sanusi of Cyrenaica*, Oxford University Press, 1949, p. 65.

13. H. N. Chittick, Note in *Azania*, vol. X, Nairobi, 1975, p. 234.

14. M. Rodinson, *Islam et Capitalisme*, Le Seuil, Paris, 1968, p. 80.

15. Karl Marx, *Pre-Capitalist Economic Formations* (tr. J. Cohen, ed. E. J. Hobsbawm), Lawrence and Wishart, 1964, p. 67.

15a. K. Y. Daaku, *Trade and Politics on the Gold Coast, 1600–1720*, Clarendon Press, 1970, p. 127.

16. Summarized in P. Hill, *The Gold Coast Cocoa Farmer*, Oxford University Press, 1956, p. 103.

17.   A. McPhee, *The Economic Revolution in British West Africa*, Routledge, 1926, *in extenso*.

18.   R. O. Ekundere, *An Economic History of Nigeria, 1860–1960*, Methuen, 1973, p. 51.

19.   ibid., p. 76.

19b.   A. J. H. Latham, *Old Calabar, 1600–1891*, Clarendon Press, 1973, p. 57.

20.   C. W. Newbury in C. Meillassoux (ed.), *The Development of Indigenous Trade and Markets in West Africa*, Oxford University Press, 1971, p. 96.

21.   In T. Szentes, *The Political Economy of Economic Underdevelopment*, Akadémiai Kiadó, Budapest, 1973, p. 63.

22.   A. G. Hopkins, *An Economic History of West Africa*, Longman, 1973, p. 48.

23.   P. Hill, *Rural Hausa*, Cambridge University Press, 1972. I am grateful to her for much valuable discussion, and the reader's attention is especially drawn to *Rural Hausa*'s extremely valuable glossary of terms and usages.

24.   Hopkins, op. cit., p. 143.

PART THREE: p. 75 to p. 143

1.   In J. B. King, in *Journal of Royal Geographical Society*, 1844, quoted from E. Isichei, *The Ibo People and the Europeans*, Faber, 1973, p. 81.

2.   In R. Battaglia, *La Prima Guerra d'Africa*, Einaudi, Turin, 1958, p. 124.

3.   In P. Mille, *Au Congo Belge*, Paris, 1889, p. 114. Somewhat freely:
Who of Fifi, on one fine night,
Or else Bobo
Have had enough, and get to hell
For the Congo . . .

4.   In J. Stengers, 'L'Impérialisme colonial de la Fin du XIXe Siècle: Mythe et Réalité', *Journal of African History*, vol. III, no. 3, 1962, p. 471.

5.   ibid., p. 486.

6.   *L'Africa Italiana al Parlamento Nazionale, 1882–1905*, Rome, 1907, pp. 25 and 35. Three good books may be consulted for the early history of the little-known subject of Italian colonialism in Africa, and for socialist critiques at the time: G. Rochat, *Il Colonialismo Italiano: Documenti della Storia*, Loescher, Turin, 1973; R. Battaglia, *La Prima Guerra d'Africa*, op. cit.; and R. Battaglia, *Risorgimento e Resistenza*, Editori Riuniti, Rome, 1964. For diplomatic back-

ground to the Fascist adventure in Ethiopia, see G. Salvemini, *Prelude to World War Two*, Gollancz, 1953.

6a. In R. Battaglia, *La Prima Guerra...*, op. cit., p. 203. See also Rochat, p. 41.

7. 2nd Series, vol. 48, 15 November 1884, p. 316.

8. Alfred Rambaud in 1885, quoted from R. Girardet, *L'Idée Coloniale en France 1871–1962*, Table Ronde, Paris, 1972, p. 51.

9. 'Wolseley's Ashanti War can be seen as a rehearsal for the wars of the subsequent European Scramble for Africa...', C. Fyfe, *Africanus Horton 1835–1883*, Oxford University Press, 1972, p. 117.

10. In G. H. Mungeam, *British Rule in Kenya 1895–1912*, Clarendon Press, 1966, p. 163.

11. Mungeam, p. 173 (Churchill), p. 195 (official comment).

12. See H. Stoecker, *Kamerun unter deutscher Kolonialherrschaft*, Rütten & Loening, Berlin, 1960, p. 103, 'Die Polizietruppe'.

13. In A. Ly, *Mercénaires Noirs*, Présence Africaine, Paris, 1957, p. 27.

14. But forced labour lingered on in British territories under various names, though on a small scale.

15. Atanda, op. cit., p. 5.

16. ibid., p. 7.

17. For conveniently collected extracts and commentary, see A. H. M. Kirk-Greene, *The Principles of Native Administration in Nigeria: Selected Documents 1900–1947*, Oxford University Press, 1965.

18. D. Cameron, *My Tanganyika Service and Some Nigerian*, Allen & Unwin, 1939, p. 226.

19. Girardet, op. cit., pp. 56, 63. See Note 8 above

20. ibid., p. 37.

21. H. Deschamps, *Histoire de Madagascar*, Berger Levrault, Paris, 1961, p. 262.

22. Félicien Cattier, *L'Étude sur la Situation de l'État Indépendant du Congo*, Brussels, 1906, quoted here from J. Stengers, *Belgique et Congo: L'Élaboration de la Charte Coloniale*, Renaissance du Livre, Brussels, 1963, p. 69.

23. In R. Anstey, *King Leopold's Legacy: The Congo under Belgian Rule, 1908–1960*, Oxford University Press, 1966, p. 43.

24. See B. Davidson, *The African Awakening*, Cape, 1955, chs 14 and 15, in a report on the Belgian Congo.

25. See L. Pestalozza, *Somalia, Cronaca della Rivoluzione*, Dedalo, Bari, 1973, for detailed evidence; S. Touval, *Somali Nationalism*, Harvard University Press, 1962; and R. L. Hess, *Italian Colonialism in Somalia*, University of Chicago Press, 1966.

26. M. Caetano, *Os Nativos na Economia Africana*, Coimbra, 1954, p. 16: 'Os pretos em Africa tem de ser dirigidos e enquadrados por

Europeos mas são indispensavéis como auxiliares destes ... os negros em Africa devem ser olhados como elementos productores enquadrados numa economia dirigida pelos brancos.' For numbers of assimilated, see p. 277 (footnote) below.

27. J. Ainsworth, in Mungeam, op. cit., p. 136.

28. ibid., p. 249.

29. See C. Coquéry-Vidrovitch, *Le Congo au Temps des Grandes Compagnies Concessionnaires, 1898–1930*, Mouton, The Hague, 1972, *in extenso*.

30. Marcello Serrazanetti, *Considerazioni sulla nostra attività in Somalia*, La Rapida, Bologna, 1933, quoted from Pestalozza, pp. 301–3.

31. Davidson, *The African Awakening*, op. cit., p. 205; *in extenso* in H. Galvão, *Santa Maria: My Crusade for Portugal*, Weidenfeld & Nicolson, 1961, pp. 46–58.

32. Gilbert Vieillard: in J. Suret-Canale, *French Colonialism in Tropical Africa 1900–1945*, C. Hurst, 1971, p. 252.

33. For these citations, and a wealth of other evidence on the same subject, see the reports of the Commission published in successive issues of *Bull. Trimestriel* of Centre d'Étude des Problèmes Sociaux Indigènes (CEPSI), Elizabethville: in this case No. 21 of May 1953, pp. 247, 347.

34. C. C. Wrigley in V. Harlow, E. M. Chilver, A. Smith (eds), *History of East Africa*, vol. 2, Oxford University Press, p. 230.

35. In S. T. van der Horst, *Native Labour in South Africa*, Oxford University Press, 1942, p. 149.

36. Cameron, op. cit., p. 133.

37. R. Delavignette, *Service Africain*, Gallimard, Paris, 1946, p. 138.

38. ibid., p. 184: 'Le gouverneur intérimaire de la Côte d'Ivoire, Richard Brunet, qui dénonçait le travail forcé et organisait le travail libre, fut rappelé et disgracié. Il paraît qu'on lui demanda s'il se prenait pour Jésus Christ.'

39. Quoted from *Report* of Central African Council, Salisbury, 1943.

40. Lists of frontier delimitations in R. Robinson and J. Gallagher, *Africa and the Victorians*, Macmillan, 1961, p. 473.

41. N. Leys, *Kenya*, Hogarth Press, 1926, p. 303.

42. Total losses of French 'colonial' troops in the First World War were 205,000 according to Girardet, op. cit., p. 118.

43. C. Leys, *Underdevelopment in Kenya: The Political Economy of Neo-Colonialism 1964–71*, William Heinemann, 1975, p. 27 and *in extenso*.

44. For citations and facts in this and following passage, see 'La Terre en Algérie', *Économie et Politique*, Paris, vol. II, no. 17, November 1955.

45. P. Kalck, *Histoire de la République Centrafricaine*, Berger Levrault, Paris, 1974, p. 164: 'Sa population durement atteinte ne se relevera jamais.'

46. Coquéry-Vidrovitch, op. cit., p. 313.

47. W. K. Hancock, *Survey of British Commonwealth Affairs*, vol. 2, *Problems of Economic Policy, 1918–19*, Oxford University Press, 1942, p. 188.

48. FO/2/83, Macdonald to Sir Clement Hill, pte 26.3.1895, quoted from J. L. Flint, *Sir George Goldie and the Making of Nigeria*, Oxford University Press, 1960, p. 207.

49. McPhee, op. cit., p. 95.

50. See Samir Amin, 'La Politique coloniale française a l'égard de la Bourgeoisie commerçante sénégalaise (1820–1960)', in Meillassoux, op. cit., p. 362.

51. C. Coquéry-Vidrovitch, 'La Mise en Dépendance de l'Afrique Noire: Structures économiques et Organisation sociale, 1800–1970', address to African Studies Association of the United Kingdom (ASAUK), Liverpool, 1975.

52. Hancock, Vol. 1, p. 290.

53. N. A. Cox-George, *Finance and Development in West Africa: The Sierra Leone Experience*, Dobson, 1961, p. 265.

54. P. J. Vatikiotis, *The Modern History of Egypt*, Weidenfeld & Nicolson, 1964, p. 282.

55. 'In 1936–7, after the (N. Rhodesian) Copperbelt had recovered from the slump, the mining companies paid over £300,000 in royalties to the British South Africa Company. From the remaining profits of just over £4 mns., the governments of Britain and Northern Rhodesia each took in tax £500,000; they also took about £40,000 each from the British South Africa Company's income from royalties. The total levy, in royalties and taxation, on the profits from mining was about 30 per cent, but only 12½ per cent went to the N. Rhodesian government ... In 1943 it was calculated that from 1930 to 1940 Britain had kept for itself £2,400,000 in taxes from the Copperbelt, while N. Rhodesia received from Britain only £136,000 in grants for development.' A. Roberts, *A History of Zambia*, William Heinemann, 1976, p. 193.

56. Penguin edition, 1962, p. 185. Castro Soromenho's *Terra Morta* is available in the original Portuguese, Sá da Costa, Lisbon, 1976, or in French, *Camaxilo*, Présence Africaine, Paris, 1960.

57. SLOTFOM (Service de Liaison avec les Originaires des Territoires de la France d'Outre-Mer), Service des Archives Nationales (Section d'Outre-Mer), Série III, Carton 56, 'Notes sur les Activités de l'Internationale communiste dans la Domaine coloniale', Paris.

58.   Quoted from E. A. Brett, *Colonialism and Underdevelopment in East Africa: The Politics of Economic Change, 1919–39*, Nok, New York (and William Heinemann, London), 1973, p. 118.

59.   Hopkins, op. cit., 1973, p. 262.

60.   For these schemes, see T. Barnett, 'Gezira and Zande'; and D. C. Dorward, 'Socio-economic aspects of Nigerian benniseed exports': both ASAUK conference, 1975.

61.   Rita Hinden, *Plan for Africa*, Allen & Unwin, 1941, p. 105, quoting *Report of Committee appointed to make a Survey of Nutrition in Northern Rhodesia*, 1939, p. 2.

62.   P. Hill, *Studies in Rural Capitalism in West Africa*, Cambridge, 1970, p. 23; and, for previous passage on cattle population, p. 83.

63.   J. Berque, *Le Maghreb entre deux Guerres*, Le Seuil, Paris, 1962, p. 116.

PART FOUR: p. 147 to p. 196

1.   Quoted from private correspondence published in *West Africa*, 13 October 1962.

1a.   Evidence in Reichs-Kolonialarchiv, and other official sources, summarized in H. Dreschler, *Süd-West-Afrika unter Deutscher Kolonialherrschaft*, Akademie Verlag, Berlin, 1966: e.g. pp. 197, 252.

2.   B. Ogot, 'British Administration in the Central Nyanza District of Kenya, 1900–60', *Journal of African History*, vol. IV, no. 2, 1963, p. 249.

3.   O. B. Mapunda and G. P. Mpangara, *The Maji Maji War in Ungoni*, East Africa Publishing House, Dar es-Salaam, 1968, p. 14.

4.   T. O. Ranger, *The African Churches in Tanzania*, East Africa Publishing House, Dar es-Salaam, n.d. but about 1969, p. 16.

5.   In *Papers Relating to Native Disturbances*, Cmd 1691, 1922, quoted from F. B. Welbourn, *East African Rebels*, S.C.M., London, 1961, p. 129.

6.   See R. K. Cope, *Comrade Bill*, Stewart, Cape Town, n.d. but about 1948.

7.   Address of 1870, in Alexander Crummell, *Africa and America*, 1891, pp. 169–98, passage quoted from H. S. Wilson, *Origins of West African Nationalism*, Macmillan, 1969.

8.   H. R. Lynch, *Edward Wilmot Blyden: Pan-Negro Patriot 1832–1912*, Oxford University Press, 1967, p. 244.

9.   E. A. Ayandele, *The Educated Élite in the Nigerian Society*, Ibadan, 1974, p. 9.

10.   Quoted from R. W. July, *The Origins of Modern African Thought*, Faber, 1968, p. 364.

11. 14 October 1885: quoted from D. L. Wheeler in Wheeler and R. Pélissier, *Angola*, Pall Mall Press, 1971, p. 103.

12. In A. G. Hopkins, 'The Lagos Strike of 1897', *Past and Present*, No. 35, December 1966, p. 151.

13. S. T. Plaatje, *Native Life in South Africa before and since the European War and the Boer Rebellion*, King, 1916.

14. In T. Karis and G. M. Carter, *From Protest to Challenge: A Documentary History of African Politics in South Africa, 1882–1964*, Hoover, Stanford, 1972: vol. 1, pp. 124–5.

15. In the *Lagos Times*, 9 November 1881, quoted from E. A. Ayandele, *Holy Johnson: Pioneer of African Nationalism, 1836–1917*, Frank Cass, 1970, p. 45.

16. Attoh Ahuma, pp. 10–11.

17. Macaulay Papers, Ibadan, Box 6: first citation from 'The Cult of Prince Eshugbayi', 5 March 1932; second from 'The Modernised Native Industry', n.d. but evidently 1932.

18. In *The Parting of the Ways*, probably 1925; quoted from Langley, op. cit., pp. 98–9.

19. Langley, p. 133.

20. In S. K. B. Asante, *The West African Response to the Italo-Ethiopian Crisis 1934–1942*, University of London MS. thesis, 1974, p. 105.

21. ibid. p. 374.

22. In S. Shaloff, 'The Africanization Controversy in the Gold Coast, 1926–1946', *African Studies Review*, vol. XVII, no. 3, December 1974, pp. 496–7.

23. Karis and Carter, vol. 2, p. 7.

24. SLOTFOM, Série III, Carton 151, police report of 30 June 1935.

25. *Le Cri des Nègres*, September 1933 (2 of 2nd year).

26. Issue of 4 May 1934.

27. *Dépêche Africaine*, Paris, edited by Satineau, No. 1 of February 1928.

28. e.g. SLOTFOM, Série III, Carton 73: 'Divers rapports d'agents . . .' (1935) includes a handwritten report on a meeting of the central committee of the Union des Travailleurs Nègres, held at 120 rue Lafayette, at which a US Negro, Ford, reports on the 7th Congress of the Comintern, whereupon Ebele, a Camerounian, rises and says: 'African Negroes are not afraid of the struggle, but they are lacking one thing, which is that the French Communist Party is not interested in and does not protect African Negroes as it should. They pay no heed to African Negro opinions . . .' Ford is reported as concluding: 'From all the criticisms we have heard, and the figures given, I see that the French Communist Party has done nothing for the Negro masses.'

29. SLOTFOM, Série III, Carton 73, referring to a plan of Kouyaté's, of

October 1935, set forth in detail. The same plan was mooted in Kouyaté's short-lived paper, *Africa* (1 of 1 of December 1935 in an article signed by Gaston Bergéry, but in fact written by Kouyaté, according to a letter from the Minister of Colonies to the Governor-General of French West Africa: Série 5, Carton 21). Kouyaté had been expelled from the French Communist Party in 1934.

30. Apparently shot as a resister by the German occupying authorities in 1942 or 1943, but I have not been able to obtain details. The part played by Africans in the French resistance is one that deserves study. For a moving glimpse, see Yves Farge, *Rebelles, Soldats et Citoyens*, Grasset, Paris, 1946, pp. 82–3, where that wholly admirable French patriot, then a Resistance Commissioner of the Republic, speaks of the African soldiers who joined the Free French forces in their desperate defence of the massif of the Vercors.

31. In *El Muntadiq*, no. 1, quoted here from Mohamed Harbi, *Aux Origines du FLN: Le Populisme Revolutionnaire en Algérie*, Bourgois, Paris, 1975, p. 68: ideologically, a seminal work of brilliance and perception.

32. Quoted from Suret-Canale, op. cit.

33. R. Gallisot, *Le Patronat Français au Maroc*, Rabat, 1964, p. 148.

34. SLOTFOM, Série V, Carton 2, report by 'Désiré' to Surêté Général, 28 October 1924.

35. SLOTFOM, Série III, 45, report from 'très bonne' source dated August 1933.

PART FIVE: p. 199 to p. 279

1. Letter from Poona of 17 September 1945: Macaulay Papers, Ibadan, Box 88, File 1.

2. Casualty figures in R. Cornevin, *L'Afrique Noire de 1919 à nos Jours*, Presses Universitaires, Paris, 1973, p. 140.

3. A full survey of the British African war effort remains to be made. Africans were recruited into some ten East and Central and seven West African brigades, mostly infantry but some for ancillary services. West and East African brigades formed part of 1 (E. Africa) Division which defeated the Italians on the Juba river, being formed in 1940 and disbanded in 1941. Others formed part of 2 (E. Africa) Division, later 12 Division, which also fought on the Juba as well as later at Gondar, in Ethiopia, and later again in Burma. A new Division, 11 (E. Africa), was formed in 1943 for the Burma war.

British W. African regiments existing in 1939 were enlarged, with new units to a total of 3 Nigerian, 2 Gold Coast, 1 Sierra Leonean, and 1 Gambian brigades. In 1943 these brigades were formed into 81 (W. Africa) Division and 82 (W. Africa) Division; all except one of them saw active service in E. Africa or Burma or both. (See H. F. Joslen, *Orders of Battle, Second World War*, vols 1 and 2, HMSO, London, 1960.) No overall casualty figures seem to have been estimated or compiled, though PRO records and regimental histories appear to make this possible. Most recorded casualties were in the Burma fighting. Thus the two W. African divisions in Burma are recorded as having suffered 494 killed, 1,417 wounded, 54 missing, while 11 (E. Africa) Division suffered 233 Africans killed, 976 wounded, 35 missing, in five months' campaigning there. Overall, the Imperial War Graves Commission has records for Burma of: unknown graves, 1,608 W. Africans; 733 E. Africans; 36 S. Rhodesian African Riflemen; and marked graves, 177 W. Africans; 12 E. Africans; 4 S. Rhodesian Riflemen; or a total of 2,570 graves.

4. But the Spanish system, unlike the Portuguese, could affect only very small populations.

5. The furiously chauvinist attitudes of Vichyist administrators are well displayed in a characteristic statement, by Henri Croze of the Casablanca Chamber of Commerce, when praising Pétain (1 January 1941): 'La France pantelante a trouvé un sauveur dont la main miraculeuse a pansé les blessures, l'a relevée de ses ruines, et l'a grandie, pauvre et meurtrie mais animée d'un esprit nouveau . . .' in Gallisot, op. cit., p. 253.

6. 'La situation actuelle des populations congolaises', *Bull.*, Inst. Roy. Col. Belge, vol. XVI, no. 3, 1945, p. 584.

7. *The Times*, 16 September 1941.

8. Harbi, p. 16.

9. Karis and Carter, op. cit., vol. 2, p. 199. The ANC's Atlantic Charter Committee had few illusions, but was careful, for the record, to note 'with satisfaction that the 26 other nations which subscribed to the Atlantic Charter on 2 January 1942 made it quite clear that the freedoms and liberties which this war is being fought to establish in countries which have been the victims of aggression in this war, must be realised by the Allied Powers "in their own lands as well as in other lands". This is the common cry of all subject races at the present time.' (p. 212.) It went unheeded.

10. Quoted from Langley, op. cit., p. 345, who gives more of it.

11. Popularized above all by Kwame Nkrumah early in the 1960s, the term 'neo-colonialism' is of uncertain origin. Some have attributed it to the British marxist scholar, the late R. P. Dutt. I wrote asking

him if this were right. He replied in a letter of 18 January 1974 that he had suggested in 1957 that the term 'new colonialism' should be applied to 'the new tactics of imperialism in the modern era of advance to national liberation'. He added: 'I would never have personally invented such a barbarous term as "Neo-Colonialism", since I preferred the simple English, "the New Colonialism"; but subsequently the term has become a standard one for general use.'

12. Only between 1953–63, dividends and royalties from N. Rhodesian copper-mining amounted after tax to £26 million, 'far more than the recurrent expenditure of the colonial government (of N. Rhodesia) in that period'; but 'little of this enormous sum was reinvested in N. Rhodesia' – instead, in this decade of the settler-controlled Central African Federation, 'much of it went to finance development in Southern Rhodesia and South Africa.' Roberts, op. cit., p. 214.

13. Burnham and Lippmann quoted here from R. P. Dutt, *The Crisis of Britain and the British Empire*, Lawrence & Wishart, 1953, pp. 161, 164.

14. Quoted from D. Welch and M. Wilson and L. Thompson (eds), *Oxford History of South Africa*, Clarendon Press, 1971, vol. 2, p. 190.

15. P. C. Lloyd, *Power and Independence: Urban Africans' Perception of Social Inequality*, Routledge, 1974, p. xi.

16. W. Elkans, *Migrants and Proletarians*, Oxford University Press, 1960, p. 65. See also J. Woddis, *The Lion Awakes*, Lawrence & Wishart, 1961, for extensive commentary, especially pp. 35–156.

17. R. Cohen, *Labour and Politics in Nigeria, 1945–71*, William Heinemann, 1974, p. 78.

18. C. H. Allen, 'Union-Party Relationships in Francophone West Africa', in R. Sandbrook and R. Cohen, *The Development of an African Working Class*, Longman, 1975; and see also, for a valuable summary, C. H. Allen, 'West African Labour and Radical Nationalism, 1944–51', seminar paper, University of Edinburgh, 1976.

19. In Woddis, op. cit., p. 87.

20. I. G. Shivji, *Class Struggles in Tanzania*, Tanzania Publishing House, Dar es-Salaam, and William Heinemann, 1975; but quoted from pre-publication typescript, hence no page numbers.

21. O. Awolowo, *Path to Nigerian Freedom*, Faber, 1947, p. 63.

22. Y. Person, 'Contre l'État-Nation', in *Faire*, Paris, issue of June–July 1976. Eng. trans in *Planet*, Tregaron, 37–8 of 1977.

23. *New Statesman & Nation*, 9 September 1950. (For anyone interested, this was the first article I ever wrote about Africa.)

24. M. G. Smith, *Government in Zazzau*, Oxford University Press, 1960, p. 291.

25. Alhaji Sir Ahmadu Bello, 'My Life, 1962', quoted from *West Africa*, 1 December 1962.

26. R. Schachter Morgenthau, *Political Parties in French-speaking West Africa*, Clarendon Press, 1964, p. 48.

27. Quoted by J. Mitterrand in debate of Assemblée de l'Union Française, *Journal Officiel*, 30 December 1948.

28. On 27 September 1946: *Journal Officiel*, Collected Debates, 1946.

29. Bizot, a speaker in the Assemblée (*Journal Officiel*, 30 December 1948) quotes statement by a General Garblay to mission of inquiry sent by Assemblée that numbers of dead were 89,000; 5,000 killed in the fighting and the rest by hunger. Mitterrand, speaking in another Assemblée debate on Madagascar (*Journal Officiel*, 25 May 1949) affirms that 90,000 were killed on one side, and 900 on the other, but quotes Governor-General of Madagascar as putting total at 80,000. Writing in 1961, however, Deschamps gives the total killed as rather more than 11,000.

30. G. Chaffard, *Les Carnets Secrets de la Décolonisation*, Calmann-Lévy, Paris, 1967, p. 294.

31. M. Staniland in C. Leys (ed.), *Politics and Change in Developing Countries: Studies in the Theory and Practice of Development*, Cambridge University Press, 1969, p. 139.

32. R. Joseph, 'Settlers, Strikers and *Sans-Travail*: The Douala Riots of September 1945', *Journal of African History*, vol. XV, no. 4, 1974, p. 682.

33. *Debates of the Northern Rhodesia Legislative Council*, 6 June 1939, col. 501.

34. *Legislative Assembly Debates*, Salisbury, 27 November 1944.

35. Much remains to be understood in this difficult subject of the interpretation of political terms. The pioneering work of William Whiteley and Pierre Alexandre has set a high standard.

36. W. Whiteley in K. Kirkwood (ed.), *African Affairs*, No. 1 (St Antony's Papers), Chatto & Windus, 1961, pp. 14, 16.

37. O. Odinga, *Not Yet Uhuru*, William Heinemann, 1967, p. 95.

38. Passages quoted from B. M. Kaggia, Fred Kubai, J. Murumbi, Achieng Oneko, in their preface to D. L. Barnett and K. Njama, *Mau Mau From Within*, MacGibbon & Kee, 1966, pp. 10–11.

39. Ethiopia's cup of woe having flowed over in great human losses from unrelieved drought, a military group dethroned the emperor and set up a 'Provisional Military Government'. As set forth in a proclamation of 1974, called *Ethiopia Tikdem*, this intended 'to provide for development through cooperation, enlightenment and

work', *Negarit Gazeta*, Addis Ababa, 25 November 1974. But these soldiers, unlike their contemporaries in Somalia next door, proved incapable of doing more than launch the revolution of which they spoke, and were soon embroiled in efforts to hold the empire together by old-style methods of force. Yet major changes seemed inescapably present, and the old régime gone for ever.

40. N. Laude, *Bull.*, Inst. Roy. Col. Belge, no. 2 of 1951, p. 638.

41. P. Lumumba, *Congo My Country*, Pall Mall Press, 1962, p. 47.

42. F.-W. Heimer, *Educação e Sociedade nas Areas Ruráis de Angola*, Missão de Inquéritos Agricolas, Luanda, 1972, relevant tables.

PART SIX: p. 283 to p. 382

1. A racist counter-myth that blacks were superior to whites became part of the 'neo-colonial' cultural scene, but was not, or not yet, much more than a reaction to past white arrogance, or a weapon in the hunt for jobs held by whites. A longer period of this 'neo-colonial' nationalism would presumably enlarge its influence. See also note 57 below.

2. Odinga, op. cit., p. 242.

3. 'A Second Birthday', in H. Swanzy (ed.), *Voices of Ghana*, Government Printer, Accra, 1958, p. 204.

4. See J. Rea, 'Aspects of African Publishing', in C. Fyfe (ed.), *Twenty-Five Years of African Studies*, Longman, 1976, a comprehensive overview.

5. Quoted from J. F. Ade Ajayi and T. N. Tamuno (ed.), *The University of Ibadan, 1948–73*, Ibadan, 1973, p. 11.

6. R. Oliver (ed.), *The Middle Age of African History*, Oxford University Press, 1967, pp. 92–3.

7. H. Seton-Watson, *Eastern Europe between the Wars 1918–1941*, Cambridge University Press, 1945, p. 147. Eastern European history should surely be a subject of study in African universities, and this book required reading.

8. Often done in reference to E. Europe as to Africa. For a case of application to Africa, see the curiously ahistorical *dicta* of S. Andreski, *The African Predicament: A Study in the Pathology of Modernisation*, Michael Joseph, 1968, at many points.

9. R. Dumont, *L'Afrique Noire est Mal Partie*, Le Seuil, Paris, 1962, p. 129.

10. Simeon Adebo Commission, Interim Report, 1970, p. 11.

11. Quoted from 'The Kariuki Affair', in *Africa Currents*, Africa Publications Trust, London, no. 2 of 1975.

12. Of 29 October 1975.

13. *The Times*, 4 June 1976.

14. In issues of 22 March and 29 October 1976.

15. D. H. Houghton, *The South African Economy*, Oxford University Press, Cape Town, edition of 1976, p. 110.

16. P. Hill, 'Socio-Economic Conditions in Rural Nigerian Hausaland in 1900 and Today', *Cambridge Anthropology*, vol. I, no. 3, 1975. See also her *Population, Prosperity and Poverty*, Cambridge, 1977.

17. Leys, *Underdevelopment in Kenya*, op. cit., p. 168. For discussion and dissent, see articles in *Review of African Political Economy*, London, 8, 1977.

18. W. W. Rostow, *The Stages of Economic Growth*, Cambridge University Press, 1960.

19. Ekundere, op. cit., p. 383.

20. Programmatic statement by Gen. G. Ramanantsoa, 27 July 1972, quoted (in my translation) from *Moniteur Africain*, Dakar, 26 October 1972.

21. Quoted from *The Times*, 3 November 1976.

22. S. Touval, *Somali Nationalism*, Harvard, 1963, p. 85.

23. I. M. Lewis, 'The Politics of the 1969 Somali Coup', *Journal of Modern African Studies*, no. 9 of 1972, p. 399. Lewis continues: the National Assembly's 'members were ferried about in sumptuous limousines bearing the magic letters AN (Assemblea Nazionale) which the inveterate poor of the capital translated with bitter humour as *anna nolahay* – "I'm all right, Jack" . . .'

24. T. Solarin, 'A View of Nigerian Independence' in P. Judd (ed.), *African Independence*, Dell, New York, 1963, p. 246.

25. G. Fagbure, *Sunday Times*, Lagos, 15 December 1963.

26. Quoted from J. de St Jorre, *The Nigerian Civil War*, Hodder & Stoughton, 1972, p. 30.

27. Quoted from J. Waterbury, *The Commander of the Faithful: The Moroccan Political Élite, A Study in Segmented Politics*, Weidenfeld & Nicolson, 1970, p. 90. Waterbury adds that Ben Barka saw the task of his new party as that of 'an indispensable conversion . . . in order to transform the Istiqlal from the movement or *rassemblement* that it was into a structured, homogeneous, efficient party, capable of playing a role in the execution of reconstruction'. (p. 188.) Ben Barka was clearly a pioneer of the politics of liberation.

28. Gen. L. Okai in issue of 9 November 1976.

29. From 'Brève Analyse de la Structure Sociale de la Guinée "portugaise"', 1964, in A. Cabral, *Unité et Lutte*, Maspero, Paris, 1975, vol. I, p. 45; an English version is in A. Cabral, *Revolution in*

Guinea, Stage One, London (and Monthly Review Press, New York), 1969, p. 57.

30.   J. K. Nyerere, *Report* (to TANU National Conference), Government Printer, Dar es-Salaam, September 1971, p. 13.

31.   Shivji, as cited in Note 20 to Part Five.

31a.   Shivji.

32.   For this and other programmatic statements, see Pestalozza at relevant points. (Note 25 to Part Three.)

33.   Quoted from *Afrique-Asie*, Paris, 15 November 1976.

34.   Much remains uncertain about Mulele's thinking, and he was killed too soon to explain himself. Offered an amnesty on Mobutu's 'word of honour' in 1968, he returned to Zaire and was at once seized and finished off. See J. Chomé, *L'Ascension de Mobutu*, Maspero, Paris, 1974, p. 188.

35.   B. Verhaegen, 'Les Rébellions Populaires au Congo en 1964', *Cahiers d'Études Africaines*, vol. VII, 1967, p. 354.

36.   I am grateful to the President of Guinea-Bissau and deputy secretary-general of the PAIGC, and to other leaders of the PAIGC, for the communications here reproduced and for permission to publish them. For general background, see my *Liberation of Guiné*, Penguin, London and Baltimore, 1969.

37.   Luiz Cabral in *Nô Pintcha*, Bissau, vol. II, no. 228, September 1976.

38.   Agostinho Neto, president of MPLA and of independent Angola, in B. Davidson, *In the Eye of the Storm: Angola's People*, Longman, London, Doubleday, New York, 1972, Penguin, 1975: p. 179 of Longman edition.

38a.   For a more detailed treatment of events and ideas, see B. Davidson, 'The Politics of Armed Struggles in the African Colonies of Portugal', in B. Davidson, J. Slovo and A. R. Wilkinson, *Southern Africa*, Penguin, 1976.

39.   There is reason to think that the Armed Forces Movement which overthrew the dictatorship had its origins in Guinea-Bissau. Its branch there in any case bore witness to the influence of the liberation movements, declaring as early as June 1974 that 'the colonized peoples and the people of Portugal are allies. The struggle for national liberation has contributed powerfully to the overthrow of fascism and, in large degree, has lain at the base of the Armed Forces Movement...' 'MFA na Guiné', in *Boletim Informativo*, Bissau, no. 1, 1 June 1974.

40.   No other parties stood, but 84 per cent of the then eligible voters turned out to vote under Portuguese supervision, and 92.17 of these voted PAIGC. Secretary-general of PAIGC, Aristides Pereira, became president of the new republic of Cape Verde.

41.   A little later, UNITA began military cooperation with the Portu-

guese army against the MPLA. See wartime correspondence (published after the Lisbon *coup* in *Afrique-Asie*, Paris, 8 July 1974) between Savimbi and Portuguese army chiefs; and memoirs of the deposed Portuguese prime minister, Marcello Caetano (in his book, *Depoimento*, Sao Paulo, Brasil, 1974, pp. 180–81) where Caetano writes: 'The enemy's [that is, the MPLA's] opening of the Eastern Front [in Angola] constituted a tremendous preoccupation and [General] Costa Gomes, on assuming responsibility for Angola's defence, approached the case with intelligence and decisiveness. [General] Bettencourt Rodrigues was given the task ... of pacifying the region, which he undertook by reaching an understanding with the people of UNITA, an insurrectionary group which under the leadership of Savimbi operated with the disagreement of the MPLA.' And see Davidson, Note 38 above.

42. Samora Machel, *Mozambique: Sowing the Seeds of Revolution*, Mozambique, Angola, Guiné Information Centre, London, 1974, p. 39.

43. A. Cabral, 'Libération Nationale et Culture', in *Unité et Lutte*, vol. 1, pp. 332–3.

44. A. Cabral, 'Resistência Cultural', seminar paper at PAIGC conference of cadres, 19–24 November 1969.

45. As late as January 1969, a Zimbabwe nationalist leader able to move around the world could ask me, of the liberation war in Guinea-Bissau then six years old, 'But is it true they're really fighting there?'

46. In the reliably leaked NSC Memorandum 39 of that year.

47. Quoted from *Big Flame*, Liverpool, December 1976, p. 7.

48. Quoted from *Africa Digest*, June 1975, p. 148.

49. In *New Society*, 21 November 1976.

50. Quoted from B. Davidson, *Report on Southern Africa*, Jonathan Cape, 1952, p. 62, drawing on evidence reproduced in report of official Native Laws Commission, 1946–8.

51. Issue of 20 October 1976.

52. 'Und willst Du nicht mein Bruder sein, dann schlag ich Dir dein Schädel ein.' For South African armaments, see *Southern Africa*, Stockholm International Peace Research Institute, Praeger, 1976.

53. Quoted from *Le Monde Diplomatique*, Paris, June 1971.

54. Houghton, op. cit., p. 242.

55. J. H. Plumb, *The First Four Georges*, Fontana, Collins, 1966, p. 54. He adds of that England: 'No nation rioted more easily or more savagely – from 1714 to 1830 angry mobs, burning and looting, were as prevalent as disease, and as frequent in the countryside as in the great towns.' (p. 15).

56. Quoted from *West Africa*, 3 January 1976 (in a series of weekly articles devoted to the drafting of the new Nigerian constitution).

57.   For why should a non-revolutionary nationalism, essentially a bourgeois nationalism, prove any better in its outcome in Africa than in Europe? The hymns of African nationalism have sung a generous tune, but so did Europe's. One thinks of Mameli's 'Marseillaise of the Italian Risorgimento', singing in 1847 the very same theme as African nationalists of a century later:

Noi siamo da secoli   We have remained for centuries
Calpesti e derisi   Downtrodden and derided
Perché non siam popolo   Because we are not one people
Perché siam divisi . . .   Because we are divided . . .

Yet within a score of years of Italy's unification Italian armies were doing their best to tread down other people, and were eagerly deriding them. They were far from being alone among the nationalists of Europe.

58.   Private communication.

59.   A. Pereira, Relatório, published serially in Nô Pintcha, Bissau, 31 August, 2, 4, 7 September 1976. The whole report is of the highest general political interest; as is also, defining state and party and their mutual relationship in new and original terms, the long report of the same authority presented to the 3rd Congress of the PAIGC in November 1977; ibid., Relatório do CSL, Bissau.

59a.   Requiring, of course, a rigorous analysis of class structure, as, for example, in Cabral's of Guinea-Bissau and Cape Verde: in ibid., Unité et Lutte; and cf., Lionel Cliffe, 'Rural Class Formation', Jnl of Peasant Studies, vol. 4, no. 2, January 1977.

60.   As well as its political, agrarian and legal policies of structural change, the educational concepts of EPLF gave a striking illustration of what I have called 're-formulation theory'. In language teaching, 'British colonialism divided society on religious lines and so created Christian schools and Muslim schools, the one using Tigrigna, the other Arabic. Then, after annexation, Ethiopia imposed Amharigna. Up to now the language problem has been a source of division; now we mean to make it a source of unity. [In our schools] every child begins to study in the language it knows best. But the child learns others because it lives collectively, and in later years it will be able to study in the language of its choice. In this way we mean to remove religious and regional barriers, and, at the same time, conserve and develop our national languages and cultures.' Statement of Osman Dafiha (EPLF) to Guido Bimbi in 'I Contadini di Medri Zien', L'Unitá, Rome, 18 March 1977.

61.   Quoted here from K. Brown, in E. Gellner and Ch. Micaud, Arabs and Berbers: From Tribe to Nation in North Africa, Duckworth, 1973, p. 203.

INDEX OF TERMS AND DEFINITIONS

The following is a guide to some terms and 'labels' used in this book, and to definitions of the meanings attached to them here.

INDEX OF NAMES